PENGUIN BOOKS

ULTRA GOES TO WAR

Highgate Litera... ...y was in tur...
...eading BBC official and a dis-
...orian. Following his war service as an
...cer in North Africa and in the Normandy invasion,
... ,oined the BBC, becoming Chief of the Home Service in
1963. Retiring early, he turned to military history. His biography
of Field-Marshal the Viscount Slim, *Slim: The Standardbearer*,
won the 1977 W. H. Smith Literary Award. He also wrote studies of Field-Marshal Wavell (*The Chief*) and General Vyvyan
Pope (*Man of Armour*), and of *Rommel as Military Commander*,
Montgomery as Military Commander and *Churchill as Warlord*.
He edited *Freedom's Battle: The War on Land 1939–1945*, and also
wrote *The Life and Death of the Africa Korps*. His ground-break-
ing book *Ultra Goes to War: The Secret Story* was followed by *The
American Magic: Codes, Ciphers and the Defeat of Japan* (entitled
in the UK *The Other Ultra*). His book on *Hitler's Mistakes* was
published posthumously. He was awarded the Chesney Gold
Medal of the Royal United Services Institute in 1982 and
appointed CBE in 1983.

Ultra Goes to War

The Secret Story

RONALD LEWIN

PENGUIN BOOKS

PENGUIN BOOKS

Published by the Penguin Group
Penguin Books Ltd, 27 Wrights Lane, London W8 5TZ, England
Penguin Putnam Inc., 375 Hudson Street, New York, New York 10014, USA
Penguin Books Australia Ltd, Ringwood, Victoria, Australia
Penguin Books Canada Ltd, 10 Alcorn Avenue, Toronto, Ontario, Canada M4V 3B2
Penguin Books India (P) Ltd, 11, Community Centre, Panchsheel Park, New Delhi – 110 017, India
Penguin Books (NZ) Ltd, Private Bag 102902, NSMC, Auckland, New Zealand
Penguin Books (South Africa) (Pty) Ltd, 5 Watkins Street, Denver Ext 4, Johannesburg 2094, South Africa

Penguin Books Ltd, Registered Offices: Harmondsworth, Middlesex, England

First published by Hutchinson & Co. (Publishers) Ltd 1978
Published as a Classic Penguin 2001
1

Copyright © Ronald Lewin, 1978
All rights reserved

Printed in England by The Bath Press, Bath

To the Poles who sowed the seed
and to those who reaped the harvest

Contents

List of Illustrations

Acknowledgements

I owe a principal debt of gratitude to Group Captain F. W. Winterbotham, CBE, who shared with me his memories, his files and his friendship.

For those who were admitted to the Ultra secret during the war there was a troublesome uncertainty even after 1974, when the tip of the iceberg first broke surface, about the extent to which they were free to speak. To all who felt such inhibitions I am grateful for the consideration and constructive discretion with which they talked to me, as I am to Rear-Admiral Kenneth Farnhill, Secretary of the Defence, Press and Broadcasting Committee, for his constantly helpful courtesy.

For their advice, information and encouragement I am particularly indebted to Sir Philip Adams, Lieut.-General Sir Terence Airey, Mrs Joan Bright Astley, Tony Allen QC, Corelli Barnett, Commander Barrow-Green, Keith and Mavis Batey, Professor Geoffrey Barraclough, Patrick Beesly, Ralph Bennett, Colonel John Bevan, Lord Briggs, Air Vice-Marshal Sydney Bufton, Wing Commander Bugden, Peter Calvocoressi, Lord William Cavendish-Bentinck, Air Vice-Marshal Sir Edward Chilton, Ronald Clark, Wing Commander Crawshaw, D. M. Davin, Vice-Admiral Sir Norman Denning, Giulio Divita, Colonel Peter Dunphie, Marshal of the RAF Lord Elworthy, Norman Evans, Squadron Leader Fawssett, Professor M. R. D. Foot, Josef Garlinski, Frank Gillard, Harry Golombek, Professor I. J. Good, Peter Gray Lucas, S. J. Hamer, Field-Marshal Lord Harding, Peter Hennessy, Miss Wendy Hinde, Professor Stuart Hood, Major D. M. Horner (Australian Army), Professor Michael Howard, Mrs Roger Howard, Sir David Hunt, Miss Judy Hutchinson, David Irving, Lieut.-General Sir Ian Jacob, Professor R. V. Jones, Paul de Laszlo, Asher Lee, Lieut.-Colonel Tadeus Lisicki, Colonel Kenneth MacFarlan, Vice-Admiral Sir Ian McGeoch, Major K. J. Macksey, Sir Herbert Marchant, Sir John Martin, the late Sir John Masterman, Colonel S. A. Mayer, Sir Stuart Milner-Barry, the late Brigadier C. J. C. Molony, John Monroe, David Mure, Professor Oeser, Professor and Mrs Roland Oliver, John Poole, the Rt. Hon. Enoch Powell MP, Mrs Anthony Quayle (Dorothy Hyson), Professor B. Randell, General Sir Charles Richardson, Colonel T. A. Robertson, Squadron Leader Robinson, Group Captain Shephard, Brigadier John Shearer, Marshal of the RAF Sir John Slessor, the late General Sir James Steele, Dr Ian Stewart, Field Marshal Sir

Gerald Templer, Edward Toledano, Professor Hugh Trevor-Roper, Professor E. R. Vincent, Gordon Welchman, Sir Edgar Williams, Sir Ronald Wingate, the Hon. C. M. Woodhouse and Kenneth Young.

In the United States I received the most generous assistance from Yorke Allen, Ernest Bell, William Bundy, Professor Raymond Callahan, William J. Casey, General Ira Eaker, Alfred Friendly, General James M. Gavin, Landis Gores, Miss Kay Halle, Benjamin King, Dr Forrest C. Pogue, the Hon. Lewis Powell, General E. R. Quesada, Professor Edwin O. Reischauer, Adolph G. Rosengarten, Professor Telford Taylor, Langdon van Norden, Robert Wolfe and the Hon. Inzer Wyatt.

R.L.

Glossary

ABWEHR   The military intelligence division of the German General Staff.

'A' FORCE   The British deception organization in the Middle East.

AVALANCHE   Code-name for Salerno landings.

B1A   Section of MI5 responsible for handling double agents.

BODYGUARD   Overall deception plan to cover Second Front in 1944.

BP   Bletchley Park.

C   Head of British Secret Service.

CIGS   Chief of the Imperial General Staff: titular head of the Army.

COBRA   Code-name for American breakthrough at St Lo in Normandy.

COSSAC   Chief of Staff to Supreme Allied Commander: a temporary appointment for General Morgan as the preliminary planner of OVERLORD. Hence 'the COSSAC plan'.

CROSSBOW   Code-name for counter-offensive by Allied air forces against V-weapon launching sites.

DIADEM   Code-name for final break through the Gustav Line in Italy in 1944.

FHW   Fremde Heere West: section of the German Army staff responsible for evaluating intelligence about Anglo-American forces.

FORTITUDE   Code-name for deception element in BODYGUARD specifically related to Normandy landings.

FUSAG   First US Army Group: phantom formation created by Allied deception to persuade Germans that apart from NEPTUNE assault force many divisions were waiting in England to land in Pas de Calais.

GAF   German Air Force: the Luftwaffe.

GCCS   Government Code and Cipher School. The pre-war British code-breaking organization, responsible through MI6 to the Foreign Office, which administered Bletchley Park throughout the war.

GOODWOOD   Code-name for biggest British armoured attack in Normandy, to the east of Caen.

G2   The intelligence section in US formations.

13

HUSKY Code-name for the invasion of Sicily.

ISK Intelligence Services Knox: a section at Bletchley under Dillwyn Knox which concentrated on special machine ciphers.

ISOS Intelligence Services Oliver Strachey: a section at Bletchley concerned with signals enciphered by hand.

JIC Joint Intelligence Committee: a tri-service committee which evaluated intelligence for the British Chiefs of Staff.

KONDOR Code-name for German attempt to plant Abwehr agents in Cairo in 1942.

LCS London Controlling Section: the central unit for the co-ordination of strategic deception.

MAGIC Code-name for the intelligence derived from the American ability to decipher Japanese signals.

MINCEMEAT Code-name for pre-HUSKY deception plan popularly known as 'The Man Who Never Was'.

MI5 Department of the British security services responsible for security within the United Kingdom.

MI6 Otherwise known as the Secret Service or The Secret Intelligence Service (SIS): responsible for all security matters external to the United Kingdom.

MI 14 Section of Military Intelligence concerned with German military organization and intentions.

NEPTUNE Code-word for the D Day landings and establishment of a beachhead in Normandy in 1944.

OIC The Operational Intelligence Centre of the Admiralty which included among its sections the Submarine Tracking Room.

OKL Oberkommando Luftwaffe: the High Command of the German Air Force.

OKW Oberkommando Wehrmacht: the High Command of the German Armed Services.

OVERLORD Code-name for invasion of north-west Europe in 1944.

RAAF Royal Australian Air Force.

SEAC South East Asia Command.

SEALION Code-name for German plan to invade England in 1940.

SHAEF Supreme Headquarters Allied Expeditionary Force: headquarters of General Eisenhower in command of Anglo-American forces during the invasion of Europe.

SHINGLE Code-name for Anzio landings.

SLU Special Liaison Unit: the section responsible for handling, distributing and ensuring the security of Ultra signals transmitted by Bletchley. Sometimes linked with its communications section as SLU/SCU.

TORCH Code-name for the Anglo-American landings in north-west Africa.

USAAF US Army Air Force, the overall American Air Command.

USAF US Air Force: a subordinate air grouping.

WAAF Women's Auxiliary Air Force.

WRNS Women's Royal Naval Service: the Wrens.

XX Committee Inter-service group responsible for overall policy in connection with strategic deception, employment of double agents, etc.

'Y' Service The British radio-intercept service.

ZEPPELIN Code-name for 'A' Force's plan to persuade the Germans that an Allied invasion of the Balkan area was intended in the summer of 1944.

Prologue: 'The Battle is the Pay-off'

A quarter of a century after she had been in charge of the Intelligence War Room in Field Marshal Alexander's headquarters at the Royal Palace of Caserta in Italy, Judy Hutchinson began to suffer from a brain haemorrhage. Her condition was critical. As she was rushed from her country home to the Oxford hospital where a long operation saved her life she was in great pain and confusion of mind. Yet when she later looked back she remembered how the only fear she had felt was not about herself: it was the terror, over-riding all other concerns, that in delirium she might give away the secret of Ultra. There could hardly be more poignant evidence of the dedicated attitude that throughout the Second World War – and for three decades afterwards – guarded the most comprehensive and effective system for penetrating an enemy's mind that has ever been evolved.

Thousands of others in Britain and the United States honoured their wartime oath of silence. Their range is extraordinary. The most senior statesmen and officers of government, the most responsible leaders of the armed services and an outstanding generation of scientists shared their private knowledge with a multitude of humble signallers and cipher-clerks, as well as with the great host of ordinary young girls from the Navy and the RAF who operated the essential machinery. There were no leaks. Perhaps never before has there been such a prolonged corporate act of silence. This compelling sense of security was built into the Ultra system from the start, and its power can be simply illustrated. During the severe second half of the war the man who had the immense burden of running Bletchley Park in Buckinghamshire was Commander Edward Travis. Everything to do with Ultra stemmed from the complex operations at Bletchley. Yet when, at the end of the war, Travis's services earned him a knighthood his wife simply asked 'What for?'

We can talk about Ultra now. Until 1974 no open reference was permitted. In that year, however, Group Captain Winterbotham

17

was authorized to publish *The Ultra Secret,* which at last brought this vital aspect of the war into the public domain. A pioneer work can scarcely be encyclopaedic, or always precise, and the Group Captain was writing from memory, without access to reserved papers, and about only a limited area of an enormous enterprise which no single man ever witnessed as a whole. Nevertheless he opened the door and Clio, the muse of history, owes him her gratitude.

The door is not yet wide open. Since 1974 a few of those who used Ultra intelligence during the war at varying levels of responsibility have been allowed to publish books in which they have described what, in each case, could only be a partial experience. The operation was so compartmentalized and so enormous that no individual could envisage the wood that stretched beyond his particular clump of trees. There have been other and more fanciful books written by authors whose imagination has exceeded their grasp of the facts. And then, in October 1977, the British Government decided to make available a substantial number of the actual Ultra signals. The release of these in the Public Record Office at Kew has been a boon for historians, but though access is now possible to many thousands of signals, they cover, as yet, only very limited areas of a world-wide landscape.

And this is not enough. The intelligence acquired through Ultra affected the whole of the war against Germany, Italy and, not infrequently, Japan. From the Battle of Britain to the planning for D Day and the conflict in Normandy: from the Mediterranean shores to the islands of the Pacific and far away China: in the war at sea and the great bomber offensive over Germany: in schemes of deception and the handling of double agents, the influence of Ultra was direct and often immediate. It is visible as an energizing vein that runs through the whole conduct of the war. Churchill and his Chiefs of Staff drew constantly and even insistently on this secret source. And when the Anglo-American alliance was forged, United States commanders in the field paid as close attention to Ultra as did General George Marshall at his daily staff meetings in the Pentagon.

Since Ultra was all-pervasive, there seemed to be an urgent need for a book in which the system could be considered as a whole. Studies or reminiscences of parts of this great enterprise have an obvious value, but it was the cumulative effect, the long-sustained endeavour, the extraordinary range of application that made Ultra unique. In war, moreover, military intelligence is not a matter of romance. It is valuable precisely in so far as it contributes practically to the defeat of the enemy. The battle is the pay-off. An attempt to indicate how, on all the Allied fronts and in all the Allied theatres, Ultra was a positive factor of the highest importance in battles by land, air and sea ought therefore to promote a deeper understanding of the way the Second World War was actually won. Without this dimension the picture is incomplete.

In the British, American and German archives much that is relevant to Ultra's story can be discovered by the informed and inquisitive student, though far too many documents are still classified and reserved. Nevertheless, Goethe's remark is true of military history: 'The most important things are not always to be found in the files'. This is specially so where intelligence is concerned. The over-riding need for secrecy, never more rigorously applied than in the case of Ultra, creates exceptional conditions for the historian. I saw that I could not get close to the reality unless I could seek out and interrogate those who, as producers or users of Ultra, knew the important things that never get into the files.

Since the stage was the whole war the cast was enormous. At the centre of action were the intelligence staffs of Wavell, Auchinleck, Alexander and Montgomery during the march from Cairo to Berlin. Behind them lay the men and women who, ultimately in their thousands, created and expanded Ultra's power-house – the establishment at Bletchley Park where, as will be seen, the secret war was won. Then there were the interceptors and, further back in time, the Poles whose pre-war achievement in cracking the German ciphers was critical for the whole story. The brilliant team in the Navy's Operational Intelligence Centre; the men who directed the Bomber Offensive; the co-ordinators of world-wide deception schemes; those who, from Ultra information about German agents, picked them up and 'bent' them to our purpose – all were essential witnesses, as were the officers and sergeants, so little known, who in their Special Liaison Units passed on intelligence from Bletchley to commanders at the battlefronts.

And then in the United States there were the men to be found who had master-minded the American involvement in Ultra both in Europe and in the Far East, as well as the specially selected officers who looked after Ultra at headquarters in the field. The vast American air offensive in the west used Ultra as a fruitful source: what had staff officers and commanders of the USAAF to say?

In all these areas of inquiry the key figures shared with me their recollections – and much of what I heard is certainly missing from the files!

*   *   *

Put in the simplest possible terms, the operation called Ultra involved intercepting enemy signals that had been mechanically enciphered, rendering them intelligible, and then distributing their translated texts by secure means to appropriate headquarters. During the great campaigns on land or in desperate phases of the war at sea, exact and utterly reliable information could thus be conveyed, regularly and often instantly, mint-fresh, to the Allied commanders. The key concept was that of security: this whole operation trembled on a razor-edge, for if the Germans had come to believe that their most important ciphers were being broken the disaster for the British would have been immeasurable and perhaps final. The Americans, too, would have been gravely discomfited had the Japanese abandoned a complacency akin to the Germans', and recognized that their own signals were vulnerable. It is the weak, however, whom intelligence most befriends: and in real terms, the British were never strong. Ultra's victory was vital if they were to be victors in the field. But there was a pre-requisite for success. No radio, no Ultra. Ultra was manna from heaven, the child of a radio war without parallel. Certainly radio was employed by the main belligerents in 1914–18, but only in the Second War did advanced technology and increased sophistication make the wireless set a common tool of communication at every level from Prime Minister or President, Duce or Führer down to the smallest infantry or armoured sub-unit. Ultra was the fortunate parasite of this proliferation.

Throughout the war the world's atmosphere was criss-crossed by immense, complex and ever-changing patterns of radio traffic. The great physiologist Sir Charles Sherrington, seeking for a phrase to describe the central nervous system of the human body, called it 'the enchanted loom'. This image beautifully captures the notion of infinite patterns constantly woven throughout space by the incessant radio signals of the Axis and the Allies – of their High Commands, their armies, navies and air forces, their diplomats, their secret establishments. It was this very multiplicity that Ultra exploited, for as long as the Germans had confidence in their ciphers (and they never, in spite of occasional suspicions, lost that confidence) high-level communication on the greatest scale – reaching thousands of signals a day – was conducted over the air. This was fundamental. Had the Germans been able to intercommunicate at all times by telephone over land-lines, there would be no Ultra story to write. Clandestine tapping into portions of a telephone network is technically possible, (as the patriot workers in the French Post Office, for example, demonstrated by fruitfully tapping some of the trunk lines from occupied France into Germany), but obviously no such intrusions could have provided the flow of intelligence about the German war effort which Ultra's cornucopia supplied.

There was thus a psychological factor – German self-complacency: there was a technical factor – radio is a convenient means of communication in war: but there was also a geophysical factor of profound importance. In the highly industrialized, highly urbanized areas of western Europe the Germans, at a pinch, might have managed to function via the telephone and only a most restricted use of radio. But the Mediterranean divides Europe from North Africa. The vast expanses of Russia set a premium on radio. There are no land-lines to U-boat packs, yet without some measure of central direction and control from a shore base the use of a pack-technique in the Battle of the Atlantic would have been inhibited. As the war progressed, moreover, Hitler's increasingly centralized control of all military operations meant that wherever he established his headquarters signals winged to and fro between the supreme Führer and his commanders on the distant battlefields. The effect, therefore, was that the Germans were not only happy to transmit their high-level messages by radio: they were compelled to do so. Ultra had an enormous hunting-ground.

Many other predators invaded this rich territory. Between 1939 and 1945 all the belligerent nations continued and intensified their peacetime practice, keeping the wireless traffic of both hostile and friendly countries under constant surveillance – surveillance unremitting, increasingly sophisticated, and conducted over the widest possible range. Outstanding among a myriad examples is, of course, that combination of intelligence derived from decoding and deciphering Japanese signals to which the Americans gave the umbrella-title Magic, whose command of the Japanese diplomatic and naval ciphers and codes should have taken the surprise out of Pearl Harbor and did make it possible for the United States themselves to spring a decisive surprise at Midway. The Germans' highly efficient naval interception unit, the *Beobachter Dienst* or B Dienst as it is usually known, for many long months after the outbreak of war possessed a fatal ability to read British fleet signals, while its mastery of the convoy code had a disastrous impact on the Battle of the Atlantic well into 1943. Even Heads of State were not exempt. Roosevelt and Churchill held apparently confidential conversations by transatlantic radio-telephone, but it is now known that the research department of the German Post Office was able to record and unscramble at least a useful portion of this secret duologue.

Magic and B Dienst produced spectacular results, but their performance at its most dramatic merely represented peaks in what was a continuous and world-wide activity, ardently practised by every country capable of applying the necessary techniques. Hundreds of intercepting and decoding units existed – the ammunition they provided being as welcome to the military staffs as the shells for their guns. In such a perspective, therefore, it becomes immediately apparent that the general characteristics of the Ultra system were not unique. Both the Allies and their enemies exploited the pattern woven on the enchanted loom. They all caught signals out of the air, broke the relevant code or cipher, and passed on the resulting information to their staffs and governments. What differentiates Ultra from the wide variety of signal-intelligence services is not that its nature was *inherently* different: it was simply the best.

Supremacy, in a field where some of the finest intellects of the combatant nations were stretched to the limit, was neither achieved nor maintained without exemplary and ceaseless effort – particularly on the part of Ultra's cryptanalysts. For at the heart of this intelligence coup lay their ability to make comprehensible the many thousands of scrambled signals which the Germans entrusted to the air in the certainty that their chief ciphering machine had rendered them impenetrable. This machine, Enigma (of which the Germans constructed some 100 000 in the course of the war), was the regular vehicle for the Reich's secret traffic from the 1920s until, in early May 1945, the latest versions ceased their clattering in the headquarters of Hitler's brief successor, Grand Admiral Karl Dönitz. But there was probably no moment before VE Day when the experts in England were not afraid, openly or subconsciously, that some new variant in Enigma's intricate mechanism would end, or at least significantly diminish, their command over the enemy's communications. Like the intellectuals and technologists who struggled at Los Alamos to perfect the atom bomb before the enemy stole a march, the cryptanalysts and their colleagues were daily haunted by *tomorrow*, when some radical change in the German ciphering technique or, still worse, a leak in the security of their own system might lead to frustration or catastrophe. The price of continuing success was eternal vigilance.

1 The Glow-lamp Machine

'It is a riddle wrapped in a mystery inside an enigma; but
perhaps there is a key.'
WINSTON CHURCHILL

Enigma is unique. No other machine has started life as an ordinary
piece of merchandise and ended as a major influence on the outcome of an international conflict.

The commercial career of Enigma began in the aftermath of the
First World War. It was in 1919 that a Dutchman, Hugo Alexander
Koch, registered a patent for the design of an enciphering machine.
The *'Geheimschrijfmachine'* or 'secret writing machine' envisaged by
this man of Delft embodied ideas that were possible but not yet
practical, and it was an engineer from Berlin, Dr Arthur Scherbius,
who was the true pioneer. By July 1923 Scherbius was sitting on the
board of directors of a *Chiffriermaschinen Aktiengesellschaft* (Cipher
Machines Corporation) which had been established at 2 Steglitzerstrasse, Berlin, to make and market the invention which Scherbius
christened Enigma.

A detailed description of the fully developed Enigma is given
later at a more appropriate point. To avoid confusion – for the
technicalities *are* confusing – it will suffice to say here that the
Scherbius model, which went through various stages of improvement, contained many of the basic concepts finally incorporated in
the Germans' military versions. All the same, the Cipher Machines
Corporation cannot have seen much financial return on the
300 000 000 marks of inflated currency with which it purchased a
controlling share in the exploitation of this new device.

Yet the Corporation was not slack. David Kahn in his masterly
book on *The Codebreakers* has recorded that 'it exhibited the
Enigma before the 1923 congress of the International Postal Union,
and the following year got the German post office to exchange
Enigma-enciphered greetings with the congress'. And an elaborate
sales-pamphlet* was produced (in English) under the title 'The
Glow-lamp Ciphering and Deciphering Machine "Enigma"'. What

*A photograph of the cover appears facing page 80.

25

persons is it calculated to serve and how?' With words that now
sound ironical it opened its attack on the customer. 'Decisive battles have been lost, by land and by water, in the air and in debating
with each other, because the adversary had a better method of
keeping his correspondence secret.' It was the Germans' failure to
do precisely this that kept Ultra alive from 1940 to 1945.

But in the twenties trade was stagnant. The businessmen of the
world, to whom Glow-lamp's pamphlet was addressed, showed no
enthusiasm. The concept of industrial espionage had not yet been
invented. Why spend money on protecting one's correspondence?
Enigma had arrived too soon. Scherbius himself went bankrupt and
his patents passed into other hands. Nevertheless, the interest
shown in his machine during those years by four countries – his
own Germany, Poland, Japan and the United States – had consequences so enormous that they are impossible to calculate.[1]

Of all the nations Germany was the first to detect and rapidly
exploit Enigma's possibilities for the secret purpose of making her
military communications secure. And there was a good reason: in
the years immediately following her 1918 defeat and the Treaty of
Versailles Germany had a great deal to hide. Though the Peace
Treaty restricted her armed forces to 100 000 men her brilliant
Commander-in-Chief, General von Seeckt, was using every illicit
device to increase his country's war-potential – including the training of his troops in communist Russia. A system which enabled
military messages to be transmitted in an apparently unbreakable
cipher was irresistible. On 9 February 1926, therefore, the latest
Scherbius model (a modified version of his Enigma C) was introduced into the German Navy and used regularly until October
1934, when it was replaced by a better type. (This, the Enigma M,
became the standard equipment of the Reichsmarine – a basic
design capable of progressive refinement.) It was natural for the
Navy to come first. Ships depend on radio whose signals are
exposed to interception: armies can use the telephone. Nevertheless, at least by 1928 the German Army had also adopted Enigma –
the Luftwaffe could only follow suit when Hitler came to power in
1933 and began the expansion of his air force. (The commercial
model, incidentally, was now withdrawn from the market.) As the
troubled thirties moved towards another Armageddon the Nazi
Reich thus had a head start in the area which all professional soldiers rate most highly: secrecy and security.

There is no evidence that the British showed any positive interest in these developments – unlike the Americans, who at least took the precaution of acquiring for themselves a model of the Scherbius machine. This transaction was carried out between the Chief Signal Officer (working through the Assistant Chief of Staff, G2) and the US Military Attaché in Berlin, Colonel A. L. Conger, who on 17 October 1927 forwarded to Washington no less than five copies of the Glow-lamp pamphlet. Conger had done his homework, for he also attached a report by Captain Koot of the Dutch Army's Staff on a two months' test of Enigma which he had carried out at the end of 1926 and in early 1927. Koot declared:

Considering the machine with reference to the security it offers against unauthorized deciphering, I dare say that it satisfies all requirements be they ever so high. Being an expert in ciphering and deciphering matters I don't shrink back from saying that even the possession of an equal machine with the same electrical connections both in the ciphering cylinders and in the other parts of the machine will not enable an unauthorized person, though he may be an expert in deciphering, to decipher a certain document or to find out its solution by scientific methods, unless he knows the whole key. . . .

'Finding the key'. 'The key of the day'. As Ultra's story unfolds it will be seen that these phrases summarize the constant quest of the cryptanalysts who sought to resolve what Churchill called 'a riddle wrapped in a mystery inside an enigma' – the words are so beautifully relevant, though it is fair to recall that he actually used them about the Soviet Union! Meanwhile, on 29 November 1927 the Chief Signal Officer in Washington sent a message: 'it is requested that the cost of a single machine, including packing, crating, and transportation charges, prices to be expressed in dollars, be furnished this office.'

In fact the price of a Scherbius machine in 1927 was 144 dollars, packaging involved another three dollars eighty cents, and as the machine was too heavy for the diplomatic pouch it set the United States back another eight dollars fifty cents for Enigma to be shipped from Bremen to New York on the SS *President Harding*. The act of acquisition is recorded in a signal to the Assistant Chief of Staff from Colonel Conger in Berlin on 12 May 1928: 'One "Enigma" cipher machine was purchased by this office and paid for on voucher No. 3 in the accounts of Major H. H. Zornig, Ord.

27

Dept., for the month of May 1928.' By June the machine had reached the General Depot of the Quartermaster Supply Officer in Brooklyn, carefully addressed to 'Signal Property Office, Research and Engineering Division.'[2]

With hindsight it can be seen that this particular piece of property was cheap at the price: 144 dollars plus transportation! Yet the result was an anticlimax. Enigma reached the United States just as the famous (or, as many felt, infamous) Black Chamber was running into trouble. Under the skilful cryptanalyst Herbert Yardley the Black Chamber unit, working covertly for Army Intelligence or the Signal Corps, had specialized in breaking codes or ciphers used by foreign diplomats in the USA for reporting secretly to their governments at home. But in May 1929 a new Secretary of State, Henry Stimson, announced the principle that 'gentlemen do not read each other's mail' and, like a man of honour, shut down the Black Chamber. 'This fine gesture', commented the *Christian Science Monitor*. 'The practice is a left-over from the secret diplomacy which the World War was supposed to have overthrown. It has no place in a world which is working for peace based on trust and good will.' Cryptanalysis was under a cloud.

Actually the practice did retain a foothold in a world where certainly not everyone was working for peace. A manuscript document in the George C. Marshall Research Library, Lexington, Virginia, entitled 'US Army in World War II: The Signal Corps', states specifically that 'The Military Intelligence Division which had subcontracted its cryptanalytic work to Yardley now transferred it to the Office of the Chief Signal Officer, and transferred the responsibility too.' The manuscript makes clear the inner meaning of the phrase 'transferred the responsibility too'. Although open authority was now only granted for the reading of 'gentlemen's mail' in wartime, in practice undercover attempts to break the ciphers of other countries were to continue. It is an argument familiar to the CIA: how, otherwise, could the United States intelligence staffs be ready in the event of war? And so a new organization was created, the Signal Intelligence Service, which took over all the files of Yardley's Black Chamber and simply carried on with the job. At its head was one of the most brilliant cryptanalysts of the century, William Friedman.[3]

The first reason why the arrival of a commercial Enigma machine in the United States was followed by an anticlimax is thus evident.

28

The climate of opinion was not favourable for an intensive attack on the German cipher system which the possession of an Enigma would certainly have facilitated. It is true that Ronald Clark, Friedman's biographer, says that 'Friedman knew as much as anybody outside Germany about what was possible with Enigma, and his papers in the Signals records contain page after page of his efforts to discover a method of deciphering Enigma messages.' But the truth was that the cipher could only be effectively and *consistently* broken with the aid of sophisticated mechanical devices, and though certain equipments were developed in the United States during the thirties, even by the time of Pearl Harbor the Americans had not gone this distance in respect of the German ciphers.

Pearl Harbor provides the clue, for the second reason that distracted America's cryptanalysts from a solution of the German Enigma was Japan. After the Mukden incident of 1931 and the Japanese occupation of Manchuria it was inevitable that the main weight of Friedman's effort – and of the able cryptanalysts in the US Navy – should have been directed across the Pacific rather than across the Atlantic. Japan had, in fact, been the second foreign country to purchase a commercial Enigma from the *Chiffriermaschinen Aktiengesellschaft* in Berlin. After modifications, this was first used for signal security by the Imperial Navy. Then the Japanese Foreign Office adopted it, and after further improvements Tokyo produced in 1937 the model 97-shiki-O-bun In-ji-ki: Alphabetical Typewriter 97. This was the famous Purple machine whose ciphers were to run like a thread through American history until the bombs burst above Hiroshima and Nagasaki. For the next few years Purple would be Friedman's preoccupation. And so it happened that the answer to the problems set by Enigma, which Scherbius had devised for peaceful purposes and his fellow-Germans had converted into a weapon of war, came in the end from the third purchaser of 'the secret writing machine'. With the British apparently indifferent and the Americans otherwise concerned, the burden of discovery descended on the Poles.

Between 1926 and 1928, when the German armed forces first began to use Enigma, the Poles were like a man who suddenly realizes that he is about to lose his sight.

Pinned since 1918 between revolutionary Russia and a humiliated, vindictive Germany, they knew well enough that for them at least the Treaty of Versailles had not established a permanent

29

peace. They were fully aware of the clandestine activities of General von Seeckt, and of the small but highly trained army that was emerging from the ruins of Kaiser William's Empire. For monitoring these developments the Poles had one outstanding advantage – their highly developed skills as code-breakers. These had already stood them in good stead during the struggle for national independence that followed the First World War, and until 1926 they had continued to read in comfort the German's most secret signals. Although the shades of the Teutonic Knights might still haunt them with centuries-old reminders of invasion, at least they could read the German mind. But now, suddenly, in 1926 they discovered that the Germans were also employing a cipher, produced mechanically, which defeated the best of their cryptanalysts. In the field of intelligence this was equivalent to going blind.

The Poles were deeply disturbed by baffling signals which their intercept stations at Poznan, Starograd and Krzlawice began to register. They knew the German way, unrelenting, meticulous, tireless: and it now seemed hauntingly possible that across the border their ancient enemy would make steady advances in the practice of mechanical enciphering. The first step, therefore, was a form of capital investment in brainpower.* At the University of Poznan, in 1928, a small group of students was selected, from those already reading mathematics, to be prepared by a special course in cryptology. (One was later sent to Germany, to study at Göttingen.) The three men of outstanding brilliance in this covert body were Marian Rejewski, Jerzy Rózycki and Henryk Zygalski, all of whom, by 1932, had been set to work in the Polish Secret Service under Major Maksymilian Ciezki, the head of the German department in the cryptological section of the General Staff. The problem of the elusive cipher was now directly assaulted.

The nature of the riddle can best be understood from a description of the machine itself, since the Poles had to discover not only how it was put together, but also the theoretical principles that governed its performance. Consider Enigma, then, from the point of view of a young German soldier under instruction in a signal school.

---

*During this year Polish intelligence also had a German *military* Enigma in their hands for a weekend. A box addressed to the German Embassy in Warsaw was tactfully removed from the Railway Parcels Custom Office one Friday afternoon and returned, after examination, before the next Monday morning. (Source: Colonel Lisicki.)

He would see something that looked like a clumsy, solid, primitive typewriter or cash register. In front, as on an ordinary typewriter, there would be an alphabetic keyboard. But the first thing the trainee would learn would be that pressure on, say the letter X on the keyboard did not result in an equivalent X being typed, as would normally happen. He would see instead that on the flat top of the machine another alphabet was displayed and that here, as he pressed X on the keyboard, not X but another letter, for example K, would stand out because a light was illuminating it from below. X had become K: and what happened in the course of that substitution was the riddle presented by Enigma. Here was the core of the German cipher-system.

Pressure on the original letter X had created an electrical contact. Between X and the lighting-up of K the impulse thus generated had followed a crazy route, thought by the Germans to be beyond calculation, as it raced through Enigma's highly elaborate wiring. There were two main sources of diversification. At the rear of the machine were three circular drums, wheels or rotors which, as the name implied, could in fact revolve. When X was struck on the keyboard, the electrical impulse produced was carried through the complicated wiring within each of the three rotors in turn. It then hit a reflector, and made its way back through the rotors but following, this time, a different route along the wiring.*

And so, for any one setting of the wheels, the impulse passed through a succession of seven permutations – produced by the three drums, the reflector, and the three wheels again. But the wheels were not fixed in position. They had twenty-six contact points set equidistantly around their circumference. Each time they functioned, they automatically revolved just sufficiently to bring the next contact point on the wheel's perimeter into the operating position. Thus, if X produced K the first time, it was impossible for this to happen twice: different contact points were now in touch with one another, and the electrical impulse would pass through a different section of the wheel's internal wiring. Put simply, this time X might produce J – but never K. Moreover, each wheel could be

---

*This capability was foreshadowed in the Scherbius machine. The specification in the British patent of 1927 states that 'the slidable end drum is arranged so as to act as a reversing drum, i.e. has its electric connections such that the electric current arriving through the rotatable drums returns through the same drums'.

lifted out and put in the seat of another wheel. All these possible variations produced huge elements of incalculability.

As if all this was not distracting enough, the trainee signaller would be introduced to a further refinement. This had a beautiful simplicity. By providing each Enigma with extra wheels it was possible to take off one of those in position and replace it by a spare whose wiring had a different effect on the circuit, thus creating an immense new area of confusion. For example: with three wheels there were only six possible combinations by which to vary the order in which they were placed in the machine. But three wheels with two spares made no less than sixty variations possible.* And there were other diversifying elements, of which the chief was an array of plug holes in the upright front of the machine. Into these apertures connecting jacks were inserted, which extended the circuit between the wheels and the illuminating lights under the alphabet displayed on the top surface of the machine. By varying the plugging of the jacks it was thus possible to vary the connections between wheels and lights. This increased the imponderables. With the jacks plugged in one way the completed circuit would cause a tap on the keyboard's X to produce a light beneath K. If the jacks were plugged in another way the result might be an illuminated R.

The soldier at his signal school must learn to unscramble ciphered messages as well as how to concoct them. He would therefore be told that if he was a cipher clerk at the receiving end he would need not only an Enigma but also a list telling him the correct current setting for his machine. So equipped, he would be able to place his three wheels in the machine in the right order, revolve each of them until the right contact points (out of the twenty-six on each wheel) had been positioned properly in relation to one another, and push the jacks into the right plugs. Then, if he had to process a message, he would simply type out the enciphered text on his keyboard while a companion read off the letters of the original signal as they appeared illuminated amid the alphabet on the upper surface of the machine.

Such (and it is a very simplified version) was the riddle confronting the Poles. Not only had they to learn how Enigma worked: if they were to be able to read the Germans' signals it is obvious that

---

*By the beginning of the war the Navy's Enigma M was using four and then five spare wheels. Four spares allowed 210 alternative wheel-positions: five spares increased the options to 336.

they would have to find not only how to construct the machines for themselves but also the means of discovering, for every day, the correct method of setting them up. The keys to the setting were vital. There were so many possible alternatives and combinations that without the right key a cryptanalyst was lost. The mathematician I. J. Good, who worked at Bletchley during the war, has estimated that for a three-rotor Enigma the number of possible permutations was about 3×10^{18}: the incorporation of a fourth wheel raised the figure to 4×10^{20}.[4] Another Bletchley man, Peter Calvocoressi, has referred to 'an astronomic figure not far short of six thousand million million million'.

Unfortunately for the Poles, they had far more to master than an ordinary German cipher clerk. Like the Americans and the Japanese, their Secret Service had acquired a model of the commercial Scherbius machine. Major Ciezki probably got what he wanted through Antoni Palluth, a partner in the Ava radio equipment factory in Warsaw which was to play an important part in the Polish technological achievement during the next few years. But Scherbius had only produced a basic structure – the system of internally wired wheels, for example, rotating with their contact points: the glow-lamp alphabet. But the Germans had introduced ingenious sophistications in their military version – the improved reflector or *Umkehrwalze:* the arrangements of jacks and plugs, the *Steckers*. The fact of these and other modifications meant that for Poland's Signal Intelligence – in spite of its possession of a Scherbius – Enigma at first was truly 'a riddle wrapped inside a mystery'.

It might have been worse. Just about the time that the brilliant trio of Rejewski, Rózycki and Zygalski were due to return to Warsaw from Poznan University, an event occurred which, seen over the long perspective of the Second World War, now seems incredible. On 2 July 1931 Major P. W. Evans of the US Signal Corps, then Assistant Military Attaché in Berlin, filed a report which went straight to the Assistant Chief of Staff G2 (Intelligence) in Washington. It was headed 'German (Military). Subject: Cipher Devices used in Army Signal Communications'.[5]

Evans began by referring to a previous report of 4 October 1930 in which he had described the signals communications in the recent German Army Manoeuvres, and incidentally revealed that 'the German Signal Corps were using a typewriter type of enciphering device in the field'. He continued:

The German authorities have recently given to the undersigned a demonstration of the types of enciphering devices used in the Army and War Department.

The machine used in the field is one made by the 'Enigma' Company. It is quite similar to the commercial machine which has three enciphering wheels, each of 25 contact points, which serve to conduct a current through varying (enciphering) channels from a contact made by a key on a keyboard to a final lamp or visual indicator on the top of the machine. This machine is the one now in the office of the Chief Signal Officer in Washington. The military machine is very similar to the commercial machine and is made by the same company. It has three enciphering wheels each of 25 numbered points on its periphery and the keyboard and lampboard are the same. The only difference in the military machine lies in the fact that at the front of the machine, just beneath the keyboard, there are a series of jacks with double contact plugs with cord connections which can make variable electric circuits in the machine.

At the German War Department in the principal station of the German Army radio net there is another 'Enigma' machine of more elaborate design. This larger machine weighs approximately 200 lb. and has ten enciphering wheels each of 25 points. This machine is built to give a typed copy of the enciphered message in groups of five characters or to give a typed clear message when the operator puts the enciphered message on the keyboard.

A still more elaborate machine is in use in the message center of the Naval communications which is in the same building (*Reichswehrminis-terium*) as the War Department. The machine has 20 enciphering discs each with 50 numbered contact points. The whole machine occupies the top of a table and must weigh 400 to 500 lb. Its operation is apparently similar to that of the War Department radio station.

Many speculations are provoked by this remarkable document. One's first and obvious reaction is to wonder how and why a foreigner like Major Evans was allowed to enter these secret sanctuaries. Was it an attempt to impress – like the visits of senior RAF officers arranged by the Germans later in the thirties, to show off the strength of the Luftwaffe? Was it contempt for American capitalism apparently slumping to collapse? Or was it a case of over-confident self-satisfaction? Certainly the year, 1931, is significant, for after 1933 and Hitler's stranglehold on Germany there would have been no welcome for Major Evans in the bowels of the *Reich-sministerium*. Secondly, the Evans report heavily underlines a question already considered earlier in this chapter. With the Attaché's previous report on the 1930 army manoeuvres, this new eye-witness, and their own Scherbius on which – as Evans pointed out so specifically – the German version was based, US Signals Intelligence had the necessary incentives for a direct attack on the German cipher system. But Enigma, as has been seen, escaped by a default in Washington. Too many eyes – with considerable justification – were turned across the Pacific.

If the report is considered from the point of view of the Poles in 1931, however, a third and sinister reflection results. What are these mammoth machines in the German War and Navy Departments? What further problems would their complications offer for Major Ciezki and his young cryptologists in Warsaw, now on the eve of their assault on Enigma? The elaborate War Department model with its ten wheels; the fifty contact points on each of the twenty wheels in that 400/500 lb table-top version? A cryptologist's nightmare. Fortunately what Major Evans had seen was some examples of the inherent German tendency towards elephantiasis – a tendency which, after their defeat in 1945, left Europe littered with specimens of tanks and guns swollen beyond the limits of efficiency. In practice, the many thousands of Enigmas manufactured by the Germans for military purposes conformed in scale to 'the machine used in the field' as described in Evans's report. The mammoths were aberrations from a standard pattern. That, at least, was some alleviation for the Poles.

Nevertheless, by contrast with that electrically-stimulated computer the human brain, Enigma might have seemed a relatively simple affair when considered in perspectives of today. With its 10 000 million nerve cells, its 10 000 miles of fibre per cubic inch, and neurons pumping in their signals at a possible rate of 1000 impulses per second, the cerebral cortex has a complexity and subtlety far beyond Enigma's scope: yet the great investigators and research teams have brought at least large areas of this infinitely complicated system within their understanding. What, then, made Enigma so grave a challenge for the Polish General Staff? Time, money, secrecy. Unlike modern brain-research teams, their Cipher Bureau could not exchange information and discuss difficulties freely with colleagues all round the world: it had to work like a clandestine cell in a resistance movement. There was no great wealth in secret service funds for the lavish purchase of equipment. Above all, they were aware of a time-clock, invisible, imperious, whose minutes as they ticked away drew Poland steadily nearer to what seemed an inescapable war with Germany. Lonely, silent, and haunted by the sense of urgency, the youthful team settled down in Warsaw under Ciezki, concentrating on abstract reasoning for their main line of attack. By intensive efforts within such mathematical fields as group theory and the theory of cycles, ideas were evolved which proved fundamental for the rapid solution of Enigma.

Throughout this quest the only direct assistance came from the French. The head of the cryptological section in the *Service de Renseignement* or Intelligence Division of the French General Staff was Captain Gustave Bertrand, who was making his own tentative explorations and now set about building a working liaison with the Poles. There was nothing to be learned from the British. Throughout the thirties Polish Intelligence knew and had contact with the current representative of the British Secret Service in Warsaw, but their impression was that these gentlemen were primarily interested in Russia. In any case, the political climate of opinion in these years was scarcely favourable for confidential exchanges between Warsaw and London about the most delicate areas of national security.

Bertrand, during his post-war retirement as a General, published in 1973 an overblown account of his career entitled *Enigma*. One leading French historian commented: '*en ce qui concerne Enigma, l'épithète "boastful" appliquée au général Bertrand est un* "understatement".' And this, for the student of Ultra's pre-history, is the dilemma presented by his book. All those witnesses, Polish, French, British, who were associated with him in this shrouded world agree that he made a genuine contribution: none would agree with his own large claims. He was no cryptologist: he was vain and self-seeking. After the publication of his book he wrote to former contacts asking them to sign a certificate affirming that his, and his alone, is the authentic Enigma story! And Bertrand is perhaps the only senior officer of some standing who, in his autobiography, has printed *in full* the citations for the decorations received not only by himself, but also by his wife.

It is with an acute scepticism, therefore, that one must assess his account of how, in October 1932, an officer in the German *Chiffrierstelle* or Cipher Bureau made overtures to the French Secret Service, and how thereafter this figure code-named Asché supplied Bertrand and his 'Section D' with an impressive collection of documents relating to the German organization and procedure for encoding or enciphering their military signals. By 1939 nineteen clandestine meetings between Asché and French officers had occurred, we are told, at rendezvous in Belgium, Denmark, Switzerland, Czechoslovakia and France. This is in the high tradition of the Great Game: but has it any more validity than the oft-repeated but baseless legend that the Polish construction of an Enigma was due to the surreptitious courage of a worker in a German factory who – according to the myth – removed a machine by parts and smuggled it over the border? Bertrand is not an attractive personality, but the answer must be 'Yes'.

The best estimate seems to be that in the early 1930s Bertrand did indeed hand over a number of relevant documents to the Poles, and that during the next few years he established a relationship of some confidence with Colonel Gwido Langer – the 'Luc' of Bertrand's memoirs – who was the able head of Poland's Cipher Bureau, *Biuro Szyfrów:* Bertrand's own cover-name, incidentally, was 'Bolek'. But it is to be doubted whether Bertrand ever understood, or indeed whether the Poles allowed him to have much inkling of, the *theoretical* effort by which they solved the Enigma problem. As for the documents themselves, emanating from the shadowy Asché, perhaps the verdict may lie with Colonel S. A. Mayer, head of Polish Intelligence from 1930 onwards. In May 1974 Mayer wrote, privately, a long paper entitled 'The breaking of the German enciphering machine Enigma by the cryptological section in the 2nd Department of the Polish Armed Forces' General Staff'. In this he affirms that *two* documents, dated 1931, were subsequently handed over by the French. In the context of Polish research at that time, he says, 'these documents appeared not to be indispensable for the final solution of the problem. But unquestionably they facilitated it'.*

Bertrand makes large claims about the material conveyed by Asché to the French, but what matters is the nature and quantity of the papers he himself actually handed over to the Poles, since it is the latter who, so far as a victory over Enigma was concerned, were the front runners. The main items that Langer obtained from Bertrand, in December 1932, were certain German documents relating to the past year. These included tables giving precise instructions

*Later in 1974, following the publication of Bertrand's and Winterbotham's books, Colonel Mayer wrote a Supplement to this memoir. He made available to the author his personal copy of both papers.

for the setting of Enigma (there were different tables for each service network, Army, Navy, Abwehr, etc.), and lists of the dates on which Enigma settings should be changed. Further documents included training or informational papers about how actually to use Enigma.

At first some of these Asché papers look out-of-date and valueless. This impression seems confirmed by the fact that the setting keys received by the Poles applied only to two months in different quarters of 1932 – the summer and autumn. In practice, however, Colonel Mayer knew what he was talking about when he said that they facilitated a solution of the Enigma problem. For the Poles in this exploratory phase were naturally keeping the texts of all German signals they intercepted, even if they could not immediately decipher. Thus the possession of actual keys, even if out-of-date, was a significant aid. By working back over old signals with precise keys in their hands the Poles could discover a good deal about the theoretical and mechanical principles of the Enigma cipher.

Whatever the relative merits of all these different lines of attack – though cryptologists would surely agree that the successful theoretical approach was crucial – the Poles with astonishing speed found themselves able not only to understand how Enigma worked but actually to build a machine for themselves. Once they had mastered the inner wiring of the wheels they moved quickly into production. Under the supervision of Major Ciezki and the technical direction of Palluth a whole series of Enigmas was turned out at the Ava factory in Warsaw, so that by the time of the German invasion in September 1939 no less than fifteen machines already existed.

And these were put to work. For most of their traffic in peacetime the Germans naturally used the telephone, but their training exercises (and emergencies) gave the Poles good opportunities for monitoring Enigma. A classic instance occurred on the night of 29 June 1934. This was the eve of the notorious purge carried out by Hitler to shatter his Brownshirt organization, the SA, and eliminate its head men including its leader, the pig-like homosexual Ernst Röhm. (The 'night of the long knives' was used to dispose of other 'unwanted' personalities, including General von Schleicher, who was shot with his wife on his own doorstep.) Thus it was that in Poland the cipher team found itself decrypting an urgent signal: 'To all airfields. Röhm is to be brought here dead or alive.' Apart from routine but invaluable 'order of battle' intelligence – the location and strength of German units – much was learned about the Reich's armaments industry, about espionage in Poland, and even about French politicians of a collaborative mind. By the end of 1937 Langer's department was comfortably at home amid the German cipher traffic.

In January 1938 a test was carried out over a period of two weeks which confirmed that about seventy-five per cent of intercepted matter was being deciphered. Colonel Mayer himself made a spot check, by picking out signals from a set of intercepts and ordering them to be deciphered in his presence. 'The result', he remembered, 'was perfect'. Yet this halcyon period was sadly brief. In the summer of 1938 the Polish Secret Service was warned, by an agent in a Luftwaffe signal section, that the Germans were intending to use two additional wheels in their Enigmas. On 15 September – the eve of Munich – this change occurred: disastrous for the Poles at the time, but in a larger perspective one of the turning-points in Ultra's pre-history.

Operation *Wicher* ('Gale' – the Polish code-name for their pioneer version of Ultra) was in disarray. From the previous description of Enigma it will be seen that by introducing two spare rotors into the system the Germans had enormously increased the intricacy of their encipherment. The Poles, for their part, had by now acquired so firm a grasp of the machine's theoretical and technical principles that even this new development would not have disconcerted them had it not been for the one dominating factor – time. In the autumn and winter of 1938, as Hitler's aggressive intentions unfolded almost monthly, time was golden: yet the Poles, suddenly incapable of reading the German signal traffic,* knew that unless some miracle happened a desperate and prolonged intellectual effort would be necessary before their brilliant team could establish a re-entry into the cipher. The ice was now very thin.

Confidence that the cipher would *ultimately* be broken again was supported not only by the skills and experience of Colonel Langer's young men, but also by a phenomenon once described as 'like a mad scientist's console from an old Fritz Lang film'. This was the

---

*Initially the signals of the three armed services were impenetrable. The signals of the SD, the German security service under Himmler, were still decrypted for a time but by July 1939 these too had been brought into line.

'Bomba', the high-speed calculating mechanism which the Poles developed as an essential complement to the human brain. For though the correct setting for an Enigma on any particular day could not infrequently be worked out by the cryptanalysts, the necessary calculations might – and often did – run on for weeks. But a signal decrypted after long delays may be a matter of professional pride in peace time: in war it is normally and often dangerously useless. The Bomba, though no more than a primitive forerunner of those great and sophisticated installations later used by both the British and the Americans, did make it possible for the Poles to tackle some of the problems posed by Enigma at speeds far beyond the scope of human thought. Indeed, built into the concept of the Bomba was the notion of in some sense paralleling the actual processes occurring within Enigma itself. Turing, the outstanding British mathematician who was to have a prime role in Ultra, once declared: 'A sonnet written by a machine will be better appreciated by another machine.' Similar thinking produced the Bomba, which in fact had portions of six Enigmas wired into its circuits.

But neither Bomba nor brains could provide an instant solution for the new dilemma. The difficulty was that Bomba could only cope effectively with the six alternative positions for the drums which, as has been seen, were the most that were possible in a three-rotor machine. The Poles had developed other devices too technical to describe, but like Bomba they too were unable to master the sixty alternatives available in an Enigma with five drums. The French, whatever their contribution, had little to add of strictly cryptanalytical value. But Bertrand, who had visited London in 1938 with some of his Asché documents and been greeted by the British cipher experts with what he called a *délirant* reception, now acted as a catalyst. By his contrivance a meeting was held in Paris on the 9th and 10th of January 1939 between two Poles (Langer and Ciezki), and two French officers, (Bertrand and, part time, an expert cryptologist), and three British (including Commander Alastair Denniston, Head of the Government Code and Cipher School). We are moving a step closer to Ultra. But the extraordinary fact is that if Bertrand had had his way neither this meeting nor Ultra itself might ever have happened.

Before the Paris conference was set up Bertrand proposed to Langer a course which he himself considered Machiavellian.[6] Since no significant progress was being made with the breaking of the five-rotor cipher, he trailed across the Pole's mind the notion that the French Secret Service should leak to the Germans, via an agent, apparently definite evidence that Enigma was an open book. If the Germans could be persuaded that both the French and the Poles were reading their most secret signals, they would be compelled to change their whole system on what seemed to be the eve of an unavoidable war: indeed, their change from the three-rotor to the five-rotor method had been accepted in Warsaw and Paris as a move towards mobilization. There is some sense in Bertrand's proposition. It is difficult to assess the effect on the German war-machine if, at the beginning of 1939, the need had suddenly and unexpectedly arisen for a new and impregnable method of ciphering all top-secret and operational signals. Certainly the High Command and the three fighting services would have been severely inhibited, and the time-scale of events in 1939 and 1940 might have been significantly affected. What cannot be doubted is that if the Germans had abandoned Enigma, Ultra might never have been born. Fortunately, Langer was not convinced.

In January, therefore, the three little groups of experts met in Paris. (In his old age Bertrand still treasured the menu of Drouant's restaurant where they dined.) Their discussions could only be tentative and exploratory, for the attitude of each delegation was different. Langer and Ciezki, eager though they were for any clues that would help them to solve the new cipher, had been strictly ordered to reveal nothing of what they knew about Enigma unless it became clear that the others had something to give by way of results from their own explorations. Not surprisingly: that knowledge was a jewel to be guarded to the death. The British, by contrast, must be presumed to have put together their own theoretical picture of Enigma, (though its scale and accuracy has never been revealed), but they could hardly bring to Paris that intimate awareness, derived from actually possessing and operating the machines, which by now seemed second nature to the Poles. The French, in effect, stood waiting in the wings. And so, as Mayer recorded, 'No positive result was achieved at this conference. Langer and Ciezki were under the impression that their partners were straightforward, but had nothing to say about Enigma.' So the Poles themselves said nothing: but at least the three groups parted with expressions of esteem, and friendly proposals were made for further meetings in Warsaw and London.

Then, on 31 March, Neville Chamberlain announced in the House of Commons that in the event of any action which clearly threatened Polish independence 'His Majesty's Government would feel themselves bound at once to lend the Polish government all support in their power', a guarantee to which the French were also openly committed. Whatever the viability of this optimistic promise in purely military terms, it certainly created a new situation and a new climate of opinion for Langer and Bertrand. Thunderheads now darkened the international scene, but the five-rotor cipher still defied all attempts at a solution. The consequence was a clandestine meeting in Warsaw during July between the Poles, Bertrand and a small British team: it occurred, unlike the Paris conference, entirely as the result of a Polish initiative. If one had to pin-point the time and place of Ultra's first decisive move from the unimaginable into the possible, this secret rendezvous in the Pyry forest would be the occasion.*

It represented a confluence of two virtually independent streams. There was the strong current of Polish expertise, strengthened by recent years of profound study and stretching back at least as far as the post-1918 struggle for national independence, when code-breaking proved itself to be a powerful weapon in the Polish armoury. On the other hand British practice, tradition and authority stemmed directly from a legend which was founded on truth – the achievements during the First World War of Admiral 'Blinker' Hall and his Room 40, the cryptological section of Naval Intelligence whose feats in connection with the Zimmermann telegram, for example, made it world-famous. Two of the three British representatives at the July conference were an embodiment of this legend. Commander Denniston's Government Code and Cipher School was a rough equivalent of Poland's *Biuro Szyfrów*. What gave the meeting its historic propriety was the fact that both he and his companion, Dillwyn Knox, one of the most brilliant and original of Britain's cryptanalysts, had served their apprenticeship together in the Admiralty's Room 40.

An extremely rare little booklet recalls this relationship: *Alice in I.D.25*, by F. L. Birch, verses by A. D. Knox, illustrations by G.

---

*The British were lodged in the Hotel Bristol in Warsaw. The meeting took place in 'the house in the woods', a secret signals-intelligence post constructed of dank concrete and buried underground under the forest's thick cover at Mokotov-Pyry.

P. Mackeson. 'Composed for', the subtitle runs, 'and read at a Concert to I.D.25 at 19 Edith Grove, Chelsea, on Wednesday December 11, 1918'. The Great War was over: the code-breakers of Room 40 were bidding farewell to one another. As an offering for the valediction Frank Birch (whom a later page will disclose in action again at his old trade) composed this deft pastiche, in which Alice falls beneath Whitehall into a subterranean Wonderland peopled by strange beings who recognizably combine the characteristics of Lewis Carroll's creations with those of Room 40's wartime denizens. Of Dillwyn Knox's amusing verses the most relevant is the last. A rousing final chorus to be sung by all the company begins:

'Oh, if a time should ever come when we're demobilized
How we shall miss the interests which once life comprised!'

Then, having sardonically listed the varied horrors of Room 40 from which demobilization will in fact release them, the chorus ends:

No more delights live there for us: But *Denniston* will never
Desert his solitary post: *He* will go on for ever!

Well, Denniston had not deserted: and here he was in Warsaw, in July 1939, with Dillwyn Knox beside him. (Knox had not deserted, either. When Room 40 was transferred from the Admiralty to the Foreign Office after 1918, and re-named The Government Code and Cipher School, like Denniston, Knox worked for it continuously between the wars. His brilliance as a classical scholar gave him good cover.)

A third man had also come from London, as observer rather than participant. In the guise of a Professor from Oxford, which he assumed without difficulty, Colonel Stewart Menzies was present, the unannounced Deputy Head of the British Secret Service. At an official lunch for the visitors Colonel Mayer found himself shaking hands with this distinguished academic 'who actually did not belong to the cryptological branch but closely co-operated with it'! After 1945 Mayer ran into the Professor again, and recalled their previous encounter.[7] 'Yes,' said Major-General Sir Stewart Menzies, who throughout the war was at the head of the Secret Service. 'Yes. It was over Enigma.'

According to Colonel Mayer there had been frequent discussions in the Intelligence Department of the Polish General Staff about the action to be taken over *Wicher* material in the event of hostilities. A clear policy emerged – 'in case of a threat of war the Enigma secret must be used as our Polish contribution to the common cause of defence, and divulged to our future allies'. When a new man, Colonel Smolenski, took over the Department in January 1939, this was the briefing he received from his predecessor. Now, in July, it seemed to the Poles that the moment of truth had arrived. They decided to give.

Denniston and Knox were astonished when, on the morning of 25 July, at the first session in the Pyry forest, Langer disclosed that his team knew everything about Enigma – how to construct it, how to break its ciphers: though not, alas, the current series produced by the five-rotor version. When he produced an actual model *'ce fut'*, Bertrand recalled, *'un moment de stupeur'*. (Bertrand says that 'it was now, perhaps for the first time, that the pride of the British technicians was lowered by the achievement of the Poles'. He does not, however, disclose that he himself was staggered, or that Rejewski, who was present, found that Knox's theoretical grasp of Enigma's principles was so sound that they could discuss the actual machine on level terms.) The British pair immediately asked to be allowed to borrow drawings and to send to England for electrical and mechanical specialists. But there was another surprise for Knox and Denniston. Langer now revealed that from the Poles' stock of replicas two Enigmas were to be handed over, one for Britain and one for France, as well as technical drawings of the Bomba and other cryptanalytical devices which Polish ingenuity had originated. The Poles were making an outright bequest from their accumulated capital. Transport was to be Bertrand's responsibility: there was a convenience in using the French diplomatic bag from Warsaw to Paris.

Everything went smoothly. On the evening of 16 August Bertrand arrived in London, accompanied by a courier from the British Embassy in Paris, (with an Enigma in his diplomatic bag), and a

---

*In fact as in fiction, Victoria Station was a focus for the secret war. It was from the baggage room there that in January 1939 the first effective British double agent, code-named Snow, collected the wireless set which had been deposited for him in a suitcase by his German master. After war broke out he used the set for regular transmissions to Germany under British supervision, from his cell in Wandsworth Prison.

member of the Secret Service. At Victoria Station* they were welcomed by Menzies himself: according to Bertrand he was going on to a party and therefore turned up in evening dress with, appropriately, a rosette of the Legion of Honour in his button-hole. *Accueil triomphal!* In any case, here was Enigma: and Bertrand could reasonably rate himself as one of the *accoucheurs* of Ultra although, as has been seen, he might well have effected an untimely abortion.

While it is evident that in this summer of 1939 the British understanding of Enigma was far less than that of the Poles, it is difficult to establish the precise extent of that knowledge. Yet if over a decade earlier GCCS in the autumn of 1927 had sent a man round to the Patent Office he would have been able to read a complete technical description, in English, of the Scherbius machine and to examine the relevant drawings. For on 17 January 1927 'We, *Chiffriermaschinen Aktiengesellschaft,* of Steglitzerstrasse 2, Berlin W.35, Germany . . .' filed application for a patent to cover British rights in the invention already registered in Germany the previous March. The specification was accepted and registered at the British Patent Office on 11 August 1927. As was mandatory, the papers provided the most minute technical details. Stress was laid on the importance of being able to change around the order of the three wheels in the machine, and (a sinister note for the future) 'It is also possible to replace one or all of the ciphering drums 1, 2 and 3, by other ciphering drums which are differently interconnected.' There was another claim which, had it been studied in GCCS, might have provided food for thought. '*In the case of war there is the further advantage** that, for instance, when surprised by the enemy it is only necessary rapidly to remove the set of drums or even only one drum, thus rendering the ciphering machine useless for deciphering purposes.' As if this was not enough a second specification entitled 'Improvements in Coding Machines' (which had been registered in Germany in November 1928) was accepted by the British Patent Office on 16 February 1931.

The historian's hindsight, so deceptively quick to notice the interconnection between events, instantly perceives the significance of these documents in relation to the future military history of Enigma and all that this entailed. It must be presumed, however,

*Author's italics.

PATENT SPECIFICATION

267,472

Convention Date (Germany) : March 10, 1926.

Application Date (in United Kingdom): Jan. 17, 1927. No. 1385/27.

Complete Accepted : Aug. 11, 1927.

COMPLETE SPECIFICATION.

Improvements in and relating to Ciphering Machines.

We, CHIFFRIERMASCHINEN AKTIEN-GESELLSCHAFT, of Steglitzerstrasse 2, Berlin, W. 35, Germany, a German company, do hereby declare the nature of
5 this invention and in what manner the same is to be performed, to be particularly described and ascertained in and by the following statement:—

Electric ciphering machines are
10 known, in which from one operating point an electric current is sent through a plurality of ciphering elements, for instance, sliding members, drums or the like, and produces at an indicating
15 point, for instance glow lamps, keys of a typewriter or the like, a cipher letter which corresponds to the particular position of the ciphering members with respect to one another and to the ter-
20 minal members connected to the same. When, for instance, rotatable drums are used as such ciphering members, a plurality of such drums is mounted rotatably one behind the other on one
25 shaft and are provided with actuating means, for instance toothed wheels or ratchet wheels, which, driven by other toothed wheels or ratchet wheels produce a rotary motion of the drums with
30 respect to one another each time they are actuated. The drums are provided on both sides with contacts, for instance of the same number as the letters of the alphabet. The contacts on one side are
35 connected to the contacts on the other side in an irregular manner by intermediate conductors. At both ends of such a set of rotary drums fixed end drums are provided, the electric current
40 entering at one end drum and leaving by the other. When deciphering the electric current travels through the rotary drums and terminal drums in the opposite direction.
45 Such ciphering machines have the disadvantage that they thus have entirely

separate positive paths for the electric current and there was a certain possibility of anyone having a knowledge of the connections of the machine decip-
50 hering the cipher with the aid of existing cipher texts and a machine having similar connections. Such a ciphering machine is in any case a relatively bulky apparatus which for the sake of secrecy
55 must of course be kept under lock and key and occupies a considerable amount of space.

According to the present invention these drawbacks are overcome, by the
60 most important part of an electric ciphering machine, viz. the ciphering elements, being removable, from the ciphering machine and having its separate parts interchangeable and
65 removable.

At the same time means are provided for a particularly favourable way of conducting the electric current through the ciphering device.
70 In the accompanying drawing a constructional example of the invention is shown,

Figure 1 being a side elevation, partly in section of a drum ciphering device of
75 an electric ciphering machine in the operative position.

Figure 2 is a view from the rear of the device shown in Figure 1.

Figure 3 a side elevation of the device
80 at the moment of removing the ciphering drums from the device.

Figure 4 a rear view of the device, similarly to Figure 3, but having the parts in position, in which the ciphering
85 drums can be removed.

Figure 5 a view partly in elevation and partly in section of a detail to an enlarged scale, and

Figure 6 a section on line VI—VI of
90 Figure 5.

In such an electric ciphering machine

First page of the British patent for Enigma.

that the documents nestled undisturbed in the files of the Patent Office, since even by 1939 the British grasp of Enigma was still tentative and uncertain. In 1977 Dillwyn Knox's niece Penelope Fitzgerald published a joint biography of the four brilliant sons of a Bishop of Manchester – her father E. V. (Editor of *Punch*), the Catholic convert Monsignor Ronald Knox, the Anglo-Catholic priest Wilfred, and Dillwyn. Of the latter's work at GCCS in early 1939 she wrote: 'His section was at present concentrated full time on the solution of Enigma. . . . The Foreign Office had supplied its department with an old commercial Enigma, costing about £2,500, from which they could study the general mechanism, but no more than that.'[8] (If the cost of this second-hand machine *was* £2,500, the Americans made a far better buy when they acquired a new Scherbius for 144 dollars!) Bertrand also has described how he brought some of the documents acquired through his agent Asché over to London in 1938.

Thus the British were not entirely out of the hunt. And so, bearing in mind the reactions of the GCCS team during the meeting in the Pyry forest in June 1939, one can speculate with reasonable confidence about the progress made by the British before the Poles came to their assistance. There is evidence of theoretical study and a limited technical grasp, each falling significantly short of an effective mastery of the problem. An important witness is Professor R. V. Jones, who describes in *Most Secret War* how when he first visited Bletchley 'Travis told me that although the World War 1 generation of cryptographers, which included Oliver Strachey and Nigel de Grey (who had helped break the famous Zimmermann telegram) believed that machine codes would be unbreakable, some of his new generation of young cryptographers believed that Enigma could be broken, and that they had already got so far as working out what some of the cross wiring inside the wheels must be.'

Even to have got so far was obviously facilitated by a working model of the German military version of Enigma. For Allied Intelligence, therefore, the arrival of that squat little instrument in a courier's bag at Victoria Station was as crucial as, for the Anglo-American development of radar, was the moment almost exactly a year later when Sir Henry Tizard's mission reached the United States, to deliver its famous 'black box', the japanned metal trunk from the Army and Navy Stores (a few yards from Victoria Station) which had carried across the Atlantic the first and priceless sample of the valve immortalized as the cavity magnetron. This, 'the single most important item in reverse lease-lend', was said by the physicist Sir John Cockroft to have increased the power available to US technicians by a factor of 1000. To quantify the value of Enigma's arrival in London is beyond mathematics, but at least the play of chance in history can be clearly seen. If Bertrand's idea had been accepted, of leaking to the Germans that Enigma was 'blown', or if the Polish General Staff had decided to keep their secrets to themselves, matters might have gone differently.

Very differently: for at 4.45 am on 1 September bombs began to fall on Warsaw and German tanks rolled over the Polish frontier. In the whirlwind campaign that followed the predicament of Langer and his staff was acute. Not only were they unable to decipher German signals: even if they had been able to penetrate the five-rotor cipher they would have been frustrated, since the intercepting stations on which they depended were soon over-run or on the move. However, after evading capture and destroying or successfully hiding their *Wicher* equipment, they managed to escape to Roumania. Colonel Mayer describes the next stage:

On 26 September Captain de Winter of the French Army arrived at Calimanesti, a resort in the mountains where some of the officers of the Polish General Staff were detained by the Roumanians. He came to me, and even stayed in my apartment in the hotel. He was looking for some Polish officers, among them Colonel Langer, for whom he had a message from Captain Bertrand. Next day he met Langer and proposed that he should go to France with all his subordinate cryptologists to continue his work. Langer duly reported this to me immediately and asked for my advice.

Mayer agreed. And so by 1 October – some by special plane and some by the Orient Express – Langer and fifteen of his experts reached Paris. The British Secret Service had assisted these notable refugees – notable, in particular, because there travelled with them to France the two Enigmas which they had managed to preserve from their original stock.

But in October the relative strengths had altered. Langer's group was now in exile from a defeated country: the French, as yet unscathed, were in the optimistic early days of their own war, and the French could call the tune. On mobilization their 5th Bureau, the intelligence division of the General Staff, moved out to the area of Gretz-Armainvillers, some forty miles north-east of Paris. It was near here that Bertrand, now a major, set up his section for handling and deciphering intercepted signals. The location was the Château de Vignolles, its code-name *PC Bruno*. Three elements composed the total of seventy technicians. Apart from the French, there was a small Spanish section, *Equipe D;* seven men who had been salvaged from the ruins of the Civil War, and whose mission was to cover the signal traffic of Spain and Italy. The third element was Langer's team, now christened *Equipe Z:* for the Polish government-in-exile, realistically accepting the inevitable, agreed that the powerful and proficient unit, headed by a lieutenant-colonel, should be subordinated to a French organization of markedly less expertise and commanded by a newly promoted major. Powerful and proficient *Equipe Z* certainly was, since apart from Langer its roll included Ciezki and Palluth, Rejewski, Rózycki, and Zygalski, as well as three experts from the old Russian section of Polish Intelligence.* For tidy administration the Spaniards were embodied in the French Foreign Legion. Liaison with England, and with Lord Gort's headquarters at the British Expeditionary Force in France, was secured by the attachment of Captain Macfarlan and by a direct teleprinter circuit across the Channel. *P.C. Bruno* had become, in fact, the first allied operational intelligence centre, and *Wicher*, the Gale, would soon give way to its offspring Ultra.

The ice had cracked. Poland was submerged. Yet the treasure whose capture would have been the Germans' greatest prize now rested safely at Vignolles – two Enigmas evacuated by *Equipe Z* plus the model bequeathed to the French. And an irreplaceable team of expert cryptologists had been preserved intact. As the war ran on the Poles would work for the joint cause memorably – in fighter and bomber squadrons of the RAF: in besieged Tobruk: on the Italian heights of Cassino and the battlefield of Normandy. Nevertheless, their most distinctive achievement was their first. They had carried out impeccably the momentous peacetime decision of their General

---

*Rózycki went down with the *S.S. Lamoricière* in the Mediterranean in 1942. After the war Zygalski settled in England and Rejewski returned to Poland.

Staff: 'In case of a threat of war the Enigma secret must be used as our Polish contribution to the common cause of defence, and divulged to our future allies'. They had made Ultra possible.

2   The British Breakthrough

'Then came in all the King's wise men: but they could
not read the writing, nor make known to the King the
interpretation. Then was King Belshazzar greatly troubled, and his countenance was changed in him, and his
lords were perplexed.'

The Book of Daniel

At Belshazzar's feast the writing on the wall was plainly visible but
unintelligible. There on the plaster were the words inscribed by the
mysterious fingers of a man's hand, doom-laden but inscrutable
until one wiser than all the King's interpreters, the prophet Daniel,
deciphered their terrible message. *Mene, Mene, Tekel, Upharsin*:
division and destruction at the hands of the Medes and Persians.

At the outbreak of the Second World War the British were in a
similar case. Who could assess the potential threat of those baffling
signals, enciphered by the fingers of a man's hand on an Enigma
machine, which the intercept stations were already catching from
the air but which none of the King's wise men in the Government
Code and Cipher School could turn into sense? The *Blitzkrieg* was
scything through Poland. When Hitler moved against the Franco-
British alliance, Germany would have an immense advantage unless
the Enigma cipher could be cracked. And where was Daniel?
Although it was only visible to a few, the writing was certainly on
the wall in September 1939, and the perplexity of Belshazzar's lords
was matched, it may be supposed, by that of the Chiefs of Staff.

The Code and Cipher School had moved to its war station. As
peace ran out Denniston transferred it from the London headquarters of the Secret Service at No. 54 Broadway, near St James's Park
in Westminster, to an undistinguished establishment some fifty
miles further north, on the outskirts of a little Buckinghamshire
country town conveniently linked with the capital by a main road
and railway. (There had already been a practice occupation in the
days of Munich.) A solid red-brick bourgeois edifice in a would-be
Tudor-Gothic style, Bletchley Park owes its fame to what happened
there rather than to any charm. One of the Americans who arrived
later in the war, Alfred Friendly of the *Washington Post*, remem-

51

bered it as 'a country estate of some tycoon who built a ghastly late-Victorian mansion set on spacious grounds (by then built up with Nissen huts or worse) with a swan pond, a ha-ha (a sunken wall so as to keep out the grazing cattle but not interrupt the view) and other orthodox accoutrements'. Still, there was space, communications were excellent, and for GCCS the implausible ambience was characteristic of the secret war. Moreover, Bletchley is conveniently sited between the Universities of Oxford and Cambridge. It was from the Cam, rather than from the Isis, that men were soon to be drafted who, like that earlier cryptanalyst Daniel, in the end proved able to 'dissolve doubts, read the writing, and make known the interpretations'.

The Junior Dean and mathematical tutor of Sidney Sussex College, Cambridge, reported to GCCS on the very first day of hostilities. Still in his early thirties, Gordon Welchman had already attended a brief cryptological course at Broadway in the autumn of 1938. Of Enigma, naturally, he had been told very little. Apart from some general principles of cryptanalysis the message that had sunk most deeply into his mind came to him from Oliver Strachey, an old hand at the game. Strachey had made him see that in war there must be a systematic procedure for processing intelligence. Welchman was not merely a mathematician. He was gifted with foresight, drive and a dexterous capacity for organization and leadership. Soon after his arrival at Bletchley Park he came to see, quite simply, that in policy and practice those of the peacetime GCCS staff who were directly concerned with Enigma were not prepared for exploitation along the lines which he had learned from Strachey to be essential in war. In the view of those who worked at BP on the cryptanalytical side of the Enigma traffic during the winter of 1939–40, it was Welchman who was primarily responsible for this department being so prepared when Hitler, turning the phoney war into reality, struck against Norway and France.

Hitler himself once remarked that 'the beginning of every war is like opening a door into a dark room. One never knows what is hidden in the darkness.' Factors of personality and tradition both prevented GCCS, in the autumn of 1939, from being properly equipped to exploit the possibility of penetrating the dark secrets of Enigma. Alastair Denniston, at its head, was a skilled and experienced cryptanalyst, a man of great charm and integrity. He could also, no doubt, have become a technical expert in breaking

Enigma's machine-ciphers, but he carried the heavy administrative load involved in expanding his peacetime GCCS into a wartime organization. His health was poor. Neither he, nor anyone else in the whole world, had personal experience of exploiting enemy signals, enciphered by a machine, to supply intelligence for the British in a major war. He needed the support of a practical specialist, but the brightest star at his side, the scintillating Dilly Knox, was a man, very specifically, of letters: his quick intellect danced elegantly amid the mazes of cryptography, but he was remote from the practical necessities of the coming war.

Like other forms of intelligence-acquisition, cryptanalysis has its moments of triumph when the achievement seems spectacular and even romantic. But the glamour, though justified, is deceptive. Most of the man-and-woman-hours at Bletchley were devoted to humdrum and routine procedures, the infinitely meticulous and often infinitely boring process of checking and tabulating, calculating and cross-referring. From these essential, exact but frequently repetitive exercises the penetration of a cipher could follow. But in temperament and mode of thinking Knox was ill-adapted to routine. His contribution to the battle against Enigma was considerable, but it was made in his own way. Intuitive, original, wayward, his mind moved like the flash of a kingfisher across a pond. Whether in Room 40 during the first World War, or at Broadway between the wars, he had been the visionary dreamer rather then the painstaking conformist.

His behaviour was in keeping. At Bletchley his fits of absence of mind were legendary. 'Oh, you've come to join us?' he said to one of his young ladies. 'Good. Have you a pencil? We're cracking ciphers.' Yet beneath the apparently unsurmountable scattiness there was a layer of steel. Cancer destroyed him, but he worked on from his bed during the last months of 1942 (having been discovered in hospital reading *The Art of Dying*). Just before the end came, on 27 February 1943 in his sixtieth year, he heard the sound of his brother Ronald, the Catholic priest. 'Is Ronnie still there,' said Dillwyn, 'bothering God in the passage?' (No doubt his treasure was to be found in heaven, unlike that of his counterpart in idiosyncracy, Alan Turing. Turing in some fit of despondency converted all his money into cash and buried it in the Bletchley woods, as a reserve against disaster. The true disaster was that Turing could never find it again). Thus Knox was better suited to being a brilliant auxiliary rather than an organizer or, on anything but a small scale, a leader.

And there was another reason. Both he and Denniston had experienced war in Room 40: but whatever the individual triumphs of that remarkable team between 1914 and 1918, the Admiralty's refusal to grasp the nature and value of intelligence meant that Room 40 existed in a vacuum. There were no systematic procedures for processing, evaluating and distributing the information produced by codebreaking. It is true that after 1918 two papers, of which Denniston was author or co-author, critically and constructively reviewed the work of Room 40 and the limitations of the Admiralty's system, or lack of system, for handling cryptanalytical and other intelligence, and it may well be that his interpretation of the World War I experience was always in Denniston's mind as hé struggled to keep GCCS alive between wars and to prepare for World War II. Certainly Welchman, who was perhaps as close to the events of that first autumn and winter as anyone still alive, feels very strongly that Denniston's personal contribution to the success of Ultra has not yet been properly appreciated. When Welchman presented specific suggestions for a comprehensive organization for deciphering, both Denniston and his Deputy Director, Commander Travis, saw their implications clearly and acted swiftly – for Travis, who ultimately succeeded Denniston, had the managerial talents needed to hold Station X together and to drive it forward. But Welchman was not alone as a source of fresh ideas. Professor R. V. Jones, who was to apply Ultra with unique success in so many aspects of the air war, has ascribed the credit for the ultimate British breakthrough to 'the magnificent work of a new generation of cryptographers at Bletchley Park in the early days of the war'. Some came from far afield.

In September 1939 the British team for the International Chess Olympiad was in Buenos Aires. It had just qualified for the final when war broke out. 'With the visions of London in flames,' Stuart Milner-Barry recalled, 'most of us did not think we could go on playing chess.' And so, on the blacked-out and unconvoyed *Alcantara* which happened to be leaving the Argentine on the night of their decision, the team returned safely to England – their only alarm coming from a porpoise which Milner-Barry, watch-keeping at night, had mistaken for a U-boat.

This was fortunate. A torpedoed *Alcantara* would have gravely affected the future of Ultra, for the British team contained some key members of Professor Jones's 'new generation'. They were men of quality. Milner-Barry, an undergraduate of Welchman's year at Trinity, Cambridge, had been a British boy champion at chess and rose to presidency of the British Chess Federation: after the war he occupied high posts in the Treasury and was knighted in 1975. His friend Conel Hugh O'Donel Alexander had obtained in 1931 a First in Mathematics at King's, Cambridge: for a quarter of a century he maintained a position as Britain's leading chess player and, after 1945, stayed on in the secret service as an officer at GCCS's successor, the Government's 'communication centre' at Cheltenham. The third of a remarkable trio was Harry Golombek: a recognized international chess master, who represented Britain in no less than nine Olympiads.

Early in 1940 Milner-Barry and Hugh Alexander were recruited by Welchman for GCCS and shared a billet in 'an old-fashioned but exceedingly comfortable pub called "The Shoulder of Mutton" in old Bletchley'. Golombek arrived some eighteen months later, after serving in the artillery, but from Cambridge in particular there was a steady flow of talent – men who would achieve great academic distinction after the war and one, the brilliant young J. R. F. Jeffreys, scholar of Downing College and holder of the Isaac Newton Scholarship for mathematics, who was to die prematurely of tuberculosis in 1944.

Recruitment in wartime always presents peculiar problems for clandestine organizations. The gentler tempo of peace allows a secret service to maintain or expand its numbers with cautious deliberation. But Bletchley was a rapidly expanding universe. The personnel it required were of a special type. They were needed in ever-increasing quantities: yet it was impossible to advertise in *The Times* for twenty code-breakers or a new batch of intelligence officers, nor was it easy, except with extreme discretion, to extract them from the armed services through 'the usual channels'. Bletchley's problem was not unique. The Special Operations Executive had the same difficulty in obtaining men – or occasionally women – to work with the resistance movements. 'In one way at least,' wrote Professor M. R. D. Foot in his official history of SOE in France, 'SOE was like a club, for membership was by invitation only.' And this, in the main, was how the members of the huts and sections at Station X were recruited – on the principle enunciated before 1914

55

by that great individualist Admiral Jacky Fisher: 'favouritism is the secret of efficiency'.

Just as the City of London and Balliol College Oxford (manipulators of two of the most efficient Old Boy Nets in the country) became mainstays of SOE, so Cambridge fed Bletchley. There were strong initial connections through the older hands, like Knox and Birch of King's, or those who like Welchman of Sidney Sussex and Vincent of Corpus had been earmarked for GCCS in the late thirties. The mathematical strength of Cambridge made the university an obvious hunting-ground. On a personal basis, therefore, suitable academics at Cambridge would be approached by friends already at BP: or, by private arrangement, someone would go down to one of the colleges to interview a mystified group of undergraduates picked out as possibles by a reliable tutor. Naturally one university was not the only source. Academics of the utmost distinction and men and women of all the talents were recruited in many ways and many places to make contributions at least as notable as those from the Cam. Still, Cambridge serves as an exact example of the word-of-mouth method that was employed – and perhaps inevitably employed – to staff Bletchley Park in secrecy. It is no coincidence that when in 1943 the Americans were faced with the problem of recruiting at speed the right sort of men to serve in Special Branch as handlers of Ultra, precisely the same system of personal and covert selection was used.*

The past of each recruit was carefully screened: an obvious precaution, but particularly relevant to an organization which contained a sizeable proportion of intellectuals chosen for their knowledge of German and Germany, or Italian, or other languages – not a few of whom, indeed, might have sought refuge in Britain from abroad or struck deep roots in other countries. These always formed a leaven, but as BP expanded from hundreds into thousands far greater numbers were drafted in from the army, navy and air force – notably the swarms of Wrens and WAAFs introduced to operate technical and communications services.

Yet that very expansion was the result of an expanding war which created its own problems for Station X. During the first year or so, for example, good mathematicians could be had for the picking by Bletchley talent-spotters. As the war effort exploded, competing

---

*For the recruitment of Special Branch, see Chapter Nine.

demands for every skill increased and mathematicians were in shorter and shorter supply. Welchman was in regular touch with C. P. (later Lord) Snow, whose task in Whitehall was to exercise rational control over the allocation of scientists. In 1977 Lord Snow recalled the problem for the author:

By the time I was actually in control, that is the summer of 1940, the position had altered. Everyone was trying to get statements from Winston that they had the highest priority. Radar really did have such a statement . . . I should estimate that quantitatively Bletchley got rather more than its share. The most interesting problem was to decide how many people, and which, should go to work on nuclear energy. The radar bosses, who became increasingly imperialistic, wanted to appropriate them all.

There is an important foot-note to be added to Lord Snow's communication. Acting as a filter for the scientific intelligentsia and the flow of promising technicians, even he, nevertheless, was not on the Ultra list. The 'need to know' principle was carried very far. Yet in spite of limitations, inhibitions and shortages it can certainly be claimed that the ways and means of recruiting for Bletchley produced what Admiral 'Bubbles' James, once head of Room 40, called 'a party of very clever fellows who could decipher signals'.

Outstanding among these was Turing. With the unpredictable waywardness of genius Alan Turing impressed himself on his contemporaries and dominates their recollections. Genius is the right word, for his ability to handle abstruse mathematical concepts was innate, spectacular and creative. Born in 1912, he was the son of the Chief Engineer of the Madras and Southern Mahratta Railway. A mathematical scholar and then fellow of King's College, Cambridge, he established a reputation for originality of thought with a paper presented in 1937 to the London Mathematical Society on computable numbers. But his originality was also temperamental. Professor Good, who was closely associated with him at Bletchley, recalled that

in the first week of June each year he would get a bad attack of hay fever, and he would cycle to the office wearing a service gas mask to keep the pollen off. His bicycle had a fault: the chain would come off at regular intervals. Instead of having it mended he would count the number of times the pedals went round and would get off the bicycle in time to adjust the chain by hand. Another of his eccentricities is that he chained his mug to the radiator pipes to prevent it being stolen.

Nevertheless, it was a happy chance that in the immediately pre-war years his more serious speculations had concentrated on relationships between the processes of human thought and those of computing machines. A happier chance brought him to Bletchley Park in the first wave of the 'new generation' that now launched its ultimately successful attack on Enigma.

Reaching its peak in the spring of 1940, the attack was conducted along three main lines. From the intercept stations there was a regular intake of enciphered German signals. Though they could not yet be cracked, they could be intensively studied for clues – such, for example, as carelessness on the part of the enemy in employing his ciphers. It was fortunate that in these early days much of the Enigma traffic was transmitted by the Luftwaffe, for throughout the whole war the German air force was helpfully insecure and slapdash in its use of Enigma.

The second line of attack was mechanical. A firm base existed for future advances, in the shape of the Enigma machine now at Bletchley along with the technical information about their Bomba and other devices which the Poles had handed over in Warsaw. With extraordinary speed the British theorists and technicians pushed forward the Polish methodology to a new point of sophistication: developing, in fact, their own form of data-processor which has passed into history as the bombe. As has been seen, the human mind is incapable of assessing with sufficient speed the almost infinite possibilities presented by the Enigma system. The bombe, of which many models would be brought into play at Bletchley during the war, had this essential function.

An initial contract was put out at an early stage to the British Tabulating Company at Letchworth. Harold Keen, who worked as Chief Engineer on its construction, recalled that 'what it did was to match the electrical circuits of Enigma. Its secret was in the internal wiring of Enigma's rotors, which "the bombe" sought to imitate.' In his lecture on 'Early work on computers at Bletchley' Professor I. J. Good, another Cambridge mathematician, was slightly more explicit. 'It obviously could not be sufficient merely to simulate the Enigma and to try all possible setups for a message, because no machine even now would be capable of running through the 3×10^8 possible states in a reasonable time. So there had to be some further ingenuity in the bombe. This I cannot describe, but I can only say that Gordon Welchman had one of the basic ideas and Turing another one. My impression is that Turing's idea was one that might not have been thought of by anyone else for a long time and it greatly increased the power of the bombe'. This is a fair judgement, for though the bombe is often reasonably called 'the Turing machine' Welchman supplied a powerful theoretical support which greatly increased its efficiency.

And certainly it was Welchman who was responsible for the third necessary element in the attack – that of organization and procedure. Rigorous rules were established for the methodical recording and analysis of all evidence – the pattern of German signal traffic, the tell-tale call signs, the mistakes and careless repetitions on the part of the enemy's signallers which offered vital leads to the cryptanalyst. In the Great War William Friedman, who in 1940 broke the Japanese Purple cipher, was successfully reading German codes on the Western Front. 'The German operators', he commented, 'often showed what we called an unintelligent pedantry, failing to alter the form of punctuation of messages and thereby helping the cryptanalyst. They also made a habit of sending proverbs as practice messages.' Repetition of the proverb made it identifiable and thus led to a solution of the code. Precisely similar pedantries and habits were now being noted and classified at Bletchley. The whole of this carefully structured and disciplined effort became centred, under Welchman's command, in Hut 6 – just one of those temporary wartime erections that covered Britain like leprosy, but in this case a central domain in the heartland of Ultra.

It is not surprising, therefore, that when Colonel Langer came over during the winter on a visit from Vignolles he was impressed by the atmosphere of energy, dedication and progress.[1] This he found in striking contrast to the attitude of his French colleagues back at *PC Bruno*, who made little use of their Enigma machines for investigative work and seemed mainly concerned to keep them in good condition. The Polish group at Vignolles, on the other hand, continued to attack the five-rotor cipher as assiduously as in the past decade. Indeed, Langer's papers record that on 17 January 1940 they achieved their first breakthrough by establishing the key for the Enigma settings on the previous 23 October, a genuine step forward in understanding, even though such a time-lag would be unacceptable in a full-scale war.

The truth was that the real concentration of mechanical sophistication, intellectual ability and financial backing was now in Bletchley Park. More and more the effective work on finding keys for the cipher came to be centred there. But BP and *PC Bruno* were now joined by a teleprinter link along which new information or ideas could be rapidly passed in either direction. And the British liaison officer at Vignolles was well fitted to monitor and assist this relationship, for Captain MacFarlan was an experienced signals-intelligence officer from the Secret Service, trained in cryptography, a skilled linguist, who had acquired valuable insights and practical knowledge while reading Italian codes during the Spanish Civil War.

And then, suddenly, the breakthrough came. 'It was just as the bitter cold days of that frozen winter were giving way to the first days of April sunshine,' Winterbotham recalled, 'that the oracle of Bletchley spoke.' Not completely – for there was a variety of Enigma ciphers of which the naval, for example, would not be penetrated for another year. Not continuously – for whilst there was never a time when breaks could be absolutely guaranteed, in those early days there was a huge element of hit-and-miss. Still, Enigma signals were now being translated into sense, and though some at BP felt deflated when it was realized that the earliest deciphered intercepts were practice messages – often nursery rhymes, like those Great War proverbs – Welchman grasped the long-term significance. You practise on a machine so as to use it efficiently, and soon the Germans would be using Enigma for battle. At his insistence, therefore, and against some opposition Hut 6 was immediately placed on a twenty four-hour footing, and manned continuously by three watches of staff. Early in April the first 'real' signals were deciphered.[2]

The Germans made many mistakes, and though the breakthrough was the result of immense effort in several fields it was one particular error that led directly to the conquest of Enigma. When the operator had set up his machine according to the instructions for the day, and was about to encipher a signal, he would begin by tapping at random a small group of letters. The machine gave him an encipherment of this group, which he now incorporated at the start of the signal. A recipient of the message would then know, from these few letters, how to set the rotors of his own machine for deciphering that particular text. It was, one might say, a key built into the message itself. In their meticulous way, however, the Germans repeated the group at the beginning of each message. To Hut

6, once the significance of the letters was realized, this duplication offered great possibilities.

The main flow of intercepts at this time came from the station at Chatham. One of Welchman's sensible and necessary steps in establishing Hut 6 as a smoothly-working organization had been to improve and streamline its connections with the very source of its material, the interceptors. Good liaison with Chatham now meant that the important prefatory groups of a signal were flashed immediately to Bletchley by teleprinter, leaving the main text to follow in a despatch-rider's pouch. The teleprinter's speed was thus reserved for that part of the signal on which the cryptanalytical attack was being concentrated.

Time was running out. On 9 April the Germans occupied Denmark and invaded Norway. A month later the *Blitzkrieg* was launched on the Low Countries. But at Bletchley a few little groups of deciphered signals had already started that process of accurately reading the enemy's mind which would continue, with ever-increasing efficiency, for the next five years of war. In themselves the decrypts were insignificant, providing, for example, commonplace details about postings of Luftwaffe personnel and some Army traffic. But they were enough. If the ciphers of the five-rotor Enigma could be broken once, in principle they could be broken again, and since military operations were at last beginning in earnest there should soon be no lack of genuinely important German signals to feed the hungry cryptanalysts in Hut 6.

These considerations struck Frederick Winterbotham with peculiar force. A fighter-pilot and prisoner in the First World War, as chief air intelligence officer of MI6 he returned to Germany during the 'thirties to monitor, behind a well-sustained cover, the expansion of the Luftwaffe. For his devious purposes he became *persona grata* with the Nazi leaders, Hess, Rosenberg, Reichenau – even with Hitler himself. Nor was he a stranger to Bletchley Park and its inhabitants, since his Air Section had moved there with GCCS at the outbreak of war. Now, on the eve of the *Blitzkrieg*, an insight born of experience told him that if this new source of high-grade intelligence bore its promised fruit two additions to BP's organization were urgently required: a proper system for translating, evaluating and processing the decrypts, and a completely secure method of distributing the Enigma intelligence to staffs and commanders. In the spring of 1939 both of these were lacking.

The great thing in war is to begin with equipment whose design is so fundamentally sound that it is capable of continuous development and sophistication. The Spitfire fought in the Battle of Britain, and after being modified in many ways for many different tasks was still in action in 1945. Winterbotham's original concepts had this supreme merit: they were simple, adequate for current requirements, and suitable for almost indefinite expansion.

On the cryptanalytical side Welchman had already brought his Hut 6 to a high degree of efficiency. But what happened to its output was still inadequate. Some intelligence officers were indeed already working on shifts in another temporary out-building – able men like Herbert Marchant, who in his subsequent diplomatic career became an Ambassador. The Air Section had already moved in. But procedures were not yet geared to the needs of the fighting services. In *The Ultra Secret* Winterbotham vividly described the speed and foresight with which he transformed the situation. As the first few decrypts had come from the Luftwaffe, he persuaded the Air Ministry to supply three carefully selected German-speaking RAF officers whom he immediately installed with the intelligence team in what, for the rest of the war, was known as Hut 3. The next day, by chance, Winterbotham was able to tackle the War Office with some decrypted Wehrmacht signals in his hand, and to convince the Director of Military Intelligence that he too should send a similar small group of specialist Army officers to Bletchley. Such a direct link between the cryptanalysts and the service departments, forged under the pressure of circumstances, had an abiding importance – both practical and psychological. From now until the war's end the Hut remained on round-the-clock duty.

This small unit would expand, over the years, into an establishment of experts handling many hundreds of messages a day – their activities organized by the blunt Commander Saunders. To them the cryptanalysts of Hut 6 would pass on the texts of deciphered signals, now in their original German. After translation, evaluation, and decision as to the correct recipients, the Hut 3 specialists would distribute the resulting information according to a system of priority markings that ran from Z to the 'most immediate' ZZZZZ. Within Britain itself, in 1940, before the complex structure for conducting a world war had fully developed, distribution could be secure and simple – to the Prime Minister, the Chiefs of

Staff, the Directors of Intelligence of the services, Fighter Command, the Commander-in-Chief Home Forces.

But distribution abroad raised far greater problems of security, and it was here that Winterbotham's second innovation proved invaluable. Like the arrangements in Hut 3, it was initially simple but turned out to be capable of expansion worldwide. The device was the Special Liaison Unit, each consisting, basically, of a hand-picked officer with a small section of cipher sergeants and signallers. Located at headquarters in the field, the SLU received its messages by radio from England in a special cipher. When the texts had been returned to English the SLU officer handed them on to the appropriate staff officer or commander and also – a key element in Winterbotham's plan – made sure, by constant surveillance, that total security was preserved.*

Before the Battle of France began, therefore, SLUs had already been established across the Channel with the British Expeditionary Force at Lord Gort's headquarters, and with the Advanced Air Striking Force. A communications-base was conveniently available, for the Secret Service's transmitting station at Whaddon Hall was a natural choice, and through its ever-growing line of huts known as Windy Ridge signals passed from Hut 3 to the SLUs on what, as the war went on, became an enormous scale. To keep them inviolate they were at first enciphered by the 'one-time pad' method. (Both sender and receiver have a pad composed of tear-off sheets each of which contains specific ciphering data. The sender having indicated the relevant page, the sender uses his own copy to decipher the signal he has received and then destroys the page he has just used.) 'One-time pad' was outstanding for its security. But it involved slow, cumbrous procedures, and later in the war much of the SLU traffic would be put through the Typex machine, a ciphering system developed for the RAF along lines not dissimilar from those of Enigma. It was fast, efficient – and very safe.

Here, then, was at least the skeleton of a complete intelligence system: a source of information, and an organization for processing and disseminating it. What should it and its output be called? The name Ultra, which came to cover loosely both the intelligence-system and the intelligence itself, was evolved by Winterbotham after discussion with the Directors of Intelligence of all three ser-

*For the detailed work of the SLUs see Chapter Five

vices. Beyond Secret, or Most Secret, or even Top Secret lay Ultra Secret. Ultra seemed simpler.[3]

Since it became possible to talk about Ultra much confusion has been caused by the fact that though the code-name existed from the first it was not always used, even at Bletchley, and indeed was frequently concealed. Many of those who worked in offices or on staffs to which Ultra material was actually being supplied could only recall, as they looked back, information apparently emanating from 'a secret source', or 'from secret intelligence', 'an agent', 'prisoner interrogation' or some other cover. The trained eye, scanning wartime documents in the Public Record Office or the National Archives in Washington, will sometimes come across such shutters over the truth and realize that Ultra lurks behind them. The shutters were nearly always down in the early days. And there was another difficulty.

Certain circles invented their own private code-words for the Bletchley intelligence, whether as an insurance or as an in-joke. Churchill's entourage knew Ultra as Boniface. Churchill himself, asking for Ultra papers, would say 'Where are my eggs?': he had a way of referring to the people at Bletchley as 'the geese who laid the golden eggs and never cackled'. In the Middle East staff officers would refer mysteriously to Uncle Henry – a pleasant derivative from Jerome K. Jerome's *Three Men in a Boat*: 'Always believe what your Uncle Henry tells you.' The Winterbotham connection caused some in RAF Intelligence to speak of Ultra as 'Fred'. Officers in the Admiralty's Operational Intelligence Centre talked about Z, and, in reports from its Submarine Tracking Room and similar secret papers, 'based on Z information' was the formula used to cloak the Bletchley source. But the fact remains: before the battle of May 1940 began there was a new intelligence mechanism in being – and the name for its christening was Ultra.

At the birth of Ultra the Admiralty went its own way. From the outset it detached itself from the Hut 6/Hut 3 complex and the system of dissemination through Special Liaison Units, preferring that naval material should be handled independently and that Ultra information should be fed direct into the Operational Intelligence Centre housed first in the Admiralty's own building in Whitehall and, after 1941, in the famous concrete Citadel whose ugly bulk still looms over the Horse Guards Parade. From the beginning a separate Naval Section was maintained at BP. There was a sound practical reason for this apartheid. Unlike the War Office or the Air Ministry, even in the spring of 1940 the Admiralty was a functioning operational centre, a command post, issuing orders to ships on patrol or in action at sea against U-boats and commerce destroyers: once Norway was invaded it had a campaign on its hands. And its existing sources of information were manifold – the network of direction-finding stations, the detailed analysis of German wireless traffic, British warships and merchantmen at sea, agents, naval attachés and other informants throughout the world.

For the Navy, moreover, Ultra was at first more a matter of promise than of performance. Though the Luftwaffe ciphers were broken with increasing regularity, the varied pattern of the enemy's U-boat and other ciphers was not to be effectively penetrated for another year. During the first eighteen months of the war at sea other sources of information were always more significant, and anything garnered from Enigma had to be carefully cross-checked with them. For good practical reasons, therefore, the Navy persisted from the start in retaining control of its Ultra intelligence. When a breakthrough was finally achieved the expanding units for handling naval material at Bletchley – Hut 8 for cryptanalysis and Hut 4 for intelligence-processing – would cope with the flood of traffic as efficiently as their army and air force parallels, Huts 6 and 3.

Were there other reasons for the Admiralty's attitude towards Ultra? One, certainly, was historical. Bletchley seemed like the successor to Room 40, and during the Great War Room 40 had been naval with the brilliant Admiral 'Blinker' Hall at its head. The latest war was still young, but by the spring of 1940 the Admiralty already had in action an alert and efficient Operational Intelligence Centre, sustained in particular by an intricate system for identifying the position of enemy ships by wireless direction-finding. Initially, moreover, the navy appeared to be carrying the main burden of the war. Both tradition and confidence in its current capability, therefore, persuaded the Admiralty to believe that so far as Ultra was concerned it was the natural heir – at least in respect of naval intelligence.

But a personal factor cannot be disregarded. By tradition, also, the head of the Secret Service itself had been a naval officer. The original 'C', one-legged Captain Smith-Cumming, had steered MI6 through 1914–18, to be succeeded by another sailor, Admiral Hugh Sinclair. But in November 1939 Sinclair died of cancer, and his place was taken not by an Admiralty man but by his deputy, Colonel Stewart Menzies. For all his long service under the Foreign Office in MI6 – since 1915 – Menzies was still a soldier from the Life Guards. And there had been a power-struggle over his appointment. Its resolution is recorded in the diary of Sir Alexander Cadogan for 28 November 1939. '6.30 meeting at No. 10 with PM, H [Lord Halifax], Winston ... about C's successor. H played his hand well and won the trick.' The Foreign Office had triumphed over the Admiralty.

The Silent Service took its defeat over the Secret Service badly. The sailors were not alone in doubting Menzies' capacity, particularly as disaster had struck MI6 shortly before his appointment. The notorious Venlo incident of November 9, in which two of Menzies's agents, Major Stevens and Captain Best, were kidnapped into Germany by the SS had seemed – and rightly – to reveal grave defects in what Professor Trevor-Roper has described as a 'rickety organization'. And Menzies's non-professional air, that of a well-bred club-man, was deceptively difficult to penetrate: Paul de Laszlo, who worked close to him at Broadway during the war, said to the author that 'he posed as himself'. Since the Director of Naval Intelligence, Admiral Godfrey, was a quick-witted, complex and ambitious officer who might well, in his own view, have become 'C', it is not surprising that chagrin and suspicion combined with all the valid operational reasons to make the Admiralty ensure that it retained a large bridgehead in Ultra's territory.

Nevertheless, it was Menzies who had made the main haul. Aware of the significance of Enigma from the start, he had demonstrated his personal interest by attendance at the Warsaw meeting and by his presence at the arrival of the first machine in London. After he became head of the Secret Service in November 1939 GCCS was formally his. Now, by authorizing Winterbotham to begin the organization of Hut 3 and to plan for Ultra's distribution, he had ensured that in spite of the Admiralty's separatism he would control the main flow of intelligence from Bletchley not only to the army and the RAF but also to the Prime Minister and, as the war progressed, to a wide spectrum of individuals and departments when they came to be placed 'on the list'. This was a position of immense authority at the centre of the war effort, and it is easy to see how its opportunities might have been abused in a Nazi or Communist state. But though Menzies relished internecine struggles in the corridors of power he was essentially a man of good will, a patriot: in his hands the weapon of Ultra was always turned against the enemy. His privileged position inevitably aroused great jealousies, but the whisperers charged him with incompetence rather than corruption.

As the web of Ultra started to extend, therefore, Menzies was at its heart, like a rather elegant and inoffensive spider commanding every point of growth. And so, when Churchill had a chance to consider the matter during those breathless days of May 1940, he could see that the country of which he had just become the chief minister already possessed a well-articulated system for acquiring and distributing the most secret intelligence: a system interconnected, because 'C' was at its head, with other areas of secret work and with lines of communication to all the fighting services. This was a remarkable advance in nine months: and in retrospect it is clear that the British arrangements for handling Ultra before the Battle of France began, however embryonic, were at once more rational and more realistic than those of the Americans for handling Purple before Pearl Harbor.

Unfortunately the sequel in each case was disaster. The truth is that for Ultra the Battle of France occurred too early in the war. Bletchley was indeed a going concern, but in spite of their vital breakthrough the achievements of the cryptanalysts were still spasmodic and their deciphering often too slow. Far more relevant is the fact that if your own troops are inadequate, under-trained and ill-equipped: if your allies are incompetently led and without heart for the fight: and if your enemy, having won strategic surprise, attacks with irresistible power and *panache*, then the best of intelligence (and Ultra in France was never the best) tends merely to confirm the inevitable. So it was to be.

Yet the impression given by General Bertrand in his book is that at Vignolles the atmosphere was one of incessant and fertile cryptanalytical activity. A change of cipher procedure just before the Germans attacked on 10 May meant that no Enigma traffic could be read there during the all-important first ten days, but between 20 May and 14 June Bertrand claims that no less than 3074 signals were broken by the Polish team of *Equipe Z* at Vignolles. Among Colonel Langer's papers, now in the hands of Colonel Mayer, there is a moving little notebook in which he has made his own record of the results obtained. According to Langer some 5084 signals were decrypted during the French campaign. At first sight these seem formidable statistics.

Certainly such assiduity on the part of the Poles was in marked contrast to the atmosphere of the French mess at Vignolles, presided over by Bertrand himself. One of Kenneth MacFarlan's most vivid memories of Vignolles is of the lunch-time ritual, sanctified and timeless, the talk round the table trailing on until late in the afternoon and nobody allowed to depart until 'le commandant' had made his exit. Was it an indicator of French attitudes in 1940 that MacFarlan also noted, to his astonishment, how even after the Germans attacked on the 10th the ritual continued without a change?[4]

The central question remains: what had *PC Bruno* produced? The background to any assessment must be the fact that in Bletchley itself there was little consciousness of breaking signals of *critical* importance. And with good reason. For even if a large proportion of the decrypts claimed by Langer and Bertrand were of Enigma-enciphered signals, and not of lower-grade codes, they must have related in the main to normal order of battle material, unit locations, logistics, strength returns and so on. In anything like a static battle such data are the gold-dust from which intelligence officers gradually compile their appreciations. And it was during the tragic weeks of May and June that Bletchley became acquainted with the practice, rigorously adhered to by German commanders in battle, of sending back nightly a detailed situation report.

But in a static battle the intelligence people have time. In a turbulent fast-moving campaign like that of 1940 there was no time for deliberation over fine details – even if the information reached the right hands. For here too there is a doubt – and a reminder. A deciphered signal at Bletchley or Vignolles only had real value when it had been passed over an efficient communications-system to the commander in the field and then been applied by him in his operations. The battle is the pay-off. But Gort, who as soon as the invasion started dashed away from his main headquarters with a small staff and bad communications to fight the battle on his own, destroyed from the outset any hope of handling secret intelligence properly. Among his allies the chaos of the French command-structure combined with confusion and defeatism to produce an even worse result. Whatever proportion of the Enigma traffic that did manage to filter through to Gort, Gamelin and Weygand can have done little more, therefore, than to emphasize the obvious – that because of their armour, aircraft, generalship and efficiency the Germans were irresistible.

A day-to-day study of the manoeuvres during the Battle of France confirms, in fact, that virtually every move made by the British – and the French – was in response to some German initiative rather than because of prior intelligence from Ultra, as would so often be the case in later campaigns. We may test this by considering what all historians consider to be Lord Gort's supreme moment – the decision at 6.30 pm on 25th May to withdraw northwards to the sea. 'Thus at Britain's gravest hour', his biographer John Colville wrote, 'it fell to Gort, deprived of all instructions from higher authority, outnumbered and outgunned but not outwitted, to take a prompt and solitary decision which thwarted von Bock and saved the whole British Expeditionary Force from death or captivity.' But because of Ultra?

Winterbotham thought this was so. In 'The Ultra Secret' he refers to a series of events in the Germans' camp on 23 May, when their ring was already closing round the contracting Allied bridgehead with Rundstedt's Army Group A, containing most of the panzers, on the British western flank and von Bock's Army Group B pressing from the east on the enfeebled Belgians and the British left. The German Commander-in-Chief, von Brauchitsch, issued orders to complete the encircling pressure first by giving von Bock responsibility for the final, decisive thrust and secondly by transferring to him, from the westerly Army Group A, von Kluge's 4th Army with its panzer divisions. The signals conveying these orders were both made available to the British on Ultra. Winterbotham says that Gort subsequently told him that the first of the signals, to von Bock, had 'influenced his decision to make for the sea as quickly as possible'.* To Churchill, moreover, the Group Captain claims that Brauchitsch's signals were a reason 'for the speed-up of Operation Dynamo and the mustering of the little ships for Dunkirk'.

It would be pleasant to be able to demonstrate that Ultra was capable of so dramatic an impact so early in its career, but the facts resist such an interpretation. It is true that on the next morning, the

---

*After reading this section Group Captain Winterbotham commented to the author that in looking at the Battle of France in retrospect Lord Gort might well have over-emphasized to him the value of Ultra in that campaign.

24th, Gort ordered that plans for a withdrawal towards the Channel should be examined – but this was an option he was already exploring as an obvious precaution. As early as the 19th his Chief of Staff had already telephoned London twice, on Gort's instructions, to discuss this possibility: and it was after General Pownall's messages that the first precautionary moves were made in England to assemble small vessels at Dover 'in readiness to proceed to ports and inlets on the French coast'. On the 24th, moreover, Gort received another Ultra intercept – the famous 'halt order' which (whether initiated by Rundstedt or Hitler himself, a permanently controversial issue) firmly *cancelled* von Brauchitsch's arrangement and stopped von Kluge's armour in its tracks. The quick kill had been at least temporarily postponed. Thereafter we observe Gort far from retreating but loyally continuing to prepare, under great political pressure, for an attack *southwards* to cut off the spearheads of Army Group A and link up with advancing French forces which Weygand promised but never delivered. It was not until the late afternoon of the 25th that Gort, on his own authority, abandoned the 'attack to the south': long after the Brauchitsch signals.

But the reason he broke off his attack and moved northwards the divisions he had reserved for it was that the Belgian army, at its last gasp, had been hurled by von Bock out of contact with the British left flank. A great gap was opening, through which Army Group B might sweep eastwards and cut off the Expeditionary Force from the Channel ports. In other words, before the Brauchitsch signals on the 23rd Gort is already considering withdrawal: after the 23rd (on orders from London) he is actually preparing to advance. What crystallized his final dramatic decision was the collapse of his allies and the power of his enemy. He conformed to the realities of the situation. And so, whilst the Ultra signals may have coloured his thoughts, they were evidently not the basis of his actions.[5]

In any case, cryptanalysts alone cannot stop ten panzer divisions. It has been suggested that an addition should be made to the classic 'principles of war' taught in all staff colleges – surprise, concentration, economy of effort and so on: the extra principle would state 'and one must be more powerful'. That great American historian of the British navy, Admiral Mahan, put it slightly differently when he observed that 'not by rambling operations . . . are wars decided, but by force massed and handled in skilful combinations'. The lesson of the Battle of France for Ultra, in fact, was not only that deciphering must be swift and reasonably continuous if there is to be a pay-off in the field. It was also terrifyingly evident, as it would be in Greece and Crete a year later, that even the best of secret intelligence diminishes in value if the enemy is overwhelmingly superior. Time would have to pass before the British could abandon rambling operations and begin to use 'force massed and handled in skilful combinations'. When that at last happened Ultra would come into its own.

For the cliché that at Dunkirk defeat concealed a victory has many meanings of which one is certainly valid: Ultra survived. In spite of over-running so many French provinces so rapidly the Germans captured nothing to indicate that their most important ciphers had been broken. Its existence unsuspected, Bletchley was thus able to continue uninterrupted with the successful refinement of its techniques. Because its secret was not penetrated during the Battle of France, it never became a German target during the Battle of Britain – or thereafter.

The two SLUs at the main army and air headquarters got safely away. Robert Gore-Brown had maintained close contact over Enigma problems with Colonel Jean Joubert des Ouches, the chief cipher officer at the French High Command. They both escaped – Gore-Brown to become a key figure in the Ultra organization and Joubert des Ouches to re-emerge from the shadows, at Algiers in 1943, as the chief cipher officer to General de Gaulle. Winter-botham's counterpart Georges Ronin, air intelligence officer in the French Secret Service, also avoided capture. He had returned to action as a bomber pilot in the last days of the battle and subsequently buried himself in the Vichy Air Ministry while keeping in touch with Winterbotham on a private wireless link. When at the end of 1942 he purloined a civil aeroplane and departed for Algiers with Colonel Rivet* Menzies thought it so important that he flew out to meet them.[6] The French connection remained intact.

But the adventures of *PC Bruno* provide the most dramatic story. They form an Odyssey. On 14 June the Germans entered Paris: but a column of twelve vehicles, headed by a bus, was already on its way southwards, skirting the capital and carrying to safety the staff and equipment from Vignolles. MacFarlan travelled with them – breaking away near Bordeaux to be picked up by a British aircraft and

*Colonel Rivet was Menzies' opposite number, the French 'C'. He was in the Ultra picture in 1940, which explains Menzies' desire to meet him as soon as possible.

returned to England and Ultra. Bertrand himself, in the wild confusion of those days, managed to lay hands on three French planes by which, on 24 June, the Polish and Spanish teams were transferred from Toulouse to Algiers.

Intense and complicated arguments followed. Could they be allowed to return and work within the unoccupied Vichy zone? Would the Polish Government-in-exile allow its officers in *Equipe Z* to operate in Vichy territory? Under demobilization the French from Vignolles had mainly melted away. But by October 1940, in a new château and under a new name, Bertrand recreated Vignolles. The domain of Uzès was a modest medieval establishment in Provence, well placed between Avignon and Nîmes. Here, with the connivance of 'men of good will' at Vichy, the Polish and Spanish cryptographers set up a new station under the code-name *PC Cadix*.

It was business-like. A radio was surreptitiously conveyed to *Cadix* by British intelligence, and regular communication was thus established with the main Polish radio base in England. Bertrand made several hazardous trips into occupied France, during which he quietly collected the parts of Enigma machines from several Paris factories where they were being manufactured when the *Blitzkrieg* began. With these and their existing equipment the Poles at *Cadix* finally had four Enigmas available. Until the Germans took over Vichy in November 1942 *Cadix* was therefore able to decipher many of their signals and to constitute, in practice, a kind of outstation for Ultra.[7]

During the fighting of May and June 1940 the British army, navy and air forces were all savagely wounded. A continent had closed its doors. The loss of its agents and contacts put the Secret Service in jeopardy. Of all the main instruments of future victory Ultra alone had emerged intact: not yet mature but, as the coming months would prove, a weapon of infinite potential. In the Battle of Britain that now followed nobody had more practical experience of Ultra than Professor R. V. Jones. Looking back, he remembered that 'in the darkest nights of 1940, knowing what was being achieved by our code-breakers, I felt that if we could only hold out over the next year we must win in the end'. Here lay the true value of the British breakthrough.

3   A Plan Called Smith

'On the 8th September Sir Samuel Hoare reported that a
reliable source, returning from Berlin, stated that the
invasion of England was known in official circles there by
the code-name SMITH.'

Air Ministry Intelligence Summary
17 October 1940

At 2.23 am on 4 June 1940 the Admiralty confirmed that operation
Dynamo, the evacuation from Dunkirk, had been successfully
completed. A few days later the author, having survived the rigours
of an officer-training unit, optimistically joined his first regiment. It
was gradually re-uniting on Cheltenham racecourse as its members
filtered back from France. Every one of its guns and vehicles had
been lost on the other side of the Channel. The total equipment of
the 65th Field Regiment, Royal Artillery, at that historic moment
was one commandeered civilian truck and a few dozen rifles. With
these riches we shortly moved up into Yorkshire, to defend the
Great North Road against an airborne invasion.

How could it be otherwise? This trivial personal episode was
characteristic of the days after Dunkirk when Great Britain, her
cupboard bare, got ready to face an assault in the skies and, so it
was feared, the attack which even Napoleon had failed to launch
across the dividing sea. During the Battle of France nearly a
thousand aircraft had been lost. The day after Dynamo finished
Fighter Command could only muster 466 effective aircraft, of
which a mere 331 were the modern Hurricanes and Spitfires: the
strength states of the squadrons throughout the months to come
show that the average figure of all fighters available for operations
rarely rose above 750. As for armour and artillery, everything had
been destroyed or abandoned during the retreat to the beaches.
Most of the 900-odd tanks remaining in England were obsolete, or
thinly-armoured tin cans. Almost no up-to-date guns remained: the
welcome given to the first shiploads from America of French 75mm
weapons from the First World War tells its own pathetic story. As
for infantry, Montgomery's 3rd Division was perhaps the only one
approximately equipped and ready for action. No wonder that the

forthcoming Battle of Britain has been described as 'the narrow margin'.

In the David-and-Goliath confrontation that was imminent during the early summer of 1940 good intelligence, the friend of the weak, would be vital for the British: and it was a great advantage that on the other side of the Channel the Germans' own sources were indifferent and misleading. Few if any of the agents already planted in Britain by the Germans remained active, and replacement was difficult. The one code-named 'Summer', who arrived by parachute, was instantly arrested. 'Tate', who also parachuted in, was 'bent' and turned into a double agent. Indeed, for the twenty-five hopefuls sent over during the summer and autumn of 1940, whether by small boat or out of the sky, the future was bleak and inevitable: they were miserably trained, miserably equipped, and miserably incompetent. Compared with the Battle of France, therefore, the Germans during the Battle of Britain would lack the benefit of spies on the ground.[1]

They must first conquer the air: yet throughout the conflict the Luftwaffe consistently ignored or misunderstood the radar system on which the British Fighter Command depended. How profitable might some efficient agents' reports have proved! And the width of that ignorance is demonstrated in the 'Comparative Survey of RAF and Luftwaffe Striking Power' drawn up on 16 July 1940 by 5 *Abteilung* of the Luftwaffe Staff, headed by the chief intelligence officer, Major Josef Schmid. Schmid got almost everything wrong. He over-estimated the RAF's fighter strength by a third, and wildly under-estimated the British capacity for production and rapid repair of aircraft, and omitted the vital radar. This myopia continued throughout the battle itself, so that the German Command lived, not unwillingly, in a state of bliss about successes its aircraft had actually failed to achieve.[2]

But the British also lacked eyes in the enemy's territory. Western Europe was now occupied. It would take weary months, and the torture or death of many brave men and women, before effective links were forged with underground movements ranging in a great curve from Norway through Poland to France. Even the normal probes of air reconnaissance could hardly be pushed beyond the German front line – the Channel coast. And though the British developed to a high degree the art of radio traffic-analysis – of identifying individual units of the Luftwaffe, and their locations, by studying intently the character of their call-signs, the chatter of their pilots and the quantity of their signals – the Germans matched these efforts by their own assiduity, if not by comparable achievement, in regard to the radio communications of the RAF. When all the other means of acquiring information are noted – reports from neutral countries, even Hitler's speeches – it is clear that for the British in the summer of 1940 the most promising means of penetrating the barrier of silence about German intentions would be Ultra – if it worked.

Only a handful of men knew at the time that even before the Battle of Britain began – on the very day, in fact, that the Battle of France was formally terminated – one of the most important of all the signals deciphered in 1940 led to decisive action. Ultra was already at work.

The day was 21 June. At 3.15 that afternoon Hitler arrived in the little clearing amid the forest of Compiègne to take his revenge for the armistice of 1918 and dictate, in the famous railway carriage, his hard and merciless terms to the French delegation. A band played *Deutschland über alles* and William Shirer, the CBS correspondent who was present, noted how the defeatist General Weygand assumed that the British would be overwhelmed in another three weeks. An important piece of evidence to the contrary, however, lay behind the historic meeting that Churchill had called the very same morning in the Cabinet Room at No. 10 Downing Street, to consider what might be called the Case of the Crooked Leg.

Behind this meeting lay some brilliant recent investigations by a young Oxford scientist, R. V. Jones, who had been active in Air Intelligence since before the war and was already familiar with Bletchley and its work.[3] Since the beginning of March Jones had become increasingly aware that the Luftwaffe was developing some form of radio beam by which aircraft could be guided to a target in darkness or bad weather. About the end of February Jones had analysed a conversation between two prisoners in which they mentioned something called *X-Gerät* or the X Apparatus. They seemed to be talking about a device for guiding bombers by a system of radio pulses. This was slightly misleading since, as will be seen, the X Apparatus was not introduced until later in the year. But the speculations it aroused were confirmed shortly afterwards by a scrap of paper recovered from a crashed Heinkel bomber. The notes it contained read, in translation:

Navigational Aid: Beacons working on Beacon Plan A. Additionally from 0600 hours Beacon Dühnen.
Light Beacon after dark. Radio Beacon *Knickebein* from 0600 hours on 315 degrees.

What was this *Knickebein* or 'crooked leg'? After intensive study Jones was able to report on 23 May:

It is possible that they have developed a system of intersecting radio beams so that they can locate a target such as London sufficiently accurately for indiscriminate bombing.... The accuracy of location expected by the Germans is something like ½ mile over London from the western frontiers of Germany.

Here was a remarkable prediction of how the Crooked Leg system of *Knickebein* would work. But on what wave-length? From what transmitter? And what was the system's technology?

The arrangements for *Knickebein* were basically simple. From a single station a pair of radio beams was transmitted, one carrying dots and the other dashes. The beams were so orientated that if the pilot kept his aircraft within the very narrow central zone of sound, in which the dots and dashes had equal strength, he would be guided accurately to his target. If he strayed off course to right or left, he would hear dots or dashes in excessive strength and know that he must adjust his line of approach. As he drew near to the target another beam, sent from a second station somewhere on his flank, would act as a marker by intersecting with the dot-dash beams and producing a warning signal. While Jones had grasped the theory of this procedure, the problem was to establish how the Germans were applying it in practice.

It was here that Ultra came into play, and that Jones's awareness of what was happening at Bletchley paid dividends. On the morning of 12 June he visited the head of the RAF's 'Y' or Intercept Service, who took a bit of paper from his desk and said, 'Does this mean anything to you? It doesn't seem to mean much to anybody here'. There has been more than one historic 'scrap of paper', but what Group Captain Blandy now handed to Jones certainly came within this class. All it said was KNICKEBEIN KLEVE IST AUF PUNKT 53 GRAD 24 MINUTEN NORD UND EIN GRAD WEST EINGERICHTET. ('The Cleves *Knickebein* is beamed (or directed) at position 53 degrees 24 minutes north and 1 degree west'.) But it meant everything to Jones.

The gradual relaxation of security since 1974 allowed Jones to publish his memoirs, *Most Secret War*, four years later. Writing of this critical moment he recalled: 'I quickly recognized that it was a decoded message, because I knew that during the preceding two months Bletchley had begun to be successful in decoding some of the Enigma messages.' (The breakthrough, as the last chapter described, had occurred in April.) For those days the decrypting was reasonably prompt. At 1455 hours on 5 June the Chief Signals Officer of 4th Flieger Korps issued the *Knickebein* signal: it was deciphered by the 9th. And what it told Jones was decisive. A beam-transmitter for *Knickebein* had been set up just inside the German frontier at Cleves, the ancient town lying between the Rhine and Meuse: Cleves whence the Lady Anne had journeyed to marry King Henry the Eighth of England on 6 January 1540 and to be christened 'The Flanders Mare' by a husband who, even as they married, observed that 'I liked her before not well, but now I like her much worse'. Moreover, the position '53 degrees 24 minutes north and 1 degree west' was a point in England, indicating that the *Knickebein* beam was directed from Cleves along a course that passed over the Great North Road near Retford in Nottinghamshire. The naiveté of those innocent early days is comically illustrated by the fact that a section of the Air Staff not in the scientific picture immediately sent a posse up to Retford, under a Group Captain, on the theory that *Knickebein* referred to a fifth-columnist organization.

Everything was now falling into place. More prisoner interrogation and the technical examination of a Heinkel 111, shot down in Scotland during a raid on the Firth of Forth, established that the Luftwaffe's bombers needed no special kit to receive the *Knickebein* beam – merely the routine receiver (with which the Luftwaffe's bombers were already fitted) used for the Lorenz blind-landing system, but now tuned to the higher degree of sensitivity. Jones was thus in a position to pull strings with confidence – or at least one very powerful string called Professor Frederick Lindemann, under whom he had worked before the war in the Clarendon Laboratories at Oxford. Lindemann (ennobled as Lord Cherwell in 1941) had a friendship of long standing with Churchill, whom he had supported devotedly as a scientific adviser during the latter's 'wilderness years' out of office in the 1930s. When Churchill went to the Admiralty at the outbreak of war he took Lindemann with him as his chief consultant on scientific and economic affairs. After he transferred to Downing Street, as Prime Minister, Lindemann was ensconced as head of the Statistical Section in the Prime Minister's Private Office. In practice he was much more: Churchill's *éminence grise*. Jones thus had a formidable ally. In earlier discussions Lindemann had questioned the concept of *Knickebein*. Now, on 13 June, he succumbed to the strength of the evidence and minuted to Churchill: 'There seems some reason to suppose that the Germans have some type of radio device with which they hope to find their targets . . . it is vital to investigate and especially to seek to discover what the wave-length is. If we knew this, we could devise means to mislead them. . . .' Churchill returned the note via the Minister of Air, Sir Archibald Sinclair, with the written comment, 'This seems most intriguing and I hope you will have it thoroughly examined.' The Crooked Leg was now at Cabinet level.

'The wavelength . . . if we knew this, we could devise means to mislead them.' By the afternoon of the 17th five radar sites had been picked as ground-stations for attempting to identify the beam, and the Blind Approach Development Unit at Boscombe Down on Salisbury Plain (accustomed to using the Lorenz system) was selected to carry out in-flight detection. The initial flights, on the 18th and 20th, were unprofitable, but another scrap of paper from a German bomber had revealed the location of a second *Knickebein* transmitter, sending out its marker beam to intersect with the main dot-dash beam. It was well to the north of Cleves, at Bredstedt in Schleswig-Holstein. This must be the flank transmitter. Thus the detective had picked up most of the clues but not entirely solved the Case of the Crooked Leg when, on the morning of 21 June, he arrived at his office to discover that he had been summoned to the Cabinet Room at No. 10 Downing Street. An experienced practical joker himself, Jones assumed that someone was pulling his leg.

He was only twenty-eight. The meeting had been going for nearly half an hour when he arrived. The auspices were not good, and the atmosphere seemed tense. 'As I was shown into the room through the double doors I had an end-view of a long narrow cloth-covered table with a writing pad and blotter set before each place, and racks of black-embossed Downing Street notepaper distributed along the table. Churchill was sitting in the middle of the left side, his back to the fireplace; he was flanked by Lindemann on his right and Beaverbrook on his left.' Across the table sat a row of what Churchill in his memoirs, with a disarming throw-away, called 'various Air Force commanders'. They were in fact the Chief of Air Staff and the Chiefs of Fighter and Bomber Command, Air Chief Marshal Sir Philip Joubert (who supervised radar and signals affairs for the RAF), Sir Henry Tizard (Scientific Adviser to the Air Staff, a supporter of Jones from Oxford days), and Robert Watson-Watt (Scientific Adviser on Telecommunications and the outstanding pioneer of British radar). But Jones was a man of nerve. As discussion proceeded it became clear that the *Knickebein* situation was not fully comprehended. He therefore seized his opportunity to ask Churchill, 'Would it help, Sir, if I told you the story right from the start?' Permission granted, he spoke for twenty minutes. When he finished, Churchill recorded, 'there was a general air of incredulity'.

Jones was, in fact, a young Daniel in a den of rather mature lions. The air of tension with which he had been greeted was generated by deep and stubbornly-held convictions on the part of those around the table who now found themselves incredulous. There were two strands of opposition. Before the war the Air Staff had flatly rejected proposals for a radio guidance system to aid their night bombers. RAF navigators, it was maintained, were fully capable of finding their targets by conventional methods of astro-navigation: the heirs, as it were, of Columbus and Sir Francis Drake. By the end of 1941 conventional methods were shown to be so inaccurate that the RAF air-crews lost over Germany amounted to more than the German civilians killed: for the rest of the war Bomber Command would be compelled to rely on radio navigation. But in June 1940, in the Cabinet room, tradition still raised its voice. Why should the Germans want these complicated contraptions? Why could they not use the stars?

The other voice was that of science. Sir Henry Tizard, who had encouraged Jones in his Oxford days and was largely responsible for his present position, nevertheless spoke as an opponent – for two reasons. Intellectually, he rejected the theoretical possibility of the *Knickebein* beam. Emotionally, he was affected by a long-standing hostility between himself and Lindemann who, as has been seen, not only accepted the *Knickebein* proposition but now sat where Tizard felt he himself should be, at Churchill's side.

Neither Tizard* nor the airmen, however, had guessed what was

*Tizard had committed professional suicide. Realizing this he went straight from the meeting to his club, the Athenaeum, and wrote out his resignation as Scientific Adviser to the

going on in the Prime Minister's head and heart. Jones discovered after the war. Sitting one day at Churchill's bedside he heard him describe how 'when this young man came in and told him that they could still bomb... accurately by night, when our nightfighters would still be almost powerless, it was for him one of the blackest moments of the war. But as the young man went on the load was once again lifted because he said that there could be ways of countering the beams and so preventing our most important targets being destroyed.' In spite of the authoritative opposition, therefore, Churchill asserted his own authority. 'Once I was convinced about the principles of this queer and deadly game I gave all the necessary orders that very day in June for the existence of the beam to be assumed, and for all counter-measures to receive absolute priority.'

But the end of the meeting was not the end of the battle. That afternoon Jones attended another conference, in the office of the Director of Signals. Here T. L. Eckersley of the Marconi Company vigorously argued that a short-wave beam transmitted from as far away as Cleves could not conceivably 'bend' round the earth's curvature sufficiently for a German bomber to pick it up over England. Then, according to Jones, the Deputy Director of Signals said something like, 'Well, we now have the greatest expert on radio propagation in the country and he says that the beam theory is all wrong. This evening's flight should be cancelled.'

But Jones was standing on two solid rocks: the first his confidence in Ultra, the second Churchill's own authorization, given in the Cabinet room, that the flight should take place. There could be no further argument. On the night of the 21st an aircraft was despatched from Wyton aerodrome in Huntingdonshire, with a special team aboard. Its mission was to fly northwards and make contact with a beam which, in Jones's estimation, would be orientated on Derby, the home of Rolls-Royce where the crucial engines for the RAF's fighters were being built. Next day the flight report dissolved all doubts. It began: 'There is a narrow beam (approximately 400-500 yards wide) passing through a position 1 mile S. of Spalding, having dots to the south and dashes to the north, on a bearing of 104 degrees – 284 degrees T.' The bearings of this and a

Air Staff. Though he was to hold other less important posts, he was removed from the centre of power. Churchill never forgot his error of judgement on a day that meant so much to the Prime Minister himself, and to Britain.[4]

The Scherbius Enigma: cover of the original sales-pamphlet. (*The National Archives, Washington*)

An historic Enigma. This machine was put together from spare parts and used by Polish cryptographers in France between 1940 and 1942. After the *P.C. Cadix* unit at Uzès in southern France broke up and scattered in November 1942, the machine was hidden, to be recovered in May 1945. It is now in the Sikorski Museum in London. Taken from above, the photograph shows clearly the illuminated alphabetic display on the top of the machine, and the three rotors. Two spares were available, giving the five-rotor capability. The arrangement of plugs is in the rear: on the German military version they were in front. (*The Sikorski Museum, London*)

CHIFFRIERMASCHINEN

AKTIENGESELLSCHAFT

BERLIN W 35

STEGLITZER STR. 2

FERNSPR.: NOLLENDORF 2899
TEL.-ADR.: CHIFFRIER BERLIN

Bletchley Park: the entrance. *(The Times)*

Opposite above: The staff of *P.C. Bruno* at Vignolles.
Bertrand and Langer at back centre,
MacFarlan at extreme right.

Opposite below: The Château at Vignolles.

General Guderian's command vehicle in France in June, 1940. His Enigma machine is in the left foreground and his cipher clerk has a problem. *(Bundesarchiv Koblenz)*

second beam, identified on the same flight, tied in with the location of transmitters at Cleves and Bredstedt. *Knickebein* existed, for sure, and the next stage would be counter-measures. An adept practical joker, Jones concluded his personal report characteristically. 'If our good fortunes hold, we may yet pull the Crooked Leg'.

This was a triumph for Ultra: not because other sources of intelligence had not contributed, but because from Bletchley had come the indisputable evidence which brought into focus the other bits and pieces, none of which had alone been conclusive. And further confirmation soon followed. An Ultra decrypt of 27 June ran: 'It is proposed to set up *Knickebein* and *Wotan** installations near Cherbourg and Brest.' Then, towards the end of July, Ultra also disclosed that *Kampf Geschwader 54* (a bomber group of about eighty aircraft) would be using *Knickebein* by early August. As it was known that the operational area for KG54 ran up the west side of England (which was beyond the reach of a beam from Cleves), this must mean that the Cherbourg beam was coming into use and that major air-raids were imminent. So when intensive night-bombing finally started British scientific intelligence – as will be seen later – was prepared to counter not only *Knickebein* but also its more sophisticated successors as guidance systems for the Luftwaffe. No wonder that in 1976 Professor Jones could say about Ultra: 'Its particular value was that I could be sure of the reliability of the information that it provided. In the Battle of the Beams the short message about the *Knickebein* at Cleves was enough to transform the beam threat from speculation to reality.'

But the main Battle of the Beams was fought later in the year. In any case, it alone could not win the Battle of Britain which, after the fall of France in June, was automatically anticipated. It is not wholly certain that Churchill himself ever believed in his heart that Hitler would dare where Napoleon had stalled: yet even he assumed, as he must, that the possibility was real. The dispassionate staff officers who advised him, trained to put together the pieces of an intelligence jig-saw and draw appropriate conclusions, mainly took a different view. They felt that the inner logic and dynamism of Hitler's career must impel him to invade, and that the prepara-

---

*This was the first reference to *Wotan*. The name of German mythology's one-eyed god suggested to Jones that the Germans were bringing into action a single-beam guidance system. Later in the Battle of the Beams this early intelligence about *Wotan* would bear fruit. (See p. 98.)

tions occurring across the Channel confirmed this deduction. So for the Prime Minister, the Chiefs of Staff, the Joint Intelligence Committee, the Admiralty, the Commander-in-Chief of Home Forces and, particularly, Fighter Command the essential question was not whether but when he would try. For Luftwaffe channels had carried the gist of Hitler's famous Directive of 16 July: ' . . . I have decided to prepare a landing operation against England, and if necessary to carry it out. . . .' Through Ultra the signal was deciphered and immediately passed to Churchill, who noted in his memoirs that thanks to 'our excellent intelligence . . . it seemed certain that the man was going to try'.

And thus everything in that hot midsummer depended on a few hundred fighters of the RAF. This was recognized by both sides. The High Commands, British and German, were equally aware of one dominating fact: before a seaborne invasion could succeed the Luftwaffe must win control of the daytime skies above southern England. During July Air Intelligence affirmed in a report to Churchill that if the skies could be held until September no invasion would happen in 1940. To this central truth all else was subsidiary. Hitler himself recognized it, as he gradually postponed his invasion date in the hope that Göring's Luftwaffe might somehow convert boasts into performance. For the panzers, the guns, the infantry, the serried barges across the Channel were useless so long as enough Spitfires and Hurricanes – and pilots for them – survived.

The skies were held and the man did not try. But in the many authoritative analyses of the Battle of Britain now available one salient feature emerges: in this, perhaps the most critical conflict of the war, the margin was indeed narrow. It was a battle fought on a razor's edge. Many well-recognized factors contributed to the ultimate success – the pilots' devotion, the quality of British radar, Göring's errors. But it was in the mind of the Commander-in-Chief Fighter Command – Air Chief Marshal Sir Hugh Dowding – that those delicate, difficult, day-to-day judgements were made which, in the end, drew the fine decisive line between victory and defeat. Often they were judgements as urgent and taxing as any commander has had to take. What has not been so far appreciated is the extent to which Dowding's calculations were assisted by Ultra.

The headquarters of Fighter Command were in Bentley Priory at Stanmore in Middlesex. For the Battle of Britain the starting date is usually given as 10 July, since it is at this point that the Luftwaffe began its opening phase of attacks on shipping and on targets not far inland from the English coast. During the first few weeks of the battle Ultra intelligence passed from Bletchley straight to the Air Ministry in London, where the staff fed it on to Dowding at Stanmore – a cumbrous method. Early in August, however, and in time for the main crunch, Winterbotham arranged for a teleprinter line between Bletchley and Stanmore to be installed, supplying a small Special Liaison Unit which was lodged in a sound-proof cubicle down in the bowels of Bentley Priory and next to Fighter Command's underground operations room, 'the hole', where incoming raids were plotted and counter-attacks devised. In one way or another, therefore, Dowding was linked with Ultra from the outset.

Long after the war Dowding recalled: 'Of course, I had available all the intelligence, or what there was of it, which meant that I had information that was not generally known.' What there was of it helped him in three ways. It enabled him to understand the enemy's main strategy: it kept him informed of the strength, location and readiness for action of individual Luftwaffe units: above all, it could supply him with invaluable advance warning about incoming raids. Ultra was not alone or the most regular agency in providing such services. Nothing surpassed the swift and accurate information about the height, direction and strength of enemy raids supplied by the Home Chain of radar stations, which stood protectively around the southern shores like the Martello towers erected as defence posts in the face of Napoleon's invasion-threat. Analysis and decoding of lower-grade signal-traffic, the use of direction-finding to pin-point Luftwaffe establishments across the water, the skilful interrogation of prisoners by Squadron-Leader Denys Felkin of Air Intelligence and the examination of captured documents and crashed aircraft all contributed to the expanding scenario. But when Ultra spoke to Dowding the voice had a special authority and its source, he knew, was impeccable: the words of his opponents communicating in secret to themselves.

The Battle of Britain was not 'won' by Ultra, as is sometimes claimed. It was won, primarily, by the 900 pilots killed and wounded, and those who fought and survived, between July and October 1940. But their victory was the cumulative effect of one fierce engagement after another, day after murderous day, and Dowding's triumph was the nice judgement with which he nursed his squadrons through these recurrent individual conflicts, never wasting too many, often risking too few. 'We must regard the generalship here shown', wrote Churchill, 'as an example of genius in the art of war'. The theme of this book is 'the battle is the pay-off', and it was here, at the decisive point, that Ultra provided reinforcement. The early and authentic information that came from Bletchley about forthcoming raids was a strong buttress for Dowding in his conduct of the battle.

In assessing Ultra's contribution, nevertheless, a sense of proportion must be maintained. Compared with later years the organization at BP was still inexperienced and imperfect. The staff was still small. Some of the intercepts could not be deciphered. By the time others had been turned into sense so much time had passed that their value had disappeared, for during this savage campaign in the air hours and even minutes counted. To get an exhausted squadron off the ground so that it could effectively disrupt some new raid was a constant race against the clock in which out-of-date intercepts were mere waste of paper. All the same, there was a significant output from Bletchley of timely information. It usually emerged late at night or in the early hours of the morning, as the cryptanalysts cracked the Luftwaffe's operation orders for the following day. Even then, of course, the Germans might in fact do something different, or nothing at all, for as this was an air battle sudden changes of weather – fog, cloud, poor visibility – could lead to rapid changes in the enemy's plans.

The sample that follows shortly of signals deciphered and circulated provides vivid evidence of the variety of the warnings which prevented Dowding from fighting the battle blindfold. The signals can be dated and usually timed, for besides those sent to Fighter Command some, at least, were also received and carefully recorded in the War Office by Department MI 14 whose head, Lieut.-Colonel Kenneth Strong, forwarded them to his opposite number Brigadier Mockler-Ferryman, the chief intelligence officer at HQ Home Forces. These papers are now in the Public Record Office.[5] Their reference to air raids are sporadic and not sensational, but until the Ultra signals sent to Fighter Command itself are released, they are the best available token of Bletchley's output.

The target areas of the German Air Fleets were known before the end of June. All to the west of a line running north through Chichester – Oxford – Wolverhampton – Halifax was the zone of Luftflotte 3, commanded by Field Marshal Sperrle and working from bases in Normandy and Brittany. East of the dividing line was the territory of Field Marshal Kesselring's Luftflotte 2, whose airfields were in Holland, Belgium and northern France. Outflanking attacks on Britain's north-east coast were the role of Stumpff's Luftflotte 5, stationed in Norway and Denmark.

The flavour of the warnings about the intentions of these Air Fleets can be captured from signals sent during the earliest days of the battle, when everything was still uncertain and menacing. 'MOST SECRET, OFFICER ONLY. It is reliably reported that German aircraft have instructions to carry out on 12.7.40 harassing attacks in target area Map 3 on aeroplane factories. Ship movements are also to be attacked.' There follows the regular security instruction: 'It is requested that this information should be treated as "Officer only" and shall not be transmitted by telephone.' And then, in green pencil, comes the addition: 'Churchill informed.' (The formula 'it is reliably reported' or 'a reliable source' is normally cover for Ultra. Phrases like ' a usually reliable source' or 'a good source' suggest some less authoritative origin.) On the 15th it was useful to know that 'day attacks on England are only to be made when weather conditions offer sufficient cover against fighter attack. These raids are to be carried out by single aircraft only, and it is impressed on the pilots that they must break off the attack as soon as the weather no longer ensures surprise.' On the 16th, and again on the 19th, the news was emphatic: 'The German Air Force have given orders that for special reasons the balloon barrages at Bristol and Southampton must be attacked and destroyed whenever the opportunity presents itself.' But these were tentative early days.

As the battle progressed the signals became more specific. 'It is reliably reported that on the evening of 18th August the German air force received a warning order to expect orders for a large scale operation on 19th August; all necessary preparations were to be made.' 'From a reliable source, information has been received of an impending attack on WARMWELL aerodrome this morning. Aircraft to be ready to leave at 0700 hrs.' (The warning was issued at 0152 hrs.) At 0740 on 25 August: 'It is reliably reported that air attacks are to be expected during the course of today 25th August 1940 at WARMWELL, LITTLE RISSINGTON and ABINGDON aerodromes and reconnaissances by a single aircraft in the area SOUTHAMPTON – ALDERSHOT – BRIGHTON.' On 13 September came something more sinister. 'It has been learned from a reliable source that various

German Air Force units have received instructions for heavy attacks upon a target believed to be LONDON at times ranging from 1800 hrs on 13 September to 0300 hrs on 14 September. If the weather permits, long range bombers will be employed.' Early next morning this was followed by 'Reference statement air attacks will cease at 0300 hours on 14 September, it is now learnt that they may continue into forenoon of 14 September and also probably into the afternoon.' It is evident that precise warnings like these specimen signals were of great value in the dangerous second phase of the battle, during which the RAF's fighter airfields and sector control stations were the main objective of the Luftwaffe.

But then came the decision to destroy the fighter force in the air, by one hammer blow to be delivered on *Adler Tag* or Eagle Day. Göring's instructions to his three Air Fleets were acquired on Ultra during 8 August and passed to Dowding and Churchill: 'Operation *Adler*. Within a short period you will wipe the British Air Force from the sky. Heil Hitler.' Bad weather prevented the mass raids immediately expected, and though Ultra disclosed that 13 August had been re-nominated as Eagle Day it was not, in fact, until the 15th that the great blow fell. If the Ultra decrypt about the location of a *Knickebein* station at Cleves was the most important piece of information in regard to the Luftwaffe's night-attack, the details Dowding received in advance about *Adler Tag* were the most important contribution Bletchley made to the battle by day.

The German plan, set out in an operational order on the 14th, was that on the morrow attacks at different times and places by the combined Air Fleets should destroy the RAF. Over southern England Luftflotten 2 and 3, by assaulting airfields and radar stations, would force Dowding to commit the maximum number of his fighters, and these would be wiped out by the superior tactics and weight of the Luftwaffe – or so it was hoped. Away to the north-east it was equally expected that an intruding Luftflotte 5 would scarcely be interrupted in its business, as most RAF squadrons, it was assumed, had been or would be sucked away to reinforce the south. Instead, Eagle Day ended in a rout. During 1786 sorties the Luftwaffe lost seventy-five aircraft (not 182 as was at first ecstatically claimed). The confirmed British losses were only thirty-four fighters. Göring, significantly, now ordered that only one officer might form part of the crew of any one aircraft and made other restrictions to preserve trained personnel. (This too filtered through

Ultra.) August 15 is accepted as a turning-point in the battle.

In establishing Ultra's precise contribution to this unexpected feat one must first recall that incoming raids were detected and plotted by radar and reports from the Observer Corps. Without this immediate and accurate tactical information all else would have been useless: it was on radar that the actual fighting depended, and the Germans' gravest error was to under-value its power. But radar revealed only what was immediately happening or soon likely to happen. It was not a long-term predictor, able to forecast the pattern of a whole day's operations. Here was Ultra's opportunity. Whenever Bletchley could provide in advance deciphered German orders for a complicated series of attacks, stretching over many hours, Dowding was able to plan and orchestrate his response with ample foreknowledge instead of having to think from minute to minute, as was the case when radar alone supplied his intelligence. Such occasions were inevitably few, but *Adler Tag* offers a classic example.

Virtually the whole of three Air Fleets was committed in raids from early morning until evening in attacks first over Kent: then, two-fisted, over the north-east coast: then Kent again, then Essex, then Kent, then Surrey and Hampshire. The prime targets were British airfields, for Göring calculated that the RAF would be destroyed in their defence. But the airfields survived for another day, and though at 10 am on the 16th Luftwaffe Intelligence reported that the RAF's fighters were down to 300, in fact 700 were still available. Dowding had won by parsimony. Knowing from Ultra the staggered pattern of the raids to come, he was able to resist the temptation to commit too many of his resources too early, to weaken the defences of the north and aid the hard-pressed south, to fail to make his fighters concentrate on the German bombers instead of 'mixing it' with their escorts and risking heavy losses. He always kept something in hand to send up against the next raid. After the Battle of Britain was over and the old man had been displaced, Winterbotham lunched with him and discussed the value of Ultra in his victory. 'He reminded me of the moment when he had received the signal for the seven great raids on the big Eagle Day and of how this information was vital . . . .'

The circumstances of Dowding's removal by the Air Staff from the control of Fighter Command were deplorable. He was not dismissed until November 1940, but the arguments by which he was undermined all related to the events of that hectic summer. As this distasteful episode precisely illustrates the quandary that more than once, throughout the war, faced commanders who used Ultra intelligence responsibly, it is worth stepping aside from a chronological sequence to examine the record.

Dowding was devoted to his pilots – his 'chicks', as he called them. On 20 November, before he left his office at Bentley Priory for the last time, he sat at his desk and composed a signal for despatch to all the units in his command. It began 'My dear Fighter Boys'. If he had known Stephen Spender's lines, he would have recognized in them the expression of his feeling for the young men, so many of them now maimed or dead, whom he had led to victory in the Battle of Britain.

Born of the sun they travelled a short while towards the sun,
And left the vivid air signed with their honour.

For 'Stuffy' Dowding the pilots felt a reciprocal affection. On them as on him, therefore, his dismissal fell like a stunning blow, brutal, incomprehensible.[6]

We can understand it now. There were in fact sound reasons for transferring to some less onerous post a man born in 1882 who had been working under extreme stress not simply in 1940, but also in the pre-war years when Britain's air defence system was being re-equipped and expanded. What hurt at the time was the abruptness of his departure. This was so sudden that it seemed to be calling into account his whole conduct of a battle which, more than anything else, had saved his country from invasion. Unfortunately what seemed to be the case was actually true.

Dowding's main instrument in the Battle was 11 Group of Fighter Command which defended the vulnerable areas of southern England. Its leader, the New Zealander Air Vice-Marshal Keith Park, had previously been Dowding's chief staff officer. They were of the same mind. During the Battle, therefore, Park carried out with conviction his commander's policy of committing fighters sparingly, of always retaining a reserve, and of protecting the Luftwaffe's targets rather than shooting down German bombers as an end in itself. To the north, however, lay 12 Group – essentially a reservoir of reinforcement squadrons in case the enemy's pressure on 11 Group became intolerable. Here there reigned a different ideology. 12 Group's commander, Trafford Leigh-Mallory, was a man of driving egoism. His most brilliant squadron leader, Douglas Bader, tackled everything with the single-minded aggressiveness which had lifted him, even after the loss of both legs, back into the skies as a brave and indeed outstanding fighter pilot. But Bader evolved and Leigh-Mallory personally supported the theory that squadrons should not be committed individually against the Germans (as Park was doing with Dowding's approval). Instead, they should first be formed up into Wings, composed of several squadrons, and then be sent in *en masse*. This, the Big Wing concept, was later called a 'balbo': before 1939 Marshal Balbo had made his mark by leading groups of Italian aircraft in long-distance flights.

Though plausible, this theory involved grave practical difficulties. 12 Group, whose airfields lay many miles from the heart of the Battle, had the necessary time and space in which to gather its squadrons together into a wing formation. But the enemy's airfields across the Channel were so close to southern England that when an incoming raid showed up on the radar screen Park had to get his squadrons into action with minimum delay. Nevertheless, Leigh-Mallory and Bader pressed their case relentlessly. There were clashes of temperament as well as of policy. The sweetness of the summer victory was embittered. One of the ace pilots, (later Air Vice-Marshal 'Johnnie' Johnson, CB, CBE, DSO with two bars, DFC with bar) is a witness of unimpeachable authority. He recalled visits to fighter stations during the Battle by 'many high-ranking members of the Air Staff, senior civil servants and politicians', and how 'visitors to Leigh-Mallory's airfields heard that since September the big Duxford Wing' [of 12 Group] 'had not been given a chance.... Upon their return to Whitehall some eminent men, who should have known better than to listen to junior officers denouncing their seniors, put pen to paper, and both Dowding and Park were called to the Air Ministry to discuss the size of fighter wings.' A palace revolution was in train.

The Air Ministry meeting was held on 17 October. The heads of Fighter Command, the Deputy Chief of Air Staff, the Chief of Air Staff designate (Sir Charles Portal) and a variety of other high-ranking officers found themselves sitting round a table in the company of one young Squadron Leader – Bader, whom Leigh-Mallory had somehow infiltrated. To Dowding's astonishment, discussion took the form of a post-mortem on the tactics which had won the Battle of Britain and were now compared unfavourably – Bader

89

being allowed remarkable latitude for a junior officer – with the Big Wing policy. According to Dowding's biographer, Robert Wright, the minutes of the meeting were then rigged. In spite of protest against their drafting by both Dowding and Park, they conveyed the conclusion that the use of 'a large mass' of fighters, a 'balbo', was to be preferred.

It is now that Ultra enters the picture. There were several secondary issues on which Dowding might have taken a stand. As a Commander-in-Chief he could certainly have refused point-blank to discuss his method of running Fighter Command at a high-level conference attended, without his permission, by one of his own subordinates. What he could not do was to sway the meeting, already pre-disposed by 12 Group's assiduous publicity, by pointing out that his conduct of the battle was founded on knowledge of the enemy's plans supplied by Ultra. What would have happened on Eagle Day, for example, if he had ignored Ultra's warnings and, by concentrating his squadrons in a few unwieldy Wings, wasted valuable time? The flexibility that brought success on *Adler Tag* would have disappeared. But he could not reveal his private knowledge of Ultra to protect his own position. In his introduction to *The Ultra Secret* Marshal of the RAF Sir John Slessor wrote: 'I am glad the author gives Dowding the credit that is his due for never letting on, in the course of that unhappy (and wholly unnecessary) Air Staff conference in October 1940, that he had known so much from Ultra of the Luftwaffe's plans throughout the Battle of Britain. I was present on that occasion ... I know that in his place I should have been sorely tempted to use my knowledge of it to confute his more junior critics who unfortunately but quite rightly had, for security reasons, not been admitted to this priceless secret.' Dowding honourably kept silent, and was sacked. Keith Park was also removed: his reward was a Training Group. And his successor at 11 Group – who but Leigh-Mallory?

As the Dorniers and Heinkels, the Junkers and Messerschmitts swarmed over the battered counties of southern England during that epic summer of 1940 the subsequent fate of their cherished 'Stuffy' would have seemed unimaginable to the pilots of Fighter Command. Equally unimaginable is the effect on their morale, had they had even an inkling of what was to come. Innocent and devoted, they merely got on with the matter in hand: the defence of the skies. And this was crucial, for across the Channel the Germans were already preparing for another battle: the invasion – Operation *Seelöwe* or Sealion, as it was announced in Hitler's Directive of 16 July. Ultra was quick to produce the first intimations that invasion plans were now afoot, but Churchill was slow to accept the facts. Menzies and Winterbotham were summoned to argue the case with him, and Jones was asked to set out on paper the validity of the evidence.[7] Since he was able to demonstrate that exactly the same source, Ultra, had produced the clinching signal about *Knickebein* Churchill succumbed. Sealion had achieved credibility.

From the moment in July when Sealion was finally accepted as imminent surveillance of the German preparations would continue for many anxious months. Ultra served throughout as an indispensable monitor. But though the Sealion plan was, as Churchill used to say, 'triphibious' – involving all three of the enemy's services, navy, army and air force – the relevant signals deciphered at Bletchley during the invasion period came, perhaps entirely, from the Luftwaffe. The reasons are straightforward. German naval ciphers remained unbroken until 1941. The German army was notably secure in its use of Enigma and anyway had the land-lines of western Europe available. But the air force was not only in action, fighting a daily battle: so far as Sealion was concerned the Luftwaffe was involved in every aspect of the operation. As preparations proceeded apace, therefore, an immense amount of signal-traffic passed over the Luftwaffe's radio circuits which contained invaluable information not just about the German air force, but about arrangements being made by the army and navy as well. Since the Enigma-ciphers of the Luftwaffe, as has been pointed out, generally caused Bletchley's cryptanalysts the least trouble, here was a fertile field for Ultra.

All intelligence work involves assembling a mosaic whose key pieces are missing while others are broken or defaced. So it was over Sealion. In the records one observes the British staffs daily but painfully, with Ultra's help, building up bit by bit a significant pattern of the enemy's intentions; then gradually deciding, in the light of the evidence, that invasion is no longer imminent: but even so, even when it seems that all is deferred until the spring of 1941, watching the indicators intently.

The scrutiny was for signs, omens, portents. In mid-August, for example, even after Eagle Day the likelihood of invasion was strong. The Luftwaffe's threat still loomed. It was invaluable, therefore, for Home Forces to learn from Ultra that a conference had been called in Berlin on 19 August of the Group Commanders of 7 Air Division, because this air-landing formation, after being used in Holland during the May offensive, in early June had been hurriedly withdrawn to its peacetime stations in Germany to recoup and refit. Its aircraft were capable of carrying a division of infantry with mortars and light guns. Now, evidently, it was ready for action again, and its commanders were attending a high-level briefing. The 7th Air Division's function in an invasion was obvious. This was an important piece for the August mosaic – and it was pure Ultra, as the documents confirm.[8] When Colonel Strong sent the details on to Mockler-Ferryman at Home Forces he added a private covering note which said: 'This information is from Boniface'. Boniface was a cover-name for Ultra, used in Churchill's circle and by a very limited number of others 'on the list'.

Much of the other evidence from Ultra had immediate significance. The warning to the Luftwaffe at the end of July that it had been ordered *not* to attack the quays in harbours along the south coast was self-explanatory. On 7 August an extremely detailed inquiry by two German air units about technical equipment for producing large scale smoke screens told its own story. A day later news came that the *Anti-aircraft* School at Carteret on the Cherbourg peninsula was making trials with 'wine cask ferries' and pontoons, and practising landings. Why should an AA School be experimenting in amphibious operations? On 24 August a signal was recorded instructing all three Air Fleets to ensure the provision at seaplane bases of air sea rescue vessels, 'by order of the German Navy in connection with the Sealion operations'. The Navy's own hesitancies are reflected, for on 28 August MI 14 reported that at a recent conference at the HQ of 16th Army* naval representatives had refused to operate certain kinds of ferries and the matter had been referred to the High Command. To observe, unseen, the disputes and embarrassments of one's enemy is always diverting. So the following, dated 20 August, must have caused much pleasure. 'It has been reported by a reliable source that on 19 August the Records Office of a German Air Force formation was much agitated over the apparent loss of a package, containing, among other things, 1 gazeteer of small harbours on the south and southeast

---

*The German 16th Army was already known to be the main force earmarked for the invasion.

coast of England, 1 guide to Dundee and Firth of Tay, and 1 volume of amendments in 16 parts.'

From the organizational point of view many useful indications came from Ultra decrypts of signals to and from a unit specially concerned with logistical preparations for the Luftwaffe, *L.G. Stab ZBV 300*, whose name is constantly mentioned. Such matters are covered as the loading of men and equipment into ships: the time in the landings at which airfield construction units should come ashore; the back-up of large oil-tankers to sail in with fuel for the forward aircraft; the placing of Luftwaffe embarkation officers at appropriate ports; requests for protection from the RAF for invasion supply dumps; the dates when screened lights are to be shown along the Scheldt to enable major shipping movements to be carried out by night. There were many such signals, and for the defence staffs in Britain their value was two-fold. There was the interest of the individual details: but beyond that was the benefit that came from being able, as it were, to listen in to the Germans during the actual course of their preparations – worrying about timings, altering assembly-points, calculating the figures for replenishment of fuel and ammunition, testing new landing devices and finding them fail, altering embarkation tables to move a unit from a place in the assault landings to one of the follow-up waves. By September, certainly, the British had pieced together through Ultra (and, of course, other sources such as air reconnaissance) a meaningful mosaic which displayed with considerable accuracy the pattern of events likely to follow 'S One', as the Germans named the opening day of Sealion.

The essential point to note is that this development was necessarily gradual. Claims for Ultra must not be pitched too high. In his light-hearted 'Invasion 1940' Peter Fleming quotes wryly from the *Informationsheft G.B.*, a hand-book printed in Germany in August for distribution to the invading troops. Intelligence, it declares, 'is a field in which the British, by virtue of their tradition, their experience, and certain facets of their national character – unscrupulousness, self-control, cool deliberateness and ruthless action – have achieved an unquestionable degree of mastery.' This characteristic view of the sinister British Secret Service was not entirely supported by the facts. As Fleming pointed out and Churchill himself admitted, in one essential respect the Prime Minister, the Chiefs of Staff and their advisers at first misinterpreted Sealion. The tendency, at least until early September, was to believe that the main assault would be made against the east coast of Britain and not across the Channel. Yet this was never the intention. As General Jodl said after the war, 'Our arrangements were much the same as those of Julius Caesar.'* The decisive factor which finally led to an increase of defences along the south coast was evidence from photo-reconnaissance, which showed a new but unmistakable build-up of small ships and barges in the various French harbours between Calais and Brest. Had Ultra failed?

The answer must be, not within the limits then possible. There was a case for believing that the east coast would be the main assault area. There was also the effect of racial memory. During the First World War there was a prolonged nervousness about the possibility of a German landing in the east. Considerable forces were held available for counter-attack. It is not surprising that Churchill and his senior officers looked, at first, in this direction. Moreover, deciphering at Bletchley in this period was, it will be recalled, primarily of Luftwaffe signals. If any plans were in fact broadcast on the radio nets of the army and navy (where, for an amphibious operation, they would be most likely to be found) their ciphers were still wholly or largely unbreakable. In any case, while it was natural for the Germans to engage in vigorous signal traffic about the details of their preparations – logistics, troop movements etc. – it is equally natural to assume that the most secret matter, the actual front of the invasion, would be reserved for high-level conferences and com-munications by secure land-line. Ultra had to work within those limits. Nevertheless, its intelligence was certainly of value, not only in helping to win the Battle of Britain and thus making invasion impossible but also in assisting the staff of Home Forces, and the Invasion Warning Sub-Committee and other agencies, in building up a cumulative picture of what was actually happening on the other side of the water. The powerful evidence provided by the photographs of shipping and barges was itself strengthened by the many indications Ultra provided during July and August about the specific character of the German preparations.

*On Caesar's first raid, into Kent in 55 BC, he crossed from the Boulogne area and landed at Walmer north of Dover. On his second expedition in 54 BC he also crossed from Boulogne, landed again north of Dover near Sandwich, repelled attacks on his beachhead and pressed inland to strike north over the Thames at the present site of London. His personal commen-taries on these two combined operations vividly illustrate the problems faced by the Germans in 1940.

German intelligence, by contrast, was certainly culpable. The psychological effect on Hitler and his High Command of the Luftwaffe's famous defeat on Sunday, 15 September – Battle of Britain Day – was the more intense because their intelligence reports had suggested that the RAF was virtually destroyed. Yet here were effective squadrons, strong and dominant. German pilots reacted, too, protesting about attacks by 'ghost' units which, as they had been told, no longer existed. Two days later, on the 17th, Hitler issued instructions that Sealion should be postponed indefinitely, Winterbotham, in *The Ultra Secret,* gives a vivid account of how, that day, he attended a Chiefs of Staff meeting at which Churchill read out an Ultra signal, small in scope but vast in its significance. It was an order for the dismantling of air-loading equipment on Dutch airfields – and must, presumably, have referred to 7 Air Division. Newall, the Chief of Air Staff, spelled out its implications: 'He gave it as his considered opinion that this marked the end of Sealion, at least for this year.' How ironic that three days earlier, on the 14th, Hitler should have told Admiral Raeder that a cancellation of Sealion must not be promulgated, for it would then be known immediately to British intelligence. 'A counter-order,' the Führer said, 'cannot be kept secret.'

The jubilation in the Cabinet War Room on 17 September was understandable, and justified in the event – for the man never did try to come the way of Julius Caesar. From the view-point of 1940, however, it was premature. Sealion may have been postponed, but the menace remained. Here is MI 14 stating as late as 26 November:

A reliable source reports that the 2nd German Air Fleet, Brussels, received a message from the air formation H.Q. in charge of Air Force Equipment in Belgium and Northern France, *(L.G. Stab ZBV 300)* stating that Loading H.Q.1 was holding a conference at Coxyde near Nieuport on 28.11.40 on the subject of operation Smith. All units which were to be embarked on the first wave of operation Smith at Rotterdam were asked to send loading officers to the conference.

Ultra and *Stab ZBV 300* have come together again. An invasion still seems to be on the cards. But why has Sealion turned into Smith?

In their memoirs two first-hand witnesses, Group Captain Winterbotham and Professor Jones, date the earliest knowledge in London of a probable invasion to about mid-July, following Bletchley's decipherment of Hitler's directive of the 16th. When in due course the codeword Sealion was identified by Bletchley, Churchill felt a distaste for the name, probably in the fear that careless use of a top-secret German code-word might compromise Ultra. He therefore ordered that Sealion should always be referred to as Smith. The proposal seems characteristic of a man who throughout the war rebelled against pretentions and high-falutin' names for military operations. It was Churchill who in 1940 reduced 'Local Defence Volunteers' to 'The Home Guard'.

If this was the intention, however, it was certainly not put into practice immediately – or perhaps 'Smith' like 'Boniface' began with a very restricted circulation. What is undeniable is that as late as 24 September, in a note entitled 'Collaboration of German Navy and Air Force in Invasion Britain', MI 14 refers to 'The Sealion operation (which it has been suggested from other sources is the term used by the Germans to designate the invasion of England)'. Sealion is mentioned again in further summaries of invasion intelligence issued by MI 14 on 4, 8 and 15 October. There is a change on the 17th, when a pull-together of the enemy's plans was produced by Section AI3b of Air Intelligence under the heading 'Invasion of England (Operation Smith)': this document, incidentally, refers constantly to information derived from 'the special messages' – which means Ultra. Next day, surprisingly, MI 14 issued its own immensely detailed summary of German preparations – running to at least four foolscap pages of highly particularized information – still entitled 'Invasion of the UK and/or Eire (*Seelöwe* – Sealion Question).' On the 27th, however, another memorandum followed, outlining some of the functions of *L.G.Stab ZBV 300*. It went out from MI 14 over the name of Colonel Kenneth Strong, after whose signature an interesting postscript was added. 'NOTE. In future memoranda the operation SEALION will be referred to as SMITH.' It would therefore seem that Smith was only beginning to be generally adopted during October 1940. From November onwards Smith reigns supreme.

Though Sealion/Smith may have seemed to be dormant until the spring brought fine weather and a calmer Channel, and perhaps to have been postponed indefinitely, this was to overlook Hitler's mentality. He was a man who preferred to keep his options open as long as possible. During the winter he would examine several such options – Gibraltar, the Azores, even an airborne landing in Ireland. Invasion was far too big an option to surrender instantane-ously. And so, though ships and barges might be withdrawn from the Channel ports to escape the bombs of the RAF, training and planning for *Seelöwe* continued – if not as hectically as in the sum-mer. Indeed, on 27 October MI 14 sent to Home Forces an unam-biguous report from 'a reliable source' that Kesselring's Luftflotte 2 had ordered: 'Troops concerned in Sealion operations are to con-tinue their training according to plan'. On 18 November an embarkation HQ issued instructions about improving the approaches to the docks and quays in Rotterdam. On the 23rd a signal was recorded from Luftflotte 2 about negotiations with the navy concerning tank-ships for aviation fuel 'in the event of oper-ation Smith'.

Churchill may have sensed that the danger had passed, but it was the duty of hard-headed, responsible staff officers to confirm that this was the case. The flow of intelligence from Ultra about continu-ing preparations made it difficult to be certain. Even in the depth of winter, as a report on 12 January noted, 'German firing practices which are connected with preparations for the invasion cannot be completed in Belgium and Northern France. In order to ensure that they should be completed in time for their results to be made use of it is proposed to continue them in Southern France.' MI 14 and Home Forces therefore remained coolly sceptical. They accepted with good sense the mounting evidence that 'Smith' was postponed: but with a proper detachment they studied every indication that it could and might be re-activated. Ultra was a copious source for optimism – but also for doubt.

About one thing there was no uncertainty. On 4 September Hitler announced that 'if they attack our cities we will simply erase theirs'. Between 7 September and 3 November an average of 200 bombers attacked London every night. With varying intensity the Blitz continued throughout the winter over the capital, the ports and the main provincial centres.

Ultra's early warning about *Knickebein* now paid dividends. Immediately after the beam had been identified in June a special unit, 80 Wing, was created under Wing Commander Addison, a signals expert, to concentrate on technical counter-measures in col-laboration with the Telecommunications Research Establishment. They never 'bent' the beams, as was suggested by a rumour not yet dead. Rather, they blanketed or jammed them: initially, and in desperation, by commandeering diathermy sets from hospitals with which they imposed an obliterating crackle of sound on the Knickebein transmissions. By September these improvisations were being replaced by properly constructed jammers called Aspirins (– maintaining the hospital connection: and the *Knickebein* beams were suitably named Headaches).

The Aspirins, by sending out dashes on the same frequency as the beam, subtly distracted a German pilot. Following – as he thought – the correct course, he would suddenly hear an excess of dashes and start wandering about the sky in an attempt to pick up the dot-signals in equal strength. Perplexity followed, then loss of confidence and even a landing somewhere in England under the impression that it was a German base. The jamming of *Knickebein* became common knowledge in the Luftwaffe, and pilots' morale declined. The RAF's night-fighters and the Army's anti-aircraft guns were still virtually useless, but the misleading effect of the Aspirins, combined with a careful use of decoy fires to divert bombs from cities to open spaces, significantly limited the effects of the Blitz during that first phase of lengthening nights when it seemed to Hitler and Göring that Britain lay wide open to terror-bombing.

But the laws of challenge and response are merciless in war. As *Knickebein*'s inefficiency and unpopularity with the air crews became evident the Germans introduced alternative methods of guidance, known as *X-Gerät* and *Y-Gerät*. The enemy's possession of something called an X Apparatus had, of course, been foreshadowed by those hints picked up from prisoners' conversation early in March. Now it was in action, and identified as a system employing a complex of several beams which directed the pilot to the area of his target and at the right moment automatically released his bombs. *Y-Gerät* had the complications of simplicity, using a single beam only with a sophisticated method that caused many teething troubles. Both techniques were too refined for the average aircrew, so the Heinkels adapted for their use were brought together in *Kampfgruppe 100*, a special unit soon to be as well known to Air Intelligence as any famous British squadron. In particular, it was a familiar subject of study for R. V. Jones as it worked from its base at Vannes near Cherbourg.

Knickebein had taught Jones a great deal. At Bletchley particular attention was paid on his behalf to the ciphers in which signals were transmitted relating to the beam operations, and from this Ultra intelligence and an increasing awareness of the German techniques enough was soon known for new jammers to be evolved. Time was short, for before the end of September K.Gr.100 had paid twenty visits to London and as many elsewhere. The first jammers for *X-Gerät* were named Bromide, and were no more than modified anti-aircraft radars. Indeed, the truth is that the complete answers to the X Apparatus proved elusive until about the end of 1940. But when *Y-Gerät* was directly attacked in January Ultra and science had combined to produce a counter-measure, Domino, which ingeniously distorted the pulse-signals passing between aircraft and ground-station on which the *Y-Gerät* system depended. Domino was instantly effective.*

On one notorious night of the winter Blitz, however, neither Ultra nor the scientists had been able to save a single life.

Coventry, the ancient city of the three spires, has been twice crucified: once by the German air force, and once by those who have spread a disturbing legend that the slaughter of its citizens during the raid of 14 November 1940 was a sacrifice – a sacrifice because the raid was known about through Ultra many hours or even days in advance, yet no warning was given to the city's authorities, or to those responsible for its defence, for fear of compromising Ultra's precious secret. Since this allegation is totally untrue, it mocks those who died or suffered.

Weeks before 14 November a change in German bombing techniques had seemed probable. Unlike the RAF, the Luftwaffe had not trained its crews for night-bombing. As *Knickebein* was known in London to be failing in its promise, the assumption was logical that the Heinkels of K.Gr.100, using the more accurate *X-Gerät*, would be employed as pathfinding fire-raisers to illuminate targets for less expert pilots. Jones identified this possibility when he noticed during October that aircraft from K.Gr.100 were attacking isolated targets but dropping flares, as though they were practising. Through Lindemann he informed Churchill that a change was in the wind.

It therefore came as no surprise when the Ultra decrypt of a German signal dated 11 November reached Jones from Bletchley. Addressed to the X-beam transmitters, it referred to an

---

*The strong transmitters of the BBC's pre-war television station at Alexandra Palace in north London were the instruments in this achievement.

impending attack of considerable dimensions, possibly staggered, since three targets, 51, 52, and 53 were mentioned. What Jones particularly noted was that the instructions for setting the beam were given to the nearest minute and not, as was usual, to the nearest second. This apparent disregard for accuracy conformed with the idea of preliminary fire-raising by K.Gr.100, for which precision was less important. Next day a second and longer Ultra message revealed that the operation was called Moonlight Sonata – implying a three-phased attack beginning at the time of the full moon.

When the Air Staff considered this information during the 11th and 12th it committed two errors. Target areas 1, 2, 3 and 4 were mentioned in the Ultra signal, but their location was obscure. The Air Staff, however, decided that the evidence indicated raids on London and the south-east, a view from which it did not budge until the afternoon before Coventry was bombed. It also erred in taking 'the night of the full moon, 15 November', as meaning the night of 15/16 November: but the full moon rose at 3.23 am in the morning of Friday 15 November. Moreover, conversations were overheard between a captured pilot from Luftwaffe 2 and his cell-mate which, besides confirming a three-phase Moonlight Sonata, also mentioned Coventry and Birmingham as the objectives. It is easy, with hindsight, to criticize the Air Staff, but there is no doubt that the prisoners' conversation was given a low priority in their calculations.

The general information pieced together from the intercepts was illuminating. An attack would be carried out by both the Air Fleets, Luftflotten 2* and 3, led by K.Gr.100 which was given a variety of other functions – reports on weather and bombing conditions, and checking on the *Knickebein* beams which, for all their limitations, were to provide an aid for the main streams of aircraft. Göring would be in charge. Knowing the scale of this attack, and assuming its target area, the Air Staff on 12 November immediately organized a highly elaborate set of counter-measures named Operation Cold Water. Apart from conventional defence by jamming, night-fighters and anti-aircraft, the theme of the plan was offensive. It included widespread attacks on the enemy's airfields, (particularly

---

*In his biography of Kesselring (London, 1978), Kenneth Macksey states that the Field Marshal – then commanding Luftflotte 2 – flew on the Coventry raid himself. This would have been entirely characteristic of a man who believed in leading from the front.

the base of K.Gr.100 at Vannes), and on Germany. That the plan was based on wrong assumptions scarcely mattered, since with suitable modifications it was carried out on the night of the raid. Twenty-seven airfields and even Berlin were bombed. Cold Water alone is sufficient proof that Coventry was not martyred by default.

But the problem still remained: what were the actual targets for Moonlight Sonata? The Germans were actually planning raids on successive nights – Target No. 51, Wolverhampton: No. 52, Birmingham: No. 53, Coventry. For the three cities their code-words were *Einheitspreis*, *Regenschirm* and *Korn*. *Korn* had appeared in the Ultra decrypt of 11 November, but its meaning was never grasped before the raid: indeed neither Ultra nor any other source ever provided the data for believing *beyond doubt* that Coventry was a target. *Regenschirm* was mentioned by the Luftwaffe prisoner during the evening of the 13th, and its English translation, umbrella, immediately pointed to the home of Neville Chamberlain the Umbrellaman: Birmingham. (Birmingham, Target No. 52, was bombed on 19 and 20 November.) The meaning of *Einheitspreis* only seems to have been established after Jones had predicted a raid on Wolverhampton, which he calculated to be Target No. 51. This did not occur. But Denys Felkin reported to him: 'We've overheard a conversation between two prisoners. One said he was in the Coventry raid and what a good show it was. The other said he was in the Birmingham raid. The first then said that there was to have been a similar raid on Wolverhampton under the code-name *Einheitspreis*.' *Einheitspreis*, Felkin explained, equals 'unit-price' equals 'sixpence at Woolworths' equals Wolverhampton.

Thus everybody was groping in a darkness only partially illuminated by Ultra or any other intelligence. Coventry's code-name *Korn* remained a mystery. The Air Staff was on the wrong track, even though preparations for *something somewhere* were well in hand. Professor Jones has assured the author that 'I myself did not know in advance specifically that Coventry was the target when I went home in the evening of 14th November.'* Nor did Churchill. On the 14th, and not till then, the Air Staff addressed to the Prime Minister personally a Most Secret document which, from its tone, was evidently composed for a man to whom its contents would be news. Telling the story of Moonlight Sonata, it still defined the

---

* In *Most Secret War* he recalls driving homewards that evening through moonlit west London and 'wondering where the target really was'.

possible target areas as Central and Greater London as well as wide swathes in Berkshire and Kent. The Cold Water plan for counterattack was outlined. 'We believe that the target areas will be ... probably in the vicinity of London, but if further information indicates Coventry, Birmingham or elsewhere, we hope to get instructions out in time.' So much for the prisoners' evidence.

In any case Churchill's own movements make it clear that during the 14th agonizing decisions about sacrificing Coventry for Ultra were far from his mind. In fact he started out with his Private Secretary John Martin for Ditchley Park at Enstone in Oxfordshire, the home of Ronald Tree and his American wife who entertained the Prime Minister there at weekends 'when the moon was high' as an alternative to his staying at the obvious target of Chequers. As the car was leaving No. 10 Downing Street Martin thrust into Churchill's hand a box or envelope that had just arrived. When Churchill had examined the contents, and before they had travelled far, he ordered an immediate return to No. 10. 'My memory is clear,' Sir John Martin informed the author, 'that after the message was opened and read, the expectation was of a raid on *London.*' Martin's personal diary for the day reads: '14 November. At No. 10. False start for Ditchley (Moonlight Sonata – the raid was on Coventry)'.[9]

The surprise implicit in that bracketed sentence is emphasized by the fact that during the afternoon the staff in the No. 10 secretariat was dispersed on the Prime Minister's orders to spend the night in safe quarters, on the grounds that the beam pointed to a raid on Whitehall. It is evident that the paper by which Churchill was so dramatically affected was the appreciation by the Air Staff. London, not Coventry, concerned him – and in the spirit of 1940 he was determined not to be absent from his post.

At 1 pm in the afternoon a beam was detected, and two hours later Cold Water was put into operation. But even now there are question-marks. The Air Staff after-action report of the 17th says that at 3 pm beams were identified as intersecting over Coventry. This looks like hindsight. Jones himself has no recollection of so specific an identification, and in the conversations on the 14th between himself and Group Captain Addison, in charge of 80 Wing, about appropriate jamming procedures the most that emerged was a sense of 'the Midlands'. Winterbotham in *The Ultra Secret* describes receiving an Ultra message at this time which mentioned Coventry and telephoning the information to No. 10. The most likely source of this is Göring's headquarters at Versailles, from which, according to the Air Staff, signals were intercepted about 3 pm. None of Churchill's Private Secretaries remembers this telephone call, which is perhaps not surprising as No. 10 was like an ant-heap that afternoon. Certainly there is no evidence that the message made any impact. The log book for No. 10 disappeared, unfortunately, after the war.

In any case, Coventry was doomed. The point is not that the city was sacrificed to save Ultra, a monstrous distortion, but that the raid happened in 1940. The initial errors of the Air Staff were irrelevant, for the Cold Water counter-measures could not have been very different even if the target of the raid had been known exactly. 119 fighter sorties went up: uselessly, for the aircraft were without radar and the pilots untrained for night work. The anti-aircraft guns could only achieve a hit by extreme luck. A trivial raid over Berlin was an empty gesture. Even the Bromide jammers were incorrectly set to 1500 instead of 2000 cycles because the experts were still learning about *X-Gerät*. Britain was not ready for a Blitz. But the real disaster was the clear moonlight night. With defences so inadequate on the ground and in the air, Cold Water contained no answer, once the Heinkels of K.Gr.100 had dropped their thousands of incendiaries on the three-spired city. The tragedy of Coventry is very simple. It is told in the recollections of a German pilot, Günther Unger, who remembered that even as they were crossing the Channel they saw a small pin-point of white light ahead, like a hand torch. 'As we drew closer to our target the light gradually became larger until suddenly it dawned on us: we were looking at the burning city of Coventry.'[10]

Soon, however, many of the aircraft employed in the night-time *Blitz* over England – particularly Luftflotte 2 – would be winging their way eastwards. For if the continued preparations for Sealion kept open the option of a cross-Channel invasion, they also served as effective cover for the more dramatic option which Hitler, on 18 December, at last decided to take up: Barbarossa, the invasion of Russia – an operation that was first called Fritz! The Führer's Directive No. 21 of the 18th gave a decisive impetus to this vast improbable scheme for taking European Russia unawares by a force of three million men, three thousand tanks and two thousand aircraft. In spite of the Germans' meticulous precautions about deception and security, such a re-deployment of troops and equipment on a continental scale provided delectable opportunities for penetration by intelligence: and so it proved. Early in January 1941, for example, a copy of the actual Barbarossa Directive of 18 December was passed to an American commercial attaché, Sam E. Woods, in the darkness of a Berlin cinema by an unnamed, highly placed, anti-Nazi official. After delays in Washington for checking, the information finally reached the Kremlin – to no avail. This was the first warning from an authentic source known to have reached Moscow from the west, but like the many others that post-war investigations have disinterred it was ignored. Stalin, as we now realize, had 'made a picture'. His total disbelief in the possibility of a German attack turned all contradictory advice – whether from Washington, Whitehall or his own people – into so much waste paper.

But if hindsight shows that nothing was to be gained by using intelligence about Barbarossa to help the Russians, it also discloses that there was much of practical value to the British themselves. Their interest in the Balkans and Churchill's private yearning to acquire Turkey as an ally were obvious reasons for watching the German build-up. Far-sighted staffs, moreover, had a practical interest in knowing the time-scales and logistic factors involved in the great eastward movement of the enemy's forces. If Hitler made another surprise *bouleversement*, and suddenly switched the *Wehrmacht* back to the Channel (as seemed not impossible in those days when few believed that Russia could hold out for long) then at least London would possess facts and figures to show how long the process would take. Underlying all was another threat, awaited and feared by the British. To guard the right flank of Barbarossa's immense front – to cover his Army Group South – Hitler had also decided in December on operation Marita, a thrust out of Roumania and Bulgaria to take hold of Salonika and the coast of northern Greece. (The attack on the Greek mainland was a late afterthought).

In occupied Poland, a main assembly-area for Barbarossa, intelligence was obviously not easy to acquire by conventional means. Later in the war, for example, the Polish underground had numerous radio links with England but as yet they were meagre. Nevertheless, the Poles observed the build-up intently and reported constantly by every means – sometimes by couriers travelling across Europe at immense risk. Further south – in Roumania, Bulgaria,

Yugoslavia, Greece – until the German grip tightened, British (and of course American) diplomatic, commercial and private contacts continued: the population was in any case more amenable to penetration by agents. Thus a considerable volume of intelligence filtered back to London from a variety of normal sources not all of which, in that Balkan world, were reputable or trustworthy.

To this whirling kaleidoscope of fact, rumour and guesswork Ultra added stability, authority and precision. A test case is available. The forward movement of the Luftwaffe into Roumania and Bulgaria was carefully planned by the Germans as a step-by-step process, so timed that at no stage but the last could observers assume that a full-scale takeover was intended. In practice the British knew all the stages, all the units and senior commanders involved, and the ultimate purpose of these secretive proceedings. To a considerable degree the reason was Ultra.

On 3 March 1941 a Deputy Director of Intelligence at the Air Staff, Group Captain Inglis, produced 'An Analysis of the Move of the German Air Force into the Balkans' during the previous three months which covered every aspect of the operations in the most minute detail.[11] The initial task of the Luftwaffe Mission was to reconnoitre and prepare the ground organization on Roumanian airfields capable of sustaining a balanced force of some 500 aircraft 'such as would provide close and strategic support for an army of 15 to 20 divisions'. Each of these airfields was individually identified, and the units based on them – dive or long range bombers, fighters, army co-operation – were known by name and number. Of the fifty-four airfields in Roumania twenty-two had been selected for the Luftwaffe. Since it was also known that special orders had been issued for officers to be sought who had had operational experience in the west, there was nothing surprising about the fact that the command headquarters appointed for this distant region was that of 8 Fliegerkorps which, under General von Richthofen, had been working as a specialized dive bomber force in the Channel area.

It was noted that by February the preliminary preparations and the move into Roumania were complete, but that as early as mid-December the German air attaché in Sofia, 'ably assisted by a staff of over 300 additional personnel', was reporting on airfield facilities in Bulgaria, and that by early March fourteen aerodromes (each identified) had been selected for about 280 aircraft, supplies for which were being fed into Bulgaria in advance by forty trains as from 7 February. The evidence, as Inglis concluded, was inescapable. 'By the preparation of aerodromes in Bulgaria, and by the assembly of supplies at these aerodromes before that country has actually been taken over, the Germans have succeeded in reducing to a minimum the time-lag between the actual absorption of Bulgaria and their preparations to strike beyond its frontiers. In fact, as far as the GAF and its preparations were concerned, no pause seems necessary.' The Inglis report is dated 3 March: in fact, German troops started to move into Bulgaria on the 1st.

Much of the information is day-by-day. Consider the recorded details of the move of 8 Fliegerkorps. On 26 November, still in the west, it is in conference with an old friend, *L.G. Stab ZBV 300*, 'in connection with Operation Smith'. On 29 December it is actually choosing embarkation officers for Smith when, the same day, it is nominated for Roumania. By 5 January hutments are ordered for it in Roumania and thereafter, almost daily throughout the month, the transfer of its forward parties and main units is logged. At the beginning of February a change occurs: the reconnaissance and flow of supply trains for 8 Fliegerkorps are now seen to be mainly directed into Bulgaria. All this was known in London.

Göring's Luftwaffe HQ is mentioned as being in daily wireless contact with the Roumanian mission. It was from this and other Luftwaffe traffic that Bletchley, of course, was able to build up the Ultra intelligence on which so intimate a report could be based. Apart from information about units, personalities and movements, the wireless traffic shed light on the Germans' problems. It was a signal from Göring's HQ to Roumania on 1 January, for example, authorizing the ethylization of 23 100 tons of fuel, which indicated that the famous oil-fields were by no means the source of high-grade aviation fuel that the Germans seem to have expected.

The story of the L trains is spectacular. Between 7 January and 1 March no less than seventy-six trains were identified, each with a serial number prefixed by the letter L, presumably Luft. Of these thirty-four were known to be carrying bombs, sixteen AA ammunition, twenty-one fuel, one general ammunition, and the remainder miscellaneous items. Eight certainly and twelve probably went to Roumania. Bulgaria was identified as the destination of a further forty-seven. But many other trains carrying personnel and supplies for the army and the air force are also mentioned, one message quoting the arrival of 1098 trains by 4 February.

Though this is but a brief summary of the Inglis report it vividly illustrates the value to Churchill and the Chiefs of Staff of Bletchley's fortunate ability to penetrate the Luftwaffe cipher. The history of 8 Fliegerkorps is only a segment of the massive build-up for Barbarossa – though of special interest, in that the Germans had to move more delicately among their satellites than in the slave-state of Poland. Still, we see instantly from this specific example how Ultra enabled the watchers in London to monitor the growth of Barbarossa just as, a few months earlier, they had been free to study the secret evolution of Sealion. And a document of this nature adds, for example, a new force and authority to some of Churchill's warnings and appeals. To Wavell at his Middle East Headquarters in Cairo on 10 January, for example: 'We have a mass of detail indicating that a large-scale movement through Bulgaria towards the Greek frontier aimed presumably at Salonika will begin before the end of the month.' Or to the President of Turkey on 31 January: 'I have sure information that the Germans are already establishing themselves on Bulgarian aerodromes. . . . The air squadrons will only have to fly from their stations in Roumania to the bases they are preparing in Bulgaria, and will immediately be able to come into action.'

Ultra was not essential in Moscow for an anticipation of Barbarossa. The Russians lacked Ultra, and yet from a myriad sources the intelligence flowed in – had there been ears to hear. When Churchill called Stalin 'at once a callous, a crafty and ill-informed giant' his third adjective was wrong – at least as regards Barbarossa. What Ultra provided in London, however, was precision, authenticity, confirmation, and material which often could have been acquired in no other way. Certainly as the Barbarossa deployment unfolded, as divisions rolled eastwards to coalesce into armies, and armies into army groups, such a mass of intelligence emerged at Bletchley that maps were kept marked with dozens of flags to indicate the Wehrmacht's current dispositions. Not that these always produced the right reaction. On one visit a number of red-tabbed senior soldiers were allowed to see the maps. Some disbelieved, on the grounds that intelligence of this nature was unattainable: the rest said that if what they saw was true, Russia would be finished in a matter of weeks.

But though Churchill himself believed in Bletchley, his own personal warning to Stalin about Barbarossa, in which he took such pride, may not have been directly based on Ultra. 'It was with relief and excitement', he says in his memoirs, 'that towards the end of March 1941 I read an Intelligence report from one of our most trusted sources of the movement and counter-movement of German armour on the railway from Bucharest to Cracow.' The transfer of three panzer divisions northwards from Roumania to Poland could only mean an imminent invasion of Russia. In his first message to Stalin since June 1940 Churchill sought to convey the facts and their meaning via his Ambassador in Moscow, Sir Stafford Cripps. The Prime Minister's warning did not reach the Generalissimo until mid-April and was then ignored. Stalin, as we now know, was deaf and deluded.

But why was it that the movement of the panzers 'illuminated the whole Eastern scene', as Churchill put it, 'like a lightning-flash'? Some sixty trains were involved. The actual information about them may well have come from agents of the Secret Service, which was responsible directly to the Foreign Office, for on 28 March the Permanent Under-Secretary at the Foreign Office, Sir Alexander Cadogan, described in his diary a conversation with the Prime Minister. 'Told PM of our news of German armoured Divisions being rushed back to Cracow. This rather in line with his ideas.' Since it was not Cadogan's responsibility to inform Churchill about Ultra intelligence it may well be that he was conveying a scoop by the Secret Service.

Be that as it may, a shuttle-service of three panzer divisions cannot have been the sole reason for triggering off Churchill so dramatically. The episode is only explicable in terms of the precisely detailed picture that Ultra and other sources had been establishing about the Barbarossa build-up. For months the Prime Minister and his advisers had been carefully discussing all the implications in the light of their full and impressive knowledge. Even at the time that Churchill was signalling a warning to Stalin the Joint Intelligence Committee was concerning itself with 'a report on the possibility of a German attack on the Soviet Union'. This had a curious origin.

The JIC was formed of the Directors of Intelligence of the three services and representatives of the Foreign Office and the Ministry of Economic Warfare. Its chairman, Victor Cavendish-Bentinck, also came from the Foreign Office: a man of independent mind, whose long reign at the JIC won respect from his colleagues. Progressively, as the war advanced, he became committed to the recognition of Ultra as a main staple in matters concerning the JIC. Now, in the spring of 1941, he observed two clues which in the context of all the existing intelligence convinced him that Hitler meant business over Russia. And this was why 'Bill' Cavendish-Bentinck proposed a comprehensive report.

The first clue was small but significant. Information was coming in from Turkey that the Germans were starting to subsidize anti-Bolshevik organizations in the Caucasus. Caucasian separatism was always an Achilles heel for centralist Russia – whoever the Tsar, Nicholas or Stalin. Why now should the Germans irritate this sore spot? But the other clue was decisive. From Ultra (as Cavendish-Bentinck has confirmed to the author) he noticed reports from Poland that the Germans were both extending the length of runways on the airfields and also reinforcing them to carry heavier loads. 'It occurred to me', he recalled, 'that this was not being done for the benefit of Lufthansa!'[12]

When one smiles at Stalin for refusing to accept the mountain of evidence about Barbarossa it is, of course, salutary to remember that although the thrust of the report initiated by Cavendish-Bentinck was in the same direction, neither some of the members of the JIC, nor the Chiefs of Staff themselves, nor a number of other highly-placed personalities could easily bring themselves to recognize the truth. Like all intelligence, Ultra could not produce results automatically. It needed perceptive interpretation and understanding. Still, there was nothing non-committal about the last act, the final attempt made by the British to use their accumulated knowledge about Barbarossa. The date was 10 June – twelve days before the offensive. The scene was the Foreign Office, whither the Soviet Ambassador Maisky had been summoned. His own words tell all.

Cadogan began to dictate from documents lying before him. 'On such-and-such a date two German motorized divisions passed through such-and-such a point in the direction of your frontier.... On such-and-such a date six German divisions were concentrated at such-and-such a point on your frontier.... During the whole of May there passed through such-and-such a point in the direction of your frontier twenty-five to thirty military trains a day.... On such-and-such a date in such-and-such a district bordering on your frontier there were discovered such-and-such a number of German troops and planes....'

The catalogue continued remorselessly until Cadogan rose and stated, formally: 'The Prime Minister asks you urgently to communicate all these data to the Soviet Government'.[13] Four days later the Soviet News Agency issued a communiqué referring to 'clumsily cooked-up propaganda' and affirming that 'Germany is unswervingly observing the conditions of the Soviet–German Pact of Non-Aggression'.

In the spring of 1941, therefore, Britain was poised on the verge of an immense extension of the war, with the Balkans about to explode, Barbarossa impending, and the whole Mediterranean at risk. Ultra itself would expand in conformity with these developments. Indeed, since the breakthrough in April 1940 its value and potentiality had been fully demonstrated. That moment of curious tranquillity before the guns start firing seems appropriate, therefore, for an account of the establishment which brought Ultra to life – the secret Station X at Bletchley Park.

4   Station X

'It's a great huge game of chess that's being played – all
over the world – if this *is* the world, you know.'

LEWIS CARROLL, Through the Looking Glass

To many Bletchley Park certainly seemed like life seen through a
looking glass. For those who dropped in from the outside –
orthodox-minded generals and admirals, the occasional politician –
there was something unreal, *farouche* and even suspect about the
motley and unsoldierly crew they encountered. Churchill's famous
remark about Bletchley – which he probably never uttered – is
nevertheless characteristic of those who found the Park's menagerie
beyond their comprehension. 'I told you,' the Prime Minister is
said to have commented, 'to leave no stone unturned in your
recruiting. I did not expect you to take me so literally.'

The first other-worldly feature of this unique establishment was
that whatever the names under which it came to be known – War
Station Room 47 of the Foreign Office, Station X, BP – nobody
either inside or outside had a complete picture of what was happening there. Security naturally and properly excluded the outsider
from anything more than minimal knowledge. But within Bletchley
Park itself the ingrained sense of security was so strong that the
occupants of one Hut would have little awareness of, and usually no
desire to find out, what those in another Hut were doing – even
though they might meet socially or perhaps be old friends. The
mathematician Jack Good shared lodgings with the poet Henry
Reed: neither had the least notion of the other's commitments. This
was the accepted situation. One only discussed one's work with
those who shared it. Even those responsible at the summit –
Denniston at first and Travis during the years of expansion – cannot
have found it easy to retain a firm grasp of more than the broad
structure even though they received daily reports from the heads of
the different huts and sections. There was a large measure of
devolution and autonomy.

The diversity of the staff was indeed distracting. No stone had in
fact been left unturned to assemble in this quiet backwater what, by

111

the middle of the war, represented something like a cross-section of the British intelligentsia.

They were not all, or even mainly, masters of the chess-board, though the presence of Milner-Barry, Alexander, Golombek and other skilled players, particularly in the cryptanalytical sections, gives colour to the looking-glass image of Bletchley as part of 'a great huge game'. Indeed the range of talent, actual or potential, was extraordinarily wide. There was a future Chancellor of the Exchequer and President of the European Commission in Roy Jenkins. A non-commissioned soldier in Hut 6 would become Lord Briggs, Vice-Chancellor of Sussex University and then Provost of Worcester College, Oxford. The young J. H. Plumb rose to the Professorship of Modern English History at Cambridge. Edward Boyle passed through BP before embarking on a career which took him to ministerial rank in politics, to a Peerage, and to the Vice-Chancellorship of Leeds University. Newman was a Fellow of the Royal Society and Turing would be elected in 1951. In one of the intelligence units was Denys Page, later a Master of Jesus College and Regius Professor of Greek in the University of Cambridge. Then there was Leonard Palmer who, as Professor of Comparative Philology at Oxford after the war, devoted himself to the Mycenaean civilization. Another classical scholar was T. B. L. Webster, later President of the Hellenic Society and Professor of Classics at Stanford University. Many others either were already or later matured as professors, fellows or heads of colleges, ambassadors, or distinguished civil servants.

A civilian prisoner-of-war camp in the Germany of 1914–18 provided a curious link. E. R. Vincent, the Professor of Italian at Cambridge (who had trained at GCCS since 1937 and became BP's expert on the Italian ciphers) was caught in Germany as a young man in 1914 and spent the war in the famous Ruhleben Camp. 'Bimbo' Norman, Professor of German at King's College, London, had also been immured in Ruhleben: serving in Hut 3, Frederick Norman was an invaluable link with R. V. Jones in the struggle for scientific intelligence, paying special attention to the signal-traffic relating to the enemy's radio-guidance systems, radar, V-weapons and so on. At BP there were also two brothers, Walter and Edward Ettinghausen, whose father, a rabbi, was a Ruhleben inmate. (By a further coincidence Sir John Masterman, whose section of MI5 owed so much to Bletchley's intelligence for its system of double-crossing the German by the use of double agents,* was also a Ruhleben man.) And there was another linkage. BP acquired the future Public Orators of both the older Universities, Tommy Higham from Oxford and Patrick Wilkinson, later Vice-Provost of King's College Cambridge. Their gift for wittily and convincingly translating into Latin topical allusions and modern technicalities, the stock-in-trade of a good Public Orator at the formal ceremonies of his University, was not alien to the world of signals-intelligence.

Any academic severity – not that the academics were notably austere – was qualified by the arts: by the presence, for example, of Angus Wilson the novelist and Leslie Harrison Lambert who, as 'A. J. Alan', had diverted listeners with his stories since that first inimitable broadcast in 1924. (Lambert/Alan came to Bletchley as a professional pre-war member of GCCS, where his field was administration rather than cryptography). Alan Pryce-Jones was later Editor of *The Times Literary Supplement*, and Edward Crankshaw a fine Russian historian and correspondent on Soviet affairs. Jim Rose and Peter Calvocoressi, both of Hut 3, became respectively Chairman and Chief Executive of Penguin Books. Dorothy Hyson was not alone among the actresses. Frank Birch** of the Naval Section was as much at home on the stage as in the study, just as, for a don like F. L. Lucas in Hut 3, literature had a life beyond the merely academic. And was it before he arrived at BP, or because of some earnest hours in the Bletchley Home Guard, that Henry Reed composed 'Naming of Parts', that poem about rifle-instruction which captured the through-the-looking-glass feeling of the civilian-at-arms?

And this you can see is the bolt. The purpose of this
Is to open the breech, as you see. We can slide it
Rapidly backwards and forwards: we call this
Easing the spring. And rapidly backwards and forwards
The early bees are assaulting and fumbling the flowers:
        They call it easing the Spring.

If it was difficult for individual members of the staff to name all the separate parts of the weapon called Bletchley, security was not the only reason. Some, at least, of the teams were often too tired or

---

*For Masterman and the double-cross system see Chapter Eleven.
**His performance as the Widow Twanky in *Aladdin* was noted as the only appearance of a Fellow of King's College Cambridge in pantomime.

too preoccupied by their own work to care about what was going on next door. The round-the-clock shift system which kept the various huts permanently manned could mean that you did not even know people who were on the other watches in your own hut: it also meant that what with a bus ride, perhaps, to and from your lodgings, and sleep, and private concerns, there was often little time to spare. A lucky break in the cryptanalytical huts, whereby the 'key of the day' was determined at an early hour, might ease the pressure there, but in the main the race was against the clock, enthralling, exacting, relentless. Any portrait of Bletchley must be impressionistic. Experience was intensely personal, individual horizons were limited. Nobody's career there was precisely characteristic. One of the cryptanalysts commented on this passage: 'Even allowing for a degree of artistic licence, I am afraid this overdoes it somewhat. Many at BP worked 9–6 throughout the war; by no means all sections were permanently manned; and shift work averaged little more than eight hours a day, though shift changes involved inconvenience.' But the memories of others are certainly more stressful.

A few – but surprisingly few – broke under the strain. In 1940, after his prolonged effort in mastering the Japanese Purple cipher, William Friedman in Washington had to withdraw to a neuropsychiatric ward. But at Bletchley there were not only the great specific struggles – the 1940 breakthrough, for example: the recovery of the Atlantic U-boat cipher in 1942 and again in 1943: the Abwehr cipher and so on. For the cryptanalysts the struggle was intense and daily throughout the whole war, with not one but many ciphers as a permanent challenge, elusive keys constantly to be discovered anew, and always the haunting possibility that a breach of security might 'blow' the whole operation. That so many endured for so long certainly owed much to motivation. There was an indefinable spirit at Bletchley permeating the whole, and affecting not only the cryptanalysts and intelligence staffs – who at least had interesting and compulsive work to do – but even the lowly but vitally important Wrens who drudged away at the dull and, to them, wholly unintelligible routine of servicing the bombes. But there is perhaps another explanation. Friedman was already a veteran when he collapsed. So many of the Bletchley men and women were young – undergraduates straight from their universities, dons of only a few years' standing. Their mental and physical resilience had not yet been sapped. And, above all, they had the incomparable stimulus of feeling that in a special but recognizable way they were helping, directly and visibly, to win the war.

In due course the parts of the Bletchley organization began to function as an integrated whole. Once the growing pains were over, the full scale of the Enigma problem had been grasped, and the intelligence requirements of the three armed services had been clearly diagnosed, the main lines of the system fell into place. To the end there was innovation, further elaboration, unremitting research into areas of enemy signal traffic still unexplored or unresolved. But the central, continuing structure can be defined, and it may perhaps be understood best by following the average route of an Enigma signal from the point of interception to the moment when it arrived, deciphered and processed, for operational use at some British headquarters in the field.

Everything began with the intercept. The story of 'Y' Service, that vast and world-wide organization responsible for maintaining a continuous watch on the enemy's radio traffic, taking down its signals and identifying their sources, is of a triumph as yet untold. From the point of view of Station X it is sufficient to note that apart from providing the cryptanalysts with their raw material in the form of intercepted signals, 'Y' Service also supplied much invaluable information about the radio networks of the enemy. To know the particular network on which a signal had been transmitted was a large step towards identifying the cipher in which its message had been concealed. Accurate knowledge of the exact frequencies used by the Germans also meant that if intelligence was urgently needed about a special matter – the beams in 1940, the V weapons – intercept stations could be asked to pay extra attention to the relevant network. The intercepts on which the cryptanalysts exercised their skills arrived in ever-increasing volume from the great main centres such as Cheadle and Chicksands Priory for air force material, Flowerdown and Scarborough for the navy and Chatham, at first, for the army. In 1941 Group Captain John Shephard returned from West Africa, a casualty of yellow fever, to be told by a friend in the Air Ministry that command of a station at Chicksands in Bedfordshire, about to be developed for wireless intelligence, might prove therapeutic – 'a diverting job with some 2,000 acres of shooting'. Shephard's actual experience illuminates the scale and the problems of the intercept game.

Colin had not told me that an embryo operation there already had to be expanded something like ten times by the day before yesterday. In ten months we built a camp for airmen – and airwomen – and a technical site to replace the spooky old Priory, and we trained a thousand or so wireless operators to provide Bletchley with some of the enormous mass of German Air Force high grade ciphers.

The Germans obscured the origins of transmitted messages by changing the frequency used, and the call sign of each transmitter, daily. At midnight all change occurred and we, the eavesdroppers, had to relocate our sources. One would have thought this to be an almost impossible task, to search through the whole frequency band. Luckily the Germans themselves had to chatter away to re-establish connections and, to the accustomed ear, each transmitter and operator had an individuality as easy to recognize as if the Mona Lisa tried to simper behind a pair of false moustaches. 'Hitlerian', 'Hals Cavalerian', 'Menjou', 'Handlebar' – it only took a little searching to find the same chap. And if our friend who turned Morse symbols into Wagnerian spondees or Mozart dactyls ceased to be heard on the sensitive aerial on which we normally picked him up, and then appeared a day or two later via another aerial, we would quickly realize that some Luftwaffe Group had been transferred from the Pas de Calais to Holland.[1]

These were but a few of the technical difficulties with which the British (and German) interceptors struggled by day and by night. For Bletchley the end-product of 'Y' Service's effort and ingenuity was a stream of ciphered texts, normally exact transcriptions of the original enemy signal, though from time to time atmospheric conditions, weak signal-strengths or other reasons such as sheer human error would result in a 'corruption' or 'garble' as it was sometimes called: a text marred by gaps or containing incorrect letters. Garbles could mean anything from a brief entertaining puzzle to a prolonged nightmare.

As Bletchley expanded, the cryptanalytical centre for army and air force traffic continued to be Hut 6, where in due course Welchman was succeeded as head by Milner-Barry. For the navy cryptanalysis came to be focussed in Hut 8: and here, for a time, Turing's intellect provided an inspiring leadership supported, not surprisingly, by the most vestigial of administrative abilities. Turing passed on to even more recherché duties: his replacement by Hugh Alexander was beneficial if only because the old friendship with Milner-Barry made it possible, as the latter wrote in his memoir of Alexander, 'to resolve differences which might have had to be referred to higher authority, with disastrous loss of time.'[2] Hut 6 and Hut 8 were joined like Siamese twins in common requirement for bombes to resolve their cryptanalytical problems. At times when each Hut was handling urgent matters, and bombes were few, the possibility of internecine conflict was always there.

And of course such occasions occurred. A good instance would be that in late 1942 when John Monroe, while head of a watch in Hut 6, was visited by Shaun Wylie of Hut 8, demanding insistently that six of the bombes allocated to Hut 6 should be put at his disposal because an important 'break' was imminent. (John Monroe later became a considerable legal authority, a National Insurance Commissioner and a Bencher of the Middle Temple. Wylie was an international hockey player. He was also winner of the unarmed combat competition in the local Home Guard, and President of the Bletchley Dramatic Club.) The break was the vital re-entry into the Atlantic U-boat cipher which, it will be recalled, had remained impregnable since the previous February. Here, in relation to the Battle of the Atlantic, was an issue of the highest priority. Yet Monroe, responsible for army and air force traffic, had also to remember that at the same time Montgomery's offensive in the Western Desert was still proceeding and the Mediterranean ciphers, for him, were paramount. Bombes were still few and precious. All the same, Monroe met the needs of the Navy.[3] At such moments of peak pressure a sense of rapport between two sets of specialists dedicated to conflicting tasks was essential.

It was into Huts 6 and 8, as appropriate, that the intercepts passed on the first stage of their journey. And in those Huts the cryptanalytical processes had one essential object: on each and every day it was necessary to determine exactly how the Enigma machines producing a particular cipher had been set up. The keys, the setting: these were dominant. It was only rarely, very very rarely, that Bletchley acquired actual lists of the keys being currently used by the Germans – as happened when U-boat 110 was captured off Greenland on 8 May 1941 with the intact treasure-trove of her Enigma machine and the relevant documents.* Normally, the key to a cipher had to be home-produced at Station X. The answers were sometimes swift in coming, sometimes agonizingly slow.

*See Chapter Eight.

Many factors were at work. Since carelessness on the part of enemy operators gave the cryptanalysts one of their most fruitful means of breaking a cipher, much depended on the service from which a signal emanated. The Luftwaffe was consistently insecure in its procedure. The German army was outstanding in its professionalism, the navy sound but variable, while the secret services, the Abwehr and Himmler's SD, offered many useful openings.* By and large, throughout the war, the Luftwaffe created the least problems and it came to be normal to expect that the 'key of the day' for the Red Luftwaffe cipher would be available at least before breakfast-time.

Carelessness took many forms. If a cryptanalyst trying to break a ciphered message can match parts of its text with words, phrases, sentences already known to him he had made a big stride towards being able to obtain the key to the cipher. Some operators regularly, and some casually, made the mistake of including in a newly ciphered signal small or large groups that they had transmitted in a previous cipher. Rommel's Quartermaster at Tripoli is particularly remembered for his habit of starting all messages to his commander with the same formal introduction. Some operators would use the recognizable names of their girlfriends in the important opening section of the signal. The SD, in their uncouth way, would interpolate obscenities: so much so that a message was once deciphered at Bletchley which instructed SD units to avoid bad language in their transmissions for fear of offending female operators. This gave great satisfaction to the girls at BP. (The technical reason is that it was the SD's practice to start their ciphered messages with a random four-letter group. Ask an average man to dream up four-letter groups, and by the law of averages . . .!)

Intercepts which raised special problems went elsewhere – in particular to a section mysteriously named ISK. Though their functions were analogous to those of Huts 6 and 8, ISK and its companion ISOS remained shrouded behind initials, which in fact stood for Intelligence Services Oliver Strachey and Intelligence Services Knox. ISOS dealt with hand-ciphered messages. Dillwyn Knox and his team in ISK pitted their wits against ciphers not yet broken but thought to have originated on some kind of Enigma. They thus

---

*One who worked in this field commented to the author: 'The Abwehr and SD were not, I think, especially careless in cipher procedure. Their system was just fundamentally more vulnerable than those of the armed services, and vastly less expensive to read.'

cracked, for example, the Italian fleet cipher (produced on a version of the commercial Enigma with special rotors) and the Abwehr cipher (for which a particular Enigma was used, lacking, for example, the system of jacks or *Steckers* characteristic of the normal model). In ISK, too, intriguing Enigma-ciphers were broken from the Eastern Front – some from the forlorn Spanish Blue Division whose final signal is recalled as 'the general direction of the enemy's advance appears to be westwards'.

At the next stage in the intercepted signal's progress, recourse must be had to the bombes. The essential value of these devices, it will be recalled, was their ability to explore electro-mechanically (not electronically) a range of alternative possibilities at speeds far beyond the pace of human thought. In practical terms, what the bombes did has been defined as 'to test all the possible wheel or rotor orders of the Enigma, all the possible wheel settings and plug or Stecker connections to discover which of the possible arrangements would match a prescribed combination of letters'. When the prescribed conditions had been matched the bombe stopped. (In the memories of the Wrens who operated the bombes 'a stop', the author found, comes back with the vividness of a personal triumph.) From the result the cryptanalysts derived a potential solution to the cipher-key for which they were searching, which could then be verified by other means. Since the order of placing the wheels in the Enigma could be varied in sixty different ways, and for each order 17 576 possible settings for the individual wheels had to be checked, no human brain could conceivably compete with the electromagnetic bombe in reaching, and very consistently reaching, an answer to questions of such magnitude.

Much of the effort and flair of the cryptanalysts was devoted, therefore, to identifying from scrutiny of the intercepts the correct set of questions to feed into the bombes: in other words, to establish 'the prescribed combination of letters'. This provender was known as 'the menu'. But it was often a matter of nice calculation as to when a menu should be proffered, for in the earlier years of the war, certainly, bombes were in short supply. And since it took a varying but appreciable time to run a bombe, this could not be pre-empted lightly. The Wrens who operated the bombes – sometimes, as the war progressed, in out-stations detached from Bletchley – deserve much praise for their staunchness in an unending routine whose reason must have defeated them. But they too had the spirit of

Station X. They too – post-war wives and mothers – kept their secret from their families. And one of the most endearing stories of Bletchley is that of a Wren who, whenever a 'stop' occurred on her bombe, took off her hat and put a mark inside it. Churchill would have liked that.

Once an intercept's cipher had been broken, whether swiftly or slowly, it was usually, but far from always, simple to convert its message into the original German. At this point the text moved onward for processing – in the case of army and air force signals to Hut 3, in the case of the navy to Hut 4. ISK worked to an intelligence unit for handling, in particular, the Abwehr and SD traffic: it was in this field that the future Professors of Greek and Comparative Philology, Denys Page and Leonard Palmer, exercised their arts.

As the system got into gear the amount of decrypts passed on their flimsy strips of paper into the intelligence Huts was enormous and, without orderly control, would have been unmanageable. As Hut 3 coped with both the Luftwaffe and the German army, its intake was inevitably the largest, and the treatment of an intercept in the hands of its staff may therefore be taken as the most evidential. To translate the deciphered signal, to understand and evaluate its meaning, and to decide who should receive the information it contained – such were the duties of this inter-service Hut whose members, some Army, some RAF, some of the Foreign Office establishment, developed a remarkable *esprit de corps* more akin to that of a good Senior Common Room at Oxford or Cambridge than to the ethos of a composite wartime unit.

'Hut 3', Peter Calvocoressi recalled, 'revolved round its watch. Imagine a room about 30-40 feet across, roughly square and pretty bare except for a large horseshoe table. The head of the watch sat in the middle of the horseshoe, with some ten other members of the Watch facing him round the outside. They all knew German and that is the one thing they had in common. Some had been schoolteachers, others came from museums, universities, and business. Three times in the twenty-four hours one watch replaced another; to the end of the war the room was permanently peopled.'

But more happened to an intercept than merely to be handed round a horseshoe table. When the German text reached Hut 3 for the translators and analysts anything of interest in its contents was also marked up for filing in the Index, that extraordinary memory-bank which grew into perhaps the most comprehensive storehouse of intelligence in the country. Its beginnings were modest. The basic principles were established, appropriately, by a man from Kelly's Directory, Flying Officer Cullingham, who set up an Air Index. But when Jean Alington joined BP in June 1941 and with Margaret Hensley and Kate Holt (the future wife of a Bishop of London) worked on a shift system to maintain an Army Index their stock-in-trade, at first, was no more than a few boxes graced by a meagre batch of cards.[4] Yet by the peak of the war the Index of Hut 3 (the naval section had its own) filled a large room manned – or rather womanned – by a large staff on shifts all round the clock. Meticulous extraction of figures, names, dates and so on from the multitude of incoming signals meant that the Index contained not only the most minute and accurate details about the enemy's order of battle, developing plans and production states, and personalities high and low in the German commands, but also records of points which, when they first cropped up in a signal, might have seemed trivial and meaningless: later, however, when they appeared in another intercept the item already noted on a card in the Index could help to throw a sudden light on some secret, unsuspected weapon or the hidden deployment of a German unit.

The Index was in fact unique. At the height of the war, when Ultra signals poured into Hut 3 and its staff was often under extreme pressure to keep pace with them, effective processing of the intercepts would have been virtually impossible without this invaluable check-point. As a precaution, a copy of its contents was maintained – and presumably up-dated – at the Bodleian Library in Oxford. Perhaps the most generous (or mordant) comment on the Index was made by one of the Americans who came to work in Hut 3 early in 1944. Surveying the Index room, its shabbiness, the dog-eared much-used reference cards with their precious contents, Alfred Friendly remarked to his colleagues 'The difference between British and American intelligence is this. You have –' and he gestured at the unspectacular scene. 'If this was in the Pentagon,' he said, 'there'd be rows of shining new filing systems – and nothing in them!'

It cannot be repeated too often that the Ultra material did not consist of a flow of intercepts coming from a single source in a single cipher. The ciphers themselves were numerous and the units, headquarters and commands using a particular cipher on a particu-

121

lar day could proliferate. In his study of Ultra and the naval war, *Very Special Intelligence*, Patrick Beesly lists no less than thirteen main ciphers employed by the different departments and units – the heavy ships, the U-boats, the surface raiders and so on – under the control of the German Admiralty, OKM, the *Oberkommando der Marine*. For the German army and the Luftwaffe similar standard variations in cipher-usage were registered in Hut 6, each being identified by Bletchley's own code-name or colour-reference: Chaffinch, for example, or Red or Brown.

For Hut 3 the significance of such a variety was that intercepts could not simply be handled piece-meal as they came tumbling in from the cryptanalysts. Order and system were necessary. And so, as the decrypts arrived, they had to be sorted according to the ciphers in which they had been transmitted, and processed according to the priority which, on that day, it was estimated that a particular cipher should receive. As the volume of traffic increased over the years, this became a matter of nice judgement. By October 1942 Wing-Commander Oeser was directing 3L, a small unit within Hut 3, whose special task it was to assess the day's traffic and establish priorities of treatment. Oeser (later Professor of Psychology at Melbourne University) was another Cambridge man and a friend of Winterbotham, by whom he had been inducted into Hut 3 in the summer of 1940. A minute section with great responsibilities, 3L was largely feminine – Christine Brooke Rose, Jean Alington and a few others. Telford Taylor, the spearhead of the American involvement in Ultra,* recalled that when in 1943 he was seeing off a visiting USAAF officer at Bletchley station the latter, having noticed Oeser and his ladies at their work, exclaimed: 'Wing-commander! And *what* a wing!'[5]

As a back-up for the watches round their table there were 'advisers' on both army and air force matters. When the intercepts, in the next stage of their journey, were passed to the watch – of which one was always on duty – the first task was translation: often a swift and routine exercise, for the translators were soaked in German military terminology and the shapes, the shorthand, the standard patterns of the enemy signals. Still, the exercise could sometimes be painfully slow. If the text was corrupt, or letter-groups were missing, it could prove difficult to re-establish the original German

---

*For the details of this involvement, see Chapter Nine.

and, if the message looked important, it might be necessary to ask the cryptanalysts to 'run' the intercept again. A signal, moreover, might contain an unfamiliar word – perhaps scientific jargon relating to a new weapon, or the name of a German to whom, as it were, the watch-keeper had not been personally introduced. And here, if he or she could not discover the answer by their own intuitive skills or recourse to the advisers or the Index, the corporate wisdom of the Hut, something actual and palpable like a group mind, would often come to the rescue.

Since knowledge of German was mandatory for the watch-keepers, it will be evident that many or even most of those in Hut 3 had learned the language in Germany itself before the war. Some had been in universities: some had stayed with friends. It was an extraordinary experience to overlook through Ultra the *Götter-dämmerung* of a nation containing their own friends or relations: even, occasionally, to follow in the signals the fortunes and perhaps the fate of one they had known. Yet they were able to discuss such matters together quite objectively and openly. The overtones of friendship or kinship did not, of course, affect their work, which became a sort of dedicated obsession: but there was a penumbra of concern and, sometimes, sorrow. Only a limited number, of course, was so affected: and such feelings were certainly balanced by the emotions of those at Bletchley who were Jews themselves or had Jewish friends or connections in Germany or occupied Europe.

After translation and assessment, distribution. The head of the watch, usually a senior in experience, had to decide to whom, out of a range of possible recipients at home and abroad, the translated text should now be forwarded. And it was the *text*: there was a draconian law at Bletchley that Ultra signals should be distributed 'raw', without evaluation. The reason was obvious. Whatever the store of knowledge in the heads of the staff or on the cards of the Index, Station X was in essence a cipher-breaking establishment rather than a fully equipped intelligence centre. There would have been grave dangers and much possible confusion had Bletchley interpretations been allowed to circulate authoritatively beyond the bounds of the park. Indeed, it is possible to diagnose the existence there of a natural and inevitable affliction which might be called the Ultra syndrome: the assumption that because the intercepts on the table, so authentic and so eloquent, told so much they must tell everything.

'We couldn't *understand* why Montgomery didn't move quicker after Alamein. Rommel's situation was quite clear to us.' Remarks like these, made by members of Hut 3 in retrospect, are a reminder that for those running a battle there were often many other factors to take into account besides the voice of Ultra – other sources of information, the condition of one's troops, the state of one's supplies, political considerations and so on. The staff in Hut 3 were highly intelligent men and women handling intelligence of the highest authority, and it was not surprising that sometimes they thought they knew best. But Bletchley could not be aware of all the factors in the minds of the Chiefs of Staff or of army commanders in the field. It was certainly prudent, therefore, to issue the signals without comment.*

When issued, the texts of the decrypts were marked, according to the judgement of the head of the watch, with those signs of priority ranging from Z to the most insistent ZZZZZ. One advantage of such a method was that a signaller or staff officer at the receiving end would have no doubt that a ZZZZZ message was not for the pending tray, but genuinely urgent. Whatever the scale of importance, the intercepts would proceed on their journey by two main routes.

At home teleprinter links carried the texts, as seemed relevant, to some or all of those who 'needed to know': the Chiefs of Staff, the Directors of Intelligence of the three services and the Joint Intelligence Committee, the Admiralty's Operational Intelligence Centre, the headquarters of the Air Commands and of the USAAF, Combined Operations HQ and so on. A link to Broadway fed Menzies and Winterbotham, through a teleprinter room permanently staffed by officers of the WAAF, and from Broadway Churchill's personal diet of Ultra messages sped a few hundred yards eastwards to Downing Street or his war room. All command headquarters abroad, both British and – later – American, had a communications system through their Special Liaison Units which (as Chapter Five describes) were in action at their fullest scope not only in North-West Europe and throughout the Mediterranean but also on the Japanese fronts, from the China/Burma/India theatre down to the islands of New Guinea. For the fleets at sea the SLU system was

---

*Comment, that is, of a subjective character. The Ultra messages sent out from Bletchley often contained *elucidatory* comment – to explain a technical detail, or draw the reader's attention to a significant point. But evaluation was generally avoided.

hardly practical. Such Ultra information as had to be communicated was therefore transmitted by the Admiralty on secure naval channels.*

However brilliant the galaxy of exceptional men and women at Bletchley it would, nevertheless, have been difficult for the Ultra organization to maintain its efforts at an increasing tempo through six years of war unless its value had been recognized – and obviously recognized – in the right high places. Fortunately the atmosphere was wholly different from that of 1914–18. During those years the main equivalent to BP was the Admiralty's Room 40: for most of them the attitude of the Naval Staff towards cryptanalysis was hostile or indifferent. Lieutenant Clarke, a member of the Room, recalled how at the time of Jutland Rear-Admiral Sir Thomas Jackson, Director of the Operations Division, 'displayed supreme contempt for the work of Room 40. He never came into the Room during the writer's time there except oη two or three occasions, on one of which he came to complain that one of the locked boxes in which the information was sent him had cut his hand, and on another to say, at a time when the Germans had introduced a new code book, "Thank God, I shan't have any more of that damned stuff".'[6] Though the breach between Room 40 and the actual conduct of the war at sea was narrowed in the course of 1917, as a result of the U-boat crisis and disastrous shipping losses, the idea of profiting from the interception of enemy signals was never fully developed at that time – even for the Navy – into a recognized and essential weapon. During the first German war too little reliance was placed on Room 40. In the second, by 1944 at least, the danger was that Ultra might be relied on too much!

This transformation owed a great deal to Churchill. The respect accorded to Bletchley was, indeed, also a reflection of the general regard in which intelligence units came to be held by the British as the war progressed. The character of the Joint Intelligence Committee and its supporting teams: the ability of intelligence officers in the field – whether professionals like Kenneth Strong and Terence Airey or militarized intellectuals like Bill Williams and David Hunt, Enoch Powell and Noel Annan: the style and achievement of the Navy's Operational Intelligence Centre were unparalleled in any

---

*Readers should not be confused by the success of B Dienst in breaking the code used by the Admiralty for communicating with convoys. From 1940 the Navy's *operational* signals were secure.

previous conflict. Intelligence rose to a higher plane from which, after 1945, it was not to be wholly dislodged in the Whitehall revolutions of peacetime. But from the beginning Churchill gave Ultra his particular attention and placed behind it the formidable weight of his approval.

His personal interest in this 'secret source' – described in Chapter Seven – was only too evident to the Chiefs of Staff, General Ismay and his other close advisers. But as they and, in due course, commanders in the field realized that the Prime Minister himself was one of Ultra's most satisfied customers, regularly receiving private copies of the same intercepts as reached their own hands, the whole Ultra organization from Bletchley outwards was impregnable. No Rear-Admiral Jackson would have dared to talk about 'that damned stuff' in Hut 6 or 8! And Churchill's authority was of particular value in the field. The indoctrination of senior commanders by Winterbotham or his representatives was always a delicate matter, as was the question of reproof if they had committed or permitted some breach of security. At times of difficulty the knowledge or reminder that there was an ultimate sanction – reference, *on his orders*, to the Prime Minister – was invaluable. This Churchillian authority, evident from the beginning, was restated to Winterbotham by Menzies in August 1942, on the eve of Torch, and complemented, so far as the Americans were concerned, by a directive from the Joint Chiefs of Staff to Eisenhower. It persisted to the end.

Churchill thus provided a context in which Bletchley Park was always, as the resistance movements used to say, 'a safe house'. But BP's own achievements were the real justification: and here, too, things were different – for in this war the Admirals who called came in gratitude. After the sinking of *Bismarck* and the first breaking of the U-boat cipher the First Sea Lord, Sir Dudley Pound, came down from Whitehall. When Admiral Cunningham returned from the Mediterranean after the battle of Matapan, which BP had made possible, he too paid a call. And when *Scharnhorst* was finally sunk, with so much help from Ultra,* Admiral Sir Bruce Fraser arrived at Bletchley to give his thanks. When Brigadier John Shearer returned from the Middle East in the spring of 1942, after serving since the beginning as Director of Military Intelligence to Wavell and

*For *Bismarck*, Matapan and *Scharnhorst* see Chapter Eight.

Auchinleck, he made a special point of visiting BP to explain grate-
fully how invaluable he found Ultra to be in the battles against
Rommel. Before a greater battle, the one launched on D Day in
June 1944, Brigadier Williams was also at pains to make the trip to
Bletchley and, as Montgomery's chief intelligence officer, to give
people there a picture of how the return to Europe was likely to
develop, so that they would have a proper background against
which the intercepts they would be handling could be effectively
interpreted. He promised, too, that when the battle began he would
supply BP with regular situation reports so that the staff could be
kept up-to-date.[7] We have travelled light-years from Room 40.

The most memorable guest, of course, was Churchill himself,
who was careful to keep his finger on the pulse of Station X. Sometimes a surprised officer in Hut 3 would find himself taking a telephone call from the Prime Minister, who in his eager way was as
liable to ring up Bletchley for the latest news as he was to put in a
personal call to the Duty Officer at the BBC or to the Admiralty's
Operational Intelligence Centre. Sometimes a translated intercept
would be returned by Churchill to Bletchley with a query in his own
handwriting about the precise accuracy of some English word used
in the translation. (Mistakes could indeed be made during work
under stress: much confusion was once caused by the phrase 'parachute horse' that had crept into a translation. This new-style
Pegasus was simply the product of a scribbled 'parachute losses'.)
But above all there was the presence of Churchill himself, the most
important of all the visiting Very Important Persons. Standing on a
tree stump before an assembly of the staff he began to address them
inimitably. 'You all look', he said, 'very ... innocent.'

They were young: they had, in the main, acute minds honed by
the nature of their work: they were sceptical, inquisitive, original,
iconoclastic, and like all good troops in wartime they tended to
affect boredom at inspection by the great and the good, christening
them 'conducted tours'. (It is interesting, nevertheless, to observe
how such visits remain vivid in the minds of Bletchleyites thirty
years later.) But Churchill's joke was not irrelevant. A certain inno-
cence about war's realities did in fact prevail. Through no fault of
their own they were insulated. They became masters of the signal-
traffic, but they were far from the battlefields. Pound's visit was
dismissed by some as that of a tired and unimpressive old man: he
was in truth exhausted, but how could they comprehend the impact

127

on the First Sea Lord of the recent nerve-wracking chase of *Bismarck*, the concurrent battle for Crete and the preceding evacuation of Greece with their crippling losses for the British Navy? Still, the laugh was sometimes on Station X. There was a day when the USAAF Generals Spaatz and Doolittle paid a surprise visit and caught the naval section unawares. One watch-leader after another seemed unavailable. Finally the room of the last possible was entered. He was cleaning a golf club and ignored the visitors. 'Ah,' said Spaatz in a constructive way, 'Golf!' 'No,' came the reply from a bored officer who had not bothered even to look up. 'It's just for dusting the strip-lighting.'

Laughter was never far-distant nor, for that matter, love. At the time or later Bletchley, not surprisingly, was the origin of successful and lasting marriages: of less permanent passions, too. Is an affaire appropriate amid bombes, Enigmas and garbles? A. E. Housman's line replies: 'But young men think it is, and we were young.' There were practical advantages, too. 'We vied in picking up new recruits,' one Hut 3 senior recalled. 'I always chose pretty girls, since if they turned out useless one could always trade them to the wolves in other departments. A modern slave market, since no one, once in, could be dismissed!' And not least of Bletchley's affinities with Bloomsbury was its penchant for the practical joke, from the days of the earliest visit of GCCS to BP in 1938 – an intensely Bloomsbury episode – to the latter stages of the war when Dillwyn Knox's son Oliver was a notable perpetrator. (His assembly of a group of senior officers for an entirely fictitious conference was 'blown' by tracing the invitations back to the typewriter Knox had employed.) But laughter was most concentrated, perhaps, at Bletchley's unique revues.

Group Captain Shephard came over from Chicksands to attend one and found 'an entertainment whose brilliance was undiminished by having to appeal to an audience whose IQ was not less than 200'. The script-writers could take the strain – Patrick Wilkinson, for example, then a fellow of King's College, Cambridge, and a classical scholar of extreme distinction, or Patrick (later the 11th Viscount) Barrington whom war had arrested in full career as a contributor to *Punch*. There were clever actresses about the Park, and theatre-minded men like Frank Birch of the naval section and Bill Marchant of Hut 3. At first the revues were staged in a school outside the demesne: later, as new buildings rose, there was a large
128

hall available on the spot. The tragedy in this comedy occurred when Charles Morgan, drama critic of *The Times*, was inveigled down to 'do a notice', and Commander Travis for the sake of security firmly but sensibly refused to give an *imprimatur*.

In other words, Bletchley was a long-stay residence for human beings, not machines: a high-spirited quick-minded group which came to number several thousands. And long-stay is the right word. In the fighting services it was frequently possible to cross-transfer men whose occupation had lost its purpose: when German bombers were few and British infantry were scarce, anti-aircraft gunners could be readily converted into soldiers of the line. But after joining Bletchley and sharing its secrets it was virtually impossible for male or female to be posted elsewhere – and this became a considerable problem in the last stages of the war, as the enemy's fronts contracted and the volume of signal-traffic fell away.

Still, the real machines in this intellectual caravanserai were of supreme importance. The bombes, of course – ever increasing in numbers and sophistication, so that for their service and other duties something like a thousand Wrens were finally assembled at Bletchley and its satellite stations. And then, during 1942 and early in 1943, another series of devices was designed and constructed – the Robinson Family: 'Heath Robinson', 'Peter Robinson', 'Robinson and Cleaver'. The joint product of the Post Office's research department at Dollis Hill, in North London, and the Telecommunications Research Establishment (famous for its development of radar), the Robinsons had a function wholly different from that of the bombes. In essence, their capability was to read at very high speeds an input of specially prepared tapes from which they supplied an intelligible print-out: significantly, their early specifications were disguised under the cover of 'Transmitter, Telegraph, Mark I'. They were wholly automatic in operation. But as they were overtaken by further and startling advances, and were used operationally to only a small degree, the true place of the Robinsons is perhaps in some niche of the complicated history of technology.

Cross-fertilization between Bletchley and Dollis Hill had, in fact, produced new ideas of such magnitude that their end-product came to be christened Colossus. At BP the centre of activity was Hut F or 'the Newmanry', set up by Max Newman after he joined Bletchley in September 1942 and persuaded Commander Travis to allow him scope for working on the concepts that led to 'Heath Robinson'. A Fellow of St John's College, Cambridge, a University Lecturer in mathematics and a Fellow of the Royal Society since 1939, M. H. A. Newman was still only half way along his road in a career of exemplary intellectual distinction. To Hut F from Hut 8 came another Cambridge man, the youthful I. J. Good – after the war Jack Good would become Professor of Statistics at the University of West Virginia – and in the small team was another future Professor, Donald Michie, who had only recently left school!

The problem for which Newman's group evolved a theoretical solution is still shrouded in security and Fish, the code-word associated with it, is still a name void of precise significance. But there are clues: and perhaps an important one is to be found in the records of a discussion at the headquarters of the German Army Intelligence Group, the *Heeresnachrichtenwesens*, held between the 15th and the 17th of April, 1943. At this meeting the Chief Signals Officer of the Armed Forces, General Fellgiebel (hanged from a meat-hook on 8 August 1944 for complicity in the July attempt on Hitler's life) made a speech in which he announced that 'before the spring of 1944 an encoding teleprinter will be introduced down to divisional level. It is fairly complicated, and only operates on perfect lines. . . .' In other words, by the spring of 1943 the Germans were already far advanced towards rendering secure and swift much of their main signal traffic in the continental-type conflict that must follow an Anglo-American invasion, when land-lines would be abundantly available. But suppose they were also trying to improve the speed and safety of their radio transmissions? The evidence suggests that this was the case; that by 1943 Bletchley knew it to be so; that this was the challenge taken up by the Newmanry and this the main reason for Colossus.

In these technical matters awareness about the enemy's intentions can derive from many sources. Since each side keeps more or less level in its grasp of what is theoretically possible, an obvious move is to ask what, logically, is the next practical step that one's opponent is likely to take. Considerations of this kind must therefore have faced the experts at Bletchley with a presumption that the Germans might seek to introduce some form of sophisticated radio teletype, capable of converting verbal signals into a code which could be hurled through the air at great speeds and mechanically restored at the receiving end, by a print-out, to the original form of

130

words. But theory was supported by more concrete indications, of which one, certainly, was a name and the other a sound.

The Germans kept referring to a 'private secretary': *Geheimschreiber*. With its other significance of 'secret writer' this was in fact the cover-name for the radio-teletype they were now developing: and the sound was its voice. When a verbal message is reduced to a digital code and pumped out by radio at very high speed, its distinctive note is different from other traffic and readily identifiable. And thus from these and other sources Bletchley knew, at least by early 1943, that an answer must be found for the *Geheimschreiber*.

One source, indeed, was more authentic than any speculation. During the fighting in North Africa the 8th Army captured two models of *Geheimschreiber*. These revealed that to encipher a signal the machine employed not three or four revolving wheels, like the Enigma, but no less than ten. The system had far greater security, for it cut out the human fallibility of cipher-clerks whose inevitable mistakes, as has been seen, provided the Bletchley cryptanalysts with their best opportunities. In the case of *Geheimschreiber* all the operator had to do was to sit in front of his keyboard and tap out the message in its original text. The machine did the rest, enciphering the signal automatically and pumping it, whether over land-lines or by radio, at the rate of sixty-two words a minute. On the receiving end a similar machine, with its wheels correctly adjusted, would take in the ciphered signal and eject it as a print-out of the original text. To the Germans such a system seemed impregnable as well as conveniently rapid. By eliminating the human element 'on line encipherment' – as the technique is called – appeared to be as safe as the safest method known to any country during the Second World War – that of the one-time pad.

For the German High Command, therefore, the apparently absolute security of *Geheimschreiber* offered great advantages. Enigma was indeed trusted, yet the technical experts were well aware that a skilful enemy might be able to break the cipher for a particular day – though only in due course and after prolonged effort. As the ciphers were altered very frequently, usually every twenty four hours, this possibility was not thought to matter so far as most of the signals sent out on Enigma were concerned. Tactical battle-messages, strength or ammunition states, artillery returns, personnel-postings and so on would be out of date by the time the British had laboriously broken the relevant cipher. But information

131

originated at the highest level of command – long-term strategical plans, for example, or diplomatic evaluations – remained valid for much longer than a signal from an army commander ordering one of his divisions to change location or from a quartermaster reporting on his stocks. And so, whilst Enigma was certainly still considered to be secure enough for much top-secret traffic, the Germans went ahead with *Geheimschreiber* as an insurance policy.

From the earliest days of the war the production of *Geheimschreiber* was in the hands of a famous company, the *Siemens und Halske Aktiengesellschaft* which specialized in telephonic and telegraphic equipment. No less than five versions of the machine were ultimately designed. The earliest model, 52 AB, was not entirely trusted by the Germans, and their doubts were justified. After their occupation of Norway during the spring of 1940 they passed signals over a telegraph line that ran through Sweden, and Swedish intelligence agents managed to tap the circuit. The *Geheimschreiber* messages so acquired were deciphered that May by a cryptanalyst called Arne Beurling, with whose aid the Swedes made a machine capable of processing the signals and producing a print-out. By the time model 52 C had been evolved, however, there were better grounds for feeling that its increased sophistication guaranteed absolute security. And by now, the central phase of the war, *Geheimschreiber*'s output could be rapidly transmitted by radio.

Speed must match speed. The family of Robinsons lacked the necessary pace, but out of the theoretical and technical effort put into them by the Newmanry and Dollis Hill a more nimble successor was born. It was T. H. Flowers of Dollis Hill who made the major breakthrough, by proposing that for the machine envisaged 1500 valves should be employed instead of electromagnetic relays, thus lifting the project into an area of electronic complexity never previously attempted. It worked. By December 1943 the first Colossus (built by Post Office initiative) was set up at BP for a trial run. 'They just couldn't believe it when we brought this string and sealing wax sort of thing in and it actually did the job,' Flowers recalled. 'They were on their beam ends at the time, Robinson just hadn't got enough output, they wouldn't go fast enough. . . .' String and sealing wax! 1500 valves!*

*See photograph of Colossus facing p. 272.

Three months later more Colossi were demanded – by 1 June: nobody knew that this meant for D Day. Extraordinary all-out efforts produced a largely re-designed version which, in the early hours of June's first day, still misbehaved. 'The whole system was in a state of violent parasitic oscillation at a frequency outside the range of our oscilloscope ... at about 3.00 am a nearby radiator started leaking, sending a pool of warm water towards the equipment.' By breakfast-time, however, all was well and Colossus Mark II was ready. Before the end of the war another six or eight models, and some small offspring, were constructed at Dollis Hill with constantly increasing sophistication and brought into operation at Bletchley Park. To have advanced in mid-war from the electromagnetic structure of the early bombes to the most advanced application of thermionic valves (that is, the most advanced electronic system in the world) was an astonishing triumph of British technology.[8]

How far does Colossus fit into the story of Ultra? No information has yet been released about the content of the signals transmitted by the *Geheimschreiber*, nor is it clear whether they were first enciphered on an Enigma machine before being fed through the teletype. What is certain is that the Germans continued to use the Enigma ciphers until the end of the war, and until specific evidence is produced we must rest on the assumption that *Geheimschreiber*'s main purpose was to achieve additional speed and security for top priority signals by the extremely high rate of its transmissions. In that sense, Colossus extended Ultra's scope and range. It was in any case a direct consequence of pioneer work by the cryptanalysts at BP: apart from Newman's team, Turing himself was in early and frequent touch with the technicians at Dollis Hill. The ideas in his famous 1936 paper, and his creative work on the bombes, certainly provided some of the significant concepts that resulted in Colossus.

Even a brief review of Colossus is a reminder that only in the nineteen-seventies has it become possible to see the work at Bletchley as a whole. Few among the hundreds of brilliant men and women assembled there had any notion, at the time, of what the Newmanry was up to even if they were aware of its existence. Mavis Batey still possesses the little pieces of silver, initialled ISK, which marked her years of service as a cryptanalyst, but even now most of her contemporaries at BP would respond with blank ignorance to any question about the section called Intelligence Services Knox.

How many entered or even knew about the Hollerith shed? Yet here were the serried machines with their punch-card operators constantly bringing aid to the cryptanalysts. Hollerith tabulating equipment was in the public domain before the war: as early as 1936, certainly, the US Army had grasped its military potential, using the system for compiling codes and envisaging its possibilities for breaking them. The high speed of a tabulator working from punched cards was exploited at Bletchley for analysing characteristics of a difficult cipher at rates far beyond human capacity.

And then there was the Japanese section, staffed to a large degree by young men of ability recruited from Cambridge who had sufficiently mastered in a six-month crash-course one of the most difficult languages in the world. The exact functions and achievement of this section have not yet been revealed, but the British possession of the Purple machine as early as 1941 makes it not surprising that, for example, the diplomatic traffic between Baron Oshima's embassy in Berlin and the Foreign Office in Tokyo proved to be a fertile source of intelligence or that in the later stages of the war the British, as well as the Americans, were supplying a regular flow of information about Japanese operations in the Far Eastern and Pacific theatres.

More closely related to the intelligence derived from decrypts of German ciphers was, of course, the Italian. Here GCCS had a substantial background, for if during the thirties the Italians were reading British signals, the British had certainly penetrated Italian communications. During the Spanish Civil War they learned a great deal from cryptanalysis about Mussolini's interventions. As the North African campaigns developed the Italian Navy was always Bletchley's prime target. Using, initially, a variant of the commercial Enigma whose cipher was so fruitfully broken in 1941 before the battle of Matapan,* the Navy subsequently settled for the Hagelin machine as its standard enciphering equipment. The Hagelin became the principle preoccupation of Professor Vincent's Italian section, whose girls, inevitably, were known as 'The Hags'.

This 'little jewel of a cipher machine', as David Kahn calls it in *The Codebreakers*, made its inventor a millionaire – unlike poor Scherbius. (The best available technical description of the Hagelin, with an admirable illustration, is indeed to be found in Kahn.)

---

*See Chapter Eight, p. 196.

Portable, compact, beautifully finished, the Hagelin also attracted the Americans by its qualities – the inventor having reached New York from Sweden in 1940 with blueprints and two machines in his bag, after a risky journey through Germany and a trip across the Atlantic on the last peacetime voyage of the liner *Conte di Savoia*. By 1942 the Hagelin was in mass-production, some 140 000 ultimately going into service.

The Hagelin like Enigma was a sophisticated device. For both the Americans and the Italians to have used it was not, however, absurd. At this level of mechanical efficiency the general rule still applied that, for the cryptanalyst, the way into a cipher is not so much the machine itself as the mistakes of its operators. Italian cipher-clerks were too often haphazard and negligent, whilst the cryptanalysts of Vincent's section – as elsewhere at BP – developed a rigorous and effective professionalism. And so, for example, it became almost customary to pass on advance information to British headquarters in the Middle East about the make-up, content, port of departure and port of arrival for the Axis convoys that transported supplies and reinforcements to Rommel's army in Africa. On these messages the successful interdiction of the Mediterranean seaways by the planned strikes of British submarines, surface warships and aircraft was very largely based.

Nor would any account of Bletchley be complete without reference to the immense and continous effort devoted by other specialists to the technical analysis of the enemy's signal-traffic; the identification of call-signs, for example, and the linking of them with a particular transmitting station or radio network was a non-stop task, for call-signs can be changed and frequencies shifted. Simply to keep abreast of the pattern of the German signal-traffic alone made great demands on many people – as did another aspect of work at Bletchley's which Ultra's fame has overshadowed. Enigma was a 'high-grade' machine-cipher. But millions of messages were sent by the enemy in the 'lower-grade' hand-ciphers or in various types of code. The regular reading of these was imperative.* For example, a great deal of the knowledge obtained about what might be called the working life of the Luftwaffe derived from the breaking of these intercepts, and to a large degree such studies rested on one of Bletchley's pillars, the endearing 'Josh' Cooper.

*Valuable information was obtained for example, from breaking the radio signals of the German police and even of the German railways.

One of the original pre-war team from the Broadway GCCS, Cooper combined in a striking manner the two features so characteristic of other notables at Bletchley like Knox and Turing. These were a high degree of efficiency and even brilliance in their specific work, and an extraordinary eccentricity in their personal behaviour. For Cooper as for Knox absentmindedness became a way of life. (It is said of him that he was once seen walking out of the gates at Bletchley with his hat in his hand and an open brief-case balanced on his head.) Unlike Knox, however, Cooper had a strong grasp of reality. His maxim, 'any report that contains the word vital is balls', speaks for itself. The story of the work at Bletchley for which 'Josh' stands a symbol is another of those operations, slightly tangential to the Ultra story yet deeply relevant, which demand a history on their own.[9]

The problem of how to see this many-sided Station X as a whole was acute. If it was difficult for Denniston in the early days, it was an even more formidable task for his successor Commander Travis who took over in 1942 after illness caused Denniston, now a veteran warhorse, to be transferred to quieter fields. The staff at BP was swelling into thousands. They came from all the armed services and from civilian life. Accommodation, food, pay, leave, the insistent routine of a great military organization had to be maintained and constantly expanded while battles were fought for money and allocations of supplies in a world of wartime parsimony. Travis, gruff, rough and burly, won little love but a muted respect. More importantly, he kept Bletchley moving and growing until the end of the war with a personal sense of security that matched the spirit of Ultra.

If administration of this large but loose-limbed empire was demanding, to keep pace with what was being done and what was being discovered presented even more intractable problems. At some mid-point of the war Travis sensibly saw the need for an improvement on mere daily reporting. This told of the trees: he needed to see the whole wood. Professor Vincent was therefore detached from his responsibilities for the Italian traffic and given the newly created post of CCR, Cryptographic Co-ordination and Records. This, in brief, meant that he had to keep himself currently *au fait* with all the cryptographic work at BP, whether in Huts 6 and 8, his old Italian section, or the other units. A matter for delicate diplomacy, since cryptographers as a race dislike disclosing their practices and processes of thought. However, once a week Vincent had to submit to Travis a synoptic report on the whole cryptographic scene. Higham similarly ran an Intelligence Exchange where he performed the daunting task of producing for Travis weekly a digest of the significant intelligence contained in all the incoming signals. Through these two channels,[10] therefore, the activities of the separate huts and sections were summarized and synthesized by acute and adept brains, and Travis could feel more precisely the stir of Bletchley's pulse.

A honeycomb – this must be the final and dominating image of Bletchley Park: a honeycomb of cells some of which may appear to have functioned independently of the main structure. But distance and perspective allow the significant patterns to emerge. It is now clear that huts and sections, individuals and teams, the Wren at her bombe, the cryptanalysts at their ciphers, the calculations of the mathematicians and the creative ingenuity of the technologists were all parts of a whole – of an organism which, like the honeycomb, had evolved to secrete a single product: in Bletchley's case, intelligence about the enemy.

But that intelligence would have little value unless it could be passed on safely to the commanders who would use it in action. The voice of Station X on the battle-fronts was the Special Liaison Unit, whose role must next be examined.

5   The Secret Limeys

'I am i' the way to study a long silence'
JOHN WEBSTER, *The White Devil* (1612)

The British Secret Service has always been the most silent service. Tradition and an iron code of practice have sustained the anonymity and discretion of its members. Names may occasionally be disclosed or an operation described, but this is more usually a consequence of disaster than of intent. The Second World War, however, imposed a similar self-effacement on a group with neither a tradition nor even a past – the officers and men of the Special Liaison Units. They, too, had to learn 'to study a long silence'.

In war this was essential: they carried Ultra in their hands. But for them – as indeed for all who served Ultra – the binding character of their oaths and the demands of security extended their silence far into the years of peace. It was not until the mid-1970s, with the publication of *The Ultra Secret*, that some of them felt able to talk about their military experiences and the character of their contribution could be weighed. It is evidently exceptional. The officers were never high in rank. The technicians were all sergeants. Working at headquarters in the field, they were subjected to strains and pressures often more severe than those affecting the cryptanalysts and intelligence staffs at Bletchley Park. Throughout they carried responsibilities far beyond their status, yet because of the secret nature of their trade this could not be publicly acknowledged.* At times the temptation to boast, to grumble or merely to reminisce must have been enormous, but there is no sign that during thirty years of post-war life anyone broke his word and babbled. Thousands of others also preserved the secret of Ultra, but in their roll of honour the SLUs have a distinctive place – for without them the system could hardly have worked. They were the voice of Station X.

The scale of their effort can best be illustrated by a summary of how they gradually spread outwards across the world. In 1940, as

---

*The ranks of officers in the field were kept low intentionally to avoid speculation in the headquarters where they worked. Secrecy also made it difficult to award decorations on an appropriate scale.

has been seen, SLUs were established at the headquarters of Gort's British Expeditionary Force in France, and with the Advanced Air Striking Force, to pass on such Ultra as might be available from Bletchley and Vignolles. During the Battle of Britain Dowding's Fighter Command was serviced. As the German war spread into the Mediterranean during 1941 and 1942 SLUs appeared with the Desert Army, the Desert Air Force and at Middle East HQ in Cairo, with a service to the Navy in Alexandria and a further SLU at Malta and Beirut. Torch, the invasion of north-west Africa, brought further extensions, to Allied Forces HQ in Gibraltar and Algiers, and to the Anglo-American armies and air forces. The leap to Italy in 1943 found SLUs working at Alexander's 15th Army Group HQ, first at Bari and then at Caserta, with feeds to 15th US Air Force, the Balkan Air Force, the American 5th and British 8th Armies.

And then came Overlord, the true invasion of Europe, when the close grapple with the Germans and the huge commitment of Allied forces threw tremendous new burdens on the SLU system. Each of the main headquarters was supplied with its vital little link to Bletchley Park – Eisenhower's SHAEF, Spaatz's Strategic Air Force, the tactical air commands (both British and American), Bradley's 12th and Montgomery's 21st Army Groups, the British 2nd and the American 1st, 3rd, 7th, 9th and 15th Armies. In South-East Asia, moreover, British and American SLUs now serviced Mountbatten, Slim, Stilwell and the US bomber commands in India and China, drawing on a world-wide informational loop that linked together Bletchley, SEAC, Washington and Brisbane. For in Australia too there was an SLU set-up which, in the last stages of the war, would reach out to the remote islands and might well, had it not been for the atom bomb, have actually established a British SLU at Manila in the Philippines.

The principles governing the work of the SLUs never varied throughout the war. They were defined by Group Captain Winterbotham, who was continuously concerned with selecting, indoctrinating, training and administering this particularly private army. 'The SLU officer was responsible for personally delivering the Ultra message to the commander or to a member of his staff designated to receive it. All messages were to be recovered by the SLU officer as soon as they were read and understood. They were then destroyed. No Ultra recipient was allowed to transmit or repeat an Ultra signal.

139

Any action taken by a commander on the information given him by Ultra was to be by way of an operation order or command or instruction which in no way referred to the Ultra signal or could lead the enemy to believe his signals were being read ... No recipient of Ultra could voluntarily place himself in a position where he could be captured by the enemy.'[1]

The existence of the SLUs was covert and shrouded. 'There was this little truck hidden among the trees', a US Air Force officer, Lewis Powell, noticed in North Africa, 'with people occasionally going to and fro. I thought it was a Direction-Finding Unit.'[2] And it was the men from just such another truck under the apple trees of Normandy, the SLU at Omar Bradley's headquarters, who in 1944 were christened 'the secret Limeys' by inquisitive but frustrated GIs after the failure to penetrate their identity. For this was the first of the SLUs' problems – to carry on, day after day, receiving at all hours the vital signals from Bletchley, to decipher them and to deliver the texts to the headquarters they were serving, all without raising a breath of suspicion about what they were doing. Difficult enough in a large British headquarters, whether that might be a desert camp or some underground tunnel at Malta or Gibraltar, their task was even more delicate when the British-manned SLU in its RAF uniforms was surrounded by the curious multitudes at an American army command-post. Security had to be meticulous. Small errors might have large consequences. Sergeant John Poole, with General Spaatz's SLU in France, remembered that amid the mud of winter it was necessary to check his boots every time he left the cipher truck, in case a strip of Typex tape, adhering to its sole, might be carried abroad and fall into unsuitable hands.[3] At General Alexander's headquarters at Caserta in Italy girls working on communications for the SLU were not allowed to share a bedroom with girls otherwise employed. 'To sleep: perchance to dream: ay, there's the rub.'

In theory the system was simple. After the Ultra signals had been deciphered, translated and evaluated at Bletchley they were then encoded again for transmission by radio from Whaddon Hall to the relevant headquarters in the field. The encoding method employed was either that of the one-time pad or the Typex machine-cipher. At a field headquarters the small SLU had two sections – a communications truck usually manned by the Royal Corps of Signals, which received the messages from Bletchley, and a cipher truck where the messages were decoded to be passed on by the SLU officer. He was then responsible for recovering the texts after they had been studied by the appropriate officers at his headquarters, and for destroying them. His cipher section in a normal SLU consisted of several hand-picked sergeants who, like the signallers, maintained between them a round-the-clock watch.

But in war, as the sage Clausewitz observed, everything is very simple but the simplest thing is very difficult. 'These difficulties accumulate and produce a friction which no man can imagine exactly who has not seen war.' 'Josh' Reynolds, who rose from the rank of sergeant in an SLU to that of Flying Officer – an infrequent elevation where promotion was almost as exceptional as decoration – recalled a Mediterranean problem.

Power supplies were a headache all the time, but we were rarely off the air, even on the move; as soon as the advance station opened up, the rear one closed down and followed up. We were often reduced to one machine working on two 12 volt car batteries and a rotary convertor. The American power was 110 volts/60 cycles, the French North African 110 volts/60 cycles, the Italian at Caserta 145 volts/45 cycles. We also had captured German and Hungarian generators. I was responsible for keeping the machines going, and often repaired them with German spares.[4]

Apart from essential power supplies, Reynolds noted that he and his officer, Flight Lieutenant Burley, had to organize messing, clothing, transport, living quarters, rations, furniture, air passages and so on 'all *without* other formations knowing what we were up to!' If this situation was characteristic of the mobile SLUs more than of those at a static headquarters, and perhaps more of the Mediterranean than of the European theatre, it nevertheless demonstrates how the simple business of keeping going was rarely easy and sometimes very difficult for these secret people.

SLU officers found their responsibilities for preserving security particularly taxing. Not an integral part of the staff at the headquarters they served, they had somehow, nevertheless, to be constantly alert for operational plans which might give away the Ultra secret to the enemy because this could be the only source of the intelligence on which they had been based. They had to look out for both carelessness and naïveté among their superiors. These could occur at the highest level. Air Marshal Coningham had a way, after a meeting, of stuffing his Ultra papers in the top of his flying boots!

Security could be shaken at the very summit. Air Marshal Sir Edward Chilton once attended a conference at South East Asia Command which was being taken, in Mountbatten's absence, by his deputy, the greatly respected American General 'Speck' Wheeler. To his horror Chilton, who had long been a user of Ultra back in England, saw Wheeler take out his keys and prepare to unlock the Ultra box on the table in front of him with the declared intention of reading some of the contents to the assembled company, virtually none of whom could have been 'on the Ultra list'. With instant tact Chilton prevented this gaffe.[5]

Sir Edward was already a senior officer in the RAF. He was capable of dealing with such an incident authoritatively. But the officers in the SLUs, Flying Officers, Flight Lieutenants, sometimes Squadron Leaders or Wing Commanders, had to make their authority felt without a weight of rank. They had this sanction: the generals and senior staff officers with whom they dealt had each been individually indoctrinated as to his responsibilities before being passed as a recipient of Ultra – responsibilities whose abrogation could be referred, in the last resort, to the Chiefs of Staff or to Churchill himself. There could be no shilly-shallying over Ultra. Usually difficulties were resolved on the spot. If not, a message back to England on the SLU circuit to Bletchley would bring Winterbotham winging out to talk sweet reason, for these were situations eminently capable of producing Clausewitz's 'friction which no man can imagine exactly who has not seen war'.

The officers in the SLUs were able to carry out their mission because they were in a real sense a *corps d'élite*: a chosen few. In the early days selection was easy: 'the old boy net' could operate. To the first SLUs in France in 1940 Winterbotham sent trusted friends: Major Plowden of MI6 to Gort's headquarters and Squadron-Leader Long to the Advanced Air Striking Force. Another friend, Robert Gore-Brown, whom we have seen working with French Intelligence at this time, continued after his escape from France to play a key role in the SLU organization, first in the Mediterranean and then in Europe. (He was to indoctrinate many of the officers and men subsequently recruited, both British and American, winning universal respect and admiration. It is striking how his name crops up in reminiscences.)

During the spring of 1941 a 'shooting war' began to envelop the Mediterranean, with German pressure through the Balkans and

Greece, the arrival of Rommel's Afrika Korps, the manifold uncertainties in the Levant and the decline of British naval and air power on and above that land-locked sea. The first Ultra unit was therefore despatched to the Middle East, and again there was no problem about the officer-in-charge, for Kenneth MacFarlan, as has been seen, had acquired invaluable practical experience as the British liaison officer with *PC Bruno* at Vignolles in 1940. (This pioneer group, incidentally, worked under the cover of 'A Detachment, Special Signals Unit', later modified to No. 5 Special Communications Unit. As the war expanded the term Special Liaison Unit came to be more generally used, though the historian can be disconcerted by the fact that sometimes – and normally in American documents – the umbrella title SLU/SCU is applied to embrace both the deciphering and communications elements within the unit. For simplicity, the brief SLU is here used throughout.)

MacFarlan, who took with him Robert Gore-Brown, was soon exposed to the frictions of war. As their convoy approached the west coast of Africa the merchantman containing their trucks, carefully packed with all their special equipment, was detached with other vessels to sail down the Mediterranean while they themselves cruised slowly onwards round the Cape. By the time they reached Cairo, towards the end of June, Wavell had fought and lost in the desert the operation called Battleaxe and, as one consequence, they found that their precious trucks had been requisitioned. It was even more deflating to discover that after their technicians, on a do-it-yourself basis, got an organization going with an office in Middle East Headquarters and transmitters some distance away at Abbassia, and after an SLU had been pushed forward to the Desert Army, there was at first very little Ultra to handle. This was a phase when at Bletchley the breaking of the Light Blue or Mediterranean cipher of the Germans was at best spasmodic. By the autumn of 1941, however, 'A Detachment' was at full stretch.

Torch and the spread of operations in the Mediterranean – Sicily, Italy – brought the first major test. As one follows the movements of the SLUs, from Algiers to Constantine and then Tunis, from Bari to Caserta, the same names emerge. The chosen few were still thin on the ground, and a significant moment came after the Casablanca conference early in 1943 when Winterbotham arrived in Algiers, to be summoned to the office of Eisenhower's deputy, Air Chief Marshal Sir Arthur Tedder. General Spaatz was present, and it was made plain that he wanted more than his ration. He already had an SLU at his main headquarters, but his Allied Air Force was using Ultra with such profit that he wanted a second SLU at his forward command post. Winterbotham was hard pressed for officers and technicians but, as he told the author, Tedder and he had long known one another. Courteously but firmly Sir Arthur conveyed the message: for the sake of Allied unity Winterbotham must produce the goods. From reserve staff in North-West Africa a second SLU was therefore constructed. It was all, of course, a compliment to Ultra.

Cover for the SLUs took many forms. A. E. Dilkes, for example, one of a small RAF group sent out to reinforce in the Mediterranean, had been serving in a statistical section of the RAF Record Office before he volunteered for overseas service. He was indoctrinated in London in November 1942, forwarded in civilian clothes by train to Bristol, and then put on a Dutch KLM airliner. Not until he was off the ground could he open his sealed orders and learn that he was making for an SLU in North Africa. Even the provision of stamps for documents raised problems, to which the answer was provided by having stamps cut locally for the word FOULTRACE and removing the redundant letters. And good cover could itself be embarrassing. One night at Caserta Sergeant Reynolds had to wake up Air Vice-Marshal Slessor, the commander of the Mediterranean Air Force, with an Ultra signal from the Chief of Air Staff in London 'to be burned after reading by Slessor only'. An American guard who disapproved of the intrusion and tried to get possession of the signal nearly shot the sergeant in the process.

Foreknowledge could be embarrassing, too. There was an awkward moment in the autumn of 1941 when the SLU informed Middle East HQ that Cairo was to be bombed. No obvious action could be taken on this Ultra warning – but fortunately the raid was slight. (The Director of Military Intelligence, Brigadier Shearer, had at least taken advantage of his secret knowledge and protected his Ultra papers in a safe place!)[6] There was the case at Constantine where the SLU learned in advance through Ultra of another impending air raid, and went to work wearing their tin hats. The subsequent raid naturally produced suspicions that they had 'known something', and the practice was sternly forbidden. At Bari on 2 December 1943, however, the case was different. Eighty eight German bombers carried out a surprise attack on the crowded har-

Group Captain Winterbotham: photographed on his farm in 1974 at the time of the publication of 'The Ultra Secret'. *(Daily Express.* Photo by Harry Dempster)

BLETCHLEY PARK RECREATIONAL CLUB

The Club Room

....

On the succeeding pages you will find a list of the various activities of the Bletchley Park Recreational Club.

If you would like to come and see me in your spare time, I shall be very glad to give you any further information you may require, and help you in any way I can.

Yours sincerely,

M. A. ROSE,

Secretary and Treasurer.

Above and opposite: Time off at station X.

ACTIVITIES AND FACILITIES

Subscription. 1/- per month or 10/- per year, payable to the *Secretary and Treasurer*, Mrs. ROSE, who (with the exception of her day's leave) can usually be found in the Club Room from 9.0 to 5.0 each day.

Club Rooms. Main Building, Ground Floor. Club membership card necessary. Coffee is served during the luncheon interval and during the evening from 7.30 to 8.30. Newspapers and periodicals. Radio and radiogram after 6.0 p.m. The Writing Room and Sports Room may be booked with Mrs. ROSE for any activity of individual Club Sections. Quiet Room in Hut 4.

Library. *Librarian*, Mrs. OWEN. In the Outer Club Room, open daily from 1.0 to 4.30. 1,500 books. 1,200 permanent stock and 300 from the Times Library, some of which are changed every week. One book may be taken out for a fortnight at a time. Fines 6d. per week. The Librarian will be pleased to take "book lists" and will make every endeavour to procure readers' requests.

Drama Group. *Secretary*, Miss LANGSTAFF, Block D. Play readings and discussions on Thursday in the Writing Room. The reading of the week is advertised on the Club Room notice board. Periodical performances as advertised.

Dancing. *Secretary*, Mr. S. SEDGEWICK, Block F. Informal dances every Monday and Thursday evening in the Assembly Hall, 8.30 to 11.0. Periodical special dances as advertised. Dancing classes are held every Monday. Application should be made to Mr. SEDGEWICK.

Fencing. *Instructor*, Miss POLLOCK SMITH, Hut 10. Fencing in the Sports Room on Friday evenings from 6.0 to 10.30. Anyone wishing to receive instruction should contact Miss Pollock Smith.

Musical Society. *Secretary*, Miss M. SAWYER, Block F. Gramophone concerts every Wednesday evening at 6.15 in the Writing Room. Lunch-time concerts as advertised. The Choral Society meets every Monday in the Sports Room at 6.0 as advertised. Periodical concerts arranged from time to time.

Badminton. Mrs. ROSE, The Club Room, Ext. 426. Players can use the equipment and court at the Senior School Hall every Sunday. Application for key of equipment should be made to Mrs. Rose.

Bridge. *Secretary*, Mr. LEECH, Block A. Bridge can be played any night in the Club Room. Anyone wishing to make up a four should contact the Secretary.

Reels. *Secretary*, Miss PARES, Block F. Meeting every Monday evening in the Sports Room (except during Summer). Instruction at lunch time on Mondays and Fridays. Dancing from 8.30 to 10.30 p.m.

Chess. *Secretary*, Mr. D. REES, Hut 6. The Section meets every Monday evening from 8 to 12 in the Club Room, Hut 4.

TWELFTH NIGHT
BY
WILLIAM SHAKESPEARE
CAST

ORSINO, Duke of Illyria — L./Cpl. Douglas Keyte
SEBASTIAN, brother to Viola — Sgt. Lesley Stuart-Taylor
ANTONIO, friend to Sebastian — Sgt. Derek Davies
A SEA CAPTAIN, friend to Viola — L./Cpl. Peter Ramsey
VALENTINE) gentlemen — L./Cpl. Ian Taylor
CURIO) — L./Cpl. Leonard Tibby
SIR TOBY BELCH, uncle to Olivia — S Sgt. David McNeill
SIR ANDREW AGUECHEEK — Sgt. John Thompson
MALVOLIO, steward to Olivia — L./Cpl. John Nash
FABIAN, servant to Olivia — Sgt. Geoffrey Mellor
FESTE, a clown — Sgt. Anne Bourne
OLIVIA — Sgt. June Rigby
VIOLA — S/Sgt. Jeanne Cammaerts
MARIA, Olivia's gentlewoman — Sgt. Cecily Giles
SAILOR and 1st Officer — Sgt. Desmond Mason
SAILOR and PRIEST — L./Cpl. James Campbell
GENTLEWOMAN — Sgt. Mary McKerrell

The Play produced by L./Cpl. Douglas Keyte.

Scene : A city in Illyria, and the sea coast near it.

Stage Manager —	Sgt. Lesley Stuart-Taylor
Production Secretary	Sgt. John Thompson
Lighting	Leslie Edwards
Scenery	L./Cpl. Cecil Waller
Stage Staff —	Cpl. Geoffrey Farrington, Sgt. Maurice Lynch, L./Cpl. John Simms
House Manager	Sgt. Sylvia Knight

Costumes by B. J. Simmons & Co. Wigs by Nathanwigs. Setting of "Come away, death" specially composed for this production by Barbara Reynolds.

There will be one interval of ten minutes and two of five minutes.

The Committee wish to express their grateful acknowledgement to the B.P. Drama Group, Capt. John Lowe and the Bletchley Co-operative Society for their help.

The next production
will take place in Mid-March.

Warren, Printer, Bletchley

Special Liaison Unit in the North African desert.

The Cottage: the secret radio station at Abbassia near Cairo which handled Ultra signals in the Middle East

bour. An ammunition ship blew up, and in all seventeen vessels were lost. There had been no Ultra warning this time. Indeed, the Official History of the Italian campaign observes that one cause of the enemy's success had been 'the discounting at Bari of his ability to stage a large-scale raid'. As the sea front was shattered the SLU officer, Flight Lieutenant Burley, was blown down the street. But his experience did not prevent a temporary loss of local prestige for Ultra. Those who knew its powers felt that it had been found wanting.

With the approach of D Day in 1944 the atmosphere became hectic, for SLUs would have to be supplied not only to the great Allied headquarters, but also to individual armies and air commands, both British and American. This was a daunting undertaking for Winterbotham, his chief administration officer Group Captain Sofino and their small central staff, on top of their routine duties of servicing Churchill with Ultra and supervising the various SLUs already in action. Apart from the problem of providing officers, cipher sergeants would now be required in considerable numbers. Much depended on finding the right man, since the combination of specialized technical ability with the temperament and character needed for this lonely, responsible work was unusual. No less than sixty cipher sergeants and a dozen officers had to be discovered and all, after passing through the filter, were personally interviewed by Winterbotham.

Many of the sergeants had already volunteered for some sort of cipher work and had received their basic training at the RAF's Code and Cipher School known as No. 5 Radio School, Oxford. Their previous experience had been diverse. Sergeant Minifie had spent the early part of the war as the coxswain of an Air Sea Rescue launch. Sergeant William Johnson had started as an orderly room clerk. Sergeant Hamer, by contrast, had joined the RAF before the war and already, in June 1939, was working at the British Embassy in Paris (as a civilian) on a secret teleprinter line. After a lively time during the Battle for France he came out through Dunkirk and continued to work on teleprinters until, in 1943, he too applied for training on codes and ciphers. When he was accepted for Ultra and met the Typex machine he realized why his touch-typing experience as a teleprinter operator had made him particularly eligible for an SLU.[7]

After they had passed through the narrow mesh of the selection

145

process the survivors were given intensive training for their new tasks, whose nature none of them could have envisaged. In the way of the clandestine services, these courses were held in obscure buildings around London like the house in Hamilton Terrace near Lord's Cricket Ground in St John's Wood, so unassertive that when one trainee arrived he wandered forlornly up and down the road trying to identify it. The individual indoctrinations, apart from so effectively teaching the need 'to study a long silence', had another wise purpose. These were intelligent men, and security would be better served by giving them a reasonable picture of the intelligence system they had now joined than by expecting them to fumble and speculate in the dark. Well before D Day the new SLUs had been formed and posted to the headquarters which they would service, so that practice drills could be carried out and working relationships established.

After crossing to the continent their treatment interestingly reflected the attitudes of individual commanders. General Dempsey of the British Second Army kept his SLU a mere fifty yards away from his own tent and gave personal instructions that it was to be looked after well. Montgomery, characteristically, required his SLU to be detached some hundreds of yards away on the perimeter of his large headquarters. 'It meant', Winterbotham noted, 'a long walk at night': but when he remonstrated with Montgomery's chief administrative officer, Major General Miles Graham, he was fobbed off with the implausible excuse that the Germans might take a bearing on the SLU's meagre radio transmissions. With the Americans the SLUs had an easy rapport, once the natural questioning of the GIs had been fended off, for the US commanders and their staffs, in the main, had none of Montgomery's ambivalence about Ultra.

Whether it was at US First or Third Armies, or at Quesada's 9 Tactical Air Command, the SLU officer's responsibilities were only slightly diminished by the presence of an American 'Ultra adviser'.* They were certainly made more delicate, for though the adviser was charged to guard the security of Ultra at his headquarters, the British SLU officer had also to be alert about infringements and if necessary to take action. He still owed an allegiance to his own masters at home: to the central Ultra organization. A pecul-

*See Chapter Nine, 'The American Involvement', for the Ultra adviser's duties.

iar degree of tact on his part was therefore demanded. The same was true at the headquarters of Eisenhower's SHAEF, whether among the 1500 officers and men at Granville on the Cotentin peninsula, or later amid the splendours of Versailles, or at the Supreme Commander's advance HQ with its township of tents and trailers scattered over the grounds of the Athletic Club of Rheims. A good instance of the sensitive inter-Allied issues that arose was a report from Colonel Gore-Brown, during the latter stages of the Normandy battle, that some American army staffs were including too much undigested Ultra information in their routine intelligence summaries, which were widely circulated. This was obviously dangerous – and as much in conflict with the Pentagon's doctrine about Ultra security as with the British. A word at the top was required – and Omar Bradley saw the point.

There was of course another invasion of Europe – the Anvil landings in the south of France. For these both Churchill and Ultra were in attendance. In *The Second World War* the Prime Minister gave an inimitable description of how, on 14 August 1944, he flew in a Dakota to Corsica and proceeded next day, on the destroyer *Kimberley*, to sail past the line of battleships bombarding the beaches towards 'the long rows of boats filled with American Storm Troops steaming in continuously to the Bay of St Tropez'. But it was all very tranquil, and Churchill noted that he spent the return trip to Corsica reading *Grand Hotel* in the captain's cabin, feeling that 'I had at least done the civil to Anvil'. What he did not record was the presence on *Kimberley* of an SLU officer, A. E. Dilkes, whose task was to feed Churchill with the Ultra signals which came in direct from England on the Navy's radio channels. 'There was very little traffic on Ultra for the Prime Minister,' Dilkes recalled, 'and when I did have any for him he was usually relaxing and sunning himself on deck.'

Dilkes himself later went on to Alexander's headquarters at Caserta, to help in handling the Prime Minister's Ultra traffic during his visit to Italy. But as the three American divisions and the French armour of General Patch's 7th Army drove northwards from the Riviera, on the tail of Generaloberst Blaskowitz's Army Group G, a service of Ultra intelligence was still maintained. Indeed, there was an impressive moment during the German retreat when, as a result of Ultra information about the enemy's weakness, an American force was able to outflank and cut off a substantial

147

column – so successfully that, according to the Pentagon records, the achievement was intentionally given no publicity for fear of compromising Ultra.

For Churchill the Italian visit of August 1944 was an exciting interlude. He was his own master, away from the pressures of Whitehall and Westminster, committees and cabinets. He was delighted by a call from Marshal Tito, wearing 'a magnificent gold and blue uniform which was very tight under the collar, singularly unsuited to the blazing heat'. Alexander drove him round the Cassino battlefield and when he looked in on Mark Clark at Leghorn he was allowed to fire a brand-new nine-inch gun. He addressed the Brazilian Brigade and inspected the New Zealand Division. The front line was his natural home. It was immensely exhilarating. But when on 27 August he went up with Alexander to observe from the battlefield itself the opening of an offensive by the 8th Army there was a new situation. 'The Germans were firing with rifles and machine-guns from thick scrub on the farther side of the valley, about five hundred yards away. Our front line was beneath us. The firing was desultory and intermittent. But this was the nearest I got to the enemy and the time I heard most bullets in the Second World War.' That was fun for the Prime Minister. It was not so funny for the officer-in-charge of the Special Liaison Unit at Caserta, Wing Commander Crawshaw.

A businessman before the war, Crawshaw began by working in an Air Raid Centre, and then entered RAF Intelligence. After training at Bletchley he went out to the Middle-East with MacFarlan and Gore-Brown, and by August 1944 was an expert in his work. Having been in charge of major Special Liaison Units at Algiers and then at Caserta he was acutely sensitive to security risks. Churchill's arrival in Italy was flattering, for the Prime Minister demanded to see Crawshaw and his Ultra papers before even speaking to the Director of Military Intelligence. Now, however, a combination of the Churchillian passions for Ultra and the front line presented Crawshaw with a problem, for a message came back that he was to proceed up to the battle-zone with the latest signals from Bletchley. He decided that it was crazy to travel around with Ultra papers in this way, so he remained where he was and awaited the lion's roar.

Writing about Churchill in 1968 one of his wartime Private Secretaries at No. 10 Downing Street, Sir Leslie Rowan, declared that 'the most vivid and lasting impression I have is ... the complete trust he placed in those who served him in what he called "The Secret Circle".[9] What followed Crawshaw's decision is a wonderful example of how the personal service given to Churchill by the SLUs included them, too, in that small circle to which the only pass-key was his confidence.

When Churchill returned to base Crawshaw was ordered to report to the Commander-in-Chief's villa where the Prime Minister was staying. A high-level conference was going on in Churchill's room, but as the generals filed out he spotted Crawshaw through the door and shouted 'I want you!' There was no further roar from the lion. When Crawshaw explained the reasons for his disobedience Churchill accepted them without demur, telling him to sit down and have a drink. After a time he said 'I suppose you'll now be too late for dinner in your mess.' Would he like to stay for a meal? So, suddenly, Crawshaw found himself dining with the Prime Minister, the head of the British Mission to Tito, Brigadier Fitzroy Maclean, and the political Minister Resident at Allied Forces HQ in Italy, Harold Macmillan. Then, after dinner, he was swept in their company towards the Map Room, where he listened spellbound as Churchill described to his guests 'off the record' the course of the Normandy landings since D Day.[10]

Nor was Crawshaw unique. Another young SLU officer during this Italian visit found himself, to his surprise, being courteously introduced by Churchill to the Chief of the Imperial General Staff – Alan Brooke having arrived shortly before the Prime Minister went up to the front. 'I don't know whether you have met the CIGS.' The truth is that Churchill felt his SLUs to be 'his people', and therefore worthy recipients of his fatherly attention. While he was convalescing at Marrakesh during the previous winter, after his dangerous bout of pneumonia, Squadron Leader Robinson was in personal attendance as his SLU link.[11] Years later, Robinson and his wife were astonished to receive, out of the blue, an invitation to the special party for Churchill's eightieth birthday. This elephant never forgot.

While Churchill was in Italy Eisenhower's armies in north-west Europe were crossing the Seine and beginning their march to the Rhine. In that great and ultimately irresistible mass the SLUs at their various headquarters were like minute invisible cells. The sort of man who in such a context observes the invisible is usually a good war reporter. One of the most acute of the British team was Frank

Gillard, war correspondent for the BBC who subsequently rose to the head of the BBC's domestic radio services. He seemed a good touchstone. In reply to a letter from the author asking him directly, as an old friend, whether he had ever suspected the existence of SLUs during his many visits to command headquarters he wrote: 'About Ultra – your surmise is entirely correct. I had no idea at all that these Special Liaison Units existed. There was never the slightest hint, from Williams or anyone else, that Ultra-type information was available to them. As war correspondents we concerned ourselves exclusively with Operations and Intelligence, and I am absolutely certain that no correspondent had even a shred of knowledge or suspicion of the Ultra source. What incredibly good actors Bill Williams and his people must have been when we tried to draw them out on enemy strengths and movements.' And not only Brigadier Williams at Montgomery's headquarters. The ordinary cipher-sergeants and signallers, living with their SLU trucks among the inquisitive hundreds of a large headquarters staff, had even greater responsibilities, for their cover-up had to be continuous.

One event in particular illustrates the difficulty for the SLUs of shrouding their unusual mission with a cloak of normality. When the Ardennes offensive started, the SLU serving General Spaatz's Air Command was at Versailles, along with Eisenhower's main SHAEF. The notorious hysteria that spread through the city of Louis XIV in those winter days was particularly awkward for Major Tommy Rhind and his clandestine unit. Their regular 'milk run' with Ultra signals from the SLU to Spaatz's headquarters became a very different matter when the roads were infested by check-points, where American military police fired catch questions about the homelier aspects of life in the United States. Then there was the Skorzeny scare, arising from an unfounded rumour that the man who had snatched Mussolini from his Allied captors was on his way to assassinate – who? Eisenhower? Top-ranking generals? Well, he was on his way: and early one morning in the Camp de Loges where the SLU was billetted Flight Sergeant Poole was aroused by a flash of light. There in the door-way of his hut stood two enormous military policemen. 'Let's go, buddies,' they shouted. 'Get your guns. German paratroopers are dropping round the camp.' Poole as the senior sergeant had the ammunition box under his bed – and one large headache. For how, few that they were, could they stand guard over the cipher truck which, as usual, was parked on its own in a quiet corner? How, without overstressing its secret importance, could extra guards be obtained in the buzzing chaos of Versailles?[12]

Fortunately the men on duty at the SLU, having heard nothing of the alarm, carried on with the routine of deciphering incoming signals, and fortunately the scare died down, so that the next 'milk run' went through smoothly. But it was no night for a secret unit to be abroad – a unit of which Spaatz himself thought very highly. In his 'Commendation for Meritorious Service' which he addressed to Major Rhind on 20 May 1945 he said:

It is with great personal appreciation that I commend SLU/SCU for the untiring effort and devotedness of purpose your unit has evidenced during the seventeen months it has been assigned to my command from January 1944 to May 1945. Your constant attentiveness to duty has been a large factor in the successful achievements of the United States Strategic Air Forces in the war against Germany.

Spaatz's commendation reads like a farewell. For some, however – including Flight Sergeant Poole – it was not a finale.

One of the most extraordinary episodes in the history of the SLUs was, in fact, only just beginning to take shape – on the other side of the globe. From the time of General MacArthur's arrival in Australia in 1942 some sort of common service had been established and developed for joint access by British Commonwealth and American staffs to signals-intelligence acquired by deciphering Japanese traffic. The history of this limited and spasmodic interchange is not directly relevant. In the winter of 1944, however, a decision was taken to draft numbers of officers and men from the European and Mediterranean theatres to run Special Liaison Units in Australasia and the islands of the Pacific battle-zone.

In retrospect this seems a curiously wasteful and even pessimistic decision to have made at the tail-end of the war. But retrospect views the facts through the distorting glass of Hiroshima. This was still a time when most responsible statesmen and commanders feared the necessity of invading an unyielding Japan: feared, even more, the casualty-list. The war in the East was still a dreadful reality. More to the point, as 1945 advanced Australian forces would begin to move tangentially from the main thrust northwards, pressing into the East Indies as a virtually independent command. On 1 May 9 Australian Division (the fine veterans of Alamein) landed in Dutch Borneo. In June Brunei and Sarawak and in July

151

Balikpapan were in Australian hands. As plans were prepared for these operations it was evident that a British signals-intelligence service would be required, for experience showed that little could be relied on from MacArthur. At the same time there was great pressure in London, that spring, to reinforce in the Pacific not simply with the British Fleet and the RAF, but even with infantry divisions. These facts provide a more convincing context for the despatch of some SLUs.

The process started in about October 1944, when Winterbotham was asked to supply liaison teams for the Pacific. The spearhead was Squadron Leader Burley, widely experienced in the Mediterranean SLUs, who was picked as Special Security Officer (Far East) to carry, in effect, the responsibilities which Winterbotham had shouldered in the West. Once again one notes the élitist quality of the Ultra organization, for in his role Burley, of no great age and no great rank, had to deal with figures like the Pentagon's staff, the Commander-in-Chief India, the Australian Prime Minister and his senior generals and airmen. When he reached Australia before the turn of the year Burley set up headquarters for himself and the embryo unit in the Australian Mutual Providence building in Queens Street, Brisbane, once a part of MacArthur's own command-post. Brisbane was the right focus, since it was here that the existing Allied and inter-Allied signals-intelligence services had been operating. That was about all that was right. As yet the Australians had no concept of the careful procedures for handling Ultra now commonplace in Europe, while the Americans were affected by MacArthur's Anglophobia and the prevalent animosity between the US Army and Navy.

The personnel of SLU 9 filtered slowly from afar into their billets at the Royal Australian Air Force barracks in Brisbane. Flying Officer 'Josh' Reynolds and two other officers from Italy sailed with a dozen sergeants in a convoy from Glasgow to Halifax, Nova Scotia, crossed North America by train, and then reached Brisbane via California, New Guinea and Queensland. John Poole left Spaatz's advance headquarters at Rheims to fly via Cairo and Karachi to Ceylon, and then, with a sizeable group of sergeants, on one of the converted Liberators which made the twice weekly 'Kangaroo' flight, 3500 miles in just over eighteen hours, from Colombo to Perth in Western Australia. Sergeant Minifie arrived from the Rhineland and the SLU at the US 15th Army. And chief among those who dropped in from Europe was Winterbotham himself, as a progress-chaser and diplomatic entrepreneur, to be followed in due course by the authoritative Commander Travis from Bletchley. SLU 9 had become, as they say, 'a meaningful activity'.

Meaningful indeed, for Reynolds had hardly tasted the peacetime pleasures of Brisbane before he, Burley and a trio of sergeants were off on a 3000-mile flight to the South Pacific island of Morotai, their one-time pads in weighted bags and a thermite bomb ready, if necessary, for destroying other secret papers. The precaution was sensible, for though the headquarters of 1 Tactical Air Force of the RAAF was perched on a part of Morotai, the Japanese held the larger portion. Here the SLU serviced both Australian and American air forces as well as the advanced headquarters of the senior Australian commander, General Blamey. From Borneo to Balikpapan the Australians now received a flow of intelligence about Japanese troop, shipping and aircraft movements whose details reached the SLU on a network ranging from Brisbane through Hawaii to New Delhi. Ultra even carried reports of U-boats working their way past Morotai with strategic materials for Japan.

It was not an easy existence. Reynolds has recorded that:

We only had the one RAAF signal link and often poor radio conditions with heavy rain and high humidity, which caused problems with our only machine. Power, too, was difficult. Our office was made of tree-trunk poles, hessian and a roof of palm leaves. We had to make it secure with wire netting and a door, and I slept in this office with revolvers and thermite bombs ready in case of Jap visitors: I also rigged up a trip wire. Being RAF we were rather conspicuous, and everyone was a bit curious to know what we did.[13]

By June 1945 SLUs had been established not only at Morotai but also at Lae in New Guinea for the Australian 1st Army, at Labuan and other centres. That 'the battle is the pay-off' had been reaffirmed as Ultra's justification, in a theatre utterly different from what had been envisaged when Bletchley was born. The affirmation was practical, for initial apathy on the part of Australian and American commanders was rapidly dispelled as the SLUs got to work. Yet Ultra had come too late to the South Pacific. John Poole was packing his bags to move with an SLU up to Manila in the Philippines when the bomb burst over Hiroshima. There was a Victory Parade in Brisbane. The men of the Special Liaison Units

153

would get no great recognition from their Government, but that day they marched, as was their right, before the long silence of peacetime descended.

6 The Mediterranean Shores

'We who pursue
Our business with unslackening stride,
Traverse in troops, with care-fill'd breast,
The soft Mediterranean side....'

MATTHEW ARNOLD

For the greater part of the war there were few weeks when the Mediterranean was not in the mind of the British public – or at least of concern to the Prime Minister and the Chiefs of Staff. This was the theatre in which their forces were most consistently engaged. But as Churchill wrote, before the battle of Alamein in October 1942 'it may almost be said that we never had a victory'. (He had overlooked General O'Connor's total destruction of an Italian army in North Africa and, in East Africa, the abolition of an Italian empire!) What, then, was Ultra's contribution during those long months of defeat and disappointment before the ultimate turning of 'the Hinge of Fate'?

A further question is often asked: 'Why, since the allies possessed Ultra, did they take so long to overcome Hitler?' Perhaps the outstanding feature of this Mediterranean phase is the variety of responses it supplies to so natural an inquiry. One has to consider the quality and the quantity of Bletchley's intelligence. One has to consider objectively the capacity of British and German commanders: the amount and efficiency of their guns, tanks and aircraft: the training and performance of their men. And when all these factors have been weighed an answer without novelty will emerge – for it had already been provided by the Battle for France. However copious its flow – and during these months of 1941 and 1942 it was sometimes in short supply – Ultra alone was impotent, if the generals lacked the military strength or the mental ability to apply it in action. As always, the battle is the pay-off. But these were the days when too much went wrong – when Ultra, far from being a source of victory, was scarcely able to diminish the effects of defeat.

In April 1941 Operation Marita swept General List's 12th Army through Greece. One of the British in its track was an intelligence

155

officer, the Hon. C. M. Woodhouse: later Monty Woodhouse would command the Allied Military Mission to the Greek resistance. What struck him that April was the precision of the information passing through his hands as a staff officer at the Expeditionary Force's headquarters. 'Astoundingly accurate,' he wrote to the author. 'We had the German Order of Battle every evening, but unfortunately we could not do anything about it, having virtually nothing to hit back with.' Had Woodhouse then known of Ultra's ability to read the battle-array not simply for Marita, but also for Barbarossa, he would have been less surprised but no more heartened. The situation he describes is, in fact, a classic example of how the best of intelligence can be nullified if you have 'virtually nothing to hit back with'. Some weary tanks, a meagre artillery, troops of fire and dash but no cohesion, a negligible air force and a frail ally – in the face of General List's panzers thrusting through Greece not even Ultra could compensate for such disadvantages.

But should Crete have been different? The omens looked no more propitious as, during the early days of May, General Freyberg resolutely sought to shape into an effective garrison his scratch force of some 30 000 British, Australian and New Zealand troops together with a few thousand enthusiastic but untrained Greeks. The enthusiasm was certainly there. To Freyberg came one of the more moving documents of the war, which ended:

> We wholeheartedly put ourselves under any service, dangerous or not, provided that the cause of our Allied effort is fulfilled.
>   Trusting we shall enjoy your proper attention,
>   We remain,
>   Respectfully yours,
>   The convicts of the Island of Crete.

There was not much else. A penny packet of antique tanks, little anti-aircraft or field-artillery, few properly organized battalions of infantry, no air-cover: and the only harbours, at Suda Bay and Heraklion, on the wrong north side of the island and wholly inadequate, anyway, for maintaining the garrison, the civil population, and large quantities of Italian prisoners. There were many other deficiencies and difficulties. Communications between units, for example, were vile: it has been said that a hundred radios would have saved Crete. And yet, in spite of all, there is a general consensus among those who have most closely considered what happened that the Germans came within an inch of losing and that the British ought to have won.

For this misfortune Ultra was not responsible. There was a shortage of guns, but not of authoritative information. 'At no moment in the war', wrote Churchill, 'was our Intelligence so truly and precisely informed': and Freyberg himself, looking back in 1949, referred to 'the wonderful Intelligence reports that were supplied from the United Kingdom'. The author of the New Zealand Official History of Crete, D. M. Davin (who fought in the battle) declares: 'It will be seen ... that the nature and strength of the invasion was not only appreciated with remarkable accuracy, but that by the time the battle was to begin there was little chance that even the obscurest fatigue man could be ignorant of what he was about to face. Thus whatever else the enemy might have in his favour he could not claim surprise; nor should the defence be able to use it as an excuse.' Woodhouse was breakfasting with Freyberg when the invasion started, 'at the moment when we saw the gliders overhead and the parachutists dropping. He was very calm, and simply remarked: "They're dead on time." So it was clear that he had an impeccable source of intelligence.'[1]

The fact is that Ultra was buoyant, and the reason is evident. It was not until 25 April that Hitler's Directive 28 set in action operation Mercury, the occupation of Crete. For the Germans a race against time started immediately, since the air element in particular was urgently needed for Barbarossa. The operation was novel, the country unfamiliar, the pressure intense. Signals flashed to and fro. The overall control was in the hands of General Löhr, commanding 4 Luftflotte: the actual assault was the responsibility of General Student and his 7 Air Division, whose gliders and parachutists were to form the bridgehead. Thus a considerable volume of Luftwaffe signal traffic poured out – and the Luftwaffe ciphers were old friends of Bletchley's Hut 6.

If the Germans worked fast, so did Station X. Considering that Hitler's Directive was not issued until the 25th, it is extraordinary that as early as the 29th the War Office received from the Joint Intelligence Sub-Committee and forwarded to Cairo an appreciation, 'Secret and Most Immediate', which reached Freyberg on 1 May and provided him with a detailed picture of Student's intentions and capability.* In London Churchill was much excited by

*The JIC had already reported to the War Cabinet on the 27th. The full text of its paper,

the immediacy of his intelligence. Winterbotham was summoned to explain the situation – as revealed by Ultra – to the Prime Minister 'on his own big new map of Crete in the War Room'. The Group Captain was also directly instructed by Churchill – as he has confirmed to the author – to ensure that Freyberg was kept fully in the Ultra picture. Of course Freyberg was not indoctrinated and could not be fed 'pure' Ultra. But when Wavell visited Crete shortly before the attack he talked privately with Freyberg – who must in any case have been curious about the source of this remarkable intelligence – and probably established its complete authenticity by some convincing fiction. This would explain why during the later desert campaigns Freyberg sometimes asked Montgomery's Chief Intelligence Officer Bill Williams, 'What's happened to that Foreign Office chap we had working in Berlin?'[2] In any case, he was more fully briefed than any previous British commander in the Second World War. What then went wrong?

Most battles have a central theme. For Crete the theme was airfields, and Freyberg misinterpreted the score. The Ultra intelligence warned specifically, accurately and in detail about both an airborne and a seaborne landing. But because Freyberg failed to perceive what Student knew (that unless 7 Air Division could seize an airfield the vital follow-up troops and supplies could not be flown in) from the start he was far more nervous about the *seaborne* approach – which was never of critical significance from the German point of view. This error in priorities was compounded by a notion that the airfields were not vital because the Luftwaffe intended to land its Junkers 52 troop-carriers on any convenient stretch of beach or flat ground – though how they would take off for the next lift is obscure. Nor did Freyberg understand that the German parachutist strength was limited – there were no reserves once Student's initial force of 10 000 was expended – which made it even more mandatory to prevent the enemy seizing an airfield to fly in his troop-carriers. Because of this failure to grasp the essential point Maleme airfield was lost: because Student captured Maleme Crete was lost. When all the other factors are taken into account, this remains the central truth.[3]

Gallant enduring Freyberg can scarcely be blamed. The command problems were too big for him, and he knew it. He was a

entitled 'Scale of Attack on Crete', is in the file PREM 3, piece 109, in the Public Records Office.

fighting general: give him his New Zealand Division and he would march to hell and back. But his handling of the defence of Crete well illustrates Ultra's perennial problem. Because of Bletchley Freyberg had all the relevant information about the enemy's strength and plans. Yet everything was marginal on Crete. In so fine-run a battle, victory awaited the man who knew what it was actually about – not in the coarse sense of winning or losing the island, but in the strictly professional sense of calculating to a nicety what must be the supremely important piece of ground. Freyberg, in effect, misread the evidence. *'De quoi s'âgit-il?'*: the question all generals should ask. With the same intelligence available Montgomery's incisive mind would surely have fastened on the one thing that mattered, and so distributed his troops that Maleme might have been held just long enough for the parachutists to have withered without support. Ultra was a shadow until the generals gave it substance.

Of all the British commanders in the Second World War Wavell, with his background of scholarship and his sense of history, responded most instinctively to the concept of intelligence. Lacking the inhibitions of more conservative officers, he looked at it in a natural way as merely a normal weapon. It is ironic, therefore, that when the war shifted southwards to the other 'soft Mediterranean side', the coast of North Africa, Wavell in his first response to Ultra made the same mistake as Freyberg on Crete: he got the message, but not the meaning.

By early February 1941 the whole of Cyrenaica was in British hands. The surrender at Beda Fomm of an Italian army on 7 February consummated an achievement by O'Connor's small but daring force in which nine Italian divisions had been eliminated and 130 000 prisoners, 400 tanks and over 1000 guns had been captured. Warning bells rang in Berlin. General Erwin Rommel was summoned to the Chancellery on 6 February, to be given command by Hitler of a token force – one light and one panzer division, the Afrika Korps – which was to stiffen the Führer's shattered allies and keep the British out of Tripoli. (During this briefing Hitler showed Rommel photographs in British and American magazines taken during the O'Connor offensive. The Desert Fox knew nothing, as yet, of the desert, and found this unorthodox form of photo-reconnaissance helpful!)[4]

But as in the case of Crete, the British were accurately warned about the transfer of Rommel and his spearhead troops to North Africa. The signal traffic of 10 Fliegerkorps, recently established in Sicily to dominate the western Mediterranean, was one fruitful source. A message informing its headquarters about Rommel also, via Bletchley, informed London. Then came the formal signal from Tripoli to Berlin reporting his arrival. As usual the Prime Minister was on the *qui vive*. Winterbotham records that 'in reply to Churchill's note to me as to how soon we could expect German forces in Cyrenaica, I was able to send over to him the OKW (High Command) signals giving Rommel the approximate dates of the arrival in Tripoli of the units which were to constitute his Deutsches Afrika Korps, coming direct from Germany. The 5th Light Motorized Division was due in April and the 15th Panzer Division in May.' (The move of 5 Light was in fact accelerated after Hitler's aide, Colonel Schmundt, returned from Tripoli with an optimistic report.)

There was as yet no Special Liaison Unit in the Middle East to connect Cairo with Bletchley. But Brigadier John Shearer, Wavell's Director of Military Intelligence, has confirmed to the author that the Ultra information about Rommel and his Afrika Korps was conveyed to them swiftly under the blanket of 'secret intelligence'. The facts were available for both current and forward estimates. What was their significance?

Immediately after the war Wavell analysed his first defeat at the hands of the Afrika Korps in a letter to General O'Connor, who was taken prisoner during the battle. 'My ... great error was that I made up my mind that the enemy could not put in any effective counter-stroke before May at the earliest ... I also thought that the Germans could never build up a supply system over the distance between Tripoli and the frontier of Cyrenaica in the time that they did.' The initial German strength he estimated, not inaccurately, as 'about a brigade group'. His staff worked out, by sound British standards, the logistic factors involved for a successful German advance and attack. In a sound British fashion Wavell decided that 'it wasn't on'.

His Director of Intelligence, Brigadier Shearer, performed the wise manoeuvre of putting himself in his enemy's shoes. On 6 March Wavell had in front of him an 'Appreciation of the Situation on 5th March, 1941, by General "X", General-Officer-Commanding German Troops in Libya'. This was a remarkably perceptive and imaginative identification by Shearer of Rommel's attitude: he put into the mouth of General 'X' sentences that read like a translation. 'As a striking force I have full confidence in my new Command. Subject to administrative preparations, I believe that the German Armoured Corps, after a few weeks' training and experience in desert warfare conditions, and unless the British substantially reinforce their present forces in Libya, could successfully undertake the reoccupation of Cyrenaica.' This was the authentic voice of Rommel.[5]

Wavell rejected Shearer's warning. By 30 March the forward units of the Afrika Korps had already advanced to El Agheila, the point where the coast swings north from the Gulf of Sirte and the great bulge of Cyrenaica begins. On the 30th Wavell signalled to his commander at the front, General Neame: 'I do not believe that he can make any big effort for at least another month.' Churchill, by contrast, was fully alert to the dynamism of Rommel's thrust and urged Wavell almost daily to 'chop the German advance', using his Ultra knowledge for encouragement – as, for example, on 2 April: 'From most secret message sent you, you will see that a squadron of Ju.88s was stopped going to Tripoli because operational focus shifted. Therefore cannot feel there is at the moment a persistent weight behind German attack on Cyrenaica.' The weight, however, was at the front: its name was Rommel. Within a week the British were scampering in retreat: the port of Benghazi had fallen, Cyrenaica was abandoned, and three senior generals were in humiliating captivity. General 'X' had fulfilled Brigadier Shearer's forecast.

It is not unjust, therefore, to claim that Wavell got the message but not the meaning. Shearer, who had been in the Middle East almost from the beginning, knew little or nothing about Rommel's record. But evidence was abundant from Poland, Norway, France and the Balkans to indicate that the doctrine inspiring any German force would be aggressive, ruthless, thrusting, daring. Also that the German system of training, based on the interdependence of all arms, gave a unit even of 'brigade group size' a cohesion and power far greater than that of its loosely-knit British equivalent. During this opening gambit of the game to be played on the great African chessboard we thus see Wavell supplied through Ultra with the basic facts but failing in interpretation. There is no evidence that he made allowance at any point, in spite of the forecast by General 'X', to insure against the fact that his opponents were German and might behave not according to the staff-solutions of Camberley but in the tearaway spirit of the *Blitzkrieg*. It was not necessary to know much about Rommel. To put his Ultra intelligence into a correct focus Wavell simply needed, as Shearer saw, to reflect on the ideology of the *Wehrmacht*. By the end of April he would be signalling to the CIGS. 'I must confess that German performance so often exceeds calculations that I am not confident that Germans will not improve on our estimate of their abilities.' Wavell was beginning to get the meaning.

But it was already too late, for in the most direct manner Ultra was about to play a part in his downfall.

The German High Command had also under-estimated Rommel's dynamism. Eastwards – to their horror – raced the Afrika Korps, encircling Tobruk and making for the Egyptian frontier. But Rommel's first impetuous attempts to force a way into Tobruk were decisively halted, the earliest rebuff to a German commander on either side of the Mediterranean. On 23 April General Halder, the Army Chief of Staff, noted in his diary: 'I have a feeling that things are in a mess ... Rommel is in no way equal to his task. He rushes about the whole day between his widely scattered units, stages reconnaissance raids and fritters away his forces.' The great black joke of the African campaign followed. General von Paulus, who would surrender at Stalingrad, was sent out by the High Command to inspect and advise on the siege of Tobruk.

Paulus arrived on the 27th and three days later personally called off Rommel's next attack, which was getting nowhere with heavy losses. After a tour of the front he signalled his report to Berlin. Since Rommel was desperately short of fuel, ammunition, food and vehicles: since the Italians would not run supply convoys by sea to Benghazi, and Tripoli was far from the battle-zone: since the weak Afrika Korps was dangerously squeezed between the Tobruk garrison and the British farther east, caution and consolidation should be the rule. No more troops should be sent to Rommel until conditions improved.

This cheerful communication, eminently satisfactory to a High Command obsessed with Barbarossa, was deciphered at Bletchley. It now becomes possible, therefore, to understand the hidden meaning of the message sent to Wavell by Churchill on 5 May. 'Have you read my telegram of 4th inst.? Presume you realise the highly secret and authoritative character of this information? Actual text is more impressive showing enemy "thoroughly exhausted" . . . also definite forbidding of any advance beyond Sollum except for reconnaissance without permission. . . .' Churchill is saying to Wavell, in effect, 'Ultra has given us the Paulus telegram. Obviously Rommel is hard pressed. What are you going to do about it?'

In his memoirs Churchill amusingly buries his Ultra information about Paulus under a meaningless sentence. 'At this time we had a spy in close touch with Rommel's headquarters, who gave us accurate information of the fearful difficulties of Rommel's assertive but precarious position.' Accurate indeed! Wavell not only received the summary to which Churchill referred in his message of the 5th: by the 7th and 8th the complete text of Paulus's report was in his hands. Ultra perfect. But now the lightning began to flash, for this was the very week in which the 'Tiger' convoy was safely proceeding down the Mediterranean with over 300 tanks for the Middle East – a personal victory for Churchill over the fears of the Admiralty. And so we now see Wavell constantly buffeted and jockeyed by a Prime Minister intensely conscious of Rommel's weakness and, in his view, British strength, to the point of 15 June, when a reluctant Commander-in-Chief launches his premature offensive, Operation Battleaxe. He had reported in advance to the CIGS, 'I think it right to inform you that the measure of success which will attend this operation is in my opinion doubtful.' Battleaxe was, in fact, another desert disaster. On 21 June Churchill switched Wavell to the post of Commander-in-Chief India.

This painful episode tells a great deal about the problems of bringing Ultra to bear on the battlefield. By any standard Bletchley's decipherment of the Paulus report was a considerable intelligence coup, yet it was profitless. The reason in this case was not the misinterpretation of the evidence, for Wavell was as capable as Churchill of deducing from the decrypt that the Afrika Korps was at a low ebb. The answer is to be found in communications theory and in what happened before Pearl Harbor. Roberta Wohlstetter, in her classic study *Pearl Harbor: Warning and Decision*, brilliantly analyses the way that statesmen and commanders were prevented from assimilating the information provided by the Magic intercepts because of 'noise' – 'noise' representing all those factors of habit and traditional practice, of individual personality, of existing obsessions with political or military goals, and so on, which distractingly inter-

posed themselves between the Magic intelligence and its distinguished recipients. Both the Prime Minister and his Commander-
in-Chief heard a great deal of 'noise'.

Churchill was confused by a private commitment to his 'Tiger-
cubs', as he called the tanks whose opportune arrival in Egypt
seemed to him, rightly, to be a great military stroke on his part. But
he yearned for them to consummate his triumph by instant victory.
Ultra had given him Paulus: the way seemed clear. Wavell's apparent reluctance caused resentment – and 'noise'. But there was a
deeper, older source of interference. Since 1940 Churchill had
nursed a sense of Wavell's incapacity: Greece, Crete and later
events extended it. 'Noise' was bred from the notion of an incapable
commander who needed to be pushed. So Churchill pushed the
desert army into Battleaxe.

For his part, Wavell knew that his army was weak. The expert
professional team of O'Connor's days had withered. The tanks from
'Tiger' had arrived in shameful condition. Simple mechanical repair
for the armour and careful training for the crews was necessary
before success could be guaranteed against the panzers. It seemed
to take the British longer than the Germans to learn how to fight
well in North Africa. These hard truths, which Churchill ignored,
set up a 'noise' of resistance in Wavell's head – resistance to a
premature offensive. But his judgement, too, was affected by personality factors. On his return to England in the autumn of 1940 he
had nearly resigned because of the Prime Minister's attitude to him
in conference. A sequence of situations in which he had argued
against the London view, and been overborne by Churchill, made
him feel like a Pro-Consul hagridden by a despotic Emperor. This
also caused 'noise'.

And thus Ultra's plain presentation of Rommel's predicament
was not, and had no hope of being, examined coolly and objectively
by the two main British protagonists. A fortunate possession of the
facts – thanks to Bletchley – was nullified by Churchill's desire to
press the evidence beyond the limits of the possible and Wavell's
sceptical awareness that he was being impelled into military nonsense. In this atmosphere there was no chance for a level-headed
appraisal of what action, granted the insight provided by Ultra,
could be sensibly undertaken against Rommel within the real and
very restricted capability of Wavell's army. Battleaxe is a textbook
example of how, before Ultra could affect the battle, a multitude of

other considerations might come into play: in this case, disastrously.

Battleaxe, it will be recalled, was also a reason for delay in establishing the first Special Liaison Unit to reach the Middle East. Until now there had been no custom-built system of communication from Bletchley to Cairo and the forward headquarters. But when 'A Detachment, Special Signal Unit' finally arrived in Egypt it discovered that the vehicles containing its technical stores, which had been sent on ahead down the Mediterranean, had been taken over because of shortage of transport for Battleaxe. By intense effort, and what the Army calls 'winning', these losses were quickly made good and a basic organization came into being. The main office was in the Middle East HQ in Cairo, the radio station at Abbassia, and a Liaison Unit went 'up the desert' to work with the army.[6]

At first signals from Bletchley were sent direct to Cairo from the Whaddon Hall transmitters, and then repeated from Cairo both to the Liaison Unit which serviced naval headquarters at Alexandria and to the unit at Army HQ in the field. But reception conditions over the Western Desert were notoriously unreliable, and later it was found that better results were achieved if Whaddon sent a single signal which all these stations could pick up independently. Each station could appreciate from the call signs if it was particularly addressed. These problems of radio communication in the Mediterranean theatre, whether over the desert sands or among the mountains of Italy, need special emphasis, for the whole Ultra system as it was perfected depended on the rapid passage of undistorted signals – sometimes over great distances. The difficulties of transmitting from Cairo up to the front may be illustrated by the fact that it was often more effective for a signal to be sent from Abbassia to Whaddon, by 'bouncing' it off the Heaviside layer in the upper atmosphere, and for it then to be re-transmitted immediately from England to the Liaison Unit with the Desert Army, rather than for the message to be sent by radio over a few hundred miles of wilderness to the battle-front. There was less interruption, distortion and fading of signal-strength. Similar techniques were, of course, employed by 'Y' Service. The essential point is that without the enormous contribution of the Royal Corps of Signals Ultra would have been impoverished, and the long monotonous toil of the signallers in the SLUs was not relieved of its tedium by their complete exclusion from the cipher work, or, indeed, from the least inkling of what the messages they handled were about. They lived in the midst of a mystery.

Weakened by the battles of the spring and early summer, both sides now concentrated on gathering strength for a winter campaign – Rommel determined to take Tobruk and Auchinleck, Wavell's successor, to relieve it. There was a lull, continuously interrupted by the loud crackle of 'noise' as Churchill tried to force Auchinleck into an early offensive and the Commander-in-Chief, more stubborn than Wavell, as resolutely refused. The relative peace had a particular value, for this was a time when the decipherment of Mediterranean signal traffic was not going well at Bletchley. Indeed, when the first SLU went forward to the headquarters of the Desert Army there was, for a while, a sense of chagrin because so little was arriving from Whaddon Hall. This was a temporary phase, which certainly did nothing to disillusion the new Commander-in-Chief: whenever Auchinleck himself went forward to the battle-zone he always took with him his personal Liaison Unit to keep in touch with the 'secret intelligence'.[7] But the ban on mentioning Ultra before 1974 has prevented previous writers from noting how Bletchley's problems during this period provide yet another reason for questioning Churchill's dismissive verdict on Auchinleck – that his 'four and a half months' delay in engaging the enemy in the Desert was alike a mistake and a misfortune'.

Plans for the actual engagement of the enemy envisaged an all-out offensive in mid-November by the newly named 8th Army; the siege of Tobruk was to be lifted and the armour of the Afrika Korps destroyed. Simultaneously Rommel himself was aiming to remove the problem of Tobruk by a direct, decisive assault. Absorbed by his own preparations, he refused to believe in the possibility of a move by the British and, in fact, his curious behaviour before and at the start of Auchinleck's operation – famous as Crusader – has caused much speculation.

His aggressive intentions and developing strength were being charted by a re-invigorated Ultra. Rommel's own secret traffic was sent out in the Enigma cipher by his No. 10 Signals Regiment to the German base in Rome and then onwards to OKW, the High Command, in Berlin. To his Italian 'superiors' other codes were used. As one of his staff, Hans-Otto Behrendt, has observed, Enigma was not employed 'for the messages to Superlibia (the Italian Headquarters in Africa) and Supercommando (the Italian High Command in

Rome). These messages in my view were always a fruitful source of information for the British side!' Additional areas of Enigma traffic for 'Y' Service to intercept and for Bletchley to seek to decipher were, of course, the signal output from Luftwaffe formations in the Mediterranean and the messages to and from Rommel's logistic base at Tripoli. As the autumn moved on Ultra from all its various sources became more abundant. By 17 September, indeed, Churchill may be observed using Ultra in his favourite way – as a means of urging on his commanders with unimpeachable evidence. On that day he thundered to Auchinleck:

> The situation has already worsened. The enemy are far better supplied with petrol. African Panzer Corps is now called African Panzer Gruppe. By waiting until you have an extra brigade you may well find that you have to face an extra division. *Various names of significant places are now creeping into the special information. Your movement of transports and formations of dumps are noted by enemy....*'*

But Rommel was now to take note of something else. Formerly his thoughts and actions in October and early November 1941 have been judged as eccentric. The Italians persistently and from the highest level warned of an imminent British offensive. Evidence accumulated – photographs of crowded airfields, the extension of the coastal railway, supply dumps, increased radio traffic. On 21 October Rommel, who vehemently rejected all such indications, told the Italian Chief of Staff, General Gambara, that the assault on Tobruk could 'begin on November 20 without our running any risk'. (Crusader was scheduled for 18 November). He then flew to Rome, meeting his wife next day, and spent the following fortnight either in her company or in conference. He did not leave until the 16th. Bad weather held him up in Belgrade for one night, and engine trouble kept him in Athens for another. By the time he was back reports of Crusader's opening gambits were already coming in. He refused to accept them. When Paulus was sent out to Tobruk General Halder said that he was probably the only man who could deal with 'this soldier gone raving mad'. Was Rommel still 'raving'?

The case for Rommel's sanity begins in a field in Palestine as far back as July. During an air raid a parachutist descended near Ramleh, and was observed by a peasant to be digging holes as if to

*Author's italics.

conceal something. The visitor was traced to Jerusalem. He carried a letter of introduction to a family of Jews from Germany whom he claimed as relatives. He looked like a Jew, and asserted that his blood had made life in the Luftwaffe intolerable, so he had deserted. He was moved to Cairo and kept in a carefully bugged room in the interrogation centre at Maadi. The respectful attitude of the prisoners towards him soon confirmed suspicion.

Brigadier Shearer, who handled the case, next ordered a search in the field at Ramleh which produced a short wave transmitter and a wad of Palestinian currency. The prisoner now broke, and confessed that he was the Gauleiter of Mannheim who had volunteered to investigate the possibility of increasing subversion in Palestine – he then intended to get away through Syria. Regular signals were therefore broadcast on his radio, using the codes, identifications and times for transmission found with the set. After a few days a station at Bari in Italy responded. The stage was ready for a masquerade. In the first act Shearer and his colleague Brigadier Maunsell sought to confirm the Gauleiter's authority by sending to Bari authentic information about troop movements and similar events which, they knew, could be easily verified by the extensive Axis spy network in Egypt. And then Bari revealed that the information was proving to be so accurate that it was being sent direct to Rommel.

With the real Crusader in mind, Shearer and Maunsell swiftly exploited their opportunity by feeding to Bari a false scenario. In this the apparently offensive preparations in the desert were presented as a cover plan for the move of a large force northwards to help Russia to protect the threatened and vital oilfields. A specially arranged visit by Auchinleck to the headquarters of the 9th Army in Palestine supported this plausible idea. Ultra confirmed that Rommel was receiving this attractive intelligence, which meshed exactly with his own ambitions. A new light is thus thrown on a remark in *The Rommel Papers* by the then chief of staff of the Afrika Korps, General Bayerlein. Discussing the situation on the eve of Crusader he says: 'Rommel did not expect the British to launch a major attack until they thought the Middle East free of the danger of a German offensive through the Caucasus.' And on Crusader's D Day, 18 November, Rommel was in Athens! At the daily meeting in Cairo that morning of the Commanders-in-Chief and the Minister in State the latter, Oliver Lyttelton, began the proceedings by saying 'First round to John Shearer' – who, from Ultra, was able to report the whereabouts of the absentee enemy commander.[8]

Crusader is one of the most complicated of the desert battles. During the six weeks or so of action the pattern changed daily and often hourly. Most of the striking events – the desperate struggle for Sidi Rezegh airfield: Rommel's notorious 'dash for the wire': General Crüwell's remarkable assault on Sunday 23 November, *Totensonntag*, the Sunday of the Dead – were the result of off-the-cuff tactical decisions made and implemented at speed. To such a battle Ultra could not contribute significantly.* Interception and decipherment of the nightly situation reports, strength states, demands for fuel and tanks and other routine traffic between Rommel and Germany may have had a marginal utility, but in a conflict of tactical manoeuvre the British commanders were more usefully served by interception of German conversations on the battlefield, direction-finding, interrogation of prisoners and similar conventional means. Churchill, however, must have had a vivid image of Ultra material at risk amid blazing tanks and intrusive Germans, for on 25 November, at a time when the turn of the battle seemed adverse, he signalled to Auchinleck, 'Please burn all special stuff and flimsies up at the front.' There should in fact have been no Ultra material further forward than Army headquarters, and the Special Liaison Unit was well prepared for the emergency destruction of its papers.

It was on 19 December that Ultra entered the Crusader story in the most striking and, as it turned out, unfortunate fashion. The Axis convoy No. 52, carrying tank replacements, had been crossing the Mediterranean – two of its ships, with forty-five tanks, were sunk on 13 December. As it approached the African coast the convoy split, its main body making for Tripoli where on 19 December *Monginevro* landed twenty-three tanks. On the same day, however, the breakaway part of the convoy – the 4700 ton *Ankara* – reached Benghazi, successfully landing its cargo of twenty-two tanks which were off-loaded with great expedition (for the 8th Army was drawing near) and handed over within a few days to 15 Panzer Division of the Afrika Korps. *Ankara* was a ship evidently blessed at her launching. Built in Hamburg for the German Levant line, fast and

---

*Auchinleck certainly received a sequence of Ultra signals during the battle. These mainly reflected Rommel's anxiety about fuel and air cover and presumably contributed to sustaining Auchinleck's confidence in final victory. He got no hard tactical intelligence from the 'special messages'.

well-equipped, with holds particularly suited for the transport of tanks, *Ankara* bore a charmed life during which her name cropped up constantly in Ultra messages as she sped back and forth across the Mediterranean. 'The Captain got quite a swollen head about his luck and would harangue the dock labourers in Naples and Tripoli on the subject.' So Sir David Hunt, who as an intelligence staff officer was as haunted by this phantom as were his colleagues and everyone in the Navy and the RAF who was concerned with cutting Rommel's supply lines.[9] Constantly hunted, *Ankara* nevertheless survived until the end of 1942 when, in spite of so many evasions, she succumbed at last to a mine laid by the submarine *Rorqual*.

Almost immediately the effect of *Ankara*'s deposit at Benghazi was felt by the 8th Army. It succeeded in pressing Rommel away from the port and out of Cyrenaica, but its troops were exhausted and fuel stocks ran low. Only a small spearhead could be sustained forward, in which the steel was 22 Armoured Brigade. On 27 December the Afrika Korps with sixty tanks viciously and unexpectedly ripped into the 22nd Armoured, destroying thirty-seven for the loss of seven. Three days later this success was repeated, the Africa Korps losing only seven more panzers while the British lost twenty-three. For the time being 22 Armoured Brigade, with little but light tanks left, was withdrawn from the front line to refit. All disasters are relative. This ignominious defeat, following a clear-cut victory in the hard-fought Crusader, had a particular impact and poignancy, since the British command had no notion that the routed Rommel could assemble so many battle-worthy panzers. The gift to the Afrika Korps of those twenty-two tanks from *Ankara*'s holds had created the conditions for a surprise coup.

For this the reason was a failure to apply Ultra. Signals from Bletchley had in fact alerted Shearer to the approach of Convoy No. 52. He knew of the delivery of tanks at Tripoli: he was aware of *Ankara*'s diversion to Benghazi. But in Benghazi, that much-bombed harbour, facilities were few. Shearer's naval advisers assured him that blocking arrangements made in the past would prevent *Ankara* from reaching a quay-side where her tanks could be off-loaded. There were no adequate crane-carrying barges to handle the panzers away from the shore. With this authoritative technical advice Shearer reckoned that *Ankara* could not deliver: inevitably, therefore, he discounted the Ultra warning, wrote down the armoured strength of the Afrika Korps, and a surprise shattering of

170

22 Armoured Brigade was the consequence. But the advice had been wrong. A current working into the blocked channel at Benghazi had gouged out enough space for *Ankara* to reach the quayside and get her tanks ashore. It was a feat characteristic of so indomitable a ship.[10]

This issue may seem small – twenty-two German tanks. But in the desert war everything hinged on a local superiority in armour: the rest was secondary. And almost immediately, as has often been told, Rommel irresistibly counter-attacked. His decision was sudden and secret – so secret that he kept it from his overlords in Rome and Berlin, and no signals passed which might have provided a warning on Ultra. The result was explosive. On 29 January Benghazi fell to him again; by early February the 8th Army had been expelled from the Cyrenaican bulge and fallen back to the Gazala line just west of Tobruk. How valuable in that hectic battle would have been the sixty tanks of 22 Armoured Brigade, surprised and destroyed as a result of *Ankara!*

The effects of these sudden and inexplicable reverses ran back to London. As the fighting swirled we find Churchill, on 28 January, using his Ultra knowledge to spur Auchinleck on. 'You have no doubt seen most secret stuff about Rommel's presumed intentions. . . . This seems to reinforce importance of our holding on. I am most anxious to hear further from you about defeat of our armour by inferior enemy numbers. This cuts very deep.' The wound would not heal. Alan Brooke, the CIGS, was also pained by the cut. The matter became a leading exhibit in the case that was built up against Brigadier Shearer, on the grounds that he was excessively optimistic in his evaluation of the enemy. As a result Shearer was replaced at the end of February (after an outspoken defence by Auchinleck) to be succeeded by the then Colonel Francis de Guingand, whose famous but wholly unpredictable role as Montgomery's Chief of Staff from Alamein to Germany was now but a few months away.

But there was a practical benefit from the mistake about *Ankara.* The episode caused much heart-searching in Cairo. One who particularly studied its implications was Enoch Powell, whose career had so far been remarkable. In 1937, aged twenty-five, he had left his Fellowship at Trinity College, Cambridge, to become Professor of Greek in the University of Sydney. At the outbreak of war he sailed from Australia by the first boat and on his return enlisted, not without difficulty, as a private in the Royal Warwickshire Regiment. Commissioned in the Intelligence Corps, he worked on the staff of an armoured division and then, in the autumn of 1941, transferred to the Middle East where he joined the section concerned with Rommel's logistics. He was aware of, but as yet not deeply immersed in Ultra. With the incisive logic necessary for cutting through conventional practices Powell saw that the lesson taught by *Ankara* must be immediately applied. Study of Rommel's supply-routes needed to be raised to a higher level of sophistication with all sources of intelligence, and particularly Ultra, meticulously and continuously surveyed. Powell's advocacy marched with the general concern. In consequence a new committee was established at Middle East HQ consisting, under Group Captain Long, of two naval officers, a brilliant young architect transformed into Flight-Lieutenant Piers Hubbard, and Major Enoch Powell himself.[11]

This small three-service unit met daily, and very early in the morning, to analyse and advise on the incoming intelligence, largely Ultra, whereby they could monitor the flow of supplies to Rommel across the Mediterranean by sea or by air. There were two aspects of their work. The first was to maintain an accurate estimate of the men and material that actually survived the crossing and reached the front. The second was to work ahead of the convoys – discover in advance what ports they were leaving, what cargoes they were carrying, the strength and number of their escorts – an exercise so refined in its development that they would know not only the name and past record of a particular ship in a convoy but also its individual cargo.* Such analysis, carried out unremittingly day by day, and based on the truths of Ultra, was invaluable for the Army in keeping it abreast of Rommel's logistic state – abreast, above all, of his fuel stocks, the life-blood of the desert war. For the Navy and the Air Force targeting information of this authority had a special value. Never, in 1942, had the British in the Mediterranean an abundance of ships, submarines or aircraft for strikes against the Axis convoys. To be able to direct a small strike to the right spot, and even to be able to indicate precisely the ship that mattered in the convoy, meant that limited forces could be used with an effective economy as radar allowed Fighter Command to be employed in the Battle of Britain.

*For the contribution of the Italian section at Bletchley to this exercise, see Chapter Four.

The Battle of Britain analogy is not false. During the early months of 1942 British resources in the Mediterranean were stretched to the extreme at a time when Hitler was paying more attention to the seaways. In December he had moved a whole Fliegerkorps into the area from Russia and re-directed eighteen U-boats into the Mediterranean, with more to follow. Between October and the end of 1941 the British had lost the aircraft-carrier *Ark Royal*, the cruiser *Galatea*, the battleship *Barham*, and two other battleships, *Valiant* and *Queen Elizabeth*, put out of action for months in Alexandria's harbour by Italian 'human torpedoes'. The clinical stroke occurred on 18 December when the only real task force available, Force K, was caught in a minefield off Tripoli and by loss and damage rendered *hors de combat*. Merely a few cruisers, destroyers and submarines remained for harrying the convoys, and with Malta under concentrated attack, Rommel controlling the most valuable coastal airfields, and strike aircraft a pitiful handful, the prospects for cutting into the Axis supply-lines were bleak. The sophisticated use of Ultra and other intelligence was therefore opportune. It was far more economical to direct a precious submarine or bomber more or less precisely to its target rather than to waste craft-hours and man-hours in time-consuming sweeps and patrols. Considering all the limitations and difficulties, the British achievement in the first half of 1942 was considerable and in the second half, when conditions improved and Ultra was functioning with a classic smoothness, it may be thought remarkable – as the figures in the Official History, *The War at Sea*, instantly demonstrate.

Between January and July 1942 the Italians lost eighty ships totalling some 163 000 tons (including a few losses outside the Mediterranean). In the Mediterranean alone German losses were ten ships of some 28 000 tons. For the period from August to December the totals jump. The Italians, 150 ships of 276 000 tons: Germans, twenty-four ships of over 44 000 tons. These sinkings were not achieved by chance or courage alone. The submarine commander who, ordered to be at a particular spot at a particular time, and, raising his periscope, found his prey in sight: the pilots flying to a successful strike apparently on the reports of a spotter plane (which, as they did not know, had merely been sent up as cover for the fact that the target was identified already) – such men, whose experiences were often repeated, represent the rewarding

173

end-product of a process that began at Bletchley and was energized by the intensive studies of Group Captain Long's committee.

Before the next major confrontation between 8th Army and Rommel, on the Gazala line towards the end of May, considerable 'noise' was generated on both sides in the exchanges between the commanders at the front and their masters at home. With the Far East lost and the fear that America might concentrate on the Pacific, Churchill desperately needed a victory in Africa both to allay public opinion and also to demonstrate to Roosevelt that the Middle East was still viable and worth American support. The record shows him using every weapon to impel Auchinleck into a premature offensive – cajolery, flattery, exhortation, but above all imperious and sometimes outrageous rhetoric (softened, when possible, by the discreet amendments of Ismay and the Chiefs of Staff). A favourite trick at which Churchill was now adept was to use as a bludgeon a judiciously selected item from the Ultra intelligence. Here, he would imply, is an argument unanswerable by a Commander-in-Chief. 'In your appreciations', he signals to Auchinleck on 15 March, 'you estimate possible by March 1 that enemy may have in Libya 475 medium tanks and by April 1,630. *We now know* . . .* that on 11th, Panzer Army Africa had in forward area 159 tanks serviceable and Italians 87, total 246, or barely half the number you credited them with by March 1.' Churchill's assurance was based on Ultra.

But accurate figures for tank strengths are notoriously difficult to establish. The numbers with units in the front line, the numbers under repair in regimental workshops or further down the lines of communication to the base, and the numbers of reinforcements expected to arrive from overseas can be juggled with in many ways to produce a deceptive result. In this matter Rommel like Patton took a liberal and unscrupulous view of the truth. His situation reports to OKW sent with no sense of delicacy the most pessimistic picture of his strength in armour or fuel, to support the strident complaints and demands he constantly signalled to Germany – the stridency, indeed, was so great that some of those who read his messages in Hut 3 at Bletchley were convinced of their implausibility. The 8th Army's assessment early in March would be based on its own wary estimate from many sources, photo-reconnaissance, constant interception of the Panzer Army's own wireless traffic in

*Author's italics.

lower grade codes, prisoner interrogation and so on. The point is that the 'noise' in the debate between Churchill and Auchinleck over the relative strengths in armour illustrates the danger, always inherent in Ultra, of accepting a deciphered signal for what it appears to be worth without looking sceptically into its background. Another good instance would be such signals from Göring about the Luftwaffe as came through on Ultra: the Marshal's tendency being to over-emphasize and overstate rather than to underplay.

But Rommel, by contrast with Auchinleck, had no wish to underplay the feasibility of an offensive. He was eager for Tobruk and, in truth, for Cairo and the Canal. The Italians, who bore the brunt of shipping his supplies over dangerous waters, were not even happy about his present eastward position, and still less so about a further advance. 'Rome is putting on the brakes,' Rommel was saying in February. But at the beginning of May Hitler and Mussolini agreed at Berchtesgaden that Rommel should attack at Gazala and capture Tobruk. Next was to follow a joint Italo-German invasion of Malta, Operation Hercules, which would take the sting out of British interdiction of the convoy routes. Until Malta fell, Rommel was to stand fast at Tobruk and make no further move forwards. He accepted his brief, and began hectic preparations for his Operation Venezia which was scheduled for 26 May.

Among those preparations was one venture, Operation *Condor*, which was so uncharacteristic of the Germans that it is not surprising to find that the man at its head was Hungarian. Broadly speaking, the Germans in Africa lacked the knowledge, the aptitude and perhaps the originality to exploit the vast desert hinterland. Rommel's operations always clung close to the coast, and the Panzer Army never developed an organization akin to the Long Range Desert Group. But in May 1942 a need arose. Rommel had been well satisfied by the intelligence supplied to him through the Italians' breaking of the code used by the American attaché in Cairo, Colonel Fellers, for his meticulous reports to Washington on British plans and capability.[12] 'The little fellows', Rommel called them. But the Germans wanted their own men in Cairo, planted with their transmitter in a safe house, as an insurance against Fellers drying up, an intelligence source under their own control, and a means of building up contacts with revolutionary anti-British elements in Egypt – men of the future like Nasser and Sadat. The task was put in the hands of the Abwehr. Two men from the Berlin HQ with African experience, called Eppler and Sandstede, were sent out along with a detachment of the specialized Brandenburger Regiment which was directly responsible to the Abwehr's chief, Admiral Canaris, for the execution of the commando-type assignments. The Brandenburgers' role was to transport the two agents safely from behind Rommel's lines to Cairo – Operation *Salaam* – so that the spy-game of Operation *Condor* might begin.

A man of experience was required to lead this expedition over its 1700 miles route from the coast of Cyrenaica deep into the hinterland of the sand seas and then north to Assiut on the Nile, whence the agents would make their own way to Cairo while their escort returned. The leader chosen was a Hungarian, Count Almaszy, who had gained much practical knowledge before the war about how to live and move in the desert wilderness. But though Almaszy completed Operation *Salaam* and conducted Eppler and Sandstede to the banks of the Nile, there was an anticlimax. The British were on the alert. The two agents, after reaching Cairo, spent a curiously ostentatious and insecure existence in a house-boat on the Nile while they contacted Sadat and his fellow-dissidents and used as a magnet for their intelligence-gathering the popular belly dancer, Hekmat Fahmi: but it was all amateur and abortive, and they were arrested in September.

Apart from the characteristically poor training of the Abwehr agents, Operation *Condor* was doomed from the start. The British were on the alert because Almaszy's name kept cropping up in Ultra. At Bletchley Jean Alington in Hut 3 became intrigued by references to this exotic figure in the decrypts and started a private investigation into his background. In Cairo Bill Williams, then working in Middle East Intelligence under its Director, de Guingand, was also made suspicious by the appearance of Almaszy in the messages and asked one of his staff, Stuart Hood, (now a Professor at the Royal College of Art in London), to find out more about him. What was this *Sonderkommando* (or special unit) *Almaszy* doing in the desert wastes? Hood found people who had known Almaszy in Egypt before the war, and in the library of Cairo University he actually discovered a book by the Hungarian which showed how he had learned, from Herodotus, that two thousand years ago the Egyptians had been able to travel great distances across the barren sands by dumping water at regular stages in quan-

176

tities of pots imported from Greece. Almaszy's *Kommando* was now playing a similar kind of game – with spies to dump instead of water.[13]

But under surveillance: for as Colonel Macfarlan of the Middle East Special Liaison Unit recalled, 'we followed them all the way'.[14] As the *Sonderkommando* came to important landmarks in its 1700-mile struggle through the wilderness it radioed progress reports to Rommel's headquarters, where special Abwehr signallers handled the decoding. Here was a simple opportunity for 'Y' service to fix its location by direction-finding and for the cryptanalysts to unscramble the signals. Moreover, when this section of Rommel's staff was captured in the opening stage of the Gazala battle, much useful documentation was acquired about *Salaam* and *Condor*. The naïve behaviour of the agents when they reached Cairo was all that was required to close the file. The story is an excellent instance of how, in the cloak-and-dagger world, many factors might play their part among which Ultra could sometimes be decisive and sometimes, as in the case of Almaszy, contributory.*

The capture of the *Condor* documents during the first days of Operation Venezia – the Axis drive for Tobruk which opened on 26 May 1942 – was only a small element in what ought to have been a major disaster for Rommel. That he recovered his poise, out-manoeuvred and outfought the British, took the prize of Tobruk, became a Field Marshal, ignored Malta and dashed onward to Egypt – all this has been microscopically examined in many books. But as battles have their central themes – for Crete, we have seen, it was airfields – that of the Gazala battle must now be defined, and considered in relation to Ultra.

The 'line' ran due south for about forty miles, from Gazala on the coastal road to the end point at Bir Hacheim where the Free French were to emulate Roland's stand at Roncesvalles. It lay about the same distance to the west of Tobruk. Rommel's options, as both he and Auchinleck knew, were either to break through the centre of the line or to come round the southern flank – or both. The difficulty was that though Ultra provided excellent warning of Rommel's intention to attack, and, with sufficient accuracy, of the

---

*The Germans at this time placed an observation post south of Alamein, in the wilderness of the Qattara Depression. Its daily reports, made with precise regularity, were intercepted and deciphered at Bletchley. Naturally they were always the same: '*Nichts zu melden:* nothing to report'. But one day there was a change. The message read 'some Arabs and a camel'.

date, Auchinleck had no hard evidence about the actual option his opponent would select. Sir David Hunt, who was chief intelligence officer at the British 13 Corps, says that 'an NCO from the HQ of one of the German armoured divisions was captured in the southern desert, and very willingly gave an outline of the plan and a list of the troops taking part'.[15] Hunt was actually present at the interrogation. The prisoner's glib readiness to speak was at first interpreted as meaning that he had been planted to give misleading information. In any case, it is evident from Auchinleck's communications with his latest commander of the 8th Army, General Ritchie, that whilst he knew from Ultra and other sources about Rommel's imminent assault, he could only guess at its route.

Auchinleck guessed wisely. He envisaged the combination of an Axis thrust through the centre and a drive round the flank at Bir Hacheim. He therefore advised Ritchie to hold his main tank force, 1 and 7 Armoured Divisions, *en masse* and well to the north so that they could cope in strength with either or both of the possible threats. Field Marshal Lord Carver, who was himself on the staff of 30 Corps at the time, has written that 'it is hardly surprising, knowing of the extensive and usually very accurate sources of intelligence available to the Commander-in-Chief, that this forecast of Rommel's intentions should have greatly influenced the minds of Ritchie and his commanders'.[16] What is more surprising is that in fact they ignored it.

On the night of the 26th, Stuart Hood, who was aware of Ultra intelligence though not 'on the list', walked along the banks of the Nile in Cairo hearing in his head the sound of the Afrika Korps's panzers rounding the flank at Bir Hacheim.[17] He heard the sound because, far away though he was, he knew that the attack was coming – and the memory remained with him for many years. Making a strong but essentially subsidiary thrust against the British minefields in the centre, Rommel with a great column of 10 000 vehicles swept by night wide to the south and then, after turning Bir Hacheim, due north to disrupt the British rear and clear a path to Tobruk. Since Ritchie and his commanders had ignored Auchinleck and left their armour scattered, the picture becomes one of piecemeal actions, units taken by surprise, and a British loss of initiative at the start which was never truly recovered until Venezia's triumphant conclusion. The theme of the Gazala battle is concentration of armour.

Rommel himself had at first disregarded the theme – hence his near approach to disaster. He too split his forces during the opening thrusts and manoeuvres. The British started with over 850 tanks and good reserves: the Axis army had only 560, of which nearly half were Italian while reserves were trivial. So Rommel's considerable initial losses and his dispersed units left him open to destruction – had the British possessed a concentrated force for counter-attack. Instead it was Rommel who saw the light, pulled his army together, and in a sequence of blows hammered the 8th Army eastwards and forced his way into Tobruk. 'Only connect', wrote E. M. Forster: it is a good theme for generals.

And thus Gazala repeats the lesson constantly taught by preceding battles. In Greece, in Crete, when the Afrika Korps arrived and before Battleaxe, Ultra alone – not to speak of all the other sources of intelligence – had supplied in advance accurate information which, if not always comprehensive, was in each case sufficient for the commander concerned to make a right judgement about his enemy's intentions and the proper method of countering them. To condemn the commanders out of hand would be absurd, for there were many countervailing factors. (Though it is difficult not to condemn Ritchie and his subordinates absolutely for the dispositions and handling of the 8th Army at Gazala). In Crete Freyberg was simply ignorant of the way a German airborne division would function. When the Afrika Korps arrived Wavell's mind was gravely distracted by the need to send troops to Greece. But the truth remains. Whether the information it supplied was total or incomplete, Ultra was in essence a service to the commanders of intercepted and deciphered German signals. Its final value lay in the skill with which commanders and their staffs understood the signals' significance and applied it to the conduct of the battle. This was beyond Bletchley's powers.

There was no need for Ultra to inform the retreating 8th Army that forlorn Tobruk had been captured. The news of the garrison's capitulation reached them in clear – announced by an uncoded German signal transmitted on the evening of 21 June. *Mit unbedingte Kapitulation der Garrison zufrieden*: 'I agree to unconditional surrender of the garrison'. Authenticated by Rommel's personal sign, ROL, it told Ritchie and Auchinleck everything – though none of those commanders knew that it was also a form of death-warrant for the Afrika Korps. Yet such was the case. When Churchill, then in Washington, told Roosevelt immediately of Tobruk's fall the President and General Marshall set in train that reinforcement of 300 Sherman tanks which was to have a crucial effect in the desert campaign from Alamein onwards.

Nor could Ultra bring much direct succour when Rommel, now backed by Hitler and Mussolini, profited from the stocks captured at Tobruk and raced for Cairo and Alexandria. As Auchinleck fought him to stalemate before the last outposts of the Nile Delta the pattern of action, sustained throughout July with great verve on both sides, was one of constant manoeuvre, sudden changes of thrust, improvised plans. Ultra could help with information about Rommel's logistic strength, an occasional indication of his intentions and reports about his convoys, but the great backs-to-the-wall struggle was fought at too great a pace for Bletchley to come in like Blücher at what proved to be Rommel's – and ultimately Auchinleck's – Waterloo.

At first there was no certainty that the wall would hold, and precautionary measures were taken in the British rear which were sometimes ludicrous and sometimes ill-starred. The notorious 'Ash Wednesday', when GHQ in Cairo set about burning documents with clumsy zeal, is better forgotten. 'Wherever one walked bits of charred paper came floating past,' wrote de Guingand. A more sensible move was the pushing up into Palestine from the Cairo Special Liaison Unit of a reserve team under Wing Commander Crawshaw – just in case. The Navy simply dispersed, the main fleet moving from Alexandria to anchorages at Port Said, Haifa and Beirut.

It was also intended to shift the submarine base from Alexandria to Haifa, but unfortunately the depot ship *Medway*, laden with spare torpedoes, was caught *en route* and sunk by U.372 (which in turn was sunk off Haifa five weeks later). 1 Submarine Flotilla was therefore transferred to Beirut, an old submarine base of the French, and here further craft were assembled from as far west as Gibraltar to form a strong striking force. Ultra was the key-note of its operations, as has been confirmed to the author by Commander Francis, the senior staff officer at Beirut. Since the base was an improvisation, Wing Commander Bugden came up from Cairo with a Special Liaison Unit to service it. The Ultra system had now, in fact, achieved the flexibility and assurance needed in an emergency.

By mid-August, however, the days of alarm were over. The

replacement of Auchinleck by Alexander, the vast inflow of troops from Britain and supplies and equipment from the United States, the impoverishment of the Axis army as its own supply ships were sunk by aircraft and submarines aided by Ultra, the changing fortunes on the Russian front – all these factors produced a sudden transformation so characteristic of the desert war. The Germans are coming: the Fleet scatters, the secret papers are burning in Cairo as the old men burned them before Churchill's eyes on that terrible day in Paris in 1940. But on that day, when Churchill asked Gamelin *où est la masse de manoeuvre?* the answer had been *aucune*. Now, suddenly, there were new divisions, new tanks, and in Montgomery a buoyant self-confident commander for the 8th Army.

Ultra's fortunes were also affected by some significant postings. When Montgomery made de Guingand his Chief of Staff, the job of Director of Intelligence to the new Commander-in-Chief, Middle East – General Alexander – went to Brigadier Airey. Terence Airey continued at Alexander's side until the end in Italy, a man with a lively and unconventional cast of mind, apt for his task and alert about Ultra. Major Williams moved from GHQ in Cairo to 8th Army, soon to become Montgomery's chief intelligence officer and to advise him until the last days in Germany. A young Oxford history don, 'Bill' Williams joined the King's Dragoon Guards at the outbreak of war and, serving with their armoured cars on the desert front in 1941, was involved in the very first skirmish with the Afrika Korps. On his return to Oxford after 1945 Bill would become Warden of Rhodes House, editor of the *Dictionary of National Biography* and, on his knighthood, Sir Edgar Williams. Two other dons worked under Airey. Joe Ewart, an immensely able Scotsman, later became a colonel on Montgomery's staff, serving there until, as the Field Marshal describes in his memoirs, at the famous surrender of the Germans on Luneburg Heath Colonel Ewart dealt with the enemy's representatives. Tragically soon afterwards Ewart died in a car accident. But with Ewart now was David Hunt, Fellow of Magdalen College Oxford, a classical archeologist who had served with the Welch Regiment and then as an intelligence officer in Greece, Crete, and the desert. Though not indoctrinated then, Hunt had actually become aware of Ultra early on in Greece when he was handling the mass of intercepts relating to the German build-up in Roumania and Bulgaria. He too would stay on Alexander's staff until the end – and beyond, for he remained with his master to write his despatches. Then – Private Secretary to two Prime Ministers, much diplomatic service in Africa and, finally, an Ambassadorship and a knighthood.

These unusual men are worth attention because, with others of similar calibre like Enoch Powell, they set in the field a standard of intellectual ability and freedom from the mental conventions of the Regular Army which matched the qualities of their brilliant contemporaries at Bletchley Park. They could understand what Ultra was about. With minds trained in evaluation, they saw that this special intelligence was not a form of esoteric magic but simply another tool, valuable, demanding a sceptical respect – but above all to be handled with imagination. For some senior regular officers, by contrast, Ultra created genuine problems of adjustment. Here, it seemed, was a revolutionary and mysterious source of intelligence which conformed with nothing they had learned in a lifetime. Better, perhaps, to carry on with normal methods and leave Ultra in limbo. In 1942, however, men like Williams and Hunt were not only battle-tested: they were also, fortunately, no more inhibited about Ultra than about any other kind of intelligence – for as scholars the weighing of evidence was their normal trade. Since the officers of this little group occupied central positions in the British commands until the end of the war, their coming-together has a peculiar relevance in the story of Ultra.

It was, indeed, a good omen. Ultra was now mature. During the great struggles that would continue until 1945 around the Mediterranean shores its intelligence would be applied in battle with regular and positive effect by commanders and staffs who, sensitive to its meaning and value, possessed in the main a sufficiency of men and *matériel*. The story is not an idyll: there would be faults and failures. But the years without victory were ending, and in the autumn of 1942 Churchill's 'hinge of fate' truly began to turn. Nevertheless the new men, like the old, would still walk within the broad and inescapable shadow cast by Churchill himself.

7   Mr Churchill's Secret Source

'Royalty and Prime Ministers must never be taken by surprise.'

Admiral Sir Hugh Sinclair, Menzies' predecessor as 'C'

Churchill had a way of demanding imperiously, 'Where are my eggs?' – by which he meant his latest box of Ultra intercepts. For when he described the people at Bletchley Park as 'the geese who laid the golden eggs but never cackled', he was referring to their product of secret intelligence not simply as an invaluable means of waging the war, but as something that was intensely precious to him because of its personal significance. For the Prime Minister Ultra was indeed pure gold.

It captured his romantic imagination. The magic and the mystery had an irresistible appeal for the schoolboy lurking inside a great man. The Wizard War – such were the terms in which Churchill thought and talked about the secret background to the battle against Germany: the electronics of the bomber offensive, Gee, Oboe, H_2S; the scientific attack on the menace from rockets and flying bombs; the alchemy at Bletchley Park which laid on his desk each morning the golden deposit of Ultra. Much of his strength as a war leader derived from this very habit of myth-making, of surrounding even the ordinary and the hum-drum with enchantment. Like Shakespeare's Glendower, he could 'call spirits from the vasty deep' – and the British believed in them. For a man with this temperament Ultra had an intrinsic fascination that Roosevelt never felt about Magic.

The intercepts also strengthened his personal position. His two great analogues, Hitler and Stalin, both impressed their authority on their subordinates by their uncanny mastery of detail, their knowledge of the technicalities and potentialities of new weapons, their grasp of the strength and locations of particular units, and so on. Churchill did the same, almost oppressively and often infuriatingly, because a fly-paper memory combined with a passionate addiction to the *minutiae* of military affairs. But Ultra helped him

183

with know-how. Down the line from Bletchley came this extraordinary facility to place himself inside his enemy's mind – to read his operation orders, to study his manoeuvres in battle almost as they took place or even before they happened, to learn in advance about his weapon development, to observe the rise and fall in the status of his commanders. It is a great advantage for a warlord, in council with his military and political advisers, to be evidently the possessor of inside information.

But at this point analogies cease. Hitler's direction of the war was notoriously furtive, wilful and incalculable: his High Command was not an open society. Stalin's mode of operating was even more centralized and authoritarian –and never more so than over intelligence. In the best of books on the Russian campaigns, *The Road to Stalingrad*, Professor John Erickson observed that 'the stream of information which flowed in from a multitude of sources Stalin could dam, divert or choke as he pleased; what he wished hidden, he could and did, in the phrase of present Soviet criticism, "wall up in a safe".' This was impossible in Churchill's régime. The only major secret he walled up for long was that of progress in atomic research, and even this sinister and deadly knowledge was carefully but necessarily dispersed among those with 'the need to know'.

Damming, diverting, choking or walling up Ultra was impossible amid the inner circle of Churchill's administration simply because, whatever its limitations, his method of running the war was one of open covenants openly arrived at. Occasionally he may have made a private rash promise to the Generalissimo in Moscow or fixed up with the President in Washington some unacknowledged agreement. But in the main he looked his advisers in the eye: browbeating, badgering, recalcitrant, slippery, but acting in the end only after he had persuaded them or they, sometimes after Herculean efforts, had persuaded him. The occasions when Churchill moved in absolute defiance of the Chiefs of Staff are very rare. His 'secret source' of Ultra, therefore, was not a treasure he hoarded for himself, like Stalin, but relevant evidence to be used in the daily debate about how best to beat the Germans.

Once the system of distribution from Bletchley was initiated in the summer of 1940 this was in fact inevitable. There was no way that the Prime Minister could become proprietary about Ultra after channels had been opened from Hut 3 to the Chiefs of Staff, the Joint Intelligence Committee, the Commanders-in-Chief at home and abroad. The list of recipients may have been restricted – even when the Americans came in it perhaps did not reach four figures – but however carefully it may have been controlled, there were always too many in the picture for Churchill to play a private game. We now know enough about his handling of the war to be sure that, in any case, such deviousness was not in his nature. His 'eggs' were used for the service of the state.

The war brought him many individual examples of Ultra which were impressive and dramatic in the quality of their intelligence. But what mattered also was the sheer quantity of the intercepts he received. Sometimes broken and sometimes thin, the chain of communication from Bletchley nevertheless continued from his earliest days in office until the final victory. He had hardly become Prime Minister before, on the afternoon of 15 May 1940, he flew to Paris for the meeting, so vividly described in his memoirs, at which he learned the full horror of the French collapse and observed, in the garden of the Quai d'Orsay, the bonfires of defeat with 'venerable officials pushing wheel-barrows of archives on them'. But Winterbotham was instructed from No. 10 Downing Street to send over any significant Ultra that might emerge during Churchill's visit. From then until the Allies successfully completed their Normandy landings during the summer of 1944 his preoccupation with Ultra was constant and insistent. If, as Winterbotham has confirmed to the author, it tended to diminish during the final months, this was because he knew that the military struggle was essentially over – because his mind was now dominated by the intractable problems of peace. But while he felt that the issue was still unresolved he kept Ultra at his elbow.

Early in August 1940, as the Battle of Britain was approaching its peak, a formal routine was evolved for servicing the Prime Minister. No longer were the decrypts sent down to Broadway from Bletchley by the car of a resolute lady in the FANYs, Mrs Barclay, or, if urgent, read over the telephone. A direct teleprinter circuit was installed. Menzies deputed to Winterbotham the responsibility, which he carried to the end, of selecting and forwarding to Churchill every important Ultra message and marking it (at the Prime Minister's request) with a brief indication of its significance – what Winterbotham called 'the headlines'. The messages were then despatched in a locked box to No. 10 or to Storey's Gate after the famous underground complex of war rooms had been established.

But before despatch the box first went to Menzies, 'for information', and he himself would occasionally deliver some Ultra by hand – either because he happened to be seeing Churchill or perhaps because it did his standing no harm if he arrived with an interesting gift. The occasional sight of Menzies in this role gave some in Churchill's entourage the impression that 'C' alone conveyed the Prime Minister's private Ultra, but this was not the case. The normal flow was from Bletchley via MI6 at Broadway and on to Whitehall. The traffic was usually handled by Winterbotham – except if he was abroad, when Menzies or some specially selected officer took over.

Those who immediately surrounded Churchill – the 'Secret Circle', as he called them – had no knowledge of the precise nature of what he was receiving. None of his Private Secretaries, Colville, Martin, Rowan, Peck, was 'on the Ultra list' or aware of the character of this hidden source.[1] 'To bring someone fully into the Secret Circle', Rowan has recorded, 'was a tremendous step for Churchill to take, for once you were in you knew and saw everything except the date for military operations and the contents of the famous "yellow boxes", the most secret enemy intelligence.' Even Sir Ian Jacob, who as a Military Secretary to the War Cabinet handled Churchill's military correspondence and minuted meetings of the Chiefs of Staff, knew nothing about his master's Ultra information or, indeed, about Ultra itself.[2] Since all these men had acute minds they were fully conscious that something was going on, but it is difficult at this distance to recreate a climate of opinion in which, if you did not need to know, you scrupulously did not seek to know. General Sir Hastings Ismay knew – but 'Pug' was the Prime Minister's principal staff officer, his right-hand man and trusted confidant, his permanent link with the Chiefs of Staff. And Pug knew about Ultra anyway.

There was one other who knew: Churchill's Personal Assistant, Major Desmond Morton. Their deep friendship ran back to a meeting in 1916 on the Western Front, where Morton, an artillery officer, was shot through the heart but survived to win the Military Cross and become ADC to Lord Haig. From 1929 to 1939 he worked under the Committee of Imperial Defence as head of the Industrial Intelligence Centre, a modest cover for its true function which was 'to discover and report the plans for manufacture of armaments and war stores in foreign countries': in particular, German plans. From his secret knowledge Morton covertly fed Churchill throughout the 'thirties with statistical and technical evidence about Nazi rearmament – the facts are thoroughly documented in Martin Gilbert's official biography[3] – and so supplied his friend with a unique stock of ammunition in his lonely campaign to put government and people on the alert about Hitler. In May 1940, therefore, it was natural that Churchill, needing support in his desperate task, should have brought Desmond Morton into his Private Office along with Professor Lindemann, 'the Prof', his trusted scientific adviser, and the indispensable Brendan Bracken.

Morton's special position was defined at an early stage. Writing in his memoirs about the advice he received from the Joint Intelligence Committee in 1941 about German preparations to invade Russia, Churchill stated that 'I had not been content with this form of collective wisdom, and preferred to see the originals myself. I had arranged, therefore, as far back as the summer of 1940, for Major Desmond Morton to make a daily selection of tit-bits, which I always read, thus forming my own opinion, sometimes at much earlier dates.' *Thus forming my own opinion*: here, for Churchill, was the profit and perhaps the peril of uninhibited access to the most secret intelligence. For the 'tit-bits' included Ultra, and it was Desmond Morton who, during the first half of the war, looked after all the intercepts that streamed from Bletchley directly into the Prime Minister's office. The 1940 arrangement to which Churchill referred was his minute of 5 August to Ismay: 'I do not wish such reports as are received to be sifted and digested by the various Intelligence authorities. For the present Major Morton will inspect them for me and submit what he considers of major importance. *He is to be shown everything, and submit authentic documents to me in their original form.*'

The minute as quoted in *The Second World War* is confusing, in that it appears to apply simply to intelligence from France and other occupied countries. When he published his second volume in 1949 Churchill was of course unable to reveal the larger truth, that he was also fed regularly with Ultra at the hands of Desmond Morton. But it was so: and the best evidence comes from Morton's assistant at the time, Arthur Benson, (later Sir Arthur Benson, GCMG, Governor of Northern Rhodesia).

Now for what we called 'the flimsies'. I was introduced to them almost immediately I arrived in Morton's office in 1940. They arrived in a double-locked box, one key of which was always attached to Morton's person, and which he opened always in the presence of Miss Gwynne, whose duty it was to count them and make a note of their number and of any (British) reference number assigned to them. Morton would make two bundles of them: those the P.M. should see, and those he need not see. Often he would dictate to Miss Gwynne a minute addressed to the P.M. which he would sign and attach to the 'flimsy' referred to with a string tag. That pile, with or without minutes attached, went into a box, which Morton locked, and which Miss Gwynne then carried away out of the office ... as I thought, to the Private Secretaries' office. Now, I know not whither.

Morton's minutes were not always to the P.M. Often they were to Ismay, often to the Prof., sometimes to the Foreign Secretary, sometimes to a member of the Joint Intelligence Committee or the Joint Planning Committee, sometimes to others, Ministers or Permanent Secretaries. Only those minutes addressed to the P.M. had the flimsy attached to them. No other minute ever referred to them, and of course none was ever copied or quoted. Each had a distribution list typed at the foot, containing never more than about five names or initials, and always including 'Prime Minister – Major Morton'.

When they came back from the P.M. there were sometimes instructions to Morton, or to someone else 'through Morton', with them. The 'W.S.C.' sometimes denoted agreement with action Morton had proposed or, much more often, that the P.M. had seen an explanatory or expanding minute. Most minutes were of this kind because the daily bundle of flimsies did not relate to each other; none was filed; nor was any note made of any of them save, as I have said, for the purpose of checking that all were returned in due course whence they came. Their full import had therefore to be explained by memory or earlier messages (and by reference to other intelligence). If we were stuck Morton would get on the scrambler to C's office. C would bring or send over the earlier 'authentic documents'.[4]

It is a curious and touching sign of the meticulous security with which these secret matters were conducted that during this period Benson and his sister used to lunch together regularly every few weeks: yet not until long after the war did either realize that he had been handling Ultra for Churchill while she had been concerned with cryptanalysis. As for Desmond Morton, 'he was', Benson recalled, 'a man of great personality and charm, whose Irish ebullience and wit and tremendous drive and energy did not make other busy but more methodical people – particularly established civil

188

servants (he was not 'established' himself) – respond fondly to the pressures he put upon them. For them he was a cuckoo in the nest.' So well had his confidential work been covered that when Morton's actual role was being investigated for this book Sir John Martin and his colleagues on Churchill's secretariat were astonished to discover to what extent the cuckoo had been sitting on the golden eggs of Ultra.

After the turning-point of the war – the winter of 1942/43 – Churchill's need for Morton waned. Ultra now seeped through many branches of what had become a highly articulated politico-military system of war administration. The volume of intercepts had greatly increased. Britain was now involved in an alliance strategy, and Churchill was no longer the monolith of 1940. So Morton was side-tracked into his earlier but secondary task, liaison with the governments-in-exile in London, and he and Benson no longer processed the 'flimsies' in their inner sanctum.

But the Great Perambulator was by no means always in Whitehall. The route of Churchill's wartime journeys forms a complicated arabesque criss-crossing the western world, Russia and the Middle East. Ultra had to go with him – not at first, and not always, for the security risk was too great for him to be allowed a supply of Ultra in Moscow. But during the central phase of the war it was customary for him to be furnished on his travels with a Special Liaison Unit which, whether he was in conference at Casablanca or convalescing at Marrakesh, brought him his personal clutch of 'eggs' from Bletchley. 'Pray make the necessary arrangements' would be his habitually courteous request to Winterbotham, but these would not always be easy to put together. The Special Liaison Units, as has been seen, were a shoe-string force: there were never adequate trained reserves, and much hard work and improvisation could be demanded from the chosen few to keep the Prime Minister *au courant* with his Ultra.

In the eyes of the Chiefs of Staff and Churchill's other senior advisers his access to Ultra on his journeyings was not so much troublesome as menacing. As a general principle, they disapproved at all times of his personal link with Bletchley, preferring, as orthodox staff officers would, that the commander should receive his intelligence through proper channels after it had been studied by trained minds and correlated with the other main sources of information. But Churchill abroad raised particular problems.

189

They were not so great at the summit conferences – Casablanca, Teheran (where Ultra was on tap all the time) – for here the Prime Minister was supported by a posse of advisers from all the services. But sometimes he was almost alone or, at least, not accompanied by many of his most authoritative officers. For the Chiefs of Staff the nightmare at these times was precisely that Churchill might start doing what he himself said Ultra allowed him to do: he might start *forming his own opinion*.

The inherent dangers are illustrated by a remarkable episode that occured on the day of Operation Valkyrie, 20 July 1944, when Hitler's rule and indeed his life were in the balance. Churchill was in Normandy at the headquarters of General Montgomery, who with his chief intelligence officer, Bill Williams, had already received some early intimations of the plot against the Führer. An Ultra box was brought in for the Prime Minister, who proceeded to ferret among the papers with devouring enthusiasm. Williams beside him could pick out some of the names on the intercepts, Fromm, Witzleben. 'Good God,' he cried, 'they've got the Home Army.' For his informed mind could see the significance. General Fromm, the commander of the Home Army in Germany, was replaced by von Stauffenberg immediately after his attempt at blowing up Hitler. (Though Fromm executed von Stauffenberg a few hours later, after the plot's failure, it did him no good, for he himself had known about it, as the Gestapo was aware, and Fromm also was eliminated.) As for the doomed Witzleben, his disapproval of Hitler had made him Commander-in-Chief designate of the German armed forces in the new administration for the Reich which the plotters intended to establish. The implications of such names in the Ultra signal were immediately evident to Williams. But what vividly and permanently impressed itself on his mind at this unique moment was the fact that Churchill had not the least idea of what was going on.[5]

There was no reason why he should. The *Wehrmacht* contained several hundred officers of high seniority and it was not the function of the British Prime Minister to be aware of the personalities and attitudes of each of them. What was mandatory, as the Chiefs of Staff rightly saw, was that when intelligence of such importance came Churchill's way through Ultra – if it *had* to come direct, and not through proper channels – he should have competent advice available to enable him to evaluate it correctly. But he had been 'forming his own opinions' for too many decades, a delicious ingrained habit which even Alan Brooke, Cunningham and Portal would never eradicate. So there was a genuine danger. Yet on balance it is probably true to say that Churchill's access to Ultra, even when he was furthest from his guardian staffs, may have occasionally warped his opinions (through misinterpreting the evidence) but rarely had an outcome in ill-judged actions. When he acted, he did so through the closely knit system of his administration, which provided many checks and balances.

Indeed, the knowledge now available of Churchill's constant access to the Germans' most secret signals makes it possible to review certain of his actions which, in the past, have been persistently criticised as ill-judged. The classic area of criticism relates to his 'bullying the generals': in particular, to the urgency with which he sought to drive both Wavell and Auchinleck into offensive operations against their will, and to the merciless speed with which each of these notable commanders was finally removed from his post.

Churchill's urgency about operations in the African desert was, of course, strategic. He wanted to re-open the Mediterranean, take Italy out of the war, entice Turkey into it, and restore the Suez Canal as a route to the Far East. But in his passion to defeat Rommel he took the measure of the Afrika Korps's commander too optimistically. As has been seen in the previous chapter, a steady flow of Ultra intercepts reached his desk in Whitehall which seemed to demonstrate that Rommel was almost permanently at the end of his tether – screams for more tanks, more fuel, more men, more aircraft: abuse of Italian incompetence: demands for better protection for the Mediterranean convoys. Churchill did not understand that Rommel was as unscrupulous as Patton: that he was always prepared to drive his tanks forward until they ran out of petrol on the assumption that when he howled for help 'they' would be compelled to take notice. All the same, Rommel was perpetually short of everything except skill, and though his signals were sometimes overstatements they revealed a true deficiency.

At the same time Churchill was proudly and painfully conscious of the precious men and equipment he himself, often at great risk, had sent out to the Middle East. A man who always looked at figures and quantities rather than quality, how could he not ask why his generals, apparently so amply provided, were unable to get on quickly with the job of defeating this starved hysterical German? It

191

is true that Wavell, obsessively silent and Sphinx-like, never achieved a *rapport* with his Prime Minister: and that Auchinleck, who could have done so with an overlord who deeply respected him, let it go by default. But beneath these personal factors ran this other current – the effect of Ultra on Churchill's mind. It is now impossible to doubt that the picture of Rommel's knife-edge condition, persistently renewed by the Ultra intercepts of his demands for reinforcement, had a decisive effect on Churchill's attitude towards his desert commanders before the arrival of Alexander and Montgomery. Moreover, the Chiefs of Staff themselves accepted and endorsed the removal first of Wavell and then of Auchinleck. For them too Ultra built up pictures of an Afrika Korps living on a shoestring, and they too, surely, must have felt that their desert generals should have dealt more drastically with an enemy so evidently weak. The stunning effect of the loss of Benghazi or the fall of Tobruk must be measured against the knowledge, in London, that Rommel's campaigns were one long victory over stinting and shortages.

But it was in the higher conduct of the war that Ultra brought Churchill the greatest support. Until the winter of 1942, when Eisenhower commanded the invasion of north-west Africa and, for the first time, an allied enterprise was American-dominated, Churchill's role was central and decisive because the British carried the burden. And even thereafter, as American and Russian power was asserted, the Prime Minister fought undaunted to retain for his country a position of acknowledged influence in the council-chamber. From start to finish, in fact, Churchill was concerned with the war in its totality.

At this pinnacle of policy-making and decision Ultra gave him advantages denied to both his allies and his enemy. In Chapter Nine it will be seen that in Washington Ultra information about the German/Italian war was studied systematically up to the level of the American Joint Chiefs of Staff, but none could maintain that Roosevelt himself enjoyed or desired that close, intimate, daily acquaintance with the signals that was part of Churchill's wartime way of life. General appreciations of the situation on the Russian front, based on Ultra but with the source cautiously disguised, were occasionally forwarded to Stalin personally through the British Ambassador, but how much that cynical and suspicious mind believed in such cosmetic documents may well be doubted. In any case, Stalin's supply of such information, with the validity of its source necessarily excluded, bears no relation to Churchill's: there was no Desmond Morton in the Kremlin busily annotating a daily flow from Bletchley. In Hitler's case there was nothing comparable. Whatever their local successes, none of the German intelligence organizations contrived to provide him with that detailed, universal picture of his opponents' intentions and actions that Ultra furnished for Churchill.* To take a single instance: a Führer and his High Command, so equipped, could never have swallowed with such avidity the massive deception schemes elaborated by 'A' Force in the Mediterranean and by all those who orchestrated the cover plan for the landings in Normandy.

But the one outstanding example of Ultra's value to Churchill in his higher direction of the war is also, unfortunately, the classic case of first-rate intelligence being rejected by a man who has already composed the wrong scenario. The example, of course, is the Prime Minister's warning to Stalin on the eve of Barbarossa that Hitler was about to invade Russia. It is sometimes said that Stalin received warnings from at least seventy different sources and spurned them all. One, certainly, came from Washington. But no other warnings were based on knowledge so exquisitely exact as that accumulated by the British over many weeks, in the main through Ultra, about the build-up of German forces in the east and the manifest preparations for a massive assault across the Soviet frontiers. The evidence presented in Chapter Three demonstrates the scale and accuracy of this intelligence. It was not Churchill's fault that Stalin at this critical time was blinded by a folly whose character has still not been fully explained. What mattered, from the point of view of Britain's Prime Minister in 1941, was that Russia should not be easily over-run by a German military machine still intact: the obvious possibility being that with Russia eliminated Hitler could turn westwards and seriously attempt to cross the Channel. At least to warn Stalin was thus vital: and it was Ultra, after all, that gave Churchill the knowledge and the authority to make the warning unqualified.

---

*Apart from the efficient naval intercept service, B. Dienst, the Germans never established a system of signals intelligence remotely comparable with Bletchley Park. In any case the *Abwehr*, from Admiral Canaris downwards, was a nest for members of the anti-Hitler opposition.

Knowledge and authority: it is perhaps these two, above all the gifts from Bletchley, that mattered most to Churchill in his supreme capacity as warlord – the man in whom the highest political and military responsibilities are united. To know meant that as Minister of Defence he could deal with his Chiefs of Staff and his commanders on level terms. They could never bamboozle him, as all staffs are prone to do, with an assumption of superior information about the enemy. But knowledge also gave him the authority he needed in his capacity as a statesman. It will be evident, for example, from the chapter on the Battle of Britain that Churchill's extraordinary delicate and devious diplomacy in 1940, during his inter-changes with Roosevelt, becomes instantly more intelligible when one relates it to the picture provided by Ultra of German capability in the air and the curious muddle that constituted the preparations for Sealion, the cross-Channel invasion. The mixture of long-term confidence and short-term concern, but above all the basic faith that the corner would be turned into 1941 and relative safety, were feelings which perhaps Churchill had to expose to Roosevelt in any case, if the American connection was to be preserved. But we can now see that they were justified: not justified with hindsight, but by the authority and the insights so fortunately made available, at the time, by Mr Churchill's secret source.

8   Ultramarine

'And they went to sea in a sieve.'
EDWARD LEAR, *The Jumblies*

The navies of both sides leaked badly. Nevertheless, the seepage of intelligence from one to the other differs critically in its quantity, its quality and its duration. Broadly speaking, during the earlier stages of the war the Germans' mastery of the Royal Navy's signal traffic, though partial, was enough to produce dramatic but not decisive results. From 1941 onwards, however, with a varying but increasing tempo the British through Ultra penetrated the wide range of German naval ciphers so successfully that it was not they, but their opponents, who finally suggest the image of a perpetually leaking sieve.

At first Bletchley was a silent aid for the Silent Service. Until the spring of 1940, as has been seen, no Enigma ciphers of any description were being broken, and even after the cryptanalysts' victory in April it turned out that for many months the really vulnerable cipher was the Luftwaffe's. All the Germans' early ventures at sea – the sorties of *Graf Spee* and *Deutschland*, the raid in northern waters by *Scharnhorst* and *Gneisenau* in the winter of 1939, even the operations of the German fleet during the invasion of Norway – occurred without those accurate warnings from Station X which in later years became habitual. Frank Birch, who had worked in Room 40 during the First World War and had joined Bletchley at the outbreak of the Second, must have felt a certain nostalgia when it appeared that the best BP could do was to offer tentative hunches based on 'traffic analysis' – that is to say, assessment of the volume, the character and perhaps the point of origin of German naval signals without the ability to decipher their actual contents. Room 40 was more advanced than this in 1917.

Ironically, it was the reputation of Room 40 itself that had caused the Germans during the thirties to organize their own equivalent, the *Beobachter Dienst* or Observation Service: B Dienst. The British assisted. For too long that element of conservation in the Admiralty which could be so fatal restricted the Navy to an out-moded system of hand-ciphering, even though the technically-minded

Lord Mountbatten, who had been Fleet Wireless Officer in the Mediterranean, wisely pressed for a machine cipher. Moreover, during Mussolini's Abyssinian campaign and perhaps during the Spanish Civil War British vessels on active duty used these ciphers so ineptly that B Dienst cracked them comfortably. Commander Heinz Bonatz, at the head of the B Service, had in fact been studying the Royal Navy's signal traffic for years, and by 1939 had produced a document entitled 'The System of British Wireless Communications'. The Germans thus held a commanding lead. During the Norwegian campaigns and at other critical stages of the early war at sea it was not Ultra but B Dienst that dominated. And later, when the great Atlantic convoys began their death-ride, the penetration by the Germans of the British and Allied Merchant Ship Code, the BAMS code, would have a prolonged lethal effect. The Admiralty's other ciphers were fortunately rendered secure by the autumn of 1940. B Dienst's exploitation of the BAMS code, however, generously supplied the U-boats with abundant prey until the summer of 1943. The Silent Service has never been more tight-lipped than about the reasons for this terrible lapse.

By a curious coincidence, the first major victory at sea for which Bletchley was responsible struck a blow at the Germans through an Italian defeat. In March 1941 the passage of convoys from Africa to Greece, carrying the British expeditionary force, naturally caused the Germans concern, and great pressure was brought to bear on the Italian Navy to make a powerful intervention. A decision was reluctantly taken to risk a fleet operation. Such is the origin of the battle of Matapan.

But even before Admiral Iachino's fleet moved to its stations Bletchley had been able to give the Commander-in-Chief in the Mediterranean, Admiral Cunningham, a complete picture of the Italians' intentions. The little team in Dillwyn Knox's section, ISK, had already penetrated the Italian naval cipher and by 25 March a signal containing Iachino's plans had been intercepted, deciphered and passed to Cunningham at his headquarters in Alexandria. Foreknowledge was essential, for if the Italians were to be taken by surprise Cunningham had to lead his battlefleet from harbour without alerting Alexandria's substantial population of enemy agents. To do this, to keep his convoys running in an apparently normal manner though he knew the Italian fleet was out, and to work his own warships into a favourable position westwards of Crete was a

196

delicate contrivance in which Bletchley's forewarning proved vital. There had been plenty of other indications – the increased scale of Axis air reconnaissance, for example, – but these could only form the basis for a guess. Thanks to Bletchley, Cunningham knew.

The Admiral decided to lead the fleet to sea in *Warspite* after dark on 27 March. His memoirs[1] give an inimitable account of his cover plan: of how, that afternoon, he went ashore with a suitcase as if intending to stay the night, and spent some hours on the golf course within the vision of a known transmitter of information about naval movements, the Japanese consul at Alexandria. 'He was unmistakable, indeed a remarkable sight, short and squat, with a southern aspect of such vast and elephantine proportions when he bent over to putt that the irreverent Chief of Staff had nicknamed him "the blunt end of the Axis".' Every ruse worked. So complete was the surprise that at 10.30 pm on the 28th appalled sailors on the cruisers *Zara* and *Fiume* (their guns still trained fore and aft) found themselves being fired on, in the darkness, by British battleships at a point-blank range of 3000 yards. Three cruisers and two destroyers for the loss of one aircraft was Cunningham's final bag at Matapan.

His victory had many important consequences. Bletchley had made its first undeniable contribution to a major success at sea.* Because of the need to work in compartments few at Station X could know about what had happened, but in the ISK section there was a sense of solid achievement after the intellectual effort of breaking the Italian cipher. Knox even wrote a poem to celebrate the event, beginning 'When Cunningham won the battle of Matapan' and mentioning the names of those in his team who had contributed. One who took a main part, Mavis Batey, remembered that when Cunningham himself came down to Bletchley in due course to thank them he was particularly eager to see the original text of the intercept on which his victory had depended.

There was a more practical consequence. The only enemy battle-fleet in the Mediterranean had been out-manoeuvred, overwhelmed and routed. For the Germans the result was that during all the complicated maritime movements carried out by the British in

---

*The most consistently successful and respected unit of the Italian navy was the 10th Flotilla, based at La Spezia, of 'human torpedoes' whose record against the British Mediterranean Fleet was exemplary. Significantly, its commander, Prince Borghese, flatly refused to allow any signals to be sent to his flotilla by radio.

connection with the battles for Greece and Crete, and the subsequent evacuations, they had to rely mainly on their own Luftwaffe rather than on the still powerful navy of their ally. Since Cunningham's resources during this hectic period were stretched to the uttermost limit, a determined effort by the Italians might have been catastrophic. Instead, the enemy's heavy ships now preferred to stay in harbour. All risk of their interfering with the troop-convoys from Africa to Greece was eliminated: and in April Cunningham's battleships could sail from Alexandria, bombard the distant port of Tripoli, and return unscathed to the eastern Mediterranean. The psychological effect of Matapan was immense.

Indeed, that effect went even deeper and lasted even longer. Knowing their own natures, and aware of the apathy or even hostility that many felt about the war, the Italian High Command was continually distracted by the idea of 'a traitor in our midst'. It is a notion that drifts through the diaries of the cynical Count Ciano: one oft-quoted passage is an instance when he refers to 'Rommel, who, according to British sources, has telegraphed accusing several of our own officers of having revealed some of his future plans to the enemy. As always, victory finds a hundred fathers, but defeat is an orphan.' The entry is for 9 September 1942. The previous day Rommel's headquarters had signalled to the German representative in Rome, General Enno von Rintelen, to protest that British prisoners had stated that a captured Italian officer had betrayed the Field Marshal's plans for the battle of Alam Halfa which opened on 31 August. Subsequently the Italians demanded and obtained an apology from Hitler.

But German suspicions were as real and as frequent as Italian self-doubt. The unreliability of his allies is a constant theme in Rommel's papers. Once, just before his surprise counter-attack into Cyrenaica in January 1942, he put the matter plainly in his diary. 'I had maintained secrecy.... We knew from experience that Italian Headquarters cannot keep things to themselves and that everything they wireless to Rome gets to British ears.' In a letter to his wife a few weeks before Alamein he actually attributed to the Italians the fact that his poor health was known to the British.

In fact, of course, it was known through Ultra, as were so many of the leakages which caused the Italians to fear the presence of traitors in their ranks and the Germans to be confident that they existed. When the battle of Matapan was analysed by the Axis commands it seemed evident that Cunningham had acted on advance information. The ciphers were surely cast-iron. Where then was the traitor? Matapan was, in fact, the first of a long series of episodes in which German distrust of their allies, and the Italians' combination of a sense of guilt with a sense of outrage against their accusers, were sustained and intensified by Bletchley's penetration of their secrets. Ultra was not planned as an instrument of psychological warfare, but in the Mediterranean this was its happy effect.

The case-history of Matapan shows, in fact, that its influence on the Italian national consciousness lasted long after 1941. In 1962 Dr Montgomery Hyde published *The Quiet Canadian*, a biography of Sir William Stephenson in whose transatlantic British Security Co-ordination Hyde himself had served during the war. And so had a seductive spy known as Cynthia, whom Hyde described as having obtained by her arts, during the winter of 1940–1, a copy of the Italian naval cipher from the Naval Attaché in Washington, Admiral Alberto Lais. The movement of Iachino's fleet, Hyde wrote, 'was correctly anticipated with the aid of the ciphers, and resulted in a resounding British naval victory off Cape Matapan. . . .' Some years later the book was translated and published in Italy with an introduction by Antonino Trizzino, already the author of a controversial work called *Navi e Poltrone*. In 1967 an action in the courts followed, brought against Hyde, Trizzino and their publisher by Mauro Lais to clear the name of his kinsman the Admiral – who was now dead. (Such an action on behalf of the dead is viable in Italian law.) The whole story of Matapan was ventilated in court and Lais succeeded, before the first panel of judges. In 1968 an appeal was lodged. The battle was fought again, but the honour of Lais was upheld. Nevertheless, the effects of a cryptanalytical coup by Dillwyn Knox's little section at Bletchley over a quarter of a century ago were still being felt.

The actions, ironically, had been contested some years too soon. In 1974 *The Ultra Secret* appeared. Here at last was a perfect answer for the Italian establishment to all those imputations of treachery. Their ciphers were the real traitors! When an Italian edition of Group Captain Winterbotham's book was commissioned, it was agreed, with good sense, that additional material of special interest in Italy should be prepared by Dr Giulio Divita, a distinguished scientist and Fellow of Clare College, Cambridge, who had an informed knowledge of the Mediterranean war. Divita assembled material which rightly demonstrated that Ultra was not the *only* means whereby the British obtained intelligence about the Italians. To his astonishment, however, he discovered in 1976 that under 'certain pressures' the publishers were now insisting on issuing merely a translation of Winterbotham's original text. Indeed, Vice-Admiral Fadda, the head of the Italian Navy's publications department, had written to them vetoing the inclusion of any of Divita's additional matter. The reason was simple. For Matapan, for the sunken convoys, for the defeats in the desert, for German sneers and for the critics in their own country the Italian authorities had found in Ultra the complete explanation. They did not wish its perfection to be blurred by the publication of any alternative possibilities.[2]

Until Matapan the Royal Navy had not fought a fleet action since Jutland in 1916, or a major engagement in the Mediterranean since Nelson won the battle of the Nile in 1798. Its impact at the time, however, was insignificant compared with that produced two months later by the sinking at 10.36 am on 27 May of a single ship: the battleship *Bismarck*. The cliche 'vital' has lost its value, yet this is a relevant adjective for the British success. In 1941 the consequences for their Atlantic convoys, had this fast and powerful vessel been free to rampage over the high seas, are unimaginable.

The high drama of *Bismarck*'s last voyage is well known – the break-out from the North Sea, the trauma of *Hood*'s annihilation, the surveillance and then the loss of *Bismarck* by the radars of the British cruisers, the agonizing hours when all contact failed, the summoning of ships and aircraft from every quarter of the compass, and the final act in the hunt when *Bismarck*, at last marked down, received her *coup de grâce* from *Rodney*, *King George V* and *Dorsetshire*, to sink on 27 May with her flag still flying.

In that month of May, and for many years afterwards, there were those who felt that Ultra had made a contribution which was even thought to have been decisive. At Bletchley this view was widespread. Some who joined about this time actually identify the date by their recollections of the prevailing excitement over *Bismarck*. Members of Hut 6 like Stuart Milner-Barry are specific about signals decrypted. Keith Batey, for example, still carries in his memory a message 'to the Military Commander Athens', which gave a position for the battleship. These impressions mainly relate to the period in the hunt for *Bismarck* when contact was lost, and there was a terrible uncertainty about whether the battleship would carry on into the Atlantic as a raider, or break southwards for safety in a French harbour like Brest or St Nazaire.

Group Captain Winterbotham's recollections are even more vivid than his book suggests. To the author he has described how in his office at Broadway a signal came through revealing that *Bismarck* was indeed aiming for Brest and that all possible naval and Luftwaffe assistance was being organized for her protection. He remembers discussing the implications of this signal with his opposite number, the naval intelligence officer at MI6, and speculating with him whether, for example, the British ships beating northwards from Gibraltar would be able to arrive in time. And yet, on investigation, it proves difficult to pin-point any moment when Ultra could in fact have affected the issue. This is certainly the considered opinion of Admiral Sir Norman Denning and Patrick Beesly, who were on duty in the Admiralty's Operational Intelligence Centre during the battle, took note of all the incoming information and observed from hour to hour the many dispositions of ships and aircraft that in the end brought *Bismarck* to bay. A reconciliation is necessary between appearance and reality.

Certainly Station X was not excluded. As soon as it was known, on 21 May, that *Bismarck* had slipped from Germany to a Norwegian anchorage Denning himself and another officer from OIC, Commander Peter Kemp, were despatched to Bletchley, where they emphasized to all concerned the urgent need for intelligence about *Bismarck*'s mission. But communications to and from the German force were being transmitted for the first time in Neptun, the operational cipher employed on rare occasions for ventures by the enemy's big ships. Neptun was beyond Bletchley's immediate capability. The hard fact is that throughout the whole drama no signal to or from *Bismarck* was ever deciphered in time. Yet how consoling it would have been for the tortured Churchill, for the Admiralty and for the Home Fleet had the cryptanalysts been able to produce instant results! For the naval files among the Ultra documents now in the Public Record Office bring the whole story to life in decrypts of the dramatic messages that passed between the hunted *Bismarck* and the shore.

At 2022 on 24 May the German Navy's HQ in France, Group West, flashes to the Fleet: 'Admiralty has announced the loss of

201

Hood. Vice-Admiral Holland on board.' Then, in the darkness around midnight, Captain Lütjens on *Bismarck* signals 'Attacked by planes from aircraft carrier. Hit by torpedo.' As *Bismarck* makes south during the 25th signals from Group West reveal a devouring activity to prepare for her arrival in a French port. At 1925 Group West radios the dispositions of fighters, U-boats and destroyers to cover an arrival by *Bismarck* at Brest or La Pallice. In the early hours of the 26th a long message reports arrangements at St Nazaire – dredging, anti-torpedo protection, readying of pilots and dockyards. By the evening of the 26th, after the great ship's mortal wound,* the radio at U-boat Command signals to all Biscay U-boats, 'Task is protection of *Bismarck* whose steering gear is at present out of action.' For so it is: at 2143 Lütjens has reported 'Am surrounded by *Renown* and light forces' and almost simultaneously, to the Navy's High Command, 'Urgent. Ship unmanoeuvrable. We shall fight to the last shell. Long live the Führer.' (By a curious slip, the original teleprint of the translation to the Operational Intelligence Centre read 'Long *love* the Führer.') Then comes the last, loyal signal to Hitler, to be followed, as the terrible hours of waiting pass, by a sighting report at 1930 on the 27th from U-boat 74 to U-boat Command. 'At 1930 in square BE 6142. Three survivors from *Bismarck*. From their account she appears to have sunk in square BE 5330 at about 1000.'

All these eloquent signals, and the others transmitted throughout the long drama, may now be studied in the up-to-date out-station of the Public Record Office beside the Thames at Kew exactly as they were teleprinted at the time, deciphered and translated, from Bletchley to the Admiralty. *Bismarck* was of course sunk in the end – with a large element of luck, for those jammed rudders were an unpredictable stroke of good fortune. But had Bletchley possessed sufficient experience of the German naval ciphers to be able to process the intercepts swiftly, they would have immediately revealed to the Admiralty the battleship's actual course and destination. Much anxiety would have been prevented and *Bismarck*'s destruction, in which chance played a large part, would have been ensured with certainty. Instead, there were delays at Station X and

---

*At about 2100 on 26 May, after contact with *Bismarck* had been regained, the torpedo from a Swordfish aircraft launched from the carrier *Ark Royal* jammed the battleship's rudders and wrecked her steering gear. From that moment the sinking that followed next morning was inevitable.

the decrypts were passed on to the Navy too late. Many hours too late, so that when they arrived they were not tools for action but already historic records. *Bismarck* had sailed during a critical phase when Bletchley was attaining, but had not yet fully acquired, the ability to process German naval ciphers at speed. Yet in a fast-developing action like this a delay of forty-eight hours in decrypting was as dangerous as a delay of forty-eight years.

Of the two decrypts that were produced at BP with greater speed the first is sometimes known as 'the diplomatic signal'. It was sent to Athens, apparently in the Red Luftwaffe cipher which Bletchley could read, in response to a query raised by a senior personality there whose nephew was aboard *Bismarck*. (The battleship carried a number of young cadets: their tragedy is not diminished by the memory that when German torpedoes sank the antiquated cruisers *Cressy*, *Hogue* and *Aboukir* off the Dutch coast on 22 September 1914 a considerable number of ex-Dartmouth cadets went down with them.) This was the message recalled by Keith Batey. But there was also some delay in deciphering this signal at Bletchley, because of errors in the original version which had to be repeated by the German transmitter. The text did not reach the Admiralty until the early evening of 25 May. By then the British fleet had already been re-orientated on the assumption (reached without Ultra) that *Bismarck* was seeking harbour in France. The same considerations of timing apply to the decrypt of the signal relating to air and naval protection for the battleship as she approached Brest.

On receipt of the 'diplomatic signal' the Admiralty did indeed broadcast a confirmation that *Bismarck* was making for western France. But this occurred at 7.24 pm and already, at 6.10 pm, Admiral Tovey had finally decided on the battleship's objective and adjusted the course of his pursuing Home Fleet to intercept the battleship before she could reach France.[3] He was still, however, 150 miles astern. How could *Bismarck* be halted before she was covered by the Luftwaffe's umbrella? We now know that at 10.30 am the next morning, the 26th, a patrolling Catalina spotted her, enabling the strike of Swordfish armed with torpedoes to attack and jam her rudders, a disaster that led to her death. The precise briefing of that Catalina would be valuable evidence. The aircraft was on an extra patrol proposed by the Commander-in-Chief, Coastal Command. Was Sir Frederic Bowhill influenced by the Bletchley intercepts in determining the Catalina's area of search? As the Admiralty and the Home Fleet had been directing their attention since the previous evening on the approaches to Brest, this seems unlikely.

If such is the correct scenario the contemporary impressions at Bletchley, Winterbotham's personal experience and all subsequent memories fall into place. Something certainly happened there: signals were undoubtedly deciphered. But even the Naval Section at BP, close though its connection was with OIC and the Admiralty, could not have known every shift in the rapidly changing pattern of moves and counter-moves. The Bletchley people were naturally excited by their decrypts. Then, suddenly, they heard that the vanished battleship had been found and sunk. Inevitably they put the two facts together and imagined a victory for Station X. If the truth seems to be an anticlimax, it is a reminder of a law which was often to be demonstrated on the battlefield, that for operational purposes Ultra could lose much of its value if its intelligence failed to be delivered in time.

By a coincidence that law was immediately fulfilled – yet not by chance. During the first half of 1941 the Navy made a determined effort to 'pinch' from German vessels at sea any documents or equipment that might help the cryptanalysts at Bletchley to achieve a breakthrough. On 23 February came the raid on the Lofoten Islands, when a boarding-party acquired from the abandoned trawler *Krebs* a set of spare rotors for its Enigma, though the machine itself had been safely jettisoned. Direction-finding later identified the presence of two other trawlers in the Iceland area, *München* and *Lauenberg*, which were transmitting regular weather reports. On 7 May the first of these craft and on 25 June the second were seized by carefully planned manoeuvres and boarded by technical experts, who were in time to grab invaluable documents but, once again, no machine. One of the most pathetic Ultra signals in the naval files in the Public Record Office was transmitted by *München*. It just reads: 'Am being pursued'. One feels for the tiny vessel in the chill Icelandic waters as the crew watch an impressive British cruiser, all speed and guns, bearing down on her.

The critical event, however, had already occurred. On 8 May U-boat 110, commander Julius Lemp, attacked a convoy. By a remarkable effort the convoy's escort commander, Captain Baker Cresswell, successfully counter-attacked and organized a boarding-party which recovered intact her Enigma with all its precious papers. The circumstances of this 'pinch' were so fraught with the possibility of failure, and its consequences so crucial, that this was one of those exceptional occasions when history holds its breath.

U 110 attacked the outward-bound convoy OB 318 at a point south of Greenland. The counter-attack by Baker Cresswell with his destroyer *Bulldog* drove the U-boat to the surface. Kapitän Leutnant Julius Lemp had a fine record in the U-boat war, but now – against all probability – he committed a double error. He gave the order to abandon ship, having set the proper explosive charges: but the detonators failed to work, the U-boat remained afloat, and he had broken the rigid rule of the German – and indeed the British – Navy by leaving aboard all his marked charts, his codebooks, his cipher documents – and his Enigma. It is thought that when he realized what had happened Lemp committed suicide by allowing himself to drown.

Bulldog hove to about a hundred yards from U 110ʼand launched a boarding-party which, in a whaler rowed by five sailors, lurched over the difficult northern seas. In charge was a twenty-year-old Sub-Lieutenant, a regular officer of the Royal Navy called David Balme. Only once before had he been involved in a boarding operation, and that was before the war, in the calm waters of the eastern Mediterranean, against one of the ships carrying illegal immigrants to Palestine. His first problem now was merely to get aboard: it is not easy to bring a row-boat alongside a bulbous submarine amid ice-cold waves off Greenland. Somehow the whaler was eased on to the curve of the craft, and Balme set off alone, revolver in hand, along the U-boat's wet and slippery spine. As he clambered down the conning-tower's ladder the atmosphere inside the deserted U-boat was eerie. On shipboard there is usually sound: at the least, a background of steady humming from the generators. But as Balme got down into the periscope control-chamber, the heart of the vessel, there was total silence: silence and a darkness fitfully broken by the blue lamps of the U-boat's emergency lighting. Only from the outside could sounds be heard – the explosions of depth-charges as the convoy's escort drove off further U-boat attacks. These, too, increased the tension, for Balme could never be sure that the shock-waves from these explosions would not detonate the destructive charges inside U 110. Nevertheless he explored inside the hull and found the shelves of codebooks, while a signaller entered the communications compartment and unscrewed what was obviously a cipher machine.

History must now have been breathing very slowly indeed, for the next step was to form a human chain up the conning-tower ladder and along the deck of the U-boat to the whaler. By this chain the documents and the Enigma were passed from hand to hand – with the strong possibility that any or all of them might have been dropped into the sea had a sailor slipped or a sudden large wave broken over the wallowing U-boat. Instead, after three or four hours of ferrying between *Bulldog* and U 110 all the cipher material, charts and many other pieces of equipment were safely transferred.

After being taken in tow U 110 – perhaps fortunately – sank, and *Bulldog*, having first made for Iceland and collected a load of prisoners, returned rapidly to Scapa Flow. Immense pains were taken to ensure that the prisoners saw no evidence of a 'pinch': thanks to this precaution, wireless security and the disappearance of U 110, Dönitz and his staff never, in fact, had any suspicion about what had happened.* When *Bulldog* reached Scotland (having sent to the Admiralty a cautiously non-committal signal about her success) she was joined by Lieutenant Allan Bacon, R.N.V.R, who worked in special liaison between the Naval Section at Bletchley and the Operational Intelligence Centre. (On 25 June he would take part in the 'pinch' of *Lauenberg*.) Bacon spent many hours examining the captured papers in the captain's cabin of *Bulldog*. His verdict: 'This is what we have been looking for.' Every page was carefully photographed – the risk of losing the originals in air-transit to London being too great. And then, finally, the intact treasure-trove arrived at Bletchley. Later in the year Sub-Lieutenant Balme, RN, received from the King a well-deserved Distinguished Service Cross.[4]

Here was the breakthrough. When a U-boat sailed on operations it carried the daily settings for its Enigma to cover the period of its cruise – normally about three months. The settings acquired from U 110 were valid up to the end of June. With the complementary material from *Krebs*, *München* and *Lauenberg*, an actual U-boat Enigma and the current settings for seven or eight weeks the Naval Section at Bletchley was in clover. With great speed the cryptanalysts in Hut 8 now penetrated Hydra, which in 1941 was the general-purpose cipher used for ships in the North Sea and the

---

*While the 'pinch' was taking place convoy OB 318 had sailed on and out of sight, thus removing many potentially awkward eye-witnesses.

Baltic; for mine-sweepers, patrol craft etc. off the French and Norwegian coasts: and, at that time, for all U-boats. At last the sieve
was leaking. Nor did the benefits of the 'pinch' run out at the end of
June. Experience gained during those two months of working with
known settings enabled Bletchley to continue to read Hydra, with
occasional gaps, until the end of the war, as well as to penetrate in
due course the 'big ship' cipher Neptun and the two naval ciphers
employed for the Mediterranean, Sud and Medusa. History is written in terms of Trafalgars and Jutlands, but by any standard the
seizure of U 110 should rate as a major victory at sea.

Its consequences were instantaneous. To support what was
intended to be the marauding cruise of *Bismarck* and her consort
Prinz Eugen, and to replenish U-boats, a small swarm of tankers
and supply ships had been stationed strategically over the vast area
from the North Atlantic down to the divide between West Africa
and South America. Ultra derived from Hydra now made their
elimination possible. By 23 June hunting groups of the Royal Navy
had deleted all the six tankers and the one supply ship assigned to
Bismarck, as well as two more supply ships intended to sustain
armed merchant raiders. Raiders themselves were sunk and harried
along with their suppliers, the whole operation being so successful
that Admiral Dönitz reached a distasteful conclusion. His Atlantic
U-boats could no longer be maintained by surface ships: they would
have to rely on underwater supply craft – the milchcow U-boats.
Compared with the *Bismarck* episode, and coming so soon afterwards, these quick and positive operations illustrate exactly the
practical value of the Ultra system when it was functioning at its
best.

Indeed, for the Admiralty's Submarine Tracking Room Bletchley's command over Hydra cipher shifted the U-boat war into a new
dimension. At last insight was possible into the whole life-cycle of a
U-boat. The trials of the vessel, the training of the crew, the name
of the captain and the scope of its operational cruise now became
accessible as never before. Assessments and predictions could often
be issued by the Admiralty with an assurance based on indisputable
evidence. Months, indeed years had to pass before the Tracking
Room could claim, with justice, to know more about the U-boats'
deployment than Admiral Dönitz's own staff, but the summer of
1941 is the point at which Bletchley moved this process from the
realm of guess-work into that of increasing authority.

The movement is graphically revealed in the series of Ultra signals issued by the Naval Section at Bletchley during 1941, which are now in the Public Record Office. Between February and May the decrypts are few, unrelated and behindhand.[5] Comparison of the German time of origin and the time of issuing the decrypt shows that Hut 8 was taking at least three weeks to break a signal. Some texts were certainly instructive. The Germans' knowledge of the composition of British convoys, for example, was disclosed by this Ultra message of 27 February, reporting a signal from Naval Group West to a Luftflotte. '18th to 23rd Feb from USA to England *Thistle Glen* (war materials, chemicals), *Manatee, Sheaf Crown, Connector* (aeroplanes), *Georgic* (war material, eight aeroplanes on deck), *City of Cape Town, Parthenon, Silver, Cedar* (war material, machine parts).'* In April another Ultra gave unmistakable early signs of that concern about their signal security which was always to nag the Germans – but never to convince them that Enigma was blown. The message of 22 April read: 'From C-in-C Navy. The U-boat campaign makes it necessary to restrict severely the reading of signals by unauthorized persons. Once again I forbid all authorities who have not express orders from the operations division or the Admiral Commanding U-boats to tune in on the operational U-boat wave. I shall in future consider all transgressions of this order as a criminal act endangering national security.'

But evidence of blustering about criminal acts was not a firm basis for identifying U-boats and building an accurate intelligence-picture. By July 1941, and thanks to the cracking of the Hydra cipher, a radical change had occurred. Consider what became known to the Tracking Room about U-boat 143. She is making for Norway.

At 0522 on the 13th Bletchley reports: 'Short signal** intercepted at 0310/13/7/41 on 5660 Kc/s was from unit with signature letters

---

*This message is identified as issued from the Naval Section at Bletchley by Walter Ettinghausen, whom the author recalls as one of the most brilliant of his pre-war contemporaries at The Queen's College, Oxford. After the war Ettinghausen, renamed Walter Eytan, served as Israeli Ambassador in Paris and later as Permanent Secretary of the Israeli Foreign Office.

**'To lessen the risk of surface vessel and U-boat locations being given away by their radio transmissions, a special "short signal" procedure was introduced during the winter of 1939–40. With the aid of a special "Short-Signal book" the text of a message was reduced by compressing sentences and phrases into single words or syllables: these were then coded by the standard method. ... Short signals were invariably prefixed by two Greek letters.' Dr Jurgen Rohwer, *The Critical Convoy Battles of March 1943*, (London, 1977).

QC (=U 143) and reads: shall be off home port in 36 hrs.' Less than two and a half hours later a second message follows. 'From Admiral Commanding U-boats. U 143 reports by short signal that she will be off Bergen at 1700/14/7.' At 0542 next morning Bletchley advises: 'intercept from U 143 at 0303/14/7. "shall be off port of arrival in 12 hrs." ' To complete the story, at 0809 Ultra supplied the text of a signal from Naval Communications Division North to U 143, confirming that her short signal about the estimated time of arrival had been received by the communications centre at Borkum. Bletchley was working very close to the grain.

In fact 14 July, the day of U 143's arrival at Bergen, copiously illustrates the new wealth of intelligence, as the following Ultra messages from Bletchley emphasize. At 1147, from U-boat Command (UBC) to U 431 and U 97, allocation of specific attack areas. At 1220, UBC to U 202 'return by stages in accordance with fuel. Squares BD20, BD30, and DE10 appear to offer good prospects'. At 1246, signal from U 146 to U-boat base, Kiel, 'will arrive Kiel about 1600'. At 1305, signal from UBC to U 203, U 431, U 372 and U 401 allocating named attack areas to be occupied. At 1352, U 432 reporting surfacing after diving exercises – presumably in the Baltic. At 1355, UBC informing U 553 that her port of arrival is St Nazaire. At 1358, signal from U 374 to the base at Kiel. At 1707 U 72's surfacing report to Kiel. At 2228, UBC ordering U 95 and U 372 to make weather reports between 0100 and 0500 the next morning.

A single day's sample of the immense variety of intelligence about the U-boat fleet that now reached the Submarine Tracking Room through Ultra is in itself sufficient to show that the war at sea had entered a new dimension. Absolutely accurate information about a dozen U-boats within twenty-four hours certainly represented a far richer haul than had so far occurred in either of the two world wars. Nevertheless, the best that Bletchley could offer was as yet far from perfection. It is essential to see this in perspective, as a reminder that Ultra was not a wonder-weapon from fairyland but the product of men and women working amid the harsh realities of wartime in a continual atmosphere of challenge and response. After the godsend of U 110, from June to December 1941 the Atlantic traffic in the Hydra cipher was being deciphered within approximately forty-eight hours. But then there came a sinister gap, for on 1 February 1942 the Atlantic U-boats were detached from Hydra and put on a new cipher, Triton, which linked them directly with U-boat Command. This cipher thwarted BP until December 1942 and throughout those long months produced an almost total stoppage of intelligence – almost, because from other sources using Hydra, and from the immense expertise of the Submarine Tracking Room, it proved possible to make many accurate estimates and assumptions and shots in the dark. Even so, this was a second-best.

The defeat might have been absolute. As it was, shipping losses during 1942 rose from the appalling figure of 700 000 tons in June to 730 000 in November. That they were not decisively greater was due, in part, to the Germans' inability to sustain one final cataclysmic offensive, but it was also due to Bletchley and the Submarine Tracking Room. For though Triton evaded the cryptanalysts and thus made it impossible to break signals to and from U-boats while they were at work in the Atlantic, BP continued to read Hydra, that general-purpose cipher used by other naval networks. From Hydra Rodger Winn* and his team, now thoroughly acquainted with the patterns of U-boat behaviour, could pick up many indicators which enabled them to make 'working hypotheses' about the cruise of a particular U-boat or the intentions of U-boat Command.

For in spite of the introduction of Triton the Admiralty was in fact still being supplied by Bletchley with a remarkable flow of intelligence. If we take as a sample a few days in June, the middle of that bad year of 1942, we find among the naval files in the Public Record Office decrypts of signals to and from the U-boat base at Kiel; the Admiral commanding Norway; the Mining and Barrage Commandant, Pomerania; the Sea Rescue Centre; Swinemünde Meteorological Station; the Admiral Commanding North Sea Defences; the Naval Dockyard, Trondheim; the Admiral Commanding the Baltic and the Admiral Commanding the Polar Coast. Even a sample taken over so short a period provides an astonishingly vivid picture of the Germans' routine naval activity from the North Cape of Norway down to the French Atlantic ports. Coastal convoys come and go, the minesweepers and escorting motor-boats make their rendezvous and report the completion of their mission,

---

*Commander (and later Captain) Rodger Winn, R.N.V.R. was the Tracking Room's remarkable leader. A successful barrister before the war, he became a Lord Justice of Appeal before his death in 1972. His achievements in war and in law were a triumph over the disabilities of polio.

personnel problems of all kinds are raised and resolved, testy Admirals inquire why a ship is not proceeding on her way, gear is lost and recovered, exercises are arranged and, particularly in the Baltic, training proceeds. All this was placed by Bletchley in the hands of the Admiralty.

For the Submarine Tracking Room the training programme in the Baltic and the movements of escort craft were of critical value. The Baltic programme had its own cipher, called Tetis, and 'Tetis', Patrick Beesly recalled, 'enabled us to follow the history of each U-boat from the moment it was first commissioned, through its months of work-up and training, until it finally left the Baltic for its first operational cruise to a Norwegian or French port. We could, in consequence, calculate not only the rate of building but the exact number of boats which, for months ahead, would be added to the operational fleet.' Additionally, the Hydra cipher supplied a flow of intelligence about the precise point of the start or finish of a U-boat's cruise. As it left or returned to base it had to be escorted by minesweepers or light craft along the safe swept channels in the German minefields. (From the Biscay ports alone a thousand such escort operations are recorded for 1942.) Since the escorts used the Hydra cipher to transmit their situation reports to the shore, Bletchley could provide the Submarine Tracking Room with a wealth of detail. What was missing, in 1942, was insight into the signal-traffic over the main battle-front: the Atlantic.

Nevertheless, in spite of delays, failures and frustrations Bletchley's achievement in 1941 and 1942 over the German naval ciphers was priceless. In the Mediterranean Ultra's role was impressive and in many ways invaluable: but it might be argued that after Russia and the United States became involved in the world war the Allies could afford to lose the Mediterranean – if only temporarily – without disaster. Loss of the Atlantic could not even be contemplated. The convoys were a blood-transfusion. Once it was cut, Britain must wither. For the ultimate victory in the Battle of the Atlantic and, consequently, for a final return to Europe Ultra would provide authentic intelligence without which all the skill and gallantry of the convoy escorts at sea and in the air, and all the phlegmatic courage of the merchantmen themselves, might have been insufficient.

The possibility that their ciphers were being broken vexed but never dominated the minds of Dönitz and the staff of U-boat Command. The clean sweep of their tankers and supply ships during the summer of 1941, for example, inevitably raised awkward questions about security and a careful investigation was carried out. The result was characteristic of all such inquiries throughout the war, whether they were naval or military in origin. The answer was always: 1) The ciphers have not been broken. 2) If they have been broken, this is only temporary, and the British would have to work on so vast a number of intercepts to establish a continuing break that the possibility does not arise. 3) Any temporary break is the result of carelessness in our ranks, which must be investigated, or of the devilish British Secret Service. That U-boat dispositions were indeed being identified was accepted and brushed off as early as September 1941, when a staff report on the 19th stated with normal confidence: 'the decoded signal from the British Admiralty of 6 September, a survey of the probable positions of German U-boats, is completely true and can only have been gained by reported sightings and radio reports. *An insight into our own cipher does not come into consideration....*'*

This blind certainty was clearly revealed in the most intensive study ever carried out by the Germans into the possibility that their naval ciphers might have been compromised. On 30 January 1943 Dönitz was appointed Grand Admiral and Supreme Commander of the German Navy. But he still remained Commander-in-Chief, U-boats, and after moving the U-boat Command from Paris to Berlin he ordered a minute inquiry into the whole Atlantic Battle.[6] B Dienst, still reading the British convoy codes, showed that the 'U-boat situation reports' and other information and instructions transmitted to the convoys and their escorts contained disturbingly accurate information. How could the British know where the U-boats were?

They knew, in fact, because months of arduous effort had enabled Bletchley to make its first break-back into the Triton cipher early in December 1942. The *how* of so prolonged and meticulous a piece of cryptanalysis is impossible to summarize. The event was what mattered. By the end of the year, and during the opening months of 1943, the Submarine Tracking Room was receiving a steady service of decrypts from the Triton cipher. Deciphering was often delayed, for the problems were acute. Still, Winn and his colleagues had their fingers on the pulse of the Atlantic battle.

*Author's italics.

U-boat locations could often be identified, the orders from U-boat Command could often be translated and countered, and convoys could be warned. One of the most important benefits from this break-back into Triton came, in fact, from a growing suspicion in Winn's mind that all was not well with the British convoy-codes. The German signals he was now able to study gave clear indications that B Dienst was reading them regularly – as was indeed the case. He pressed the argument on the Admiralty until at last, and mercifully, the codes were changed.

But this critical decision was not taken, and new codes could not be distributed to hundreds of users all over the world, until early June 1943. In the meantime, Grand Admiral Dönitz's rigorous Court of Inquiry continued. Vice-Admiral Maertens, Chief of the Navy Signal Department, swore that his ciphers were unbreakable. Two fine U-boat commanders, Günther Hessler – First Operations Officer at U-boat Command and Dönitz's son-in-law – with his assistant Leutnant Adalbert Schnee constructed a mosaic map of the North Atlantic, built up from information revealed by the British in the 'U-boat situation reports' decoded by B Dienst and the records of German operations in the files of U-boat Command. Put together, these seemed to provide consoling confirmation that the Triton cipher had still not been penetrated by the enemy. Direction-finding from shore bases and, even more significantly, detection of U-boats by airborne radar seemed a sufficient explanation for the increasing accuracy of the British reports.

The war diary of Commander U-boats for 5 March 1943 summarized the conclusion of what is called this 'systematic evaluation'. The inquiry, Dönitz decided, 'has, to some extent, allayed strong suspicions that the enemy has succeeded in breaking our ciphers'. As a matter of fact, his personal belief in the ciphers' integrity was unshaken. In his post-war memoirs (first published in Germany in 1958) he declared that 'our ciphers were checked and re-checked, to make sure that they were unbreakable: and on each occasion the Head of the Naval Intelligence Service at Naval High Command adhered to his opinion that it would be impossible for the enemy to decipher them. And to this day, as far as I know, we are not certain whether or not the enemy did succeed in breaking our ciphers during the war.'

The truth is that in spite of a professional instinct that told them something was wrong, the men in power at the head of the German armed services suffered from a limitation once defined by that shrewd sociologist Thorsten Veblen as 'trained incapacity'. Their minds had been dragooned and regimented into the belief that Enigma was totally secure: therefore they were incapable of assessing objectively any indications that it had become insecure. The error is repetitive. At a conference in the autumn of 1943 we find Generals Fellgiebel and Thiele, Chief Signals Officers of the highest grade at OKW, the High Command, reaching precisely the same conclusions as the Navy. As late as June 1944, when the Normandy battle is already raging, we are able, thanks to the diary of Oberstleutnant Meyer-Dietring, to overhear a conversation between himself and Major Laub, the Chief Signals Officer on the staff of Hitler's Commander-in-Chief in the West, von Rundstedt. 'How far', says Meyer-Dietring, 'do you think the enemy has penetrated our ciphers?' 'Not at all,' replies Laub. 'With our cipher machines that's not possible. The enemy would have to obtain 50 000 five-letter groups of cipher to be able to break it. But the cipher is changed every 24 hours.' Of course there may be a more subtle explanation of this complacency. Did the men at the top ever *want* to know that Enigma was 'blown'? Technicians are special pleaders in their own cause, and the signals people clearly had a vested interest in proving that Enigma was secure. But the senior generals and admirals? Suppose they had been convinced, irrefutably, that Enigma was *kaput*. Who would be the first to lay his head on the block and inform Hitler that the whole secret communications system of the Reich – for which there was certainly no instant alternative – was untrustworthy from Norway to the Mediterranean and from Russia to the Atlantic?

There were many respectable reasons for the confidence of U-boat Command. Few of the staff were allowed to know the precise details of the communications-system. Constant changes of cipher and even of equipment were introduced to preserve security. The lists of settings and similar documents carried on board a U-boat were printed on soluble paper to make destruction easy and to avert recovery in case of a sinking. And there was a special, secret arrangement with each U-boat whereby, on a concealed radio warning from shore, the craft's cipher was immediately changed: an item would be inserted into a signal from U-boat Command that could only have meaning for that particular crew – the date of the birthday of the captain's son, or the wedding-day of the chief engineer.

Such devices often caused delays for the Bletchley team, but in essence they were palliatives. The Germans' fundamental error was their failure to grasp that it was possible for cryptanalysis and technology so to master Enigma that even though it might be temporarily lost that mastery, once gained, must inevitably be recovered. One says 'inevitably' with hindsight: yet such was the pattern.

The Battle of Britain ended too soon for Bletchley and Fighter Command to become fully integrated. The battle against the U-boats, by contrast, was unceasing. Time, experience and necessity gradually blended the cryptanalysts and the Naval Section at BP with the most comprehensive organization ever evolved by the British for bringing intelligence immediately to bear on operational decisions. From Bletchley the deciphered signals passed directly by teleprinter into OIC and particularly into the Submarine Tracking Room. From this flow of exact evidence about the position and movements of U-boats warnings to convoys could be rapidly transmitted, and information on which counter-attacks might be based could be passed with ease to the headquarters of Coastal Command and to the hub of all anti-submarine action, the headquarters of Western Approaches. Indeed it became the practice to hold a morning conference on a three-way telephone link, enabling the staff of OIC, Coastal Command and Western Approaches to discuss and take decisions about the very latest situation reports.[7] At its best this integration produced speed, confidence and accuracy of judgement. Nothing so immediate and elaborate could be provided for the armies abroad, nor could the staff of Hut 3 at Bletchley have anything like the direct and intimate relation with their opposite numbers in Africa or Italy, for example, which the Naval Section could and did maintain with the Submarine Tracking Room. In its complexity and efficiency this bonding together of intelligence, straight from the source, and active operational decision was perhaps only approached once during the whole war: by the interlocking of Germany's vast radar-warning system, spanning western Europe, and her centres for directing and controlling the fighter arm of the Luftwaffe.

But the laws remained inexorable. Intelligence without the means to apply it was reduced in its effect: if the means were available but good intelligence was missing the practical results were disappointing. After Bletchley began to break the naval ciphers, following the capture of U 110, the second half of 1941 certainly showed diminishing returns for the U-boats. Up to June shipping losses had passed 200 000 tons in every month – and usually 300 000. Between July and the rest of the year no month's loss was over 200 000 tons: for November and December the figure was just over 50 000. Ultra was not the only factor in this improvement, but the elements in it that contained most promise – as the future would prove – all depended critically on Bletchley's reading of the U-boat cipher. These were the escort groups, the evasive routing of convoys, and the aggressive use of aircraft. Each derived enormous benefit from the Tracking Room's ability, as a result of Ultra, to pin-point the position of U-boats, whether singly or in packs, and rapidly inform the convoys and the ships and aircraft disposed to protect them.

But the figures, considered realistically, represented little more than a promise. In the early days there were not yet enough of the right ships and aircraft for anti-submarine work, nor any of the specialized weapons still being developed. Ultra was not in top gear because the means for applying its intelligence were insufficient. And then, as has been seen, for the greater part of 1942 Ultra itself lost much of its relevance to the U-boat war. Over 6,000,000 tons sunk during the year by U-boats in all waters: a total strength of 393 on the books of U-boat Command at the end of the year as compared with 249 at the beginning. The figures are eloquent, compared with what had gone before and what was now to come.

Indeed, the Battle of the Atlantic during the opening five months of 1943 presents an incomparable drama. Its most savage phase was enacted during the first three weeks of March, when seventy U-boats were operating in the Atlantic – forty-five of them in the convoys' most vulnerable area, the North. In January the sinkings from U-boats (203 128 tons) had been lower than in any month in 1942. February's total of 359 328 tons, though larger, was still less than the figure for all but two of the months in the previous year. But now, in March, the graph was to rise again menacingly to a tonnage reminiscent of the worst days of the Ultra-less past, 627 377.

It was the good intelligence derived from intercepts of the Admiralty's signals by B Dienst that helped Dönitz to concentrate a pack of forty U-boats against the converging convoys HX 229 and SC 122. During a four-day slaughter that began on 16 March twenty-one ships of 141 000 tons were sunk for the loss of only a single U-boat. The prospect for the Allies was appalling: in the first ten days of March, in all waters, forty-one ships had gone, and in the next ten days fifty-six. This was the time when the Naval Staff thought it possible 'that we should not be able to continue to regard convoy as an effective system of defence'. Faced with a similar situation in 1917 Admiral Jellicoe had decided that Germany must win the war.

It was, nevertheless, bad luck that an event anticipated and feared at Bletchley should have occurred just as the life-and-death struggle in the Atlantic was renewed. A new form of Enigma was known to be in preparation, the M4. Unlike the usual models which, as has been seen, worked with three rotors positioned in the machine, M4 contained a space for a fourth. With four rotors linked together the process of enciphering became even more complicated, and deciphering, in consequence, was that much more difficult. The alarm went on 8 March, when an Ultra signal was found to contain the code-word ordering a change to the M4 system. Next day Admiral Edelsten, the Admiralty's Assistant Chief of Staff with overall responsibility for seaborne trade and its protection, minuted to the First Sea Lord, Admiral Pound: 'The expected has happened. The Director of Naval Intelligence announced yesterday that information on U-boat movements is unlikely to be forthcoming for some time – perhaps even months.' This was a tactful way of defining a tragedy: Ultra for the Atlantic was drying up.

No technical explanation has yet been published of the miracle that followed. Somehow – perhaps because the change to the M4 Enigma had been anticipated – Bletchley managed to make its way back into the Triton cipher with astonishing speed. By the end of March up-to-date decrypts were on stream again. But the blurring and imprecision of the intelligence available during that murderous month are well illustrated by excerpts from two reports by Rodger Winn. On the 15th he advised that 'no Special Intelligence has been received since the 11th March and therefore it is not known with certainty how the U-boats are now disposed'. On the 22nd he admitted that 'Special Intelligence has been received for the period noon 15th to noon 19th but does not give a clear picture of the operations'. Yet these were the days when a wolf-pack of forty U-boats was massacring convoys SC 122 and HX 229.

From his vantage point in the Submarine Tracking Room Patrick Beesley could see the whole picture. He has confirmed, in retrospect, that nevertheless he, Winn and their colleagues were not dejected. 'It was certainly a battle lost, but there would be more, and we should win them.' They were right, for suddenly everything came together. With Ultra restored, the new 10 cm radar sets, the reinforcement of escort carriers and Very Long Range aircraft, the stiffening of Coastal Command and the mounting efficiency of warships in the escort groups a dramatic reversal occurred – almost, it seemed, overnight. In early March the Admiralty was in despair. On 24 May it was Dönitz who cracked by withdrawing his U-boat fleet from the dangerous high seas to westwards of the Azores. During April and May he lost no less than fifty-six of his boats. The ratio of loss to effort had become unacceptable, and the Grand Admiral was forced into a policy of *reculer pour mieux sauter*. But never again would the U-boats make a significant comeback. Taking the first twenty days of March as their high point, it may be said that the Germans had not experienced so extraordinary a reverse of fortune since the shattering success of their offensive launched on 21 March 1918 was followed by the decisive British victory of 8 August, 'the black day of the German army'.

In retrospect the black day of the U-boats seems less surprising than inevitable. Soon the Tracking Room was no longer working by guess and by God but, once again, by reading verbatim the signals exchanged between the captains at sea and U-boat Command ashore. These regular two-way signals were an essential conversation without which large U-boat packs could not be assembled and controlled. Their vulnerability to cryptanalysis was a risk calculated and accepted by Dönitz. Thanks to the skills of Bletchley it proved to be his Achilles' heel. The Naval Staff can certainly not be blamed for feeling – to quote its oft-quoted confession – that 'the Germans never came as near to disrupting communications between the New World and the Old as in the first twenty days of March 1943'. Yet it was a *cri de coeur* whose despondency was in fact too acute. It was natural that the Admiralty, blinded by loss of Ultra, should have felt like the sightless John Milton.

> And that one talent which is death to hide
> Lodg'd with me useless.

But the tragedy of the shattered convoys SC 122 and HX 229 emphasizes not only the consequences of Ultra's absence, but also the immense reinforcement its renewed presence brought to the battle when Bletchley so astonishingly re-started the flow of deciphered U-boat signals.

And there was a deeper truth which, when set against the enormous losses of those spring months, seemed hard to credit at the time but is evident in retrospect. From early February onwards Rodger Winn in the Tracking Room discerned in the Ultra signals increasing evidence that the morale of the U-boat crews, once of the highest quality, was beginning to flag – and that Dönitz was revealing his awareness of this in the character of his messages to them. It was partly a matter of fact – too many failures to push home attacks, too many craft returning to port with 'engine defects', too many refusals to fight back at hostile aircraft. It was partly a matter of a new tone in Dönitz's signals – a barely concealed desperation.

All this was visible in the Ultra messages. To those who lived with them from hour to hour and day to day it was therefore no surprise when Dönitz accepted defeat – indeed Winn had predicted that a collapse would occur, and that it would be sudden. The conjunction, at last, of good Ultra, skilled escort groups with sophisticated equipment, aircraft-carriers and Very Long Range Aircraft all working with the harmony of experience was – put simply – too much for a U-boat fleet most of whose best men were dead. (Over two-thirds of all U-boat men lost their lives in the course of the war.)

The retreat from the North Atlantic did not mean unconditional surrender. Attention was now concentrated, particularly by Coastal Command, on the routes across the Bay of Biscay taken by U-boats at the start or conclusion of a cruise. So fierce were the engagements during June, July and August that the conflict came to be called The Bay Offensive, and Marshal of the RAF Sir John Slessor, who was then Commander-in-Chief Coastal Command, is uncompromising in the credit he gives to Ultra. 'I have the best reason to know', he has written of this period, 'that Ultra was a real war-winner.' Fitted with the latest 10 cm radar which the U-boats were unable to detect, and using the Leigh lights which enabled them to illuminate the enemy unexpectedly in the darkness, Coastal Command's aircraft were guided to their targets, over and over again, by Ultra. From the signals passing from U-boats to base, and the instructions transmitted by U-boat Command, the Tracking Room not only mapped the routes used by homing or departing U-boats but also, by grace of the intercepts, monitored the way these routes were altered by the Germans in an effort to avoid their attackers. All Dönitz's counters – U-boats fighting it out on the surface with their anti-aircraft guns, U-boats travelling on the surface in groups for mutual assistance – were given away in his signals. During these three months, in the Bay and elsewhere, more U-boats were sunk than allied merchant vessels: seventy-four as against fifty-eight. By the autumn of 1943 the Battle of the Atlantic had been reduced to an acceptable running skirmish. There were no more disasters. Certainly the path had been cleared for those immense movements of men and supplies without which the next year's return to Europe would have been impossible.

But there was another region of menace. Few but intensely powerful, the battleships and battlecruisers of the German navy offered an insistent threat entirely out of proportion to their individual strength. With convoys passing all over the oceans of the world, it was impossible for the Allies to provide escorts everywhere capable of dealing with even a single big ship at loose on the high seas. The nervousness felt by Churchill and the Admiralty about such a nightmare is well illustrated by the frenetic gathering of British warships from all quarters when *Bismarck* made her final sortie. Not surprisingly, Ultra was a factor not only in the U-boat war but also in the dramatic surface actions which involved ships from the German battle-fleet: nor is it surprising that, as in the war on land, Bletchley's intelligence was useless in averting disaster when it was treated with insufficient respect, but a vital element in the achievement of success when those responsible for operations applied it wisely.

The successful dash of *Scharnhorst* and *Gneisenau* up the English Channel, which began during the dark night of 17 February 1942, was described by *The Times* with anguish. 'Nothing more mortifying to the pride of sea-power has happened in home waters since the 17th Century.' The event had a shock effect. Yet, seen in perspective, its course was not simple but consisted of a series of contradictions and calamities from which Hitler and Ultra perhaps emerge with the greatest credit.

It was evident that attacks by Bomber Command were rendering Brest untenable, and that the two ships must move from this useful Atlantic base if they were to live. But where? To the horror of the professionals, Admiral Raeder and the German naval staff, their Führer insisted in his adamant way that they should race up the

Channel and thus become available for the defence of Norway, whose invasion he anticipated. It was in any case a possibility which the Admiralty could hardly overlook, and much thought was given to it during the early weeks of 1942.

Ultra converted speculation into reality. All those small preliminaries necessary for the secret move of a considerable naval force were indentified from intercepted signals by Denning and his colleagues in the Operational Intelligence Centre – the particular arrangements for U-boats and the Luftwaffe's fighters, the increased and clandestine activity of minesweepers along significant channels, the assembly of extra destroyers as escorts in the dash. A full appreciation was laid before Admiral Pound, and as early as 2 February the Admiralty issued its detailed conclusions which ended: 'Taking all factors into consideration, it appears that the Germans can pass east up the Channel with much less risk than they will incurr if they attempt an ocean passage.' Coastal Command took the same view.

We thus have a situation in which the general probability was obvious to anyone who could read a map, but virtual certainty, the hard evidence on which commanders base plans for action, was produced in the main by Bletchley's ability to read, in particular, the Luftwaffe and Hydra ciphers and by the skill of OIC at extracting a coherent meaning out of Ultra traffic from a variety of sources. But just as Hitler was right about the Channel dash and his Admirals wrong, so Ultra's initial accuracy was now negatived by the errors and fumbling of the professional staffs and the responsible commanders.

The outrage caused by the passage of *Scharnhorst* and *Gneisenau* in February 1942 was largely due to the fact that it occurred on England's doorstep. The catalogue of misadventure that made it possible provokes a more troublesome thought: if, after a further eighteen months of preparation, this was the best that the British could do, how would they have fared in the summer of 1940 if Sealion's forces had actually attempted to cross their doorstep? For nothing went right from the beginning, when the Admiralty estimated that the Germans would start by daylight and slide through the Channel by dark – whereas Admiral Ciliax boldly sailed by dark and came down the Channel in broad daylight. From the radar failure in the reconnaissance aircraft which should have raised an early alarm to the pathetic last effort by doomed Commander

Esmonde and his ancient Swordfish torpedo-planes, the whole story constitutes

> a lamentable tale of things
> Done long ago, and ill done.

Ultra, which had been so valuable during the preliminaries, also played an undisclosed part in the aftermath. For during the evening of 12 February, as they were steaming in what seemed safety down the Dutch coast, both ships hit mines off Terschelling. This was known in London through Ultra but could not, of course, be used to diminish the disquiet of the British public. Yet the view of the German Naval Staff about the operation, that it was 'a tactical victory, but a strategic defeat', gains meaning when it is realized that the mine-damage to *Scharnhorst* kept her out of action for months while *Gneisenau*, dry-docked at Kiel, was so battered by Bomber Command a few days later that she never went to sea again. Nevertheless, from the strict if narrow viewpoint of this book, which is to evaluate the connection between Ultra intelligence and actual operations, it is clear that the safe transit of the English Channel by two German battle cruisers in spite of the Royal Navy, Bomber Command and Coastal Command, and after impressive forewarning from Ultra, might be explained but could hardly be excused. And soon another great warship, *Tirpitz*, would be the cause of a similar concern.

In retrospect the Channel affair seems to call in question the whole system for guarding the home waters surrounding the British Isles. By contrast, the connection between *Tirpitz* and the tragedy of the Russian convoy PQ17 (which occurred in the arctic desolation of the Barents Sea early in July 1942) was not so much the result of organizational failure as of political urgency and the faulty judgement of a single man, Admiral Sir Dudley Pound, the First Sea Lord and supreme head of the Royal Navy. The situation was simple. Russia was desperate for equipment and supplies. Roosevelt put great pressure on the British to clear from Iceland the merchantmen accumulated there with Lend Lease stocks for Stalin. Churchill accepted the requirement, stating to his Chiefs of Staff that 'failure on our part to make the attempt would weaken our influence with our major allies. I share your misgivings, but I feel it is a matter of duty.' Pound's life had been dedicated to Duty, 'stern daughter of the voice of God': since the voice was also Churchill's, he loyally undertook the obligation of running convoy PQ17 from Iceland to Murmansk. Yet those who would have to execute his orders consistently advised and even pleaded for their cancellation – particularly the commander of the Home Fleet, Admiral Sir John Tovey, who was driven to using phrases like 'bloody murder'.

Misgivings approaching insubordination derived from another simple fact – the known presence in the northern fjords of Norway of a powerful German striking force, including the pocket-battleships *Lützow* and *Scheer*, the heavy cruiser *Admiral Hipper*, a destroyer group and, above all, the battleship *Tirpitz*. The Luftwaffe had over 250 aircraft in the region of Norway's North Cape, and U-boats infested the waters between the Cape and Spitzbergen through which PQ17 must pass. It was rational for the Admiralty to calculate that the convoy would be in grave danger – particularly from *Tirpitz*, whose speed and strength outmatched her British equivalents. And this was justified, for Admiral Raeder had composed a plan, Knight's Move or *Rösselsprung*, which committed his capital ships to an attack on PQ17 once it had been located, once the presumed presence of an aircraft carrier with the British covering forces had been checked and – a vital qualification – once Hitler's permission for the Knight's Move had been obtained.

It was on 27 June that PQ17 sailed from Iceland – thirty-four miscellaneous merchantmen under British, American and Russian flags, transporting 157 000 tons of war material. By 3 July Ultra was already providing valuable confirmation of German moves northwards along the Norwegian coast to a point of concentration in Altenfjord, the furthermost anchorage for launching an attack on the convoy. But the vital question remained unanswered: had *Tirpitz* already left the fjord to engage PQ17? There were delays in deciphering at Bletchley, but at seven o'clock in the evening of the 4th the Naval Section reported that decrypts of signals passed during the last twenty-four hours would soon be available. They revealed that *Tirpitz* had certainly reached Altenfjord, but no more: and that her destroyer escort had been ordered to re-fuel.

At this point Admiral Pound made his way to the Operational Intelligence Centre deep beneath the Citadel's concrete fortress and cross-questioned Denning. The thrust of the First Sea Lord's interrogation was: can you assure me that *Tirpitz* is still at anchor? And if so, can you tell me whether she is ready to sail? Denning replied that he would know *if* she had sailed *after* she had sailed. For this there was none of the evidence that might normally be expected. Moreover, it was unlikely that she was even about to sail since there was no indication that her destroyers, who would have preceded her to search for submarines, had yet emerged from Altenfjord.

In his vivid account of Naval Intelligence, 'Room 39', Donald McLachlan ascribes Denning's conviction to his knowledge that a trusted Norwegian agent working at Altenfjord would certainly and rapidly have reported *Tirpitz*'s departure.[8] No report: therefore no departure. But this was a cover-story. Writing in 1968, McLachlan could not disclose that Denning's assurance derived from Ultra. Experience of the German Enigma traffic had taught him that when a capital ship sailed on operations it might itself maintain wireless silence, but from the Naval Command ashore – in this case Gruppe Nord, which controlled the Norwegian zone – a stream of messages would flow. The traffic was unmistakable, as had been demonstrated in March when *Tirpitz* made an abortive sortie against convoy PQ12. But now there was no such traffic – nor, for that matter, had the patrolling submarines, British, French and Russian, made any report of a battleship at sea off the North Cape. Moreover, had *Tirpitz*'s destroyers been sent out ahead to clear the way, a normal procedure, their wireless transmissions must certainly have provided a clue. Denning's deductions were correct. The menacing warships remained in or near Altenfjord 'like chained dogs', as the German naval historian Cajus Bekker puts it: for the Luftwaffe never found the Home Fleet in its distant support of the convoy, and thus Hitler's pre-requisite for the execution of Knight's Move – that British aircraft carriers must first be located and attacked – was not fulfilled. *Tirpitz* stayed meekly out of action until she was withdrawn to the south.

But Pound had not trusted his intelligence staff. He decided that the battleship *had* sailed, and that her great guns would begin the destruction of PQ17 before Admiral Tovey and the heavy ships of the Home Fleet could possibly arrive. And so, shortly after nine o'clock on the evening of the 4th, a signal went out from the Admiralty ordering the cruisers accompanying PQ17 to withdraw. Soon afterwards a further signal, written by the First Sea Lord himself, instructed the convoy to scatter. This was a death-warrant. The close escort of destroyers could hardly protect a far-flung convoy: their role was now to help the cruisers, as they thought, in delaying a *Tirpitz* which they, like Pound, assumed to be in hot pursuit.

Meanwhile U-boats and the Luftwaffe picked off the abandoned merchantmen one by one: a tragic tally of twenty-three sunk out of thirty-four.

Ultra kept pace with this inevitable slaughter. For those in the Operational Intelligence Centre who sensed that Pound had made the wrong decision it must have been agonizing to read the flimsy signals as they reached the Citadel from Bletchley, carrying one by one the mounting story of disaster. A sequence of deciphered reports from the Luftwaffe commander in the Lofotens told of relentless surveillance and attack by German aircraft: from individual U-boats Ultra carried sinister accounts of sightings and sinkings.

Two decrypts summarized the dreadful climax. At 1440 on the 5th Bletchley passed on a report from Lieutenant-Commander Bielefeld, captain of U 703. 'Have sunk 9000 ton *Empire Byron* ... Port of destination Archangel. Her captain John Rimington on board as prisoner ... *convoy totally dispersed*, course 120 degrees. Am pursuing.' *Empire Byron* was a brand-new merchantman loaded with tanks. Her captain, John Wharton, was asleep on the bridge when U 703's fifth torpedo exploded in the engine-room. After taking charge of survivors in their boats, and watching his ship go down, he avoided capture by a curious chance. Wharton had ordered all officers to remove their distinguishing uniform but an Army technical expert, Captain Rimington, (who was travelling to advise the Russians about the convoy's gift of Churchill tanks) refused to remove his fine white duffel-coat. So Rimington, the most prominent figure, was selected by the Germans for transfer to U 703 and Bletchley's decrypt identified him wrongly as *Empire Byron*'s captain. But this sinking was only one of the tragedies in a situation tersely defined by a signal from Battle Headquarters, Luftflotte 5, which Bletchley issued on the 6th. 'Reconnaissance against convoy PQ17 from 1400 to 1800' (presumably on the 5th). 'Convoy dissolved.... Total number of ships present cannot be established because they are so far spread out.' And so Ultra's intelligence service illuminated the last act of a drama which ought never to have occurred.

The man at the apex of a command pyramid, doomed by his unique status and authority to make private and lonely decisions, cannot escape their consequences. Winner takes all. Eisenhower is rightly praised for his courage and judgement in ordering the D

Day invasion, Overlord, to proceed when his meteorologists offered small comfort, the results of failure would have been immeasurable, and he alone could say 'Let's go'. Pound's reputation is diminished by the orders issued to PQ17 on 4 July, for which he was entirely responsible. By 1942 the use of Ultra by the Operational Intelligence Centre (apart from its remarkable record in the use of other sources) had been so frequently and even dramatically successful that the First Sea Lord can hardly be excused for the indifference with which he responded to Denning's appreciation. Nor, indeed, was there any warmer response when Denning's superior, Captain Jock Clayton, faced up to Pound a couple of hours after the 'scatter' signal had been transmitted and tried to persuade him to cancel it – for evidence that *Tirpitz* was still in harbour had hardened with receipt of a further Ultra decrypt, in the form of a message to U-boats in the North Cape area that no German surface ships were in the vicinity. Pound rejected Clayton as he had rejected Denning. *Tirpitz*, in his view, had sailed: he therefore sacrificed a convoy. At a time of similar tension, the evacuation of Crete, Lord Wavell recorded the reactions of another seaman. After the fleet had done its uttermost Wavell himself, the Australian General Blamey and the New Zealand Prime Minister jointly absolved the Navy from further endeavour. Admiral Andrew Cunningham simply 'thanked me for our effort to relieve him of responsibility but said that the Navy had never yet failed the Army: he was going in again that night with everything he had which would float and could bring off troops'. On the other hand Pound's supporters have argued with some force that in the absence of direct evidence from Ultra, and in view of the certain catastrophe if *Tirpitz* were to find at her mercy a convoy in close formation, the Admiral was justified in giving the order to scatter. Whatever his motives, the result was a tragedy.

Pound's subsequent death from a tumour on the brain, and earlier evidence of significant symptoms such as an excessive tendency to fall asleep in mid-conference, have suggested that during the critical evening of 4 July his faculties may have been less than acute.[9] Against this plea in mitigation must be set the established fact that on more than one previous occasion Pound had directed his fleet at sea in an authoritarian fashion. To him centralized control from the Admiralty was instinctive and automatic. What is certain is that he gave Ultra and its interpreters no chance. His mind closed, without any discussion of the reasons why serious and tested officers like Clayton and Denning believed that *Tirpitz* was still at anchor – still less of why they were prepared to risk his disfavour in backing their judgement. That many other pressures, political and strategical, affected Pound in his decision about PQ17 must be freely granted. But at the central point, the relation of intelligence to operations, it was fortunate for the Allies that other commanders were more sensitive and more flexible than this Admiral of the Fleet in applying the Ultra information that was laid in their hands.

Indeed, as it happened the next time that Ultra was involved in a major attempt by a German capital ship to break up a convoy proved to be a classic example of how intelligence from Bletchley, if prudently used, could have a radical effect in the war at sea. The mine-damage to *Scharnhorst* took months to repair, and even when she was ready to make for Norway in early 1943 her first two efforts were baulked by the RAF as a result of Ultra warnings. At last she reached Altenfjord, where her sister ships *Tirpitz* and the pocket battleship *Lützow* were soon eliminated, the former by a British midget submarine on 22 September which caused extensive damage and the latter by need of a refit which sent her back to Germany. In December 1943, therefore, *Scharnhorst* was the only seaworthy capital ship in northern waters at a time when German disasters on the Eastern front convinced Admiral Dönitz, Raeder's successor as naval Commander-in-Chief, that interdiction of the arctic convoys to Russia was essential.

One of the basic laws governing the success of Ultra now came into play. Its intelligence was derived from signals transmitted by radio. Messages sent by telephone or teleprinter were beyond its scope. By a quirk of fate the situation in Altenfjord supplied a simple but decisive demonstration of this invariable principle. The wounded *Tirpitz* lay close enough to shore for connection to be made with the mainland systems of communication: signals passed safely to and fro by telephone or telex. But *Scharnhorst* had a more distant anchorage, so that a motor-boat might carry incidental messages but the main signal traffic had to be conducted by radio. On the eve of a major operation such traffic was inevitably heavy – and capable of interception. But in December 1943 Bletchley was breaking naval ciphers with an adequate regularity. Such is the technical background to that moment during the evening of 26 December 1943 when at 6.25 pm *Scharnhorst* signalled to Hitler 'We shall fight to the last shell', and sank, an hour later, beneath the guns of *Duke of York*.

During mid-December several convoys were due to pass in both directions between Murmansk and the west. *Scharnhorst*, lying to their flank, was an obvious threat: it was equally obvious to the Admiralty, from the Ultra decrypts of U-boat and Luftwaffe signals, that the Russia-bound convoy JW55B which sailed on 20 December was anticipated. *Scharnhorst* was on the alert. But the deciphering at Bletchley, if not instantaneous, was sufficient. A signal from Gruppe Nord to the Luftwaffe commander in the North was not received in OIC until the early hours of 20 December, over a day late, but it told all. 'Urgently request air reconnaissance against convoy which is certainly to be assumed and against heavy group which is probably at sea. Battlegroup is at three hours' notice.' Battlegroup meant *Scharnhorst*.

The problem for Hitler's chained dogs was that the whistle for release must come from Berlin, where Admiral Dönitz had to satisfy himself in his distant headquarters that the tactical situation around the North Cape was favourable enough to guarantee success. Because of this limiting factor and the need to communicate with *Scharnhorst* by radio, between the 20th and the 25th (when she finally sailed) a series of signals passed between the main naval headquarters ashore and the isolated battle-cruiser, either decreasing or increasing her hours of immediate readiness – first three, then six, then three, then one – or passing to her reconnaissance reports on the eastward progress of JW55B. If some of these defeated or delayed Bletchley's cryptanalysts, the important majority were deciphered and passed not only to OIC but also to the Commander-in Chief Home Fleet, Admiral Sir Bruce Fraser, now flying his flag in the battleship *Duke of York*, and to Admiral Burnett commanding the cruisers *Belfast*, *Norfolk* and *Sheffield*. Fraser and Burnett were the convoy's insurance against *Scharnhorst*.

Thus – and here is the essential point – the officers actually responsible for bringing the enemy to action were kept up-to-date through Ultra as the Germans' plans for intercepting JW55B matured, so that after Grand Admiral Dönitz at last made up his mind and ordered *Ostfront*, the executive code-word, to be issued with effect from 5 pm on the 25th, there was no surprise in London or confusion aboard *Duke of York*. Dönitz's order was actually in the hands of Fraser and Burnett early on the 26th. One has an extraordinary sense of poise and inevitability. Indeed, when Ultra worked so effectively great simplicities became possible. A little later, at 3.19 am, a confirmatory signal went out to all in the hunt. Without frills, it tersely stated the Admiralty's appreciation: *Scharnhorst* was at sea. No more was necessary. By the same evening, thanks to the preliminary dispositions which Ultra's forewarning had made feasible, the ships of the Commander-in-Chief Home Fleet removed the threat of *Scharnhorst* for ever and earned for him, in due course, a new title: Admiral of the Fleet the Lord Fraser of North Cape.

Indeed, because of the preliminary data provided by Ultra the bringing of *Scharnhorst* to bay involved little more than the solution of a simple geometrical problem. Fraser and Burnett knew with sufficient accuracy the position, course and speed of the convoy. They knew that *Scharnhorst* had left Altenfjord to intercept. Their seamanship told them the type of manoeuvre that the battlecruiser would adopt in her attack, and therefore where she was likely to be found. The angles and distances were readily calculable. And so it was that at 0926 on 26 December, amid the snowstorms off the northern coast of Norway, Rear-admiral Erich Bey on *Scharnhorst* found to his horror that the ship was being illuminated by starshells from a wholly unexpected source. Within minutes 8-inch shells landed on the revolving cupola that contained the radar, and killed the operators. The fire came, in fact, from Admiral Burnett's cruiser force which, undetected, had been following *Scharnhorst* on its own radar screens for the last fifty minutes. One recalls the astonishment of those Italian sailors at Matapan, suddenly exposed to lethal fire from great guns at point-blank range because the cracking of their ciphers had betrayed them. And great guns were soon brought to bear on the blinded *Scharnhorst* herself, for by 1650 *Duke of York* with her 14-inch armament was in action. Within hours all that remained of a proud and beautiful ship of war was thirty-six rescued survivors.

In such an action speed is the essence of the contract. There could be no more appropriate comment on Ultra's rate of performance than that of the leading German naval historian, Dr Jürgen Rohwer. 'During the final operation of the *Scharnhorst* on December 25/6 1943,' he reckoned, 'from the time of transmission to the time the deciphered message arrived by teletype from Bletchley Park at the Operations Intelligence Centre, between 5 and 31

229

hours had elapsed if it had been sent by Admiral North Sea, 8 to 12 hours if it had been sent by U-boat Command Norway, 4 to 18 hours on the Battle Fleet net, and 3 to 8 hours if it had been transmitted by one of the Luftwaffe stations.'[10] And with *Scharnhorst* the last of the seaworthy big ships disappeared – *Gneisenau* and *Hipper* paid off, *Prinz Eugen*, *Scheer* and *Lützow* refitting or locked in the Baltic against the Russians. But up at Altenfjord there still lurked the wounded *Tirpitz*.

It was from Ultra, once again, that a warning came. The giantess was stirring after her long sleep. Decrypts in March 1944 showed that the battleship had been carrying out trials on the 15th and 16th: serious news, for on the 27th a Russian convoy, JW58, was due to sail. However, two other Ultra decrypts in swift succession disclosed first that *Tirpitz* was to make further trials at full speed on 1 April, and then that these had been postponed for forty-eight hours. A perfectly timed attack by the Fleet Air Arm was thus able to catch the battleship at the moment when her protective torpedo nets were opening as she weighed anchor. Fourteen hits immobilized her for several months. In September a force of Lancasters, working from Russia with their 12 000 lb blockbuster bombs, hit her again and drove her south to Tromsö for further repairs. This was the moment of truth, for *Tirpitz* could now be reached from England. On 12 November thirty-eight Lancasters turned her upside down. But the significant fact is that thanks to Ultra and the raid of 3 April the German Navy did not possess a single capital ship fit for action when the vast armadas of the Allies sailed in June for D Day.

By all previous standards of warfare, protection of the Normandy invasion fleet would have caused insoluble problems for the British and American navies. 138 bombarding warships, 221 destroyers and other convoy escorts, 287 minesweepers, 495 light craft, 441 auxiliaries and over 4000 landing ships and craft of various sizes: a formidable but vulnerable array. And yet, since there was no risk of intervention by German capital ships and the Luftwaffe in the west was a spent force, only two major difficulties remained to be tackled – apart from the brain-shrivelling staff work required to produce and distribute the millions of words and numerals and diagrams that composed the book-size sets of operational instructions. The outstanding problems were U-boats and minefields.

The assault shipping with its escorts and back-up would be

gathered together from every harbour and temporary anchorage from Milford Haven in Wales, around the southern coast, and as far to the north-east as Felixstowe in Suffolk. Bombarding units and blockships sailed from distant Belfast and the Clyde. But ultimately all had to be assembled, organized in orderly groups, and fed through gaps in the thick curtain of mines which the Germans had deposited along the central stretches of the Channel. No wonder an American, Rear-Admiral Kirk (who commanded the Western Task Force covering the US landings) remarked of the minesweepers that they were 'the keystone of the arch in this operation'. Adjusting the image, however, one might equally say that Ultra provided the main key for understanding the architecture of the German minefields. Not for nothing had the Naval Section at Bletchley been reading the Hydra cipher with increasing intimacy since the summer of 1941. This, it will be recalled, was the cipher used by German naval headquarters from Norway to France for the direction and control of their inshore traffic – coastal convoys, light escorting craft, minesweepers. From the decrypts a rich store of information was built up about German minelaying: the dividend on this investment was paid on D Day.

'OIC was involved throughout all the stages of the preliminary planning,' Patrick Beesly recalled, 'and the approach routes to the beaches were chosen on the information it supplied about German-swept channels and minefields. The approach routes were changed more than once in the light of the latest intelligence available, and a few days before D Day a combined surface and air operation was organized and carried out in Seine Bay to confirm that OIC's conclusions were completely up-to-date and accurate.' This was a correct judgement, for the record stands that shipping losses on D Day were infinitesimal.

Ultra had the U-boats well under control. Admiral Dönitz's counter-attack plans were identified in advance, and seen to consist (as a Tracking Room report stated on 10 April) of collecting his powerful 500-ton craft at bases in the Bay of Biscay (Group Landwirt) while maintaining over two dozen in a useless detachment along the Norwegian coast (Group Mitte) – distracted, presumably, by the ever-present fear of an Allied descent on Scandinavia. In mid-May the actual details of the German plan were revealed by Ultra, with the decrypt of a signal from U-boat Command to the headquarters of Admiral Commanding Western France. This dis-

closed that about forty U-boats would sail to attack the invasion
fleet on D Day or D + 1. The specific areas for other standing
patrols were nominated – off the Scilly Isles, from there to north
Cornwall, and in a reserve position in the Bay of Biscay. With
Ultra's accumulating evidence added to that from other sources –
air reconnaissance, direction-finding and so on – the Allies had no
difficulty in blanketing the whole of the threatened area with ten
naval attack groups while covering the western approaches to the
Channel so generously with aircraft that every square mile of the sea
was investigated every thirty minutes by day and by night. Within a
month of D Day eighteen out of the forty-three U-boats that ven-
tured against the invasion had been sunk. By the end of August, as
Dönitz confessed in his memoirs, 'I myself could no longer match
the moral fortitude displayed by the U-boat crews.' He recalled the
remainder, from a hopeless campaign in which over forty per cent.
of his best craft and men had been sacrificed for the meaningless
profit of some thirty vessels sunk or damaged.

As the Landwirt group began to assemble in the Biscay ports
from March onwards, the coming and going of U-boats was
watched with close attention by the Submarine Tracking Room. Its
accurate identification of U-boat movements were of special value to
19 Group of Coastal Command whose aircraft, working from the
west country, quartered the Bay area with reconnaissance flights
and strikes against shipping and submarines. Since Bletchley, as
has been seen, could decipher a U-boat's homing report and the
instructions to the escorts which helped an incoming craft through
the swept channels in the German minefields, 19 Group could estimate the exact moment when its aircraft ought to swoop from the
skies and catch a U-boat on the surface, its crew relaxed and off
guard at the end of a taxing cruise. Air Marshal Sir Edward Chilton,
then of 19 Group, described to the author an event during one of
these strikes which, perhaps more than anything in this book, illustrates how accurately Ultra intelligence could be applied.

For these attacks 19 Group used a small number of Mosquito
aircraft in the remarkable version which, for obvious reasons, was
known as the Tsetse. The particular structure of the Mosquito
made it possible to instal a six-pounder gun within its body. This
hard-hitting weapon, combined with Mosquito's speed and man-
oeuvrability, gave Tsetse an unusually vicious sting and several
U-boats, caught in the swept channels with their minesweeper

escorts, were damaged or sunk (U 976 off St Nazaire on 25 March, for example) so that Dönitz, as the war diary of U-boat Command records, was compelled to restrict passage on the surface to the hours of darkness. As a Tsetse was going in on one of the attacks the pilot noticed dead in his sights a Ju. 88, one of the aircraft giving the U-boat top cover. Instinctively he pressed the gun-button and, to his astonishment, saw the Junkers disintegrate before his eyes under the direct impact of a six-pounder shell. With Ultra even the improbable became possible – for it was Ultra, through the Intercept Service, Bletchley and the Admiralty's Tracking Room, that had laid the basis for this extraordinary strike.

9 The American Involvement

'You are undoubtedly aware of the supreme importance
which the War Department attaches to intelligence
known as Ultra.'
General Marshall to General Eisenhower, 15 March 1944

'Air raid on Pearl Harbor. This is not a drill.' The radio announce-
ment that stupefied the United States marked the end of many
roads. In the deepest sense it meant that the Americans would now
have to bring to the conduct of war a professionalism which had
been markedly lacking during the last twilight months of peace.
And in no field – as intensive inquiries into Pearl Harbor and its
preliminaries have demonstrated – was the American administration proved to have been more amateur than in its handling of the
cryptographic intelligence which its agencies abundantly supplied.

Colonel William Friedman, founder of the US Signal Intelligence
Service, was one of the most acute of living cryptanalysts. In the
autumn of 1940 he and a brilliant team had presented his country
with a weapon of immense power – the ability to read the cipher in
which Japanese diplomatic signals were transmitted round the
world. Not only had he cracked the cipher itself, Purple, but by a
remarkable technical feat (paralleled only by the Poles in the case of
Enigma) machines were constructed on which the enciphered
Japanese signals could be returned to their original text.[1] Now, of
course, it is well known that during the months leading up to Pearl
Harbor Friedman's weapon tragically misfired. For the intelligence
about Japan acquired from Purple (which was given a comprehensive cover-name, Magic), the Americans before December 1941 had
organized no effective system of evaluation and distribution. A mis-
conceived and misapplied sense of security – stemming from the
Chief of Staff himself, George Marshall – meant that those on the
Magic list sometimes received information too late and sometimes
not at all, while others who should have been on the list never had a
chance of being informed.

The contrast with the British system described in the previous
chapters of circulating Ultra intelligence to all who 'needed to

234

know', and of applying it effectively in operations, seems bleak and disconcerting. Lest the comparison should seem chauvinist or arrogant, it is worth remembering that the British record throughout the thirties is full of similar instances – instances of hard, factual intelligence about Germany's rearmament and aggressive intentions being disregarded, of evidence about France's military decline being misread through rose-tinted spectacles, and of home truths about Britain's own weakness simply not being recognized by those whose duty it was to be alert. The Germans' own intelligence system, as has been seen, quavered during the Battle of Britain. Stalin was blind to the facts before Barbarossa. The failure of the American administration to develop a proper doctrine and organization for handling the fruits of Magic before Pearl Harbor was not unique: with time and experience of war, moreover, it was rectified. Nevertheless it was a failure, and nobody has analyzed that failure more cogently and dispassionately than an American, Roberta Wohlstetter, in her classic 'Pearl Harbor: warning and decision'.

'Not only did we know in advance how the Japanese ambassadors in Washington were advised,' she wrote of Magic, 'and how much they were instructed to say, but we also were listening to top-secret messages on the Tokyo-Berlin and Tokyo-Rome circuits, which gave us information vital for the conduct of the war in the Atlantic and Europe. In the Far East this source provided minute details on movements connected with the Japanese programme of expansion into Southern Asia. Besides the diplomatic codes, our cryptanalysts also had some success in reading codes used by Japanese agents in major American and foreign ports. . . . They could determine what installations, what troop and ship movements, and what alert and defence measures were of interest to Tokyo. . . . Our naval leaders also had at their disposal the results of radio traffic analysis. . . .' And much more. 'All of the public and private sources of information mentioned', Mrs Wohlstetter observed, 'were available to America's political and military leaders in 1941.' The scenario sounds like that for Ultra. Why was there a different performance?

The answer is embedded in the thirty-nine volumes of the 'Hearings before the Joint Committee on the Investigation of the Pearl Harbor attack', published in 1946, but Mrs Wohlstetter gives the gist of it in a single sentence. 'The signals lay scattered in a number of different agencies; some were decoded, some were not; some travelled through rapid channels of communication, some were

235

blocked by technical or procedural delays; some never reached a centre of decision.' There was no equivalent to Bletchley, no service of Special Liaison Units: above all, perhaps, no Churchill avid for the intelligence and determined to sustain a system that could provide it. In short, there was not even a system to sustain.

Analysis of the handling of Magic on the eve of Pearl Harbor summons up the image of a group of highly placed men purblind, fumbling and nervous in the face of something they only partly understood: still, fundamentally, amateur. Above all, nobody in the United States had yet grasped the need for making such secret intelligence swiftly and comprehensibly available to commanders whose decisions, whose fleets and armies might be vitally affected by it. The misuse of Magic was not the only reason for the Pearl Harbor disaster, but it lay at its heart: 'a magic that somehow failed', according to General Marshall's biographer Forrest Pogue.[2]

And yet, with that marvellous resilience and ability to learn from defeat which so often distinguished the Americans in the Second World War, they let only three days pass after Commander Fuchida's triumphant victory signal, *'Tora, Tora, Tora!'* A non-stop process then started which, within a few months, produced the first, the perfect, the classic example of how cryptanalysis can be used to spring a surprise and achieve decisive results in a major operation of war. At Midway on 4 June 1942 everything came good.

The smoke and dust had barely settled over Hawaii before the Combat Intelligence Unit in the bowels of the Navy yard at Pearl Harbor was given a new task – to penetrate the Japanese Fleet Code known as JN25. Remorseless effort (in collaboration with the British at Singapore, and then at Colombo) made such headway that by early April the Japanese plan to press southwards against Port Moresby and, perhaps, Australia was clearly identified. Admiral Nimitz was warned. At the battle of the Coral Sea on 7 May his Pacific Fleet dealt the enemy an opening blow in that famous naval conflict where, for the first time, the ships never saw one another. But the break into JN25 was not absolute, and Japanese confidence was not shaken.

So Admiral Yamamoto with a fleet of 200 vessels set about a grander design – of moving out from the bay of Hiroshima, feinting north at the Aleutians, but actually making with his main force for Midway and, in the process, destroying American naval and air power in the Pacific. Fortunately, as his preparations advanced the

American cryptanalysts achieved an almost complete breakthrough. Towards the end of May Nimitz was fully inside his opponent's mind. A week before the actual battle he was able to issue operational orders based on 'the enemy is expected to attempt the capture of Midway in the near future,' and by the evening of June 4 *Akagi, Kaga, Hiryu* and *Soryu*, the carriers that represented the core of Yamamoto's strength, had been eliminated. 'Midway', Nimitz declared, 'was essentially a victory of intelligence.'

But two salient facts emerge. Magic, like Ultra, was a knife-edge business. Without the JN25 warnings a disaster perhaps worse than Pearl Harbor might have followed, for Yamamoto's massive superiority, allied to surprise, would have been conclusive. Yet there should have been a routine change of the Japanese code on 1 April: postponed, the change should have occurred on 1 May: it was again deferred to 1 June and when it did happen, on 2 June, the Combat Intelligence Unit was blind for weeks. Only the Japanese inability to distribute fresh code-books around their vast and sprawling empire prevented an intelligence blackout at the most critical moment for the Pacific Fleet. Luck was as necessary as cunning in the secret war.

It is more important to note that the unveiling of Yamamoto's intentions was not instantaneous but gradual: first the size of the threat, then its objective, then the actual date of the Japanese attack had to be teased out by the cryptanalysts. Yet *at every stage* of the developing picture – and here we observe the contrast with the period preceding Pearl Harbor – Admiral Nimitz was immediately supplied with JN25 intelligence on the basis of which, (along with submarine-sightings, routine analysis of wireless traffic and other indications) he could build his counter-measures. It is true that before Midway the whole complex, from cryptanalysis to command decision, was naval-controlled: but the message is plain. There was a new assurance, a new professionalism. Nimitz had a better deal than Kimmel. The Americans had quickly attained that insight which the British acquired in respect of Ultra: in war secret intelligence has a fundamental purpose – to assist in winning the battle. The battle is the pay-off: but the field-commander cannot operate effectively in blinkers.

And so, as the United States turned towards direct involvement in Ultra, significant shifts in attitude had already occurred. In the Pacific the processes, skills and procedures for reading and profiting from Japanese codes and ciphers would continue to develop apace on an enormous and fruitful scale: but that is another story. The German war, the Ultra war meant Europe, the Mediterranean, the Atlantic.

'Germany first' had long been the accepted doctrine of the US Joint Chiefs of Staff and their Commander-in-Chief, the President, but it was not until 1942, the year when Americans began to engage Germans in battle, that they first discovered the true meaning and value of Ultra. On the Far Eastern and Pacific fronts, as has been seen, there was an early intimacy of collaboration: indeed, of the six Purple machines constructed in the States after Friedman's solution of the Japanese cipher one went to England in January 1941 (and thereafter to Delhi) whilst a second was also sent to England after Pearl Harbor. But until then the British were tight-lipped about Ultra. Technical exchanges and visits by experts certainly occurred. (Friedman was to have led a small group to Bletchley in the winter of 1940: instead he collapsed as a result of his efforts over Purple – 'the insomnia, the sudden awakening at midnight, the pressure to succeed because failure could have national consequences, the despair of the long weeks when the problem seemed insoluble'.[3]) But the traffic was substantially one-way.

Or was it? From the cover of the British Passport Control office in New York's Rockefeller Center 'the man called Intrepid', William Stephenson, from 1940 onwards master-minded his country's secret activities in the United States and, as is claimed, acted as go-between for Churchill and Roosevelt.[4] But there is a persistent legend that Stephenson was also responsible for passing on from Prime Minister to President an occasional carefully selected item of Ultra intelligence. While this is not inherently improbable (whether or not the information was conveyed as undisguised Ultra, or covered as coming 'from a secret source'), the difficulty is that no firm documentation has as yet been published: we have assertions without evidence. Obviously, for example, it was in Churchill's interest to inform Roosevelt of what Ultra had told him about the German build-up before Barbarossa: obviously the warning sent at that time to Stalin from Washington could have been stimulated, at least in part, by a prophet in London. But whether this or any other communication actually revealed the existence of Ultra to Roosevelt must remain an open question. Probability suggests that he was first put in the picture by Churchill personally at the Arcadia Conference

238

in Washington between 22 December 1941 and 14 January 1942.

What is certain is that Eisenhower arrived in England on 24 June 1942 as Commanding General, European Theatre of Operations. When, early in August, Ike was appointed Commander-in-Chief for the Anglo-American landings in North Africa Churchill himself explained Ultra, its benefits and the security responsibilities it imposed for those 'on the list' to Eisenhower. It was indeed the imminence of Torch – the Allied assault on north-west Africa – which set in train a process of introducing American officers to Britain's most guarded secret. This led, in the end, not only to US commanders and staff officers regularly using Ultra intelligence in the field but also to Americans being specifically trained to advise them on Ultra matters, and even to the presence of other Americans at Bletchley Park as accepted members of the intelligence and cryptanalytical teams in the various Huts. When to this is added the vast flow of information from the Enigma intercepts which, as the invasion of Europe approached, began to stream from Bletchley to Washington it may be said that by 1944 the American involvement in Ultra was virtually complete.

Inevitably, not all of the early indoctrinations went smoothly, sometimes because of a character-defect in the officer concerned. Winterbotham has put on record[5] how in August 1942 he and Menzies called at Norfolk House in St James's Square, the centre of Eisenhower's planning for Torch, to brief his senior staff about Ultra. General Clark, Eisenhower's Deputy, and three other officers were present. 'Mark Clark was restless from the start. I explained not only what the source was, but in an endeavour to catch Mark Clark's interest gave some pertinent examples of what it could do. I had intended to follow this with an explanation of how the information would reach him, and the security regulations which accompanied its use. But Mark Clark didn't appear to believe the first part, and after a quarter of an hour he excused himself and his officers on the grounds that he had something else to do. It was a bad start, and Menzies was considerably upset. . . .' Here is advance evidence of that self-opinionated and self-centred personality which, in the summer of 1944, 'had something else to do' and, instead of carrying out a mission to cut off a retreating German army, turned aside to grab the tinsel distinction of being the first to enter Rome.

The resistance of another General to indoctrination was more pardonable, and its implications are so interesting that it is worth examining in detail.

The bulk of the American forces in England in 1942 consisted of the 8th US Air Force, dedicated (in its leaders' minds) to the proposition that with the Norden bomb-sight, and the ability of Fortress-formations to defend themselves with their own guns, its crews (after experience over France) could bomb individual targets in Germany with shattering precision. At its head was Major-General Carl Spaatz, sage, far-sighted, and beloved as 'Tooey' by kin and ally on both sides of the Atlantic. Though Germany still lay ahead, the first tentative essay by 8th Bomber Command (which with its sister 8th Fighter Command formed the 8thUSAF) occurred on 17 August when twelve aircraft made a daylight attack on the marshalling yards at Rouen. Spaatz was in business. Moreover, for present and future operations he and his staff worked closely with Sir Arthur Harris and the British Bomber Command. At an early stage, therefore, Spaatz was put on the Ultra list and indoctrinated. (A USAAF officer, Colonel Palmer Dixon, had in fact been attached to the Intelligence Department of the Air Ministry since the spring of 1942 with a normal Ultra briefing.)

In December, however, Spaatz was switched to Algiers. Co-ordination of the air effort in north-west Africa was urgently needed, and Tooey joined Eisenhower's staff to introduce logic and order: early in 1943, at the Casablanca Conference, he would be made commander of the Allied Air Force on the Torch front. In England, therefore, a successor general appeared at the 8th USAF, Ira Eaker, who soon met Churchill and (as he told the author)[6] was asked by the Prime Minister whether he knew about Ultra. He did not. Winterbotham quickly reported to carry out the indoctrination drill, but already Eaker had received from Spaatz a message and a warning. It told Eaker not to allow himself to be exposed to Ultra as Spaatz had been, since it would prevent him from flying on missions. Spaatz had regretted his own inability. When Winterbotham appeared, therefore, Eaker recalled that he was staggered to find an American general adamant in the face of his practised persuasion. Eaker said 'No', and kept on saying 'No'.

The reason was simple. Spaatz and Eaker were old friends: there was nothing hidden between them. After the war they built together and shared for years an up-country fishing lodge. Spaatz knew that Eaker was a flier, irreversibly committed to the air. He

240

knew too from his own experience that the young 8th Air Force, still to prove itself over Germany, might well require for morale's sake a flying General at its head. Most of all, he knew that whatever limitations might be imposed for a man on the Ultra list Eaker would nevertheless fly – and almost certainly be sent back to the United States in consequence. At this delicate moment in the history of his country's Air Force Spaatz had no intention of losing Eaker – who did indeed continue to fly, on sweeps over France and on at least one mission above the Atlantic coast where, to his chagrin, he observed his bombs bouncing in fragments off the impregnable U-boat pens.

Eaker was not indifferent to Ultra. On the contrary, in retrospective conversation he recalled how for his USAF, as for Bomber Command, it had proved to be a constant and invaluable source of information about the fighter strength of the Luftwaffe, about weather conditions over the Continent (so vital for day-bombing), and about targets. What Eaker valued, and kept, was personal freedom. He was content to let a trusted staff digest all the incoming intelligence and brief him: he distanced himself from Ultra rather as, for different reasons, Montgomery did. It was still an attitude of respect for Ultra – and not so cavalier as that of Patton who, when Winterbotham sought to brief him in Algiers, said: 'You know, young man, I think you had better tell all this to my Intelligence staff, I don't go much on this sort of thing myself. You see I just like fighting.' The truth is that the case of Eaker illustrates a wider problem – that of all those commanders who could not be kept out of the front line and who, if Ultra-indoctrinated, represented a grave security risk. America's General Doolittle, the bomber of Tokyo, and Britain's Air Marshal 'Mary' Coningham were both as irrepressible as Eaker or Patton. But a nation at war needs its Jeb Stuarts as well as its Grants: and how would Rommel have reacted to an Ultra briefing?

There is a more sinister connection between Ultra and the 8th US Air Force.

'Germany first' in fact meant 'Germany late' for this USAF. It was not until January 1943 that Fortresses crossed the German frontier, the first step towards that point of no return, 14 October, when in the terrible Schweinfurt raid 198 aircraft were destroyed or damaged out of 291, and the absolute superiority of the German fighter over self-defending American day-bomber formations was conclusively established. Without this trauma the US Air Staff in Washington would never have embarked on that characteristically American triumph, the crash programme for mass production of the Mustang long-range fighter which, by April 1944, gave the USAF a virtual superiority in the daytime skies above Germany.[7] It had been a murderous but essential learning-process. Nothing but such experience could teach the USAF and its masters, from General 'Hap' Arnold (the Chief of Air Staff) downwards, about what it could not – and then about what it could – do. Why did the process take so long?

In 1942 Torch abstracted from the young USAF a considerable number of aircraft and crews for operations in North Africa. That was a check. But what basically prevented Spaatz and Eaker from getting their Fortresses in strength over Germany at an early date was the U-boats' threat to the sea-lanes on which Eisenhower's Allied Army depended. Convoys must run constantly from the British Isles and the United States to support first the invasion and then the conquest of North-west Africa. But in the autumn of 1942 shipping losses, to U-boats alone, were catastrophic – well over 500 000 tons in August, rising to over 700 000 tons in November. For every possible reason, and Torch was only one, the drain must be plugged. Eisenhower therefore gave as *top priority* to the USAF a sustained attack on the great concrete submarine pens along the French Atlantic coast. To little purpose – as it turned out – this directive prevented the USAF from getting on with its prime mission, that of learning whether it could survive on bombing runs deep into the heart of Germany. Moreover, the Biscay bases of the U-boats were still registered for special treatment in the directive for a Combined Bomber Offensive issued at the Casablanca Conference on 21 January 1943.

It cannot be irrelevant that this useless diversion towards an irrelevant target occurred, as a policy of despair, during a period when Bletchley was unable to decipher the signals between the Atlantic U-boats and their Command. Throughout most of 1942, as has been seen, the Submarine Tracking Room was denied the Ultra intelligence most pertinent for the conduct of the anti-U-boat war. Yet after the Triton cipher was cracked in December 1942 the picture changed significantly, since Station X was once again able to decipher the signals passing to and from the Atlantic U-boats and the Admiralty's Submarine Tracking Room moved into high gear.

It therefore seems probable that if Atlantic Ultra had been available throughout 1942 the convoy situation would have been sufficiently under control for panic measures to have been unnecessary. The 8th USAF could then have been left to the bloody but crucial task of discovering the truth about daylight bombing over Germany. In that sense it can be argued that the absence of Atlantic Ultra in 1942 may have set back the coming-of-age of the 8th USAF by something like two critical months.*

Yet this absence, curiously enough, may have impeded but did not prevent a marriage that year between Ultra and the US Navy.

Along the Atlantic seaboard of the United States the first result of Hitler's declaration of war was mayhem. An immediate submarine assault (Operation Drumbeat or *Paukenschlag*) was organized by Dönitz against the huge quantities of shipping that were to be found off the eastern coast of America. There was no black-out. Convoys were silhouetted at night against the glow of shoreward towns. They steered by still illuminated lighthouses, followed the peacetime sealanes, used their radios without discipline, and were thinly escorted. Drumbeat took the US Navy unawares. 'Appreciations of the current situation varied in each command. There was no correlation, nothing on which an overall plan could be based, no central plot where all dispositions could be displayed and decisions taken.'[8] No Operational Intelligence Centre, in fact, no Tracking Room – and no Ultra. From January to April 1942 the average monthly loss of shipping in American waters was at least 100 000 tons of which over half consisted of invaluable tankers. *Paukenschlag* exacted a terrible toll – and a high proportion of the ships and men lost were British.

A British initiative was required to make the US Navy face the facts. Rodger Winn flew over Washington. There and in New York he set out the case, like the brilliant advocate he was, for adopting a naval intelligence system akin to the British as a means of beating the U-boats. After seeing every relevant officer up to Admiral King himself he carried the day. And so, with that incomparable American ability to do big things fast once the need is manifest, an Atlantic Section, Operational Intelligence, was immediately established.

*The author discussed this proposition with General Eaker in 1977. He said that although he had not previously considered the matter in this light, the scenario made sense. Certainly he believed that the attacks on the submarine pens had very seriously impeded the maturing of the USAF.

By June Commander K. A. Knowles was at its head: by July he was in London consulting with Winn. Looking at it from his experience of the Admiralty's Tracking Room Patrick Beesly concluded that the co-operation with its American counterpart, Op 20 (later called F21), 'that grew up during the next two and three-quarter years was probably closer than between any other British and American organizations in any Service and in any theatre.'

Knowles and his team were completely and continuously in the Ultra picture. The effect on the American Navy's operations against U-boats was dramatic, particularly after Bletchley reconquered the Triton cipher in December 1942 and intelligence about the Atlantic U-boats was restored. There was a daily exchange of Ultra information between the Citadel in London and Op 20 in Washington (and with the Royal Canadian Navy's equivalent section in Ottawa), though Knowles received his actual Ultra messages direct from Bletchley through American channels. The integrity of this Allied effort was symbolized by the fact that the British and American Tracking Rooms were connected by a direct signal link, on which only Winn, Knowles and their two deputies were permitted to communicate.

During 1942, therefore, the USAAF and the US Navy may be said – at least so far as the German war is concerned – to have been Ultra-indoctrinated both in theory and in practice. As for the Army, Eisenhower and a few of his trusted officers had been introduced to the theory of Ultra after their arrival in Britain, but it was not until November 1942, and the invasion of North-west Africa, Operation Torch, that practice taught them the true meaning and value of Bletchley's 'special intelligence'.

Indeed, the positive contribution that Ultra could make to the battle became plain to Eisenhower even before the Torch landings started. In his temporary headquarters beneath the rock of Gibraltar he learned for the first time how lonely a vigil the commander must keep on the eve of a great operation, when all is committed and nothing more can be done. Were the Germans suspicious? His fears were calmed during the anxious period immediately before the landings occurred by the absence of any indication in the Ultra signals that the Germans were preparing counter-moves.[9] This was 'negative information' of the highest value. And then, when the assault took place, a Special Liaison Unit went ashore at Algiers while gunfire was still crackling, to receive from Bletchley a decrypt of the surprised Kesselring's order for an emergency air-lift of German forces into Tunisia. This positive news, of course, was also passed straight to Eisenhower in his Gibraltar command-post. At the start of his Mediterranean experience, therefore – and thereafter in North Africa, in Sicily and in Italy – Eisenhower and numerous other American officers received clinching evidence that in Ultra they had an incomparable source of military intelligence.

But until 1943 the United States and its representatives were sharing the Ultra secret in a somewhat haphazard and coincidental fashion. There was no overall plan, shaped by the Americans themselves. It was the gathering certainty of an invasion of Europe from the north, the shadow of Overlord, that started a new advance on a broad front into Enigmaland.

The spearhead of that advance was Telford Taylor, who arrived in England during the summer of 1943 as the designated co-ordinator of the American Ultra effort in Europe. The future prosecutor at the Nuremberg War Crimes Trials who later became Professor of Law at Columbia University was an admirable choice for a mission that would require clarity of mind and firm, realistic judgement. It is to be noted, moreover, that when in 1944 an officer was sent out to co-ordinate in similar fashion the American Ultra effort in South-east Asia, the man who arrived in Delhi was a future judge in the Federal Courts of the United States, Inzer Wyatt. These two key appointments reflected principles for the selection of Ultra officers which had long been familiar at Bletchley Park but had so far been traditionally absent in the US Armed Forces. The basic criteria were quality of mind and general capacity rather than length of service, rank, or any other of the conventional symbols.

Taylor was, in effect, the first European representative of an organization set up by Colonel Alfred McCormack, whose responsibilities derived directly from the fumbling over Magic before Pearl Harbor. Sensitive to this failure the Secretary of War, Henry Stimson, appointed McCormack on 19 January 1942 to investigate and recommend. First in his class at Columbia University, a brilliant and highly successful Wall Street lawyer, McCormack was an ideal choice. He came to his task without inhibitions. Like the little boy in the fable, he could see and say that the emperor was short of clothes. And so, as a result of his report, a new organization, Special Branch of the Military Intelligence Service, was introduced in the spring of 1942 with Colonel (later Brigadier General) Carter W.

Clarke as Chief and McCormack as Deputy Chief. Its function was the intelligence exploitation of intercept material and general guidance to the US Army Signal Corps over cryptography, traffic analysis and similar recondite matters. From the firm base of Special Branch, which had the advantage of not being trammelled by service tradition, McCormack now set about choosing the Ultra team.

He sought officers for two distinct tasks. Before the anticipated D Day in Europe one group of Americans was to be fed into Bletchley itself and established as normal participating members of the community: virtually interchangeable with their British colleagues and a welcome reinforcement at a time when many of the 'old hands' at BP were now tired and stale.* McCormack's more important job was to evolve an entirely new breed of animal – the 'Ultra adviser' or 'representative'.

This was an all-American concept. In the British system the material sent out from Bletchley to the SLU at a field command was passed direct by the SLU officer to the commander himself or one of the two or three senior staff officers on the Ultra list. They then formed their own judgements. But in the new American pattern which was standardized before D Day, June 1944, and applied throughout the Overlord campaign, the 'Ultra representative' received from the SLU the intake of Bletchley signals. It was his personal responsibility to digest the material and present it regularly to his superiors – the commanding general, the G2 or chief intelligence officer, and perhaps a chief staff officer. In addition he carried the heavy burden of security – of ensuring that Ultra was not compromised either by his commander's operational plans or in any other way. But a post-war review of the Ultra representatives' work, issued by Carter Clarke,[10] pin-pointed their prime function.

At most commands, the heart of the Ultra operation was the daily briefing of recipients; this generally took place at a regular hour each morning, either preceding or following the intelligence briefing based on lower classified sources. The briefing, ordinarily lasting from 15 to 20 minutes, covered the salient intelligence received during the past 24 hours

---

*It is an index of the strain of work at Bletchley that some members of Hut 3, for example, at first resented the arrival of the Americans, fresh reinforcements though they were, because of the extra effort that would be required from a weary staff in training them. This attitude was short-lived.

plus an occasional special study or summary. The methods of presentation varied considerably, depending upon the personalities of the representative and his recipients.

So it was that on Telford Taylor's heels several dozen talented Americans reported to Bletchley Park during the winter and spring of 1943/44. Some remained, to be absorbed into the existing teams. Others, after a short course in Bletchley practices and Ultra procedures, passed on as advisers to the US commands, army and air, for which they had been pre-selected as Special Branch men or to which they were now assigned by Telford Taylor. Their backgrounds were diverse. Some had been at Harvard, and at least nine at Princeton. One had been extricated from 17 Airborne Division: one came from the 11th Airborne, and one had been a captain in the horse artillery of the 1st Cavalry Division. Their futures were as diverse as their pasts. William Bundy, who became a head-of-watch in Hut 6, was a post-war Assistant Secretary of State and later editor of *Foreign Affairs*. (In the same Hut, by coincidence, was a girl called Wendy Hinde who, in after years, would edit Britain's equivalent journal, *International Affairs*.) Alfred Friendly's distinguished career took him to the desk of the Managing Editor of the *Washington Post*. Langdon van Norden combined considerable business interests with chairmanship of the Metropolitan Opera Association. Curt Zimansky, before his death in 1973, was a notable philologist, and Yorke Allen an adviser for the Rockefeller Brothers Fund. Edmund Kellogg, Captain USAAF, had the special task of feeding Ultra intelligence from Bletchley to the Pentagon until he was appointed as Ultra officer at Strategic Air Force HQ at SHAEF: he went on to the State Department in 1946 and then into the Foreign Service. Landis Gores, a valiant conquerer of great personal disabilities, nevertheless pursued a long career as an architect of quality.

Special Branch, it might be said, picked special men. And all of them with whom the author discussed their time at Station X revealed, consciously or unconsciously, that on them as on their British colleagues BP had cast its unique spell. They too had felt that sense of monastic dedication combined with high intellectual stimulus which pervaded the Bletchley huts. After Winterbotham's *The Ultra Secret* appeared Alfred Friendly wrote about it in the *Washington Post*, and remembered BP.

There was an amazing spirit at the place. Morale was high because everyone knew the fantastically successful results of our daily-and-nightly endeavours. It was one place in the military where there was no sense of futility, of useless work or of nonsense. Had he served there, Heller would have had no material for *Catch 22*.

This was a magic that had not failed.

For Ultra representatives at command headquarters in the field the stamp of man Colonel McCormack required would have to be a clear-headed diplomat, capable of assimilating detailed information rapidly and of expounding it lucidly; persuasive, independent, authoritative. Not surprisingly, many of those chosen were lawyers: indeed, of all the twenty-eight officers who ultimately served as representatives in the European theatre the most distinguished was unquestionably a man of law. If the British involvement in Ultra produced a future Lord Justice of Appeal in Rodger Winn of the Admiralty's Submarine Tracking Room, in Lewis Powell the American involvement produced a future Associate Justice of the United States Supreme Court.

Powell's experience, if not unique, was certainly exceptional. As an air intelligence officer in North Africa, briefing for shipping strikes over the Mediterranean, he found his unit was often directed to a point out at sea where, to their surprise and pleasure, they discovered on arrival that an enemy convoy was waiting for them. Their Marauder bombers were being targeted in the same way as the North African Coastal Air Force, which used Ultra with great efficiency against Axis shipping: its deputy commander was another American, 'Pete' Quesada, who was learning here the technique of exploiting Ultra for targets of opportunity which he would apply with great profit during his command of 9 US Tactical Air Command in the battle for Normandy. Now, in 1944, Powell found himself inducted into Special Branch and posted first as Ultra representative to General Spaatz at the headquarters of the US Strategic Air Force, and then as Chief of Operational Intelligence.

At USSAF Powell found Ultra invaluable. During the Americans' all-out effort to destroy the day-fighters of the Luftwaffe, for example, the intercepts arriving from Bletchley through the SLU at Strategic Air Force enabled him to monitor the progress of repairs on a bombed German airfield, to take note of instructions for fresh units to move in, to establish when the move had occurred, and then to send in a further strike. During the pulverizing of the

248

German oil industry it was often possible, after a raid, to obtain from Ultra intercepts a good knowledge not only of the damage done but also of the rate of restoration of production, so that just when the efforts of German technicians and slave labour were bringing a plant back into effective action the Fortresses could be sent in again. From an inexperienced officer in Africa, unconsciously briefing his few air-crews from Ultra, to the Chief Intelligence Officer of Strategic Air Command, consciously using Ultra as a guide for bombers by the hundred – Powell ran through the whole gamut.[11]

If other Ultra representatives, by comparison, were short on operational experience they soon acquired it. Adolph Rosengarten advised 1 US Army first under General Omar Bradley in Normandy and then, after Bradley took over 12th Army Group, under General Hodges during the eastward advance. Langdon van Norden was the representative at General Nugent's 29th Tactical Air Command, supporting Simpson's 9th Army on the Siegfried Line and beyond. During the encirclement of the Ruhr in 1945 Lieutenant William Carnahan, who had graduated via the cavalry and an airborne division, was the representative with Gerow's 15th Army. And when the Allied Airborne Army was formed under another American, General Brereton, his Ultra adviser was an artillery Captain called Josiah Macy who after the war flew on and up to the executive heights of Pan American Airways. A few track records like these indicate the scale and variety of responsibility imposed on these able young men.

The responsibility was indeed great. For the objective historian the question is whether it was carried out in the right way.

The function of the representatives as envisaged by the US Army Chief of Staff was spelled out by General Marshall in a letter to Eisenhower on 15 March 1944; a letter which constituted the representatives' charter.[12] Marshall was not only defining their task: he was laying it on the line, without any question of misinterpretation, that these officers were in a special category, that Washington had the proper handling of Ultra much in mind, and that when the invasion commenced generals in the field were to allow their representatives – young and unmilitary though some might be – the necessary scope and authority. With so many senior American officers approaching high command in battle for the first time and tending, in some cases, to take the traditionally authoritarian and dismissive attitude towards juniors, Marshall's instructions and implicit warning were salutary. In his letter to Eisenhower a key sentence, defining the representatives' duties, read:

Their primary responsibility will be to evaluate Ultra intelligence, present it in useable form to the Commanding officer and to such of his senior staff officers as are authorised Ultra recipients, assist in fusing Ultra with intelligence derived from other sources, and give advice in connection with making operational use of Ultra intelligence in such fashion that the security of the source is not endangered.

This directive was so comprehensive and permissive that it allowed and indeed encouraged the representative to think of himself as a kind of private intelligence centre. In the field each had his tent, van or trailer as an office – under guard – in which his safe contained the Ultra papers. Most maintained very full records. One representative with an Army Group kept details of all units in his own Group's area, of all units from division upwards on the entire Western Front, and of German knowledge about Allied units. A representative at a Tactical Air Command had a card index with separate inserts for all airfields and the units located on them as well as an 'order of battle' notebook with separate pages for units down to individual *Gruppen*. Some officers produced periodical résumés of Ultra information, indicating recent changes in the enemy situation and estimating German capabilities. One air representative used to issue special papers on subjects like V-weapons and jet aircraft.

There was nothing equivalent to this in the British system. Most of the activities just outlined would be carried out by the normal intelligence staff of the commands concerned. Indeed, as the Ultra representative was not fully integrated into the complex of operational planning at his command headquarters, but acted as a sort of fifth wheel, there was a potential danger in allowing so much advisory power – by way of regular briefings and even the production of intelligence summaries – to officers who were not (and in Marshall's directive were certainly not intended to be) involved in the evolution and conduct of operations like a commander and his immediate staff. It seemed as though the representatives, since they did not merely pass on the information from Bletchley, but digested it themselves and then communicated it garnished with their own interpretations, were an unnecessary filter through which the signals from BP had to make their way before reaching their real target, the commander and his chief operations and intelligence officers. In the light of British practice since 1940 this might seem a reasonable comment.

But the system and the situation were not British. For the battles in Europe many of the British command teams, both army and air, were machines well-oiled by years of practical experience in action and those that were not had a model to follow and established doctrines to apply. To many the application of Ultra in field operations was no novelty. Some of the highest American commanders, by contrast, lacked this experience and background. There was a strong case for assisting them with men of considerable aptitude and a certain detachment, whose allegiance ran back to Bletchley and Washington as well as to their local generals. The Ultra signals, after all, were not always information handed out on a plate: they required skilled evaluation and interpretation. Moreover, as Winterbotham had insisted from the beginning and as Marshall's letter warned his subordinates, they must never be betrayed by a commander acting on them so obviously that the enemy might suspect a break of the Enigma ciphers. The mission of the representatives, to brief their generals and to monitor security, was therefore a genuine requirement in the American context. If some of them over-elaborated their role and set themselves up as intelligence officers in their own right, this was a minor and pardonable excess of enthusiasm.

For there was another justifying factor which, in practice, demonstrated that Marshall had been right in his directive and McCormack shrewd in his recruiting. Telford Taylor, by virtue of his Special Branch mission in Europe, knew as much as anyone about the representatives and their work. As he reminded the author, the status of the intelligence officer in the pre-Pearl Harbor American armed forces was low. (There is an important analogy here with the Royal Navy before 1939.) Service with active units – battalions, squadrons, divisions – was always more significant for an officer's promotion than intelligence work: in consequence there was not, in 1944, a large stock of officers equipped by training and outlook to fill the highest intelligence staff posts at field commands. Here again the British situation was different: the realities of continuous engagement in war since 1940 had, by 1944, effectively refined and expanded the group of intelligence officers capable of holding staff positions within the highest commands.

So it was that at least some Ultra representatives – relatively junior officers, in services where rank carried weight – had to work to their general through or even by-passing the titular Chief Intelligence Officer at a command, because of the latter's limitations. Some contrived to brief their generals direct, or to exercise the skills they had once employed as lawyers and businessmen in tactfully amending the appreciations prepared by their senior, the G2. At such times it was a taxing business, particularly as the representative had no deputy and was permanently and exhaustingly on the job, a strain increased by the fact that in the Army headquarters or wherever he worked the nature of his task was known, at most, to a handful. He would be camouflaged as a Russian Specialist, an SLU Liaison Officer, a German Air Force Specialist, a member of an Estimates and Appreciation Group. Over-riding all was security. Carter Clarke's report noted that 'the representative's most difficult job was to make certain that recipients did not make direct operational use of Ultra without appropriate cover'. This was a problem long and well understood by the British. But to ride herd round a Patton was not easy.

It was therefore of the greatest importance that this small body of hand-picked men – no more than twenty-eight in all, as has been seen – should have been inserted as a leaven into the American command system. Trained at Bletchley and carefully indoctrinated, they understood both the magnitude and the irreplaceable quality of what was going on at BP in a way that few field commanders were able to do. They could establish close relations with British intelligence officers, as Rosengarten at Hodges' 1st Army did, for example, with Williams at Montgomery's 21st Army Group, because in a sense they were part of the same priesthood and applied the same standards. Their work was lonely, demanding, sometimes misunderstood, but in the long view essential. Since the American armies and air forces in Europe had so preponderant a share in the victory, and since the representatives were the main channel through which Ultra intelligence flowed to US commands, their performance deserves close study in any account of Ultra's contribution to the conduct of the war.

The British shared their Ultra secret to the full. Nevertheless, before Overlord was launched there were grave reservations in London about the Americans' ability to preserve the secret intact.

The concern was over security. Long experience of the Special Liaison Units had disclosed the difficulty for a young officer of low rank in preventing occasional breaches of security at a headquarters controlled by Generals, Admirals or Air Vice-Marshals supported by senior staffs. Not imperceptive, the British sensed that the Americans' Ultra advisers might have even less muscle, responsible as these were to Washington and therefore slightly alien, as well as subordinate, figures in the commands to which they were attached. They well understood the attitude of some of the American top brass towards their juniors. From his visits to the battlefronts and his frequent use of the Special Liaison Units Churchill was keenly aware of the problem of personality and seniority. Nevertheless, he was anxious, as ever, that the precious Ultra should not be compromised and his geese stop laying their golden eggs.

It was not that there were flaws in the initial arrangements. When Telford Taylor first arrived in England to set events in train, he and Winterbotham together went over all the British operational procedures and agreed a joint system. It was Winterbotham who indoctrinated the American commanders. Marshall's instructions to Eisenhower were based on the British code of practice. The Ultra advisers were briefed at Bletchley. All the same, Churchill was uneasy.

With so much at stake, he decided to re-insure. When the Ultra organization first took shape he made Winterbotham, through Menzies, personally responsible for surveillance of the whole British system. Now, privately, he issued instructions that Winterbotham must carry an equal and personal responsibility for monitoring the Americans' handling of Ultra. This was a delicate mission for Churchill's watchdog. Between the allied camps there was always a charged field of electricity, and the least hint that the Americans were behaving irresponsibly could generate sparks and flashes of resentment and suspicion. Fortunately Winterbotham was able to play it cool.

He had a useful mechanism to hand in the Special Liaison Units which, with British officers many of whom were now veterans at the game, were located at all the main American command-posts. From the many private papers relating to the SLUs which the author has studied it is clear that these young men looked up to Winterbotham as a fountainhead and a Father Confessor: in the European theatre, particularly, there was a relationship of mutual trust and respect. A

253

quiet warning to the SLUs to keep their eyes open and report back any problems was sufficient. So warned, Winterbotham would fly out instantly to the points of trouble. Using his good personal relations with the American commanders and their staffs, he would remove any security risk in their procedures without causing heat and hurt pride. Such occasions were infrequent but important. In Normandy, for example, it became evident that a developing American habit of passing Ultra summaries and reports between army and air force headquarters was not only a contravention of the rules but also a considerable security risk. A visit from Winterbotham to General Bradley restored the situation smoothly, for Bradley was big enough and wise enough to take the point.[13] But such episodes were no more than symptoms of growing-pains such as the British themselves had experienced in the early days of Ultra. In practice there was no significant breach of security throughout the whole of Overlord.

In that European campaign the Allied armies and air forces were at least converging with some cohesion on a central point, the heart of Germany, and Ultra officers were making their contribution to what was, in essence, a single effort. But in the China-Burma-India theatre the situation was more complex.

Inzer Wyatt began his mission as the chief Ultra officer for this vast region by reporting in April 1944 to Telford Taylor's London Office at the American Embassy in Grosvenor Square. Clarke and McCormack had already briefed and indoctrinated him about Ultra in Washington. Now he saw Menzies at Broadway, spent several days at Bletchley, proceeded to Algiers (watching the handling of Ultra there), and next moved north to Italy and Caserta where, in Telford Taylor's company again, he observed the distribution of Ultra from Alexander's headquarters. This was a thoroughly professional preparation such as Marshall had envisaged in his letter to Eisenhower. 'They will have had a period of training if possible in the Mediterranean theatre,' he wrote, 'and this training will be directed towards equipping them to use Ultra intelligence effectively and securely.' All this is a world away from the atmosphere at Pearl Harbor.

When he arrived at Delhi in June 1944 Wyatt established an immediate and continuing relationship with the officer in charge of the British SLU, John Stripe, with whom he would regularly confer about Ultra problems. But his own responsibilities were inevitably far wider than Stripe's. The information he received came direct from Washington, even though some of it originated from British sources. It was his task to evaluate the incoming intelligence and to distribute it appropriately not only to Lord Mountbatten's South-east Asia Command at Kandy in Ceylon but also to General Stilwell, advancing on the northern frontiers of India and Burma, to Major-General Stratemeyer (Commanding General Eastern Air Command), to General Claire Chennault's bomber group in China, 14 USAF, and to General Curtis LeMay's 20 Bomber Command, the strategically targeted B 29s which operated from their five airfields around Calcutta and the advanced field at Chengtu in China.

Wyatt's direct link with Washington represented a clean break with American procedures. While he and his group in the Far East were theoretically subordinated to the local US commander, in fact they were at all times responsible solely to the War Department in Washington. All Ultra intelligence and all administrative messages came to them in a cipher that only Special Branch could read. No wonder McCormack chose men with a diplomatic flair – for senior officers as a class and Americans in particular look with disfavour on colonels with a private line to the Chiefs of Staff. Wingate's notorious link with Churchill is a reminder of British tenderness about command prerogatives. Similar arrangements in the Pacific drove MacArthur to a point of rebellion from which he withdrew only after a direct order from General Marshall. And in Wyatt's theatre there was a further problem – the Chinese. Stringent orders were issued and the strictest precautions taken to prevent Chiang Kai Shek and his staff from obtaining even the most minute evidence of Ultra's existence. The sieve contained too many holes.

To run his oriental Bletchley Wyatt had thirty-five American officers and enlisted men – signallers, cipher clerks etc. – whom he distributed as representatives, on the European pattern, to the various commands he serviced. But whereas in North-west Europe and the Mediterranean signal traffic between Bletchley and the SLUs was conducted by one time pad or Typex cipher, Wyatt's circuit employed the American Sigaba or M-134-C, a rotor-based ciphering machine akin to Typex or, indeed, to Enigma itself. All traffic was known as Ultra: all papers were Ultra-stamped.

Each general in the field had different needs. There was not much Japanese order-of-battle or other operational information through Ultra on Stilwell's front, but what he greatly and characteristically appreciated was the diplomatic intelligence that Wyatt was able to furnish, since this supplied Vinegar Joe with aces up his sleeve in his negotiations with Chiang Kai Shek. Chennault's requirements were strictly operational. To enable his aircraft to carry out their long missions by striking at Japanese convoys, minelaying and otherwise infesting the seas off South-east Asia he needed advance intelligence about both shipping movements and such Japanese fighters as might seek to interfere. Chennault was a dedicated user of Ultra: how else, indeed, might his men have found those long-range targets of opportunity. LeMay's 20 Bomber Command had a different problem. Its far-distant strategic objectives, dictated from Washington, were more like the static urban targets of Bomber Command in Europe and Ultra could hardly add much information about them. In June 1944 the Command had started attacking the Japanese steel industry: in August it flew 4000 miles to attack the important Palembang oilfields in Sumatra: in October it was over Manchuria and Formosa: in November the B29s from Calcutta hit the naval base back at Singapore. What LeMay needed, and what Wyatt through Ultra could often provide, was significant intelligence about the strength of the waning Japanese airforce along the extended and exposed flight-paths of his Command. Like Spaatz and Eaker, Chennault and LeMay were entirely pragmatic in their attitude. They accepted Ultra because it worked.

The whole of this American organization in the Allied theatre of South-east Asia owed much to the British system and was conducted, as has been seen, in close liaison with the British at Bletchley and in the field. But nothing illustrates this interlocking better than the way that the British organization was used to bridge a yawning gap between the US Army and Navy. To Wyatt from Washington came the intercepted signal-traffic of the Japanese army and air force, forwarded through US Army channels. But the American Navy refused to let the Army have its intercepts of Japanese Navy traffic – of which those concerning the enemy's troop and supply convoys were of such critical interest to Chennault in China. The intercepts were, however, reaching Mountbatten's HQ at Kandy, since the US Navy had no objection to passing information to the British Navy. A timely visit by Winterbotham to India and the close relations established between Wyatt and Stripe enabled this absurd anomaly to be overcome.

Winterbotham arranged with London that the Japanese naval Ultra available at Supreme Headquarters in Kandy should be fed to the British SLU. Stripe then handed it on to Wyatt who, in turn, was able to file it back to his Army superiors in Washington. More importantly, he was now in a position to provide Chennault with target information about Japanese shipping which was of central importance for 14 USAF on its remote stations in China. As Wyatt wrote to Winterbotham in 1971, 'the arrangement was bizarre in the extreme, but it was effective'. It was not unique. Benjamin King, an RAF officer transferred from Bletchley to Washington in the latter stages of the war, observed a similar gap which he bridged by arranging for US naval intelligence sent to England to be repeated back to him down the normal Army/RAF channels. He was then able to hand on the information to his deprived US Army colleagues. No wonder that as late as 8 May 1945 MacArthur's right hand man, Major-General Willoughby, testified during the Pearl Harbor investigations that 'in an otherwise meritorious desire for security (though every modern nation knows that crypto-analysis is going on) the Navy has shrouded the whole enterprise in mystery, excluding other services. . . .'[14]

Behind Wyatt, behind all the American Ultra officers sent on missions abroad – whether to Bletchley Park or to field commands – lay not only Colonel McCormack and Brigadier General Clarke but the whole panoply of the Pentagon and, in the last analysis, their Commander-in-Chief, the President. No account of the American involvement could therefore be complete without an examination of the system for processing, evaluating and distributing Ultra intelligence at the heart of the US war administration.

One of the most striking features of the American High Command in Washington is its mental distance from the *day-to-day* conduct of the German war. The Pacific separated the capital city from the campaigns of MacArthur and Nimitz, but these were still an ever-present reality. For Admiral King and his naval colleagues, of course, they were top priority, the breath of their being. But even in 1944 the Operations and Planning Division of the War Department was more concerned with the Pacific than with the European theatre. And there were good reasons. In Europe the United States had Eisenhower, a tested and trusted soldier, in supreme command of the Allied Forces. In control of the air General Spaatz acquired a virtual parity with the RAF's Chief of Air Staff. In London the British now had a war-skilled organization close to the battlefields. The Atlantic was certainly wide, but hardly ever can one observe in Roosevelt, Marshall or their entourage any urge to cross the seas and intervene in the handling of the fighting. On strategic matters relating to the German war the President and the Joint Chiefs of Staff were always active and vocal, whether it be at the great conferences, Casablanca, Quebec, Cairo, or during what was termed 'the transatlantic essay contest' in which argumentative memoranda shot to and fro. But once actual operations started the attitude of Washington, broadly speaking, was more detached.

This posture meant that at the centre of American affairs Ultra intelligence was treated in a manner markedly different from the long-established British system – a manner more leisurely and at times, it might almost be said, more scholarly. Certainly the treatment had its immediately utilitarian aspects. Of the information presented daily at the morning intelligence conference of the War Department to enable the Assistant Chief of Staff, G2, to brief General Marshall it was calculated that an average of thirty-five per cent came from Ultra sources. But in the main the Washington context was quite different from that of London. There the Prime Minister and his military advisers conducted an intimate and sustained dialogue about the current waging of the war. Churchill monitored his field commanders closely and even personally, in Normandy, in the Mediterranean, at the crossing of the Rhine. An umbilical cord connected the continental battle-headquarters and the conference rooms in Whitehall. There was a complexity of relationships.

The use of Ultra by the British war administration had, therefore, an urgency and relevance greater than its American equivalent attained. The intelligence Bletchley supplied was a tool for immediate use rather than an object for brooding contemplation. In a report[15] issued by Carter Clarke after the war on the use of Ultra by the US War Department it is significant how often a note of almost academic regret is struck over the fact that daily requirements of analysis and presentation prevented more long-term appreciations. The British, down to their last reserves of man-power (the author's division was broken up in Normandy to provide infantry reinforcements for other divisions) still retained something of the 1940 sense of fighting for their lives. Naturally long-term appreciations were produced by British staffs, but as compared with Washington the attitude towards Ultra of the service departments in London, and indeed of the Prime Minister himself, was far more that of Churchill's 'action this day'.

This is abundantly illustrated by the methods evolved in the Pentagon for processing CX/MSS material. (CX/MSS were the distinctive letters marking the huge amount of Ultra intelligence about the European theatre that was forwarded by Telford Taylor's men from Bletchley to Washington.)

The effective circulation of German intelligence began in July 1943 when Special Branch set up Section C, at first consisting of two officers and then expanded. Drawing mainly on Ultra sources, Section C prepared a daily publication known as the 'Military and Naval Supplement to the Magic Summary' which, because of its origins in CX/MSS material, went only to the Secretary of War, the Chief of Staff, the Assistant Chief of Staff G2, and the ACS of the Operations and Planning Department. As the months ran on a few more senior officers became recipients, including Admiral Leahy as Roosevelt's Chief of Staff and Admiral King, for the Navy, as well as the Commander-in-Chief US Fleet. But control was always rigorous. All copies had to be returned to Special Branch for destruction, and all distribution was by the locked pouch of a Special Branch courier. The contrast is marked with the wide and fertilizing flow of Ultra along British channels, whether in Whitehall or in the field. How much Ultra reached the President himself is uncertain. He was presumably fed by Leahy with selected items liable to interest him – for Roosevelt, unlike Churchill, was not interested in *everything* to do with running the war. There is no evidence that when Roosevelt was abroad he insisted, as Churchill vehemently did, on a personal service of Ultra through a Special Liaison Unit. Bletchley was on Churchill's doorstep, visible, exciting. He and Station X had soldiered on together since 1940. Roosevelt inevitably lacked this sense of direct involvement.

Clarke's report itself observes that at this time the work of Section C 'was uneven and its function uncertain' – even though Colonel McCormack gave much personal attention to the preparation of the Supplement. Shortage of staff was exacerbated by the posting of officers to England as soon as they were trained: even more by the restrictive security which prevented Section C from consulting outside Special Branch and stopped the Supplement from reaching

259

senior officers to whom it would have been invaluable. In 1943 not all the lessons of Pearl Harbor had yet been learned: even though at many points in England and the Mediterranean officers of the US Army and Air Force (and of the Navy too, if only over the Battle of the Atlantic) were already sharing the Ultra secret. There were, nevertheless, some practical benefits. For the morning intelligence conference held by the AC of S G2 an 'Ultra disposition map' would be marked up daily, as at Bletchley or in a British command head-quarters, showing the latest lay-out of German forces and, in particular, the varying developments in the sole European battle-zone where American troops were engaged – the Italian front. And many special studies were undertaken on aspects of the German army, on Europe's defences, on Yugoslavia, even on some German operations in Russia. Ultra was certainly being used: but it was still a limited usage.

With the coming of D Day in June 1944, however, the whole military informational system in Washington was revised and enlarged. Three new Directorates of Military Intelligence were introduced – for Administration, Information, and Intelligence – the last comprising a Research Unit, a Reports Branch, and a group of free-ranging officers called Specialists. As the Overlord campaign developed the stream of CX/MSS material channelled to Washington became a flood, but there was now a mechanism for dealing with Ultra far more expeditiously and comprehensively than in the past.

The German Military Reports Branch, as it was known, took over from Section C the daily production of the Supplement which, from 1 July 1944, was re-christened the Magic European Summary. (The blurring of Magic and Ultra in American terminology is always confusing and sometimes misleading. In fact the Summary was based as to ninety per cent of its contents on CX/MSS or Ultra material, the remaining ten per cent being drawn from conventional intelligence sources.) Under their Chief there was a good staff of about twenty, nearly all Special Branch officers, recruited under the McCormack system for 'analytical ability, judgement, scholarship and imagination'. Quality of mind was the prime factor.

The daily Summary (which even in the spring of 1945 was still only being distributed to eleven senior recipients within the War Department and to four outside) was wide-ranging, but insistently focussed on recent operational intelligence in spite of pressure from the editors themselves, and from the recipients, for more extensive and long-range appreciations: such, for example, as a brilliant analysis of German progress with the jet-fighter which the Summary carried as an appendix on 17 November 1944.* The reason for that pressure is evident and understandable: it explains the different attitudes in Washington and London towards Ultra. The 'need to know' was not the same. Churchill and his team were absorbed in the immediacy of the battle. They could do something about it, take 'action this day', and often did. A comparison between the personal involvement of the Prime Minister and General Alan Brooke and, on the other hand, of Roosevelt and Marshall in the Normandy campaign from D Day until the end would be instructive. For the President and the Joint Chiefs, remote from the day-to-day direction of the German war, it was in fact the long-term view that mattered: what great new production programme to initiate (or cut back) for tanks and aircraft, how many more divisions to ship or not to ship to Europe. Perforce they were students not of particular points on the war graph but of the curving graph itself. This was their need to know – a need that Ultra could largely satisfy.

This is not to say that General Marshall, shrewd soldier that he was, did not keep himself abreast of current events. Here the second division of the Directorate of Intelligence, the Research Unit, had an important role. It was ordered 'to study, evaluate and collate all incoming information pertaining to order of battle in the European theatre . . .' and to 'produce special studies relating to various aspects of strength, identifications, dispositions, operations or personalities. . . .' These studies would be classified Top Secret Ultra. By a regular routine, carried out at Marshall's specific request, the Order of Battle section made its summaries of the previous day's intelligence, mainly CX/MSS, and passed them on to the specialists for comment and amplification. They in turn briefed the Assistant Chief of Staff, G2, who then conveyed the most significant points to Marshall at his morning conference. Broad analogies may be drawn here with the work of the British Joint Intelligence Committee and the daily briefing of the CIGS.

Indeed, the close implication of Special Branch men in the process of intelligence briefing, already noted in the case of the US Ultra representatives in the field, persisted to the end. When Gen-

*See Chapter 12 where this appendix is discussed in its chronological context.

eral Marshall accompanied Roosevelt to the Yalta Conference, for example, an officer of the German Military Reports Branch went with him to pass on any specific items of information captured in the Ultra net which it was thought necessary for the Chief of Staff to see. When Churchill travelled abroad, as has been noted, he insisted on taking a Special Liaison Unit in addition to his normal staff.

But like the British, the Americans learned from realities of experience. The Reports Branch and the Order of Battle Section, at first too compartmentalized, gradually fused into a working whole, so that information, interpretations and evaluations could be freely interchanged. Marshall and his staff were now serviced by a single team. This lesson was increasingly understood by the British, although it was not until after the war that something like a truly unified intelligence system emerged. And there was another principle which the British at least partly grasped: to function effectively, intelligence staffs must have adequate foreknowledge of their own side's battle plans. In this respect security spread over the Pentagon too thick a blanket of the dark. The Special Branch men were too much inhibited by lack of information about the actual or projected operations of the Allies.

Nevertheless, the fact remains that after the Americans first became fully involved in Ultra they entered into an enormous inheritance which they did not squander. At every level, (from the Joint Chiefs of Staff down to the commanders in the field, the directors of the USAAF in its struggle over Germany, the naval units that shared in the Battle of the Atlantic, the far-flung bomber commands of Chennault and LeMay), the whole of the American war effort came to be interlocked with the British: not simply in terms of fighting side by side, but of drawing continuously and fruitfully on the unique source of Ultra. This was indeed not a drill.

10   Alamein to the Alps

'By indirections find directions out'
WILLIAM SHAKESPEARE, *Hamlet*

On 7 August 1942 a pair of Luftwaffe fighters, hurtling from the African skies, shot down the unprotected aircraft that was carrying the newly designated commander of the 8th Army back from the desert to take up his appointment. Lieut.-General 'Strafer' Gott was killed: a casual but poignant event, for it is now clear that the death of this admired and respected officer ensured for the British an historic victory and enabled one of their outstanding generals to establish the basis of his fame.

Few things are certain in war. Nevertheless, the considerable amount of evidence now available supports the view held by many wise judges at the time that Gott, mentally and physically enervated by long service in the desert campaigns, was incapable of securing in the autumn of 1942 that decisive rout of Rommel and the Axis army which Auchinleck had more than once failed to achieve. Gott himself sensed this. Alan Brooke, the CIGS, noted that on 6 August, as Churchill in Cairo re-shaped the Middle East commands, 'I had very serious misgivings concerning Gott's appointment in his tired state.' The hard truth is that there are no valid grounds for believing that Gott could have orchestrated the victory at Alamein.

But Gott's death was the making of Montgomery. The day before, he had been nominated to command the British contingent, cosmetically called the 1st Army, which was to take part in the projected Anglo-American invasion of North-west Africa – Operation Torch. In view of the political complexities, the difficult Tunisian terrain, the speed of German reaction and the meagre scale of the British force there was no conceivable way in which Montgomery, still virtually unknown, could have secured for himself by some sudden stroke an instant niche in the national Valhalla. As Gott's immediate successor in command of the 8th Army he was presented, by contrast, with exactly this possibility. After interminable defeat and retreat between Egypt and Cyrenaica the British public yearned for a victory, Churchill demanded a victory, and the

263

imminent Torch landings at the other end of the Mediterranean made victory a strategic requirement. Since men and equipment were reaching the Middle East in unprecedented quantities while Rommel pleaded almost daily for reinforcement, all that the 8th Army needed for success was the fresh mind and firm control that Gott could never have supplied. Montgomery seized his opportunity and provided the victory: in a flash his name became a household word. His first battles in Africa were the origin of his fame. Unfortunately, as was said of Napoleon the Third, 'his origins condemned him to success': for never, thereafter, would Montgomery risk a failure or – except rarely – confess if one occurred.

But before Montgomery could launch at Alamein on 23 October the offensive from which he later took his title he was compelled, only a few weeks after his arrival, to deal with Rommel's last desperate effort to break through. The action at Alam Halfa, which began before dawn on 31 August, was brief in duration, an absolute defeat for the Afrika Korps, and different in the clinical certainty of its conduct from any battle previously fought by the British in North Africa. The calm and orderly management and the apparent foresight of Montgomery's command seemed to reinforce the impression he had already made on his superiors and his army – of a mind and character strong, lucid, determined and, above all, efficient. His subsequent victory at Alamein merely confirmed on a larger scale the supreme confidence which both Montgomery and his countrymen came to feel about his generalship.

While all of this is true, it does not represent all of the truth. The effect that Montgomery had on the Americans during the Ardennes campaign, of a self-assured god descending from on high to tidy up a shambles created by incompetent mortals, was no more than a distressing caricature of an image formed in August 1942 and perpetuated not only by his admirers but also by himself. He arrived from England, summed up the desert situation in a trice, issued quick ruthless orders, and behold! Victory! Yet his reputation – if not his self-esteem – would have been neither harmed nor diminished if the legend had been more closely linked to the facts.

For it is indeed a matter of fact that before his army was attacked at Alam Halfa Montgomery possessed through Ultra not only a clear picture of Rommel's 'thrust line' – the direction in which the main bulk of his armour would advance – but also a sufficiently accurate knowledge of the date when the Panzer Army would assault. Moreover, Bletchley was handling the Mediterranean ciphers with good effect at this time. The constant and impassioned pleas and complaints transmitted by Rommel to his overlords in Germany and Italy were conveyed to Montgomery through Ultra, providing the general and his staff with solid evidence about the morale, supplies and order-of-battle of their opponents. Nor was it by chance, but as a result of the highly developed connection between Ultra and shipping-strikes, that before and during the battle a monotonously high proportion of the Axis transports ferrying ammunition and priceless fuel was deftly sunk – *Istria* and *Dielpi* on 27 August, *Sanandrea* on the 30th, *Picci Fassio* on 2 September and *Bianchi* and *Padenna* on the 4th.

When Montgomery died *The Times* published some recollections by his intelligence officer, Bill Williams. He recalled how:

I was summoned to the caravan on August 15 or 16, 1942. The new army commander had uncomfortably piercing eyes, and his questions, in a sharp, spinsterly voice, were much to the point. He wanted to know when Rommel would attack, where, and what with. . . . He won his first battle, the model defensive battle at Alam Halfa, by accepting the intelligence with which he was furnished that morning. . . . It meant, too, that because the intelligence had proved adequate then, he believed it afterwards.

Montgomery's greatness in these days when the hinge of fate turned rested, in fact, not merely on an uncanny gift for reading the battlefield and penetrating his enemy's mind – the contemporary legend which still persists – but on something far more reliable and professional which may not have dilated his ego so much, but certainly emphasized the quality of his military judgement. The intelligence that Williams and his other advisers provided was naturally derived from a number of sources. But a key source was Ultra. In his first command of an army in action Montgomery grasped Ultra's significance, applied it triumphantly in battle, and 'believed it afterwards'. This was admirable generalship, and he would have done better to make more of it in later years than to pretend that he was a clairvoyant. For Alam Halfa *was* a model. Rommel was allowed to enter a trap. Everything was prepared in advance. The author, whose first battle it was, took part in the exercise which actually preceded it and felt that this was a considerate way to run a war.

An unavoidable strategy of indirect approach was to carry the 8th

Army from Egypt to Tunis and then, erratically, to Sicily, the heel of Italy, and onward from one mountain chain to another until the Germans at last capitulated in the shadow of the Alps. But all began at Alamein: at that point early in November 1942 when Rommel accepted defeat and, on the 6th, General Alexander signalled to Churchill 'Ring out the bells! . . . 8th Army is advancing.' For that advance, though circuitous and sometimes interrupted, 'by indirections found directions out' and made steadily for the final goal.

Yet at Alamein – as so often in the main conflicts on land, and by contrast with the war at sea – Ultra's chief contribution was perhaps incidental: coming with most effect at the beginning and at the end. It was certainly an advantage for Montgomery to learn through Ultra of the sorry state of Rommel's health and of his return to Germany for a cure – at the end of September, some weeks before the British offensive began. 'Rommel must have taken a knock,' observed Roosevelt when the news came from London. In the Chancellery in Berlin Rommel was also taking, from Hitler's hands, the jewelled baton of a Field Marshal – and protesting violently that traitors in Italy must be betraying the convoys on which his army's fate depended.

But it was not a case of traitors, any more than it had been at Matapan: at sea and in the air the British (with some squadrons of the USAAF) were applying with increased effect the intelligence that came through Ultra about Axis shipping movements. General Stumme, who flew from Russia to replace Rommel – as Montgomery knew – began the battle short of fuel: after Stumme's death in action during the first night, and Rommel's precipitate return, the situation merely deteriorated. Throughout Alamein a lack of petrol restricted the Field Marshal's freedom to manoeuvre. Of the general cargo and fuel despatched from Italy and Greece during October forty-four per cent was lost *en route*: during November, twenty-six per cent. But even these substantial figures disguise the impact of particular sinkings. At the outset of the battle Rommel received – and knew he had received – a body blow when, on 26 October, *Proserpina* went down at sea with 3000 tons of fuel and *Tergestea*, carrying 1000 tons of fuel and 1000 tons of ammunition, was sunk at the approaches to Tobruk.

If fuel was short, so were men. Preoccupied with Russia, Hitler and the High Command spared Rommel few reinforcements. The only German division to reach Africa at this time of stress was 164

Light, and even its transfer overseas during July and August had been revealed by Ultra. There was a comic moment. Bletchley sent out a decrypt of a signal reporting to Rommel that 164 Light Division would be arriving 'by platoons'. To Enoch Powell and the intelligence staff it seemed curious that a large formation should be transported in dribs and drabs. But in the middle of the night light dawned on Powell. Bletchley had blundered. The German word for platoon or detachment, *zug*, was also the word for train. Obviously 164 Light was being fed through Greece by train-loads. Powell rushed into the intelligence office shouting 'trains, trains, trains'.[1]

With a good flow of Ultra from England Montgomery thus had a clear picture, before the Alamein barrage exploded on 23 October, of his opponent's strength and morale, his notable shortages, the disposition of his army – and the absence of its commander. But much of this knowledge had come from conventional sources. Once the battle began and the armies were locked together all the key intelligence people – Airey and Hunt at Middle East HQ, Williams at 8th Army – agree that Ultra had little direct effect compared, for example, with the almost continuous contribution of 'Y' Service.[2] Monitoring the actual battlefield conversation of German staffs and commanders, fixing enemy locations by direction-finding, and assessing the movements of units by a study of their call-signs and the changing volume of their radio traffic, 'Y' Service provided an extraordinary awareness of what was going on beyond the dividing minefields. (Rommel's similar capability had been drastically reduced by the capture of his intercept unit during the July fighting. Moreover, the documents then acquired taught the British much about their own lack of radio security and led to a marked improvement.) Apart from the many tactical moves during the twelve days' fighting Rommel made only two of major significance – the transfer of 21 Panzer Division from the south to the north of his line and his commitment during the latter stages of his last reserve, 90 Light Division, from its lay-back position westwards along the coast. Each of these critically important shifts was identified and known to Montgomery – but through 'Y' Service rather than Ultra.

Yet Ultra had its full share in what must be considered the most dramatic single episode of the Mediterranean campaign. By 2 November Rommel was finished – about two dozen tanks left, with little fuel or ammunition, and a large part of his artillery and infantry dead, wounded or captured. At 7.50 pm that evening he signalled to OKW a detailed estimate of the need to retreat. Hitler's response was telephoned to Rome next morning at 11.05 and radioed to Rommel at 11.30. It was the famous and foolish order which began by declaring that 'in your present situation nothing can be thought of but to hold on, not to yield a step' and ended: 'You can show your troops no other road than to victory or death.' Mussolini chipped in with a similar exhortation. Rommel's despair: his agonized discussions with his staff and his commanders: his immediate reply to Hitler giving details of the hopeless position and his final signal at 11.15 on the 4th specifically asking for permission to withdraw – all these are recorded, as were the responses from Hitler and the Duce during the evening of the 4th which gracelessly accepted the inevitable.

Here was certainly high drama. But the relevant fact is the speed with which this significant interchange was deciphered at Bletchley. Ultra was soon circulating the good tidings. At the Foreign Office Sir Alexander Cadogan noted in his diary for 3 November: 'C had news, which he phoned me this morning, which certainly seems to show Rommel is in a fix.'³ Alan Brooke, out in the country inspecting an airborne division, was called to the telephone at lunch-time and told that incoming reports showed the Axis position to be desperate. Returning to London next day, he found Churchill wildly excited, already talking of ringing the church bells and 'busy dictating messages to Roosevelt, Stalin, Dominions, Commanders, etc.'

But the information so swiftly disclosed about Rommel's difficulties and his dialogue with the Führer related, after all, to a battle. What use was Ultra to the victor? The triumph at Alamein, and Montgomery's pretence that everything went according to plan, conceal the fact that as the fighting progressed he had many grave problems and no absolute certainty of a breakthrough. The infantry in his best divisions was waning away. As usual, the German line was solid. If his last big thrust, Supercharge, had failed Montgomery would have been a very worried general. Of course he had many indications from battlefield intelligence – prisoner interrogation, 'Y' Service, reports from his own troops – that Rommel was in straits. But from the Ultra intercepts he now knew all this for certain: knew both the scale of his victory and Rommel's own estimate of his losses and deficiencies.

The evidence about Ultra's deciphering of the Rommel-Hitler

exchanges, so recently available, must therefore puzzle still further those military critics who, ever since the Second World War, have been unable to understand why Montgomery failed to cut off and destroy Rommel's army after Alamein. There was no lack of pressure from his own people. General Briggs, commanding 1 Armoured Division, wanted to prepare it logistically for a dash to head off the Afrika Korps, but was refused.[4] De Guingand, Montgomery's Chief of Staff, put up a proposition for a mobile encircling force, but to no effect. Even without Ultra the disparity between the strength of the British and the Germans in early November was evident enough: the Ultra signals not only confirmed this, they also disclosed that for the time being Rommel was in no mood to fight. Nevertheless, whatever the explanations and justifications, the hard core of his army got away. It is those who worked most closely with Montgomery who feel most strongly that Alam Halfa and Alamein 'condemned him to success': that his method thereafter was to plan certainties and put his bets on them, but never to take risks – in particular, never to risk the fate that his predecessors Wavell and Auchinleck had met along the desert road, of running disastrously into a Rommel at bay.

But there was another factor. Both Montgomery and Rommel knew that the Axis forces falling back from Alamein were ultimately doomed, because of the Anglo-American landings at the western end of the Mediterranean which began on 8 November. Rommel learned about Torch when it happened, but his plight was already known to Torch's commander, Dwight D. Eisenhower, for the diary kept by his aide Harry Butcher records that on 7 November, D Day minus one, Churchill sent the general a top secret signal to inform him that 'a message from Rommel to the German General Staff had been intercepted in which Rommel begged for aid immediately, or his force would be annihilated.' And thus Ultra, which illuminated the end at Alamein, shed a bright light on the eve of Torch. Montgomery, of course, was aware of the impending operation well in advance, though his knowledge seems to have put him under greater pressure to achieve a victory than to exploit it.

Eisenhower gained more from Ultra than a comforting report about the success of a distant 8th Army. His immediate concern was whether he could get his troops ashore and move them eastwards in time to secure Tunisia before French politics, German reinforce-

ments or the rigours of the winter prevented him. All three produced unexpected obstacles, but Ultra was 'a very present help in
trouble'.

The foundations had been well laid. During the preliminary
months of planning Eisenhower and all his senior staff officers and
commanders, Generals Bedell Smith and Mark Clark, Spaatz who
would direct the USAAF in North Africa, General Anderson who
succeeded Montgomery at 1st Army and his opposite number Air
Marshal Sir William Welsh had been individually indoctrinated
about Ultra by Winterbotham. This was the first Allied operation in
history for which the leading soldiers and airmen were briefed in
advance about the source and quality of the intelligence they might
expect to receive. And the significant fact is that during the six
months it took to get to Tunis the appetite of these men for Ultra
increased through experience rather than diminished from disillusion.

When Eisenhower arrived at Gibraltar early in November to set
up a provisional command post in the dark and dispiriting tunnels
within the Rock – he later recalled it as 'the most dismal setting we
occupied during the war' – one of his many fears on the eve of his
first campaign was the likelihood that U-boats would get among the
assault and supply convoys now converging on North Africa from
British and American ports. But this fear, at least, was unfounded.
Rodger Winn had estimated, from the accumulated experience that
Ultra gave to the Submarine Tracking Room, the maximum
number of craft that the Germans and Italians might assemble to
the west of Gibraltar and within the Mediterranean itself. The Navy
made dispositions accordingly. Fortunately the Germans, taken by
surprise, failed to re-deploy their U-boat fleet effectively before the
landings or to achieve heavy concentrations thereafter. Inevitable
sinkings followed of Allied transports and warships, but by
December the U-boats were being forced away from the Straits of
Gibraltar, the danger passed and, as the Official History of the War
at Sea puts it, 'The great stream of shipping from America to Casablanca continued to pass on its way unhindered.' On the other
hand, in the five weeks after 7 November no less than fourteen
German and Italian submarines were sunk in the Mediterranean or
its immediate approaches. Eisenhower owed much to Ultra for the
safe-guarding of his enterprise.

And there was another consolation from Ultra. Until the assault force was securely ashore nobody knew for certain whether the Germans would anticipate the invasion and take steps to prevent it. The fact that Bletchley produced no decrypts of signals indicating that Hitler was having one of his intuitions or, more practically, that Kesselring, the Mediterranean Commander-in-Chief, was hurriedly moving troops to protect North-west Africa was negative information of the most positive value – especially to a worried Eisenhower in the bowels of Gibraltar. In fact Hitler's intuition assured him that the Allied preparations, which were suspected by the Axis, were directed not against Algeria and Tunisia but at a number of possible points further east: nor did his military advisers oppose him. The security surrounding Torch was outstanding: but so was the work of the British deception teams, who so deeply relied on Ultra intelligence in their delicate task of keeping German eyes on the wrong target.

Such consolations were short-lived. Predictably, the German response was ruthless once the Allied objectives had been disclosed. Winterbotham, who was in Gibraltar at the time to check on the functioning of his Special Liaison Units, recalled how Kesselring 'in an Ultra signal to the German Commission in Tunis, ordered immediate agreement by the French for the Germans to take over the aerodromes and port facilities, both at Tunis and Bizerta. Shortly after Kesselring had sent this signal another one arrived from Hitler which gave permission "to seize these areas and prepare forces despatch to Tunisia".' And then Ultra revealed Hitler's orders to the German Commander in Paris to occupy the regions of Vichy France – news which produced in London a flurry of activity to prevent the French fleet at Toulon from falling into German hands. The French disposed of this threat themselves by scuttling their ships, but nothing stopped the airlift of German troops for Italy to Tunis and the transfer to Africa of fighter aircraft. Ultra, making all this plain from deciphered Luftwaffe signals, was warning Eisenhower that he had lost the race while still on the start-line.

The winter campaign settled into stalemate: a pattern of actions by Allied task forces, usually under strength and always under-experienced, against tough and tenacious German opposition. Such a war, of skirmish and manoeuvre, was not indeed for Ultra, though an episode on 12 November illustrated its occasional value. On the 11th Ultra produced an order from Kesselring for a parachute battalion to seize the airfield at Bone, on the coast a hundred miles west of Bizerta, before Allied spearheads arrived. By a laudable reflex British paratroops in American Dakotas were successfully flown in first, a quick operation which not only showed that Ultra could be decisive in a purely tactical situation, but also secured the best all-weather airfields for the RAF in a region where, as the Tunisian rainfall revealed, most runways disintegrated in a slough of mud.[5]

As the German defences stiffened in eastern Tunisia Eisenhower's forward troops were at the end of a long line of communications. A poor rail-link, bad and mountainous roads, atrocious weather and not the best of staff-work prevented a build-up in impressive strength. While Rommel conducted his brilliant withdrawal westwards along the African shore, it was still stalemate on the Tunisian chessboard. And then, in January 1943, radical changes occurred. One of the results of the conference held at Casablanca that month between Churchill, Roosevelt and the Combined Chiefs of Staff was the appointment of General Alexander to head a new 18th Army Group comprising the British First Army and the American formations in Torch. Since disunity of command and control had so far distinguished the Allies' operations, this was a major improvement. But the Axis, too, was consolidating. By early February the danger to which the eastern flank of Torch had always been exposed now became real: the Afrika Korps linked up with the garrison of the Tunisian bridgehead.

Had Rommel and General von Arnim, who commanded 5 Panzer Army within the bridgehead, felt less than detestation for one another this combination might have been disastrous against an Allied command set-up which has itself been described as 'a tangled skein of misunderstanding, duplication of effort, over-lapping responsibility and consequential muddle'. Instead, the rapid sequence of German successes in mid-February 1943, known to history as the battle of Kasserine Pass, ended in defeat where proper co-ordination and a determined final thrust might have resulted in a breakthrough as significant for the Tunisian campaign as that at Sedan had been in the Battle of France. The topographical details and tactical moves are complicated, but the central issue is easily discerned. Emerging through the passes that breach the mountainous eastern flank of Tunisia, von Arnim carried out a private offensive in the north while Rommel (with Montgomery still at Tripoli and the defences of the Mareth Line between them) risked a sortie in the south, hoping to strike a blow of strategic significance before

Ultra confirmed. In their last days in Tunisia the Germans in desperation used their 'Gigants', the huge six-engined Me323 transports, to ferry supplies. When the news of this plan arrived on Ultra, Squadron Leader Tony Allen, senior intelligence officer at Tactical Air Force, could not believe the enemy would be so mad. As a check, a man was sent through the German lines to photograph a 323 on the ground. This is his photograph, which confirmed Ultra's warning. Most of the 323s were shot down.

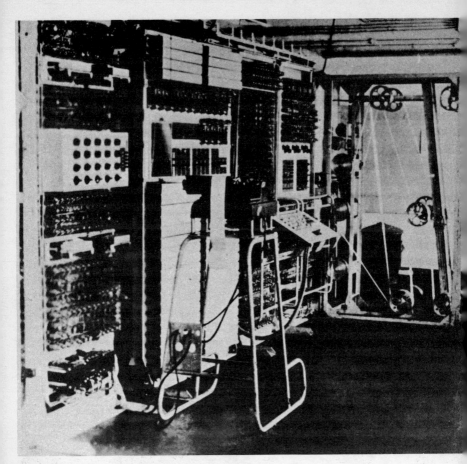

Bletchley's Colossus: 'the driving of the tape could be
entirely by pulleys'. (*The Public Record Office
London)*

Opposite above: The man behind Colossus.
T.H. Flowers receiving a doctorate at the University
of Newcastle in 1977. (Photo by Allen Glenwright)

Opposite below: Geheimschreiber. (BBC)

'Burn after reading'. In this elegant incinerator at the
Royal Palace at Caserta in Italy all Ultra signals sent
to General Alexander's Allied Force headquarters
were destroyed after use.

he had to turn back again and face the 8th Army. He was in his Stonewall Jackson mood.

Instead of co-ordinating his attack with Rommel's, von Arnim wilfully went his own way, and was later roasted by Kesselring for doing so – of small help to the Field Marshal, whose final drive to the head of the Kasserine Pass was halted by a thin red line of British tanks and American guns. Rommel fell back: so near, and yet so far. In the course of these scattered but substantial operations the Americans suffered ignoble losses of men and equipment; but they were their own harshest judges, they learned quickly from their blooding, and the British, bearing in mind their own African follies in the past, had no grounds for comment.[6]

From Eisenhower downwards, the Americans' self-examination was intense. And perhaps it was the bitterness of this appraisal that caused the removal of a British officer from his post. The facts are curious, but well-documented. A post-mortem on the battle suggested that the intelligence appreciation of the Germans' intentions had been at fault. Its drift had been that the enemy's main attack would come from von Arnim in the north: the danger in the south was underplayed. Acceptance of this scenario had naturally restricted the transfer of troops from the northern zone to what became their exposed right flank. And the chief intelligence officer at Eisenhower's HQ was Brigadier Mockler-Ferryman, who was last noted as handling Ultra intelligence at the headquarters of Home Forces during the Battle of Britain.

Eisenhower asked London for the relief of Mockler-Ferryman on 20 February at about the same time as Rommel's 10th Panzer Division was moving into Kasserine Pass. In his major biography of Eisenhower, *The Supreme Commander*, Professor Stephen E. Ambrose gives a cryptic explanation for this exceptional request to the British CIGS: 'he decided that Mockler-Ferryman was too wedded to one type of information'. But the real answer is to be found in the full and unpublished text of the diary kept for Eisenhower by his aide, Harry Butcher. The entry dated Algiers, 20 February 1943, reads:

An explanation of the defeat, as seen by Ike, lies in a misinterpretation of radio messages we regularly intercept from the enemy. This source is known as 'Ultra'. It happens that our G.2 Brigadier Mockler-Ferryman, relies heavily upon this source. It has frequently disclosed excellent information as to the intentions of the Axis. However, the interpretation placed

273

by G.2 on the messages dealing with the place of attack – an attack that has been expected for several days – led Mockler-Ferryman to believe that a feint would be made where the attack actually occurred through Sidi Bou Zid, and that the real and heavy attack would come farther north. . . . Basing his judgement on the reliability of Ultra, Mockler-Ferryman was confident the main attack would come in the north. . . . General Paget left this morning *en route* to the UK and is to handle with Sir Alan Brooke (the CIGS) the replacement of Mock in such a manner that he will not be discredited. . . . However, Ike insists we need a G.2 who is never satisfied with his information, who procures it with spies, reconnaissance, and any means available.[7]

Pity the poor intelligence officer! By relying insufficiently on Ultra over the *Ankara* affair in December 1941 Brigadier Shearer had contributed to the defeat of his own armour and ultimately lost his job. Now, in February 1943, Brigadier Mockler-Ferryman was removed for over-reliance on Ultra. The issue was not clean-cut. He had been used to Ultra for some two and a half years. The American ground commanders to the south were certainly uneasy and conscious of a German presence. On the other hand, those positive identifications of units and their locations which 'Y' Service established so readily in the open desert were much more difficult to achieve amid the hills and valleys of the Tunisian uplands.[8] What the episode does confirm is the view held by all commanders and senior staff officers who handled operations in the field, that in the battle zone Ultra information was usually most valuable when buttressed by good local intelligence from the conventional sources.

But in one sense the defeat at Kasserine was to Eisenhower's benefit, since Mockler-Ferryman was replaced by his old colleague of 1940, Kenneth Strong, who was to continue as Ike's chief intelligence officer throughout the Mediterranean campaigns and in the key intelligence post at SHAEF from Normandy to the end in Germany. After the war Strong became the first Director-General of Intelligence at the Ministry of Defence. Nor, incidentally – in spite of Butcher's romantic words – was he a man prone to rating spies more highly than Ultra.[9]

Rommel also received a temporary benefit after Kasserine. He was put at the head of Army Group Africa, consisting of his own old command (now re-named 1st Italian Army, under General Giovanni Messe) and von Arnim's 5th Panzer Army. But he was ill and deflated. It was with uncharacteristic apathy that he set about his next venture. Nevertheless, it looked promising, for Montgomery had been ordered to provide a distraction from the fighting in Tunisia and had pushed forward two divisions, 51 Highland and 7 Armoured, up to Medenine on the approaches to the formidable Mareth Line. With three panzer divisions Rommel planned to destroy this relatively weak spearhead before it could be reinforced.

But this time Ultra intervened with devastating effect. Decrypts from Bletchley provided ample forewarning of an attack. By a considerable feat of organization and down the single coastal road a Guards brigade, the New Zealand Division and a brigade of tanks were rushed up to Medenine in reinforcement. A position was calmly prepared in text-book fashion for anti-tank defence. The date of attack, 6 March, was precisely known. In consequence three seasoned panzer divisions were made to turn tail ignominiously, with the loss of some fifty tanks. The British lost no armour, and little else. In his *Papers* Rommel observed that 'the attack had been launched a week too late. The operation had lost all point the moment it became obvious the British were prepared for us.' Three days after Medenine, at the Palazzo Viminiale in Rome, Rommel talked with Mussolini. 'Did they know about our attack in advance?' asked the Duce. 'Yes.' And that same day Goebbels was noting in his diary how he had heard at Hitler's headquarters that the defeat was due to Italian treachery. Could this, he wondered, be a British cover-story? Perhaps Goebbels was right – for the real reason was Ultra.

Sick in body and spirit, Rommel left Africa for ever on 9 March, to be replaced by von Arnim who pressed on Kesselring the Desert Fox's own view that the Afrika Korps should fall back into Tunisia as fast as possible. But no: the orders from on high were to stand fast in the Mareth Line, that strong necklace of fixed defences which the French had built to protect the frontier of their pre-war empire in Africa against the Italians. During the policy-making debate within the Axis over this issue many signals passed between Africa, Italy and Germany, from which Ultra was able to supply Montgomery with a full picture of the layout of the enemy's troops. This showed that the Line, as it ran southwards from the sea behind the useful anti-tank ditch of the Wadi Zigzaou's watercourse, was manned mainly by Italian divisions, with just the German 90th Light in the centre and 15th Panzer lying back in reserve.

But Montgomery knew a great deal more about the Line. He had available for consultation the former Garrison Engineer at Mareth and another invaluable French officer, General Rime-Bruneau, the late Chief of Staff in Tunisia. Last-minute photographs from air reconnaissance were abundant. With all the other evidence from patrols, prisoners, 'Y' service, and the confirmatory voice of Ultra, Montgomery was better informed about Mareth than the Germans about the Maginot Line in 1940.

It remains for his definitive biographer to unravel what nobody as yet has satisfactorily explained – why, with this wealth of knowledge, Montgomery chose to begin with a direct assault on the northern defences of the Line itself instead of pressing from the start with the outflanking movement far inland on which he was compelled to fall back when the frontal attack, ill-conceived, ill-prepared and ill-fated, ended in total failure. His desert army, fresh from the open spaces, was not suited mentally or technically for smashing its way into a stronghold – though its spirit was high. The author, whose battery by chance was the foremost of the 8th Army at this moment, recalls the elation of the infantry as they passed through his guns to the assault: remembers, too, the cool confidence of the tank crews, most of whom were to be shot to pieces when 15th Panzer counter-attacked them on the far side of the Wadi.

After Pearl Harbor the unfortunate Admiral Kimmel quoted a phrase from the Roman philosopher Seneca: 'It is better to have useless knowledge than to know nothing.' And sometimes better, perhaps, than to know too much. It is difficult not to feel that the authority of Ultra and his other sources of intelligence combined with Montgomery's well-founded contempt for the defensive will of the Italians to make him feel that an abrupt assault by his infantry, supported by generous gunfire, would 'bounce' the Young Fascist and Trieste Divisions into a rapid retreat. Foiled by their tenacity and the German riposte, he was finally forced to execute the brilliant outflanking move by the New Zealanders and 1st Armoured Division which levered General Messe's army back into Tunisia.

Once the Axis forces were boxed inside the bridgehead surrounding Tunis, and once Alexander began to knit together in effective unity the British, American and French elements within his 18th Army Group, the question was not how a collapse would come but when. With the front lines meshed together along the great half-moon of valleys and mountains, Ultra as usual became complementary to other intelligence rather than a critical factor in itself. But there was one region where its impact continued and even increased – the air. After the early days of inferiority and sodden landing-strips the Allied air force, thriving and multiplying under Air Chief Marshal Sir Arthur Tedder and General Spaatz, achieved a virtual mastery. Ultra was of constant value in the identification of targets for what had become a flexible and efficient strike-force. Nowhere was this more evident than over the seaward approaches, where with Ultra aiding airmen (and the submarines and surface craft), Axis convoys and their escorts were so precisely eliminated that when the end came a quarter of a million men had to face a Dunkirk without any ships. The paralysis can be illustrated by a single example. In desperation efforts were made by the Luftwaffe to ferry over fuel in the huge, slow, six-engined Messerschmitt 323 transports, each of which could haul twenty tons of freight. One member of Hut 3 at Bletchley recalled how, as the news came through on Ultra, her sympathy went out instinctively to these doomed and lumbering giants. When the Germans' intention to use the 323s came through on Ultra to the Tactical Air Force in Tunisia the senior intelligence officer, Squadron Leader Tony Allen, could not believe that they would be so foolish. The Axis bridgehead was now small, so he was able to arrange for someone to penetrate the enemy lines and photograph a possible 323 on an enemy airfield. Tiny though the resulting photograph was, the evidence was con-clusive: the characteristic tail, the six engines, the high wing, the bulky body.[10] Of the twenty-one despatched on 22 April, sixteen were shot down.

A decision to proceed from Africa to Sicily had been taken early in the year at the Casablanca conference, not so much for profound reasons of strategy as because its capture would clear the Mediter-ranean as a secure route to the Far East and save two million tons of shipping – and because the masses of men and equipment in the 18th Army Group could not lie idle until the Normandy invasion was ripe. Allied strength meant that Sicily must succumb – but only if the troops could be got ashore. If the Germans became suspici-ous, it was feared that to produce another Gallipoli they would not need to reinforce the island beyond their capability. Thus, though the actual fighting was over in thirty-eight days, it required the largest amphibious operation in history, highly complicated plan-ning and a sophisticated deception scheme to ensure the result. As

Alexander said in his subsequent despatch, the operations in Sicily are less interesting than the preliminary planning because the conventional words are justified: operations proceeded according to plan.

It is therefore relevant to note that during the preparations for this enormous Allied enterprise Ultra played its part in an unprecedented fashion. For no previous venture, not even for Torch, had its intelligence and its facilities been so comprehensively employed. Winterbotham toured the Mediterranean during the planning phase to check that his Special Liaison Units – in Alexandria, Algiers, Cairo and Malta – were tuned up for Husky, the operation's codename. He recorded what was happening.

I found that at all the main SLU stations a great deal of high-level traffic was being sent over the SLU channels by the chiefs of staff in London to Eisenhower and Alexander, and also between the various commanders-in-chief in the Mediterranean area.

This was primarily because so much of the planning for Sicily and Italy was based on Ultra information and any discussion or change of plan based on this intelligence had rightly to be sent over our own channel; added to which the top brass as well as Winston Churchill found our channel quicker than the normal signals organization, and its maximum security was useful when personalities had to be discussed. The SLUs were, in consequence, working flat out.[11]

The SLU at La Marsa near Carthage, for example, was handling some 200 signals a day, often very long ones. The Ultra system had expanded, in fact, from an organization for acquiring and disseminating intelligence into a maximum-security communications network.

Since surprise was the essential factor for the success of Husky, deception was paramount in its planning: not tactical deception, which seeks to confuse the enemy within the micro-war of the battlefield, but strategic deception which seeks to persuade one's opponent that the battle itself will be fought in some quite different region or even country. By 1943 the British were developing a highly centralized system for orchestrating their deceptive schemes, so that for Husky a whole range of techniques could be brought to bear on the central problem: how to make the Germans look in the wrong direction.

Nearly always, the best deception trades on the enemy's own

preconceptions. If he already believes what you want him to believe, you have merely to confirm his own ideas rather than to undertake the more difficult task of inserting new ones into his mind. So it was with Husky. Hitler was obsessed with the Balkans – perhaps because this Austrian could not forget the exposed underbelly of the Old Empire, more probably because the Reich relied on Balkan metals – copper, chrome, bauxite – and on Roumanian oil. For him, as for his High Command, the chief alternative threat seemed to be to Sardinia. Only Kesselring and the Italians worried about Sicily.

Into this ideal context of preconceptions, therefore, the British deception team dropped 'Captain (acting Major) William Martin, 09560, Royal Marines': dropped literally, for the body of the fictitious Man Who Never Was went overboard from a submarine off Huelva on the Spanish coast at dawn on 30 April. Chained to Major Martin was a briefcase containing documents prepared with exquisite care to establish his authenticity – love letters, a jeweller's account, a document from his Bank. More importantly, papers from the Vice-CIGS to Alexander and from Lord Mountbatten to the naval Commander-in-Chief Mediterranean, Admiral Cunningham, suggested delicately but conclusively that Sardinia and Greece were the next targets for the Allies.[12]

Ultra was fundamental for strategic deception – fundamental for knowing in advance which of the enemy's forces were stationed where (the order of battle): fundamental for observing immediately his secret reactions to any attempts to deceive: and fundamental for monitoring any redeployment of his troops which might confirm that he had been taken in. The case of the planted courier showed the machine at work with absolute precision. The documents in 'Major Martin's' brief-case were quickly photographed by an agent of the Abwehr, their contents reported to Berlin and copies forwarded to Germany while the originals, as was seemly, came back to London via the Spanish Foreign Office and the corpse of 'William Martin' was interred at Huelva in the presence of the British vice-consul and a Spanish firing-party. As the German documents now disclose, the poisoned bait was swallowed by Hitler himself. Operation Mincemeat was only part of the complicated deception plan for Husky, but it was not only the most famous, it was also the most convincing. A few days later, on 12 May, Hitler issued a directive about the Mediterranean which down-graded Sicily and stated that 'measures regarding Sardinia and the Peloponese take precedence over everything else'.

Though the total German reaction has only been ascertainable since the war, there were many indicators comfortably evident at the time. The Abwehr radio circuit from Madrid to Germany was one of the 'main lines' and a rich fount of intelligence for Bletchley. Within three days of what Churchill called Major Martin's swim it was known for sure in London, through Ultra, that the plan had been accepted as genuine. And then there was the negative intelligence so important in deception: to know what the enemy has *not* done can be as conclusive as some positive act. Between early May and 10 July, when Husky was launched, the Germans made many redeployments – 1st Panzer Division from France to Greece, more divisions switched from Russia to Greece, reinforcement for Sardinia. At the end in Africa the Luftwaffe had 415 aircraft in Sicily and 125 in Greece and Crete: when Husky began there were 305 in Greece and Crete and 290 in Sicily. From Ultra and elsewhere these significant shifts of emphasis could be identified. What did *not* emerge was any evidence of concern about Sicily where, when the invasion started, the Germans had only two reconstituted divisions, the Herman Göring and 15th Panzer Grenadier (whose presence was known) which in the course of the battle were reinforced by less than their own strength. The unknown warrior buried at Huelva had done the state some service.

But though the presence and indeed the location of the two German divisions in Sicily was very precisely known, the attack itself posed an old Ultra problem: who should share the secret? Alexander and his immediate staff at 16th Army Group, as well as the two army commanders Montgomery and Patton, were of course in the Ultra picture. Yet the Americans' North African Theater of Operations Intelligence Summaries had nothing to say about the Hermann Göring and the 15th Panzer Divisions. General Gavin, who was later to win great distinction in command of the 82nd Airborne Division at Arnhem, dropped on the 10th with his 505 Parachute Regimental Combat Team to cover the landward approaches to the harbour of Gela – soon to become an important point of entry. But he knew nothing about the Hermann Göring Division though its armour was lurking within striking distance: Patton's staff had strict instructions not to inform Gavin's command because of the likelihood of their being captured.[13] D Day for Husky vividly illustrates, in fact, Ultra's inescapable limitation. It was impossible to risk disclosing its intelligence to those in actual contact with the enemy, or liable to capture for other reasons, even though the knowledge might improve their chance of success or survival. Nor could private pain be allayed. When Colonel David Stirling of the SAS Regiment was captured in Tunisia on his final foray, Brigadier Hackett of Raiding Forces back in Cairo knew what had happened, because the good news was immediately radioed to Germany, intercepted, reported by Ultra to Egypt and passed to Hackett who was on the Ultra list. But Stirling's brother, in the British Embassy in Cairo, was not on the list, and Hackett had to fob off his anxious inquiries until Colonel Stirling was removed to Italy in a U-boat and his arrival reported in a lower-grade code, knowledge of which it was safe to admit.[14]

As the landings occurred General Airey at Alexander's headquarters, with his full knowledge of the German dispositions, 'listened in on the network of 15th Panzer as they toiled over the hilly and bad tracks in response to Dudley Clarke's deception plan and was delighted to hear them, just after the landings started, sending a *stellungswechsel* (change of location) which meant them retracing their steps from near Trapani and toiling back again'.[15] Here Ultra was truly assisting the battle, for since the German strength and positions were already known and since the Anglo-American beachheads were on the eastern shores of Sicily it was important to use this knowledge to inveigle one of the enemy's divisions to the west. Brigadier Clarke's brilliant 'A' Force, the Middle East deception team, mounted a simulated assault on the plausible harbour of Trapani, and off went 15 Panzer Grenadier Division. They had been false-footed.

Once the Allied armies made their lodgement on the mainland of Italy and Hitler accepted Kesselring's policy of holding a line south of Rome rather than pulling back to the Alps, it might seem that during a campaign which often looked like a prolonged siege Ultra would have been at a disadvantage. In the main this was positional warfare, with the opposing forces at close grips along the whole front. Moreover, the normal land-line communications down the peninsula were not contemptible, whilst a campaign as static as the Italian allowed the Germans abundant opportunities to establish their own telephone and teleprinter circuits. In theory, this was not a good hunting-ground for Ultra.

In practice, Allied intelligence throughout the campaign was usually of a high order. Indeed it could be maintained, in general terms, that the slow and painful advance to the Alps was impeded and frustrated less by lack of information than by the terrible character of the terrain, the quality of the German generalship, the ferocious endurance of their troops and the departure of Alexander's divisions for Normandy or Southern France. Radio was used by the Germans for important signals more regularly than might have been anticipated. Communications within the battle zones; traffic to and from Germany; the feeding into Italy, particularly at crisis moments, of divisions from all over Europe; contact with the considerable German forces in the Balkans (where radio was at a premium) – all these networks laid Kesselring's signal system wide open to the interceptors. And then, of course, there was the helpful Luftwaffe which, in all the theatres of the war, offered itself so generously to the cryptanalysts. The constantly marked-up map of the Italian front that was maintained at Bletchley reflected this surveillance by its graphic presentation of the German order of battle.

Ultra's direct impact on the Italian campaign was nowhere more evident that at its heart, the command post from which Alexander concerted and controlled the operations of Montgomery's (later Oliver Leese's) 8th and Mark Clark's 5th Armies. After the capture of Naples Alexander's headquarters were established amid the splendours of the Royal Palace at Caserta, and it was here that the intelligence War Room reached a high degree of efficiency. Into its files and on to its maps there was filtered, of course, all the selected information from other sources that would be of value at the level of an army group, but the essential flow came from Ultra.

The running of the war room was the direct responsibility of Captain Judy Hutchinson. Its sentry-guarded doors were closed to all but the limited number of headquarters officers or visitors who were 'on the Ultra list'. Maps on the walls displayed the latest information about unit locations in the battle zones, movements of enemy reserves or reinforcements from a distance, the complicated pattern of Yugoslavia and the Balkans, and the Germans' own construction of what they thought to be the Allied order of battle. A strong Special Liaison Unit maintained an unbroken connection with Bletchley. As the Ultra signals came in Captain Hutchinson would bring her maps up to date, and the texts were kept available in open files marked 'U' for consultation by any authorized visitor – from Alexander downwards. But all material, as soon as it had served its purpose, was scrupulously destroyed in an incinerator whose elegance befitted a palace of Kings.

By breakfast-time the overnight Ultras had to be sorted and assessed, and the maps marked up ready for General Airey to digest the latest information before attending Alexander's morning conference to give an intelligence briefing. But unlike some other commanders – Montgomery for example – Alexander's interest in Ultra was personal, direct and alert. He did not rely entirely on briefing by his staff. He would often stroll into the War Room alone, perhaps two or three times a day, and stand in quiet reflection in front of a map or ask some gentle question. Before the invasion of Sicily Winterbotham walked with Alexander among the sand dunes at Carthage and was struck by his eager and perceptive reaction as the Group Captain explained the complexities and significance of the Ultra system. Throughout the Italian campaign Alexander never lost sight of this weapon that Bletchley had placed in his hand. His attitude towards Ultra is confirmed by both Field Marshal Lord Harding and Airey, who together served for so long at Alexander's side.[16]

Yet in Italy as elsewhere all the accumulated weight of intelligence from Ultra and other sources was only of practical value in so far as the generals applied it effectively on the battlefield. And there were times, particularly during the earlier phases of the campaign, when the wilfulness or incompetence of individual commanders diminished that effect. Montgomery's unopposed crossing from Sicily to Italy over the Straits of Messina, supported by a cascade of fire from his own artillery, from naval guns and from the air, was pure *opéra bouffe* in which it is said that the only casualty was a puma that escaped from the zoo at Reggio. But the landings at Salerno on 9 September 1943 were a serious business and a near-disaster. There was no failure of basic intelligence. From Ultra Alexander and his staff well knew that the German divisions which had escaped from Sicily – Hermann Göring and 15th Panzar Grenadier – were over 100 miles away. Near Salerno there was only 16th Panzer, and a Parachute and a Panzer Grenadier division not far to the north around Rome. The landings were a calculated risk which took this knowledge into account.

The gamble nearly failed because of the muddle over the Italian

Ultra goes to War

surrender, which the Germans had anticipated, and the speed and ruthlessness (not anticipated by the Allies) with which Kesselring applied the 'Axis' plan for taking over Italy. At Bletchley the vigour of the German reaction was visible as the signals came into Hut 3. For nine days and nights it was a more vivid reality at Salerno, as repeated counter-attacks almost drove the beach-head divisions back into the sea. The gamble finally paid a dividend because of the dour quality of the troops, the weight of naval gunfire, and Alexander's unflurried presence. General Dawley, commanding 6 US Corps, was not a man for this moment, and all the evidence indicates that at the critical point of the action Mark Clark's own nerve was beginning to tremble.

It was the old story. Once battle was joined, the issue depended on the quality of the commanders. Ultra could hardly affect a dogfight like Salerno. But Churchill's reliance on the system as a means of keeping him in immediate touch with a battle is well illustrated by his frequent inquiries to Winterbotham in London, as the beach-head conflict raged, for the latest news from the front. And when all was over Ultra, as so often in the aftermath of a battle, reported the decision of an enemy who had accepted defeat, with a decipherment of Hitler's instructions to Kesselring to fall back north of Naples and establish a continuous 'winter line' from coast to coast for the forward defence of Rome. Hitler himself, oddly enough, was convinced that he had administered a 'thrashing'. 'No more invasions for them!' he said. 'They are much too cowardly for that. They only managed the one at Salerno because the Italians gave their blessing.' This thought greatly comforted the Führer.

However, after prolonged frustration before the apparently impregnable Gustav Line, with Cassino at its core, the 'cowards' did attempt a further amphibious assault in the hope of outflanking the enemy. The operation, known as 'Shingle' at the time, is immortalized as 'Anzio'. But this time it was the Germans who were taken by surprise. When the first wave of a force that would swell to over 100 000 men landed on the Anzio beaches in the early hours of 22 January 1944, the alert was given by a corporal in the railway engineers who departed on his motor-cycle into the darkness in search of someone to whom he could report. Purely by chance he found an officer of 200 Panzer Grenadier Regiment. Lieutenant Heuritsch informed the Town Mayor of Albano who, at 4 am, telephoned the German command post in Rome. And so, ultimately, the news reached Kesselring who first transmitted some details of the landings to Berlin at 12.45 pm. OKW immediately assumed a major assault on the outposts of Fortress Europe.

We now know that what Churchill hoped was a wild cat hurled ashore became, in his splendidly mixed metaphor, a stranded whale. The story has often been told of how the cramped beachhead of the first days survived a sequence of vicious counterattacks, only to persist for months as no more than a shallow and overcrowded death-trap. Discussion of tactical detail is irrelevant here. But on the central issue, around which all controversy about Anzio revolves, Ultra becomes very relevant indeed. Should General Lucas's 6 US Corps, under Mark Clark's army command, have moved further and faster once it was ashore on a virtually unoccupied coast?

From their intimate knowledge of the German order of battle which Ultra in particular provided, General Airey and the intelligence staff at Caserta constructed a table which set out, with what proved to be remarkable accuracy, the scale of German opposition to be expected on the D Day beaches and the daily rate of enemy reinforcements that might reach Anzio.[17] These calculations correctly forecast that the assault troops could walk ashore unopposed, that during the first few days Germans would assemble round the beach-head in increasing but not unmanageable strength, and that thereafter the build-up would develop more formidably. The first forty-eight hours were crucial. Yet General Lucas, who seems to have believed that he might actually have to fight his way ashore, made no attempt at an immediate move inland. He sat by the sea while his supplies piled up and Kesselring wove a ring of steel around Anzio.

But Mark Clark, when questioned by Alexander's biographer Nigel Nicolson about Lucas's caution, a reflection of his own policy, sought to defend it by referring to his Ultra intelligence. 'We had broken the code and could read the messages from Hitler to "drive us into the sea and drown us". He also ordered several divisions from France, Germany, Yugoslavia and from other sectors of Italy to the bridgehead. Knowing of the impending onslaught, it was necessary to dig in, for had we advanced, we would surely have been defeated.'[18]

This is specious self-justification. It is true that as soon as the German High Command heard about the landings at Anzio they ordered reinforcements to be moved from outside Italy – three Grenadier Regiments and artillery from Germany itself, an infantry division and a regiment of Tiger tanks from southern France, substantial Luftwaffe groups and so on. And certainly these plans were revealed through Ultra to Alexander's headquarters, and to Clark. But men and armour from such a distance could not arrive by a magic carpet. The landings began on 22 January: by 28 January, though most of the German reinforcements had crossed the Italian frontier they were still delayed by the need to detrain before moving south of Florence. In other words, it is absurd of Clark to suggest that it was necessary to 'dig in' from the start because of a threat that could not possibly materialize for at least a week. Of course intelligence and not the commander is often at fault. Has it not even been maintained that the error of a cipher-clerk precipitated the Franco-Prussian war? But it is a distortion of the facts to use Ultra as an excuse for what happened at Anzio.

The real and immediate threat was the combination from his local resources that Kesselring, though taken by surprise, flung together with astonishing speed and efficiency to seal off the bridgehead. By the fourth day elements of six German divisions were already closing the ring. But Airey's calculations, as has been seen, had taken this into account when measuring the time-scale of local reinforcement. What was more important was the fact that for the first day or two Lucas's troops had a considerable freedom of manoeuvre. Bearing in mind that time was short before the opposition became too great, and that from Ultra Clark knew about the even heavier opposition to be expected in due course, it seems extraordinary in retrospect that more vigorous efforts were not made instantly to 'peg out claims', as Churchill put it, further inland: to establish a zone of sufficient depth to take the shock of the powerful counter-attacks known to be impending. Instead, the stranded whale gasped on the beach.

In Alexander's war room, however, there was little gasping for information. Putting all other sources on one side – and they were many – it is impossible to convey in words the wealth and variety of intelligence about German activities throughout the whole of the northern and eastern Mediterranean that poured into Caserta from Bletchley. If one takes the half-year from November 1943 to May/ June 1944, as represented in the thousands of Ultra signals now available in the Public Record Office, one sees that no previous commander was informed so extensively and so accurately as Alexander. A particular instance would be that of shipping movements, so essential for the German garrisons along the Mediterranean coasts and islands. It seems at times as though no little convoy, or transfer of gun-boats, or shift of Siebel ferries could occur anywhere between southern France and the Dodecanese without the times of departure and arrival, the precise course, the arrangements for escort and so on being registered in the signals that passed from Hut 3 at Bletchley to the Liaison Unit and thence to the Caserta War Room. Kesselring's complete strength returns to OKW, recording as a routine the composition of his armies in Italy: German operations, strengths and locations in Yugoslavia: Luftwaffe reports: the Germans' capability in divisions, ammunition, guns, and armour all along the Italian front: the dislocation of their communications by Allied bombing and sabotage[19] – all are on the file in almost prodigal variety. Signals about cross-posting of officers, promotions, casualties and even change in command at the highest level kept the War Room's register of the enemy's personalities up-to-date. An outstanding example is that of 27 November 1943. Hitler had at last decided to opt for Kesselring's policy of defending Italy inch by inch rather than one of withdrawal to the Alps, as had been advocated by Rommel at the head of Army Group B in northern Italy. At 10 pm on the evening of the 27th Bletchley sent this message. 'Twenty-first. Kesselring took over command the whole Italian area as C-in-C South West and G.O.C. Army Group C. No further information as to possible continued existence of Army Group B, but latter not believed to remain in Italian area.' This was not surprising, for on the 21st Rommel had made his farewell to Kesselring and departed from Italy for ever.

The stranded whale at Anzio lay gasping on the beach until the following spring. Kesselring's will and the German genius for defence turned the mountainous Gustav Line, which wound across Italy south of Anzio from sea to sea, into an apparently impregnable barrier. Neither Clark's 5th Army in the west nor the British 8th Army in the east could force a way through or round. Their successive futile assaults on the great fortress-height of Monte Cassino, and the stubborn tenacity of the Germans, created a Stalingrad legend for the Italian campaign, unique in ferocity of attack and defence. It was not until Alexander secretly transferred 8th Army to his eastern flank and, on 11 May 1944, launched one of the most beautifully orchestrated offensives of the whole war, operation Diadem, that his divisions broke through the Gustav Line at Monte Cassino and streamed up the Liri valley towards Anzio, Rome and the north.

The logic behind Diadem was simple: under Kesselring – and Hitler – the Germans would refuse to relax their hold on the Gustav Line, whatever the pressure. But the planning was complex, involving a high degree of successful deception. Since the lateral move of the 8th Army could not be concealed, every device was used to suggest that it would not be ready to attack until mid-June. And though the divisions at Anzio were intended to break out of their bridgehead once the Gustav Line was cracked, Kesselring's attention was diverted from this threat by a more persuasive menace. As the Germans always believed that the Allies had more shipping available than was the case, the idea was spread abroad that in due time a major amphibious assault would be launched even further to the north, at Civitavecchia. The bait was swallowed. 'Hitler called an investiture at Obersalzburg at the end of April which was to be followed by a senior officers' indoctrination course. Von Vietinghoff, von Senger and Baade of 90th Panzer Grenadier Division, together with other important senior officers, were called away from the Italian front to attend, and *several were still on leave when Diadem broke on 11 May*. Von Senger had told his corps before he went on leave *to be ready from 24 May onwards*.'[20] Next to Normandy's D Day, Diadem was deception's consummation.

Churchill was fully aware of what Ultra could tell him about the progress of a battle. He knew in advance about plans for Diadem. Winterbotham was ordered by the Prime Minister to report to the underground war headquarters at Storey's Gate with any Ultra intelligence about the early progress of operations around Cassino.

It was a cold evening for May and the Prime Minister was sitting in his boiler suit deep in his green leather chair in front of a good fire. He looked tired. As he asked me to sit down and tell him my news, he was puffing gently at a large cigar. I had the distressing feeling that he took my normal quiet, but factual, opening of the conversation as my own way of telling him something exciting. I had given him the various small details of the fighting which had come in during the afternoon. When he said 'Is that all?' I had to say that I was afraid that was so ... Churchill was obviously puzzled and disappointed. In his usually courteous manner he thanked me for coming over and then, with a broad smile, he said, 'See that I get anything more first thing in the morning. I think you will find there will be something more of interest.'[21]

What Churchill, aware of Alexander's plan, was awaiting from Ultra was news of the famous breakthrough by French mountain and mobile divisions under General Juin whose remarkable penetration of the grim mountains to the west of Cassino created the lever with which the Gustav Line was split asunder. And the reason why there was no immediate Ultra is interesting. The German command on the French front failed to realize the scale of Juin's success, which indeed was hard to credit, and simply left Kesselring in the dark. By noon next day, however, Ultra was conveying Kesselring's urgent demands for a situation report.

Indeed, as the battle developed so much Ultra intelligence poured in – mainly *current* information, as decrypting at Bletchley seems to have been running smoothly – that it is best, perhaps, to select a phase which for the Germans was a crisis and for the Allies a climax. By the 23rd a breakthrough was near. With 12 000 French colonial troops, the famous Goumiers, General Juin had clawed a way over the mountains to outflank the Gustav and reserve Hitler Lines in the west. The Poles, at last, had entered the shattered monastery of Cassino. The Canadian Corps was thrusting up the Liri Valley towards Pontecorvo. Between the western mountains and the sea 2 US Corps was on the way to Fondi and Terracina. Ultra quickly disclosed the enemy's reactions.

At 0554 on the 22nd a composite message from Bletchley supplied situation reports for the previous day from Flivos or air liaison officers with divisions all along the line, 94, 15 Panzer Grenadier, 1 Parachute, 5 Mountain, 334, as well as 715 at Anzio: a panorama of the German front. Early on the 23rd a signal gave precise details of the boundaries of 15 PG division 'after complete execution of withdrawal movement ordered on 22nd'. At 0231 on the 24th came another batch of situation reports for the previous evening from 70 Corps, 94, 305 and 15 PG Division. Then, just two hours later, there arrived the decrypt of a signal sent from 90 Division at 1515 on the 23rd which encapsulated the achievement of Alexander. 'The deep penetration in centre of front could not be cleared up owing lack of reserves and was leading to withdrawal of main defence line. Pontecorvo being evacuated.... Terracina to be evacuated that night.' By the 25th General Keyes's 2 US Corps was beyond Terracina and linking up with patrols from Anzio. The 8th Army, clogged by its transport, was nevertheless out and away beyond Pontecorvo and the whole German defensive system. Even Hitler, that night, gave permission for a 'methodical and economical' retreat. This was the moment for the stranded whale at Anzio to turn into Churchill's wild cat.

There is no question that Alexander's strategic objective for Diadem was the destruction of the German 10th Army as it fell back in disorder from the Gustav and Hitler Lines. Rome was certainly now within reach, but Rome was incidental. Even Churchill wrote to him: 'a cop is much more important than Rome, which would anyhow come as its consequence.'* (It is ironic that in the last days of the war Eisenhower was criticized by Churchill for ignoring Berlin and concentrating on strictly military objectives, whereas now, exactly a year earlier, Churchill and Alexander disregarded Rome for the sake of the proper military target.) And whatever apologists may say, it is clear that Mark Clark was intended by Alexander to make the cop by breaking out from Anzio and cutting off the retreating 10th Army as it fell back inland from Cassino. Instead, he suddenly turned his main force north-west, to strike over the Alban Hills to Rome. 'That', as Churchill blandly observed in his memoirs, 'was very unfortunate.'

The details of this complicated story fill many pages in the appropriate histories, nor is it a simple matter of right and wrong. But when Clark decided to abandon the mission given to 5th Army and to make for Rome (which, from the beginning, had been agreed as his prize in due course), he must have known with great clarity the condition of the Germans retreating ahead of him. Apart from abundant air reconnaissance and 'Y' Service, there was Ultra. Even at Bletchley people observed the German dispositions on their map and could not understand the 5th Army's behaviour. Clark was fed with Ultra which, as has been seen, was coming quickly and copiously from the cryptanalysts. From the very start of Diadem constant decrypts from Bletchley and reports from the recce aircraft had provided a vivid picture of the 10th Army's deterioration. It must therefore be assumed that it was not for fear of the unknown that Clark turned aside from a broken enemy, but for personal

*Cop=capture, as in 'it's a fair cop'. One of Churchill's private selections from the dictionary of slang, with which he loved to salt and pepper his conversation and his memoranda.

reasons which have scarcely been disguised. And that was unfortunate. Much of 10th Army lived to fight another day.

It was not until noon on 6 June that Churchill asked the House of Commons to 'take formal cognisance of the liberation of Rome by the Allied Armies under the command of General Alexander' – who shortly became a Field Marshal. But this was a mere *hors d'oeuvres*. Ten minutes later he presented the *pièce de résistance*. 'I have also to announce to the House that during the night and the early hours of this morning the first of a series of landings in force upon the European continent has taken place. In this case the liberating assault fell upon the coast of France.' Instantly, and irrevocably, the Italian campaign had been reduced to a sideshow. The final defeat of the German armies that Alexander's skill continued to hold down in Italy would occur at Bologna and the crossing of the Po. He was never to fight his way into the heart of Europe over the ancient threshold of the Alps.

11 Overture and Beginners: the Prelude to D Day

'Who going through the vale of misery use it for a well ... they will go from strength to strength.'

Psalm 84

During the desperate early years of the war many men's minds were seized by the conviction that only massive raids on Germany by heavy bombers could bring Hitler to his knees. Some persisted in their delusion until the end – particularly Sir Arthur Harris, the chief of Bomber Command. Even Churchill wavered at first. During the strains of the Battle of Britain and the threat of invasion he warned the Cabinet, on 3 September 1940, that 'the Fighters are our salvation, but the Bombers alone provide the means of victory'. But he learned quickly. Before the end of 1941, the year during which more British airmen were lost over Germany than German civilians were killed, he knew the truth.

In October of that year he was under fierce pressure to commit more of Britain's scarce resources to the bomber offensive. To the Chief of Air Staff, Sir Charles Portal, he wrote on the 7th that 'I deprecate placing unbounded confidence in this means of attack.... If the United States enters the war, it would have to be supplemented in 1943 by simultaneous attacks by armoured forces in many of the conquered countries which were ripe for revolt. Even if all the towns of Germany were rendered uninhabitable, it does not follow that the military control would be weakened or even that war industry could not be carried on.... One has to do the best one can, but he is an unwise man who thinks that there is any *certain* method of winning this war, or indeed any other war between equals in strength. The only plan is to persevere.' Back in 1941 he was a year out in his forecast of a date for the return to Europe, but in every other way this remarkable minute was prophetically accurate. Its thrust is obvious. The role of even the most powerful force available, Bomber Command, was really to act as John the Baptist to Overlord: to prepare the way for an inevitable Allied invasion. Nothing, not even 'Bomber' Harris's four-engined Lancasters, could be an effective substitute for the men who, one day, would clamber from their landing-craft and trudge into Europe.

Eighteen months later, with America now well in the war, Churchill's view of bombing as essentially preparatory for an ultimate D Day was sanctified in an Allied Directive. At the great Casablanca Conference in January 1943 when Roosevelt, Churchill and the Combined Chiefs of Staff took so many fateful decisions, a definitive instruction was issued 'to govern the operations of the British and United States Bomber Commands in the United Kingdom'. 'Your primary object', it declared, 'will be the progressive destruction and dislocation of the German military, industrial and economic system, and the undermining of the morale of the German people *to a point where their capacity for armed resistance is fatally weakened.*' An invasion of the continent is assumed: and when that happened, the directive stated, 'you will afford all possible support in the manner most effective'.

To see that those great fleets of Lancasters and Fortresses flying to Germany by day and night were not aiming at a final solution, but sacrificially clearing the way to one, makes it easier to grasp that all the other developments in the middle phase of the war were equally preparatory. All, in different ways, and for different reasons, were focused on a single target – making possible those beachheads across the Channel from which, in due course, the troops and tanks of the Allies would batter their way across the Rhine and liberate the West.

This is true of the fostering and arming of the resistance movements: of the subtle game of deception: of the quiet nursing of 'double agents': of the frantic attempts to understand the nature of the V-weapons before they were launched. It is true of the campaign in Italy, which for long months before D Day was the only continental theatre where British and American troops were fighting Germans: if the campaign had any strategic justification, it was that by clawing their way from one mountain range to another the Allies were drawing and holding south of the Alps divisions which, when the day came, might otherwise be used against them in Normandy. 'The only plan is to persevere': but when the airborne divisions landed on 6 June 1944 and the great armada came into view off the French coast their presence was the result not simply of dogged perseverance but also of long-term preparation: sometimes very long-term. In this extended prelude to D Day Ultra, not surprisingly, was an active and often a crucially important instrument.

Sharing a common objective – to break the nerve and pulverize the resources of the German people as a preliminary to invasion – the American airmen by day and the British by night had also a common need: to execute their long flights in maximum safety and to find their targets with precision they required accurate and up-to-date information about Europe's weather. The Luftwaffe and the German Navy had similar needs, but they suffered from one grave disadvantage which Ultra enabled the Allies to exploit to the full. The weather mainly came from the west. Eisenhower's chief meteorological officer, Group Captain Stagg (on whose personal judgement D Day was launched), described the German predicament.

Deprived of weather reports from the British Isles and the ocean areas to the west and north, German forecasters could be kept in ignorance of the development and movement of weather systems over an area which is always important for forecasting throughout north-western and central Europe – in ignorance, except in so far as the Germans organized their own reports from their own reconnaissance aircraft or submarines, and they were known to go to great lengths to do this.[1]

The lengths were indeed great. From lonely German weatherships, from U-boats, from regular Luftwaffe 'Met' flights and other special sources a steady stream of meteorological information was reported in signals which were constantly intercepted – and deciphered at Bletchley. From BP the data passed to the Meteorological office at Dunstable (which served the RAF), to the Admiralty, and to the main US forecasting office which, feeding both US air and army units, came to be centred on Widewing, the headquarters at Bushey Park, to the west of London, of Eisenhower's SHAEF command post and of the Strategic Air Force.

Obviously the information acquired from the Germans was mixed by the forecasters with all the other considerable intelligence at their disposal. It is thus not easy, as in the case of a battle, to point to a particular Ultra signal and say 'that was decisive': such was not the nature of the operation. But it will be clear that German meteorological messages from the North or South Atlantic were an invaluable addition for the Allies' Met-men as they strove to build up their daily pictures of the weather moving inexorably towards Europe, pictures whose inaccuracy might result in a night-bomber stream caught in the moonlight (as happened to the disastrous Nuremberg raid) or in Fortresses high over Germany being blinded by unsuspected cloud.

And there were other benefits. An ability to read the Germans' 'Met' ciphers meant that their weather reports could be acquired not only from the westward seas but also from the inaccessible continent itself. Much weather information was signalled back and forth about conditions over Germany and the occupied countries, weather which the Allied bombers might soon be penetrating. Sometimes, indeed, a weather system might actually be moving across Europe from the east. There were other but limited sources. For example the Polish radio station in Britain, constantly in touch with the clandestine transmitters in the homeland, received a flow of weather reports from the Polish resistance movement.[2] But Bletchley's gift of the Germans' own meteorological intelligence was manna for Widewing and Dunstable.

Bletchley was also doing itself a service. As the Germans circulated their meteorological information to the various headquarters and units which needed it, the text was inevitably transferred from one communications network to another and often, therefore, from one Enigma cipher to another. If Bletchley was able to read the current cipher for one network it could obviously establish the original German text of the Met signal. And so, when this was repeated in another cipher for which Bletchley lacked the key, it was a wonderful assistance for the cryptanalysts, since knowledge of the original text is clearly invaluable when seeking to penetrate a difficult cipher. In fact German meteorological traffic was studied meticulously at Bletchley for precisely this reason. The weather reports sent regularly to an obscure naval unit on the Baltic could provide a means of cracking ciphers of far greater importance. Harry Golombek broke the cipher used for the Abwehr in Turkey because he was able to identify a weather-signal.[3]

As a guide to targets for the Combined Bomber Offensive Ultra's value varied. For the night-bombers of the RAF it was perhaps marginal. In discussions with the author neither Marshal of the RAF Lord Elworthy (who both commanded a bomber group and also served on the staff of Bomber Command), nor Air Vice-Marshal Sydney Bufton (Director of Bomber Operations at the Air

Ministry), nor Squadron-Leader Fawssett (Target Intelligence Officer at Bomber Command) felt that Ultra had been of key significance in the selection of targets.* Since so much of the Command's effort was devoted to the area bombing of large cities this is not surprising: Hamburg, Berlin, the Ruhr define themselves. But in one vital area of intelligence Ultra could bring massive support. Its great strength, always, was the ability it provided to build up an accurate picture of the enemy's order of battle. As far back as 1940 it was making this major contribution, which continues visibly throughout the land campaigns. For the staff of Bomber Command, as they plotted the best routes to Germany for each night's offensive, it was essential to have up-to-date knowledge of the location, strength and plans of the Luftwaffe's night-fighters and to keep abreast of the deployment and development of the German radar system. Here Ultra was an essential complement to the other brilliant signals-intelligence organizations which, without breaking ciphers, identified the structure of the German air force by the study of call signs and the meaningful pattern of radio traffic.

The study of the Luftwaffe was truly in depth. Estimating its current battle order was the task of a section of Air Intelligence called AI3b. But in a strip-lighted underground room in Horseferry Road in Westminster another small unit, AI3c, worked continuously on the longer-term problem of piecing together the whole organizational structure of the German Air Force. AI3c was a small group of able men like the Oxford don, C. S. Emden, a First War pilot. Their fodder was Ultra – what one of them called 'the daily arrival of stapled-up mss. from Bletchley which had to be understood and in some way analysed and recorded'. (When Emden joined in mid-1941 he asked for six or eight weeks in which to read through all the Ultra material from the beginning – a measure of the volume even of Bletchley's early output.)[4]

All these different categories of information – and its own flow of teleprints from Bletchley – became equally available for the US Army Air Force in Britain as the graph of its offensive effort rose from 1942 to 1944. For the day-bombers good weather was of

* These three officers were all members of the German Bomb Target Information Committee, a high-level staff group which at first met weekly and then, after its 45th meeting on 14 August 1941, fortnightly. In the minutes of these meetings there is naturally no direct reference to Ultra. But neither are there any to 'the special intelligence' or 'secret sources', or other cover-names for Ultra.

course essential. That General Spaatz recognized the contribution of Ultra in this critical area is illustrated by Winterbotham's recollection of a briefing session.

As we sat in what had been one of the old classrooms of the famous Wycombe Abbey Girls' School, and which was now the US headquarters, I would watch the care with which the meteorological officer would outline the weather all the way to the target and back. No one, I am glad to say, asked him how he knew it, but if someone queried the forecast, 'Tooey' Spaatz would look across at me with a twinkle in those shrewd eyes behind his gold-rimmed glasses and say quietly, 'I think you can rely on that'.[5]

For plotting the routes of those vast fleets of Fortresses and their escorts Ultra information about the capability of the German day-fighters was obviously as invaluable as similar knowledge about the night-fighters for the RAF. It was in the field of target selection that the Americans differed from the British.

For this we have what might be called an affidavit from a Justice of the Supreme Court of the United States. In a letter to the author Lewis Powell – onetime Operational Intelligence Officer at Strategic Air Command – wrote:

As the GAF relied heavily on Enigma for transmitting information, we had an invaluable – and reliable – source on its order of battle: location of combat units and headquarters; changes of location; strengths and serviceability; and, sometimes, planned GAF operations. It also provided GAF casualty information in the air and on the ground. The Ultra information was not always complete, and was supplemented and corroborated by excellent aerial reconnaissance photography.

But Ultra was important to strategic bombing in the target information it supplied. This was especially significant in 1944 when the primary objective of our strategic air operations was to destroy the GAF and gain total air superiority. Damage assessment, essential to the conduct of strategic air operations, was enormously aided by Ultra information. This was especially true of the remarkably successful campaign against the German synthetic oil refineries.

The achievements of air operations were immeasurably aided by the genius of the British intelligence service that made Ultra available. *

The elimination of the Luftwaffe was certainly a main theme in the prelude to invasion, for Eisenhower laid down air superiority over the battlefront as one of the essential preconditions for launch-

*Author's italics.

ing D Day, while the virtual absence of hostile aircraft on 6 June 1944 accounted in considerable measure for the success of the landings. Ultra and the USAAF worked hand in hand. It would go something like this. The Fortresses would be sent in against an airfield or airfield complex of known vigour. Its defending fighters would be decimated, its run-ways holed. Through Ultra the extent of the damage would be monitored, the progress of repairs carefully noted, the replacement squadrons identified and then, when the field was ready and the new aircraft had moved in, hey presto, another strike of Fortresses. The same system helped to intensify the great oil-interdiction programme. A heavy raid pounds the installations at Leuna. From several sources such as Albert Speer's damage-repair organization Ultra can pick up German assessments of the damage done and, with such aids as photo-reconnaissance, keep track of the rate of repair so that when production is just beginning to reach a tolerable level the Fortresses can move in again. If we except the operations of specialized units like 617 Squadron, the Dam-busters, Bomber Command's task was essentially to drench large urban areas. But from the start the philosophy of the USAAF, pickle-barrel bombing by daylight with its sophisticated bomb-sights, was one of flexibility and precision. Ultra helped that philosophy to achieve its terrible efficiency in practice: as Justice Lewis Powell put it, 'immeasurably'.

Though the Combined Bomber Offensive was essentially preparatory, it was nevertheless a public event, dramatic and impressive. The swarms of aircraft sweeping towards Germany, the photographs of gutted cities, the terrible casualty lists of Allied crews and enemy civilians had a direct and immediate significance for the free world, for the waiting millions in the occupied countries, for the Germans and even for the Russians. Hitler's *Reich* was being visibly pulverized. But other preparations were also in hand, so secret that their scale and importance are still only gradually emerging. Two things, however, are certain: their impact on the invasion of Normandy in 1944 was decisive and their achievement would have been impossible without Ultra.

Their development was long-term. Indeed, a study of the two most important of these clandestine operations provides a telling answer to those who maintained that Churchill and his advisers had no intention of risking a return to Europe, for while their central purpose was to assist an invasion, and while they were authorized

298

and supervised at the highest level in Whitehall, their gradual advance towards a peak performance in the summer of 1944 occurred over a period of several years. They were, in fact, intentional.

The first of these activities was the organization of strategic deception, centred on a small unit called the London Controlling Section whose very existence was known only to a few throughout the war. Its head was Colonel John Bevan. The second of the activities that would bear fruit at the time of D Day was the 'bending' of German spies in Britain so that they could be used in the ancient role of double agent to radio back to their masters in the Abwehr signals whose content was dictated by the British. This devious system was in the hands of a section of MI5 called B1A, with Lieutenant-Colonel T. A. Robertson at its head. Bevan and Robertson have jointly testified to the author that without Ultra the great web of deception spun round the Germans could never have been devised. Yet without their efforts Overlord might have been a disaster.[6]

Tactical deception consists of misleading the enemy about one's intentions within a specific battle-area. (A good example would be the dummy vehicles and tanks, the false water-pipeline and other devices used to persuade Rommel at Alamein that Montgomery would attack his line in the south and not in the north.) In strategic deception the object is to persuade one's opponent that the real battle will occur in an entirely different place – even in a different country: to create an imaginary threat, by suggestion or simulation, which will make the enemy divert large forces from the area where something is about to happen to a region where nothing is going to happen at all. The range of such deception in a world war can obviously embrace whole continents and even become global. It was General Wavell who, as far back as 1940, wrote a pioneer paper in which he argued that such schemes should 'not only have the maximum effect in their own theatre, but should fit in with the general plan of campaign of other theatres'. The place for such co-ordination, Wavell maintained, was under the eyes of the Chiefs of Staff in London.

Wavell's ideas germinated: and this was just, for in his own theatre, the Middle East, the deception team called 'A' Force which developed under Brigadier Dudley Clarke was outstandingly successful in the arts of confusion, both in the tactical area of the battlefield and in the wider realm of strategic deception. The persuasive efforts of 'A' Force were certainly a main reason, for example, for Hitler's maintenance of unnecessarily large numbers of divisions in the Balkans because of a wholly fictitious threat of invasion: Dudley Clarke, it used to be said, was worth an Army Corps. But it was in London rather than Cairo that the complete network of strategic deception could be centrally manipulated, and so, in October 1941, the London Controlling Section was born. At first its head was Colonel Oliver Stanley, a Conservative politician and former minister, but his heart was not in the trade, nor was his head best suited to it. In 1942 he was succeeded by John Bevan, a stockbroker with wide contacts who had already gained much experience of intelligence work in both World Wars.

In *Bodyguard of Lies* Anthony Cave Brown wrote: 'His appointment as the Controlling Officer of the LCS was in the tradition of the post – it was an aristocrat's job. For the LCS had, in turn, been headed by a son of the Earl of Derby, by a brother of the Earl of Scarborough, and now by Bevan, who was by marriage a member of the family of the Earl of Lucan and connected through his mother with the Viscounts Hampden and the Dukes of Buccleuch'. That is verbiage. The post had no tradition because in 1942, when Bevan took over, it barely existed. That something should be done was clear – Wavell had made the point lucidly – but so far nobody knew exactly what to do. On his appointment Bevan had the greatest difficulty in obtaining from the Chiefs of Staff any precise definition of his functions and responsibilities. They emerged as he got down to work, and what he did was not simply the result of a piece of aristocratic jobbery any more than was the presence of his brother-in-law, Harold Rupert Leofric George, Field Marshal Alexander and son of the 4th Earl of Caledon, in supreme command of the Anglo-American armies in the Mediterranean theatre. As the war advanced, merit mattered more than coats of arms.

The small team at LCS headed by Bevan was in fact less aristocratic than able. Certainly it was mixed: it included Major Ronald Wingate, a former Indian Civil Servant with immense experience of intelligence and politics both in India and in the Middle East: Dennis Wheatley, who had switched his imagination from best-selling fiction to interpreting the German military mind; Derrick Morley, a financier, and Harold Peteval who is described as 'the manager of a soap factory'. Some worked on intelligence and plans, some on organization. It is a measure of Bevan's immense respect for Ultra and his intense concern for its security that even within this close-knit and top secret unit he only allowed the few who handled plans and intelligence to have access to the Ultra messages. The safeguard of 'need to know' was ruthlessly applied.

The principles on which the LCS operated were as old as war itself. What Bevan and his unit brought to them was sophistication and finesse. But all the main elements in their technique can be observed, for example, in this account of an episode during the American Civil War, when at the time of the battle of Gaine's Mill in 1862 Robert E. Lee needed to keep the bulk of the Union Army under McClellan out of the fight. General John B. Magruder did the trick.

Magruder all day long played the part of a general who was just about to launch a shattering offensive. His skirmish and patrol parties were constantly active, his batteries were forever emitting sudden bursts of fire, he kept bodies of men in movement on open ground in the rear where the Yankees could see them, and with drums and bugles and human voices he caused noises to be made in the woods like the noise of vast assembling armies – and all of it worked.

It worked, partly because Magruder was very good at that sort of thing, and partly because the Federal command was fatally infected by the belief that Lee had overwhelming force at his command. This was the grand delusion that brought other delusions after it.[7]

To distract Hitler and his High Command from the real intentions of the Allies by fatally infecting them with grand delusions, and by convincingly creating a threat where none in fact existed, was precisely the task of the London Controlling Section.

In spreading this infection a prime carrier was Colonel Robertson's section B1A. It was 'an old-established firm', whose foundations had been effectively laid as far back as 1940. During the second half of that invasion year the Abwehr headquarters directly concerned with infiltrating into Britain, the Hamburg *Stelle*, made vigorous but abortive attempts to plant their agents. Some came by parachute, some by sea: some tried to insinuate themselves as refugees or as neutral businessmen. All were apprehended. Those who refused to 'bend' and become double agents under the control of B1A were imprisoned or executed. By early 1941, at the latest, the British had a firm grip – never subsequently relaxed – on the German spy network.

And now began the great game which, ever-expanding in its subtlety, reached its peak during the D Day period. Those agents who had proved malleable were used, each under the careful individual surveillance of a B1A 'case officer', to radio back to their Abwehr masters in Hamburg, Madrid or Lisbon, (that international focus of the secret war) messages which contained a nice blend of innocuous fact and a shrewdly calculated measure of misinformation. Some of the agents were actually anti-Nazi and willing collaborators: the best of them, and the clever men in B1A, made the system of misleading the Abwehr – and thus the German High Command – immensely more fertile by inventing sub-agents supposedly working at key points in Britain and by sending back from them, too, radio messages to Germany which the Abwehr happily swallowed. There was an important psychological factor which B1A could profitably exploit. Many of the Abwehr spy-masters actually *wanted* to believe in the trustworthiness of their agents and the validity of their reports, since to be handling an apparently fruitful source of intelligence redounded, in the lax German way, to their personal credit. Whereas the British attitude in this shadowy underworld was one of acute scepticism the German, only too often, was credulous and permissive.

While the efficiency of the Abwehr was diminished and distorted by its own internal rivalries and the self-seeking of individual officers, there was a deeper schism within the German war-organization which also benefited the British deceivers. This was the *guerre de course* or running fight between the Abwehr itself, under Admiral Canaris, and the SS 'state-within-a-state' which Heinrich Himmler steadily expanded in his capacity of *Reichsführer SS* and Chief of the German Police. Himmler sought predominant power: Canaris – it is now well established – had as his private aim the fall of Hitler and the end of Nazism, for which he was to pay with his life. This friction at the very core of the intelligence-gathering machine meant that items of information were often served up not because they had been scrupulously checked for accuracy, but because they could be presented as scoops with which to score credit and advantage in the dog-fight between Germany's principal security systems.

To keep the efforts of Bevan, Robertson, Clarke and their colleagues in a proper perspective it should nevertheless be remembered that there were limiting factors which certainly, from time to time, thwarted their attempts to deceive. The tendency of German agents to send in reports that were less accurate than likely to enhance their prestige produced a homegrown crop of untrustworthy claims and rumours which competed with false information projected from London and Cairo. Thus the British always faced this danger: if there were an intelligence staff in Germany capable of making cool and objective evaluations its members would have become so accustomed to doubting unreliable reports that deceptive material filtered to it by the agencies of LCS and B1A would be dismissed as yet more nonsense.

And there was such a staff. Compared with the Abwehr and Himmler's empire, a distinctive professionalism pervaded *Fremde Heere West* or Foreign Armies West, the section of the General Staff's intelligence division responsible for assessing the strength and intentions of the Anglo-American forces. (Its counterpart, *Fremde Heere Ost* under the ambivalent General Gehlen, had the same function in respect of the Russians.) At the head of FHW from 1943 onwards was Colonel Freiherr Alexis von Roenne. Of this severe and dedicated Prussian his predecessor in the post, General Liss, recorded that 'he had a perception of political and military matters that was akin to genius. He had a clear and realistic mind, and he was able to make decisions with the speed of lightning.'

It was therefore inevitable that when a department under an officer of such quality came to evaluate British schemes of deception they should sometimes fail to convince. Roenne's judgements were conditioned, of course, by the fact that he too was opposed to Hitler: indeed, he was executed after the assassination-attempt of 20 July 1944, writing to his mother that he was dying like the thief on the cross at the side of Jesus. Undoubtedly on occasion, and particularly before D Day, his subjective inclinations affected his objectivity. Sometimes it suited him, in other words, to accept as true what he knew or guessed to be false. Still, there was an inherent risk, and post-war scrutiny of the German documents has confirmed that not all the fictions of the Allied deception teams were swallowed by *Fremde Heere West*. But in war what matters is the effective concentration of strength at the critical point. During the great operations when deception was vital, its success was absolute. Trial and error may have involved frustration and failure, but in the end the battle is the pay-off. The Allies landed safely on D Day.

The patient long-term build-up of certain double agents against the time when they could be deployed as powerful secret weapons in the invasion of Europe may be illustrated by two classic examples. The first is the man code-named Tate, who was parachuted into England in September 1940, bent, and employed with a consistent record of success up to the last minute when, a few hours before Hamburg was captured on 2 May 1945, his masters signalled to him to keep in touch. Between those dates the Germans had bestowed on him, for his 'efforts', the Iron Cross both First and Second Class. In the pre-D Day deception, as will be seen, his role was of the first importance.

Later, in 1945, Tate had a remarkable individual success. U-boats were now using the Schnorkel, a breathing device which enabled them to remain under water while re-charging their batteries or taking in fresh air. Off the southern coast of Ireland the contours of the sea-bed are such that with the aid of their echo-sounders and Schnorkels U-boats could travel considerable distances submerged – and did so. An ideal area for a minefield, but no minelayers were available. Tate was therefore used by B1A to pass on to the Abwehr in Hamburg first-hand information from an invented 'minelaying friend' about 'a new deep minefield' off the Irish coast. Pure chance produced confirmation for the Germans. A U-boat hit a stray mine, its survivors landed in Eire, and Red Cross reports about them validated the story. And so, very soon afterwards, an Ultra signal arrived in the Submarine Tracking Room at the Admiralty. It was the text of a special operation order from U-boat Command, which forbad all U-boats to enter a prohibited area to the south of Ireland – 3600 square miles, a sanctuary now denied to the dangerous Schnorkel U-boats and secure for Allied convoys as they passed through the Western Approaches. The minelaying Tate is an exquisite example of Ultra and the double agent working in harmony.[8]

But even more remarkable is the case of the Spaniard code-named Garbo. A key figure in B1A was Sir John Masterman (later Vice-Chancellor of the University of Oxford) who in 1972 published as *The Double-Cross System* the departmental report which he wrote for MI5 immediately after the war: a record of the double agent story unequalled in its authority. 'Connoisseurs of double cross', Masterman declared, 'have always regarded the Garbo case as the most highly developed example of their art.' Certainly Garbo made

304

a good beginning. When in April 1942 MI6 smuggled him from Lisbon to England Ultra had recently disclosed that U-boat Command was preparing to intercept a large Liverpool–Malta convoy. Actually the convoy was entirely an invention of Garbo! It was part of the elaborate game he had played with the Abwehr during the last nine months, in which he fed them to their complete satisfaction with a flow of supposedly eye-witness reports from the British Isles. These, in truth, he had concocted in Lisbon from 'a Blue Guide, a map of England and an out-of-date railway timetable, supplemented by meagre gleanings from Portuguese bookstalls.'

In June 1944 Garbo (who the following December received the MBE) was also awarded the Iron Cross. There were some difficulties about his Spanish nationality, and the long plea on his behalf sent from the Madrid Abwehr to Berlin has a wonderful irony. 'The extraordinary successes of Garbo have been made possible by his constant, complete and express confidence in the Führer and our cause.' Hitler had indeed much to be grateful for. Soon after his arrival in 1942 Garbo built up a team of half a dozen imaginary sub-agents: by the spring of 1944 he was 'chief of an organization comprising fourteen active agents and eleven well-placed contacts, especially one at the Ministry of Information: all, with the exception of Garbo himself, being in fact notional, though fully trusted by the Germans. He had also furnished himself with a deputy and a substitute wireless operator, and had established his principal assistants at Glasgow, Methil,* Harwich, Dover, Brighton, Exeter and Swansea.' In 1945 his range extended. He contrived for one of his inventions, a Wren, to be sent out to Lord Mountbatten's Southeast Asia Command in Ceylon. Her 'reports' to Garbo – composed, of course, in London – went first to the Abwehr and then, via the Japanese military attaché in Berlin, to Tokyo. The Allies' ability to decipher signals from the Berlin embassy to Japan provided a useful check.

Apart from aces like Tate and Garbo, about 120 double agents came on to the books of B1A. Some were trivial, and a few were worked from stations abroad like Ireland and Canada. But the great scale of the organization, as it matured, and the formidable exchange of messages between the agents and their Abwehr spy-

---

*Methil, on the northern shore of the Firth of Forth, was well situated for 'observing' the movement of naval units.

masters on the continent produced two continuing problems for Colonel Robertson and the other officers responsible for operating the system in conditions of total secrecy. How could the system be kept under control? That is to say, how could B1A enter and stay inside the mind of the Abwehr; know how it was reacting to both the true and the false information passed over; be forewarned about German plans to plant new agents in Britain; scent suspicion and anticipate trouble? And an even more delicate question: how, and by whose authority, could decisions be taken about the truths that might be told and the lies that must be insinuated?

One reliable source of control existed within the actual messages exchanged. The replies by the Abwehr to their agents' reports, the kind of questionnaires they sent them as a basis for further reports, the very tone of their response was evidential. (The nature and timing of their queries, of course, were also invaluable guides to current German preoccupations about such matters as Allied troop or convoy movements, airfield or factory locations, technical innovations and so on: they helped the British High Command and, in particular, the officers concerned with deception.) But all this was a dialogue between the Abwehr and its agents. Through Ultra the Abwehr could be overheard talking to itself.

For over two years from the outbreak of war the highest-grade signal traffic of the Abwehr resisted penetration by Bletchley, for the Abwehr's Enigma machine had certain important differences from the standard model. Signals enciphered by hand were indeed being read: but it was not until the winter of 1941 that the ISK section at Bletchley found a way into the Enigma traffic. This was crucial. All the 'main lines' of the Abwehr communication network, connecting their chief operational bases like Hamburg and Madrid or Istanbul, used the Enigma cipher: it was the 'branch lines' to less important out-stations that normally employed hand-ciphers. The decrypts now made available through ISK thus enabled B1A and LCS to know without a shadow of doubt exactly how the Abwehr was responding to some planted falsehood, or beginning to suspect one of the bent or invented agents, or setting up a scheme for infiltrating a fresh agent. 'The final confirmation of the belief that we controlled the whole', wrote Sir John Masterman, 'came gradually from a study of secret sources.' By secret sources he meant Ultra; had his book been published some years later than 1972 he would have said so. To Colonel Bevan these Ultra decrypts were of such vital significance that he kept a personal file of them in his office for private study and reference.

Those concerned with processing the Abwehr intelligence after it had been deciphered included no less than three future Professors – Sir Denys Page, Regius Professor of Greek at Cambridge from 1950 to 1973 and Master of Jesus College: L. R. Palmer, Professor of Comparative Philology at Oxford from 1952 to 1971: and Hugh Trevor-Roper, Regius Professor of Modern History at Oxford since 1957. Page and Palmer dealt with the evaluation of the decrypts before they left Bletchley. Trevor-Roper, after Byzantine manoeuvres within MI6 (his membership of which is partly but pungently described in *The Philby Affair*), came to act as a sort of central clearing-house and point of reference on Abwehr intelligence. Receiving all the Ultra information, he was constantly relied on and respected by Bevan, Robertson and their units. It might not have been so, for when the Abwehr cipher was broken elements in MI6 argued speciously that the handling of the intelligence should be purely their concern, on the ground that coping with German agents was their special province. This might have led to a restrictive attitude, and a withholding of the intelligence from other essential users. Fortunately Trevor-Roper with enviable dexterity established an independent position for himself, and the future Regius Professor of Modern History was able to take a broader view.[9]

But the second difficult question raised by the practice of deceiving the enemy was one that could not be answered by those immediately involved in the planning and execution of deception – that is to say, by either LCS or B1A. The device of supplying the Germans with just sufficient truths about British armaments, industry and intentions for them to accept as valid the lies which they also received was fraught with such immense issues of major national policy that no Colonel in charge of a special unit could be expected to take such decisions alone. The solution was found in a typically British way – by forming a committee. From January 1941 until the end of the war the Twenty (or XX or Double-Cross) Committee met weekly for precisely this purpose. 'The essential purpose of the Committee', wrote Masterman, who chaired it, 'was to decide what information could safely be allowed to pass to the Germans, and what could not.' Very appropriately, the first XX conference took place in the prison at Wormwood Scrubs. It included representatives from MI5 (Robertson and Masterman), MI6, the Admiralty, the War Office, the Air Ministry, Home Forces and the civil authorities. As the time for invasion approached the Overlord planning team, COSSAC, and later Eisenhower's supreme headquarters at SHAEF also had a voice at the table.

A group of this strength was well equipped to compare and co-ordinate the activities of the double-agents, to prevent dangerous contradictions in their reports and to assess the risk in using them to convey to the enemy true statements of fact as the bait for misinformation. If problems of policy arose that were insoluble even at this level, it was through the Twenty Committee that guidance and instruction could be obtained from 'approving authorities' higher in the stratosphere. This was not a world of private armies carrying out self-indulgent enterprises. The issues were too great. It may have been tiresome or frustrating, but the successful history of British deception in the Second World War is founded on the fact that no such operations were undertaken without full endorsement from the policy-makers or, a fundamental principle of Colonel Bevan's, without the understanding and agreement of those who would actually have to conduct the fighting.

B1A and LCS pursued long-term objectives. The first was to nurse the credibility of certain agents in the eyes of the Germans, over patient months and years, so that as D Day approached the vitally important misinformation they signalled to the Abwehr would be swallowed without suspicion. The second was to maintain an unrelaxing grip on the German spy network so that when the time of invasion arrived there would not be a single free-ranging enemy observer in Britain able to supply his masters with accurate reports. For this dual achievement Bletchley's deciphering of the Abwehr's own most secret communications was obviously invaluable. It explains, to a large degree, why both Bevan and Robertson believed that without Ultra they could not have succeeded.

Yet the agents, though essential, were only one tool in the planning and conduct of strategic deception, whose basic purpose is to persuade the enemy to move large forces to the wrong place and keep them there while you are attacking in the right place. Evidently, therefore, you must know as much as possible about those large forces and what the enemy is doing with them. This is merely a simplistic way of saying that the Allies' deception plans for D Day depended critically on an exact knowledge of the German order of battle. Just as it was vital for Harris and Spaatz to know the strength and location of the Luftwaffe's fighters, or for Montgomery and Alexander in the Mediterranean to have an up-to-date picture of the armies opposing them, so it was imperative for the deceivers to maintain a running check on the overall disposition of the German armed services – the deceivers being LCS, the XX Committee, and the department at SHAEF called Ops B which handled much of the detailed planning for the deception plan before Overlord. And just as Ultra provided the battle-commanders with facts and figures about the enemy on their respective fronts, so the deceivers could monitor through Ultra the large forces whose deployment they sought to manipulate.

It was not by chance, for example, that Hitler consistently retained an excessive number of divisions in Norway, even though the technical problems of launching a major Allied invasion on that forbidding coast were appalling. The figures are self-explanatory. In November 1943, when there were still only fifty divisions in France and the Low Countries, there were eighteen in Norway and Denmark. In January 1944 there were sixteen. In January 1945, as the Allies approach the Rhine, seventeen divisions are still loitering on the sidelines in Scandinavia. The heavy ships of the German Navy, moreover, were regularly concentrated by Hitler in Norwegian harbours – and not merely as a threat to the Russian convoys. He was deluded into fearing as genuine what even Churchill was not allowed to promote as a reality. All the Prime Minister's personal and ill-judged efforts to launch an actual invasion of Norway were thwarted by his sensible Chiefs of Staff: but the men at OKW joined their Führer in swallowing the deceivers' bait and believing that, whereas they themselves had not dared to cross the Channel, the Allies would not be daunted by the hazards of the wide North Sea.

Since Hitler's mind was infected from 1940 onwards with delusions about the importance of Norway, the deceivers were in that classic situation which General Magruder exploited at Gaines's Mill: they had merely to persuade the enemy to continue to believe what he already wanted to believe. For a start, a useful though not dramatically significant deception game was played in latter 1942, as part of the cover plan for the Torch landings in North-west Africa. During 1943, Masterman recorded about Norway, 'even the most retentive memory would have difficulty in recalling just when and how often our agents helped to put into effect a threat against

309

that country'. For the deceivers the fundamental need at all times was to know, and to know for certain, whether in spite of their efforts substantial forces were being moved out of Norway for use on other fronts – or whether no such moves were occurring.

In this surveillance Ultra was pre-eminent. There were other good sources, such as the intelligence links between Britain and the Norwegian resistance (whose efficiency and courage were outstanding) or the British service attachés in Sweden, that whispering gallery of Scandinavia. Ultra itself supplied conventional information about order of battle, from decrypts of German strength returns, personnel appointments, weapon states and so on – powerfully supported as usual by 'Y' Service's radio traffic analysis, study of call signs, direction-finding, the routine of Signal Intelligence. But it was geography that gave Ultra its peculiar strength. There are only two routes from the continent to Norway, by air and by sea. Bletchley's mastery of the Luftwaffe cipher meant that any considerable airlift must be betrayed by its accompanying signal-traffic. As for the sea, BP's equal success with the Hydra cipher meant that no major convoys of troops could be organized and sailed without the unavoidable signals relating to mine-sweeping, escort vessels, transport arrangements ashore and many other administrative matters alerting the London Controlling Section.

On Sherlock Holmes's famous principle about the importance of the dog that did not bark in the night, the significant fact for the deceivers in London was that no such major movement of troops from Norway was disclosed on Ultra up to and beyond the time of D Day. Here was clinching evidence that the deception plans were working. Moreover, when movement did occur later it was instantly spotted. After the conference at Hitler's HQ on 22 October 1944 where instructions were given for the Ardennes offensive, the 'Battle of the Bulge', the Admiralty's Operational Intelligence Centre was quick to note the indicators. On the 30th Denning reported to the First Sea Lord: 'The gross tonnage of shipping which has made the passage from Oslofjord to Denmark from the middle of October amounts to 97 000 gross registered tons. It is estimated that this is sufficient to have lifted at least one division from Norway. Elements of the 269th Division previously stationed in the Bergen area have been identified on the Western Front during the last few days and have evidently been transferred from Norway to Denmark since mid-October.'[10] Up to 16

December, when the Ardennes battle began, OIC reported weekly on the continuing southward movement from Norway. This positive intelligence from post-D Day, like the negative intelligence pre-D Day, emphasizes how with Ultra's aid the deceivers were well placed by practice and capability to infect the German mind with delusions about the Northern Flank. Bletchley, in effect, provided a telescope through which they could observe what the enemy was – or was not – doing.

Far away to the south, moreover, there was another great region where reality and fantasy were combined to focus the Germans' attention: the Balkans. Hitler had, indeed, valid grounds for fearing an Allied attack: the loss of bauxite, copper and other rare but essential metals, the threat to Ploesti and the vital oilfields, the opening of historic invasion routes from the Mediterranean into the heart of Europe. So here too was a will to believe, and a basis of truth which the deception experts of the Middle East's 'A' Force distorted into delusion with increasing authority. (As one of them observed, 'truths do not constitute the truth'.) Employing real and invented double-agents (like B1A in England) and ingenious techniques of visual deception (master-minded by that past master of magic, Jasper Maskelyne) they perfected their arts during the battles of the North African campaigns. By the summer of 1943, therefore, in the cover plan for Husky, the invasion of Sicily, 'A' Force was able to provide massive misinformation to validate the papers washed on to the Spanish shore beside the corpse of 'Major Martin' in the London-mounted Operation Mincemeat. From the War Cabinet Office to Churchill in Washington the signal flashed: 'Mincemeat swallowed rod, line and sinker by right people and from best information they look like acting on it.' 'Best information' was Ultra: but it was not to Mincemeat alone that the Germans responded.

David Mure was an active deceiver in 'A' Force. (In the winter of 1942/3 he was indoctrinated into Ultra and signed on to 'The Prime Minister's List', thereby swearing that he would not enter a war zone or divulge the secrets into which he was initiated.) Mure recalled how between the end in Africa and D Day for Husky the orchestra of double agents, real or imaginary, began under the baton of 'A' Force to play its delusive tune – 'Cheese and his allies in Egypt and also in Tripoli, Algiers and Casablanca; Quicksilver, Pessimist, Humble and Alert in Syria and Lebanon; Lemon in

Cyprus: arranging the truth with the skilful emphasis to turn it into a lie.' The lie was Cascade, the deception plan for Sicily in which 'the man who never was' played his posthumous part. Its object: to convince the Germans that the Allies' real targets were the Peloponnese, Rhodes, the Dodecanese islands, leading to penetration of northern Greece and the Balkans. The success of the cover was such that before Husky began the movement of German reinforcements was not to Sicily but, precisely, to Rhodes, the Peloponnese, Crete and Corsica.

The span and variety of 'A' Force's activities, which ranged from Algiers to Baghdad, was so considerable (and often so comic) that only a full-scale history of deception could do them justice. But they worked. And the essential reason for their success was the same weapon that Ultra placed in the hands of the London deceivers – penetration of the Abwehr's cipher system. Up and down the communications network linking Germany with the Abwehr's main centres in cities like Sofia, Istanbul and Ankara, and with the smaller outposts scattered around the eastern Mediterranean, there was a constant flow of traffic in signals which, whether enciphered by Enigma or hand-ciphered, were thought by the German intelligence service to be secure. But Ultra had blown their security. 'A' Force was thus armed to deceive both by its carefully cherished miscellany of double agents and by its ability to keep track, from the Abwehr's own sources, on what its opponents were *actually* thinking, suspecting, planning.[11]

During that Sicilian summer of 1943, however, the first outline plans for an Allied return to North-west Europe were being worked out by the team under General Morgan, COSSAC (Chief of Staff to the Supreme Allied Command – the latter as yet non-existent). When Churchill sailed in *Queen Mary* with his Chiefs of Staff to the August summit conference at Quebec he took the COSSAC plan with him for endorsement – which it received – by Roosevelt and his Joint Chiefs. All that remained was the simple matter of overcoming a million difficulties and actually putting into effect the 'invasion' (or as Eisenhower preferred, 'liberation') of France and then all western Europe, whose comprehensive code-name was now Overlord, with Neptune as the name for the initial landings of D Day. Morgan, looking back in his memoirs, wrote of the situation at that time: 'ever present must be the ultimate aim, which was to arrange that the eventual blow would come where the enemy least expected it, when he least expected it, and with a force altogether outside his calculations'.

What this meant in practical terms was, first, that though a landing in northern France seemed the obvious objective for the Allies, the Germans must be persuaded to anticipate attacks elsewhere – in Norway, in the Balkans – and if they nevertheless felt that the cross-Channel threat was the most sinister, then they must be led to believe that 'the eventual blow' would fall not along the Bay of the Seine and the Cherbourg peninsula (as was intended) but well to the north in the Pas de Calais whose proximity to south-east England, it might seem, would offer the Allies a short sea-crossing and good fighter cover. Secondly the Germans must believe that the blow or blows would fall some weeks after the planned D Day. And thirdly, the build-up of British and American divisions in England must be concealed.

The ultimate aim, as General Morgan put it, must therefore be deception. To this end an all-embracing, indeed a global plan was devised under the name of Bodyguard, an echo of Churchill's oft-quoted remark at the Teheran conference in November 1943 when the plan's basic principles were agreed by himself, Roosevelt and Stalin: 'In war-time, truth is so precious that she should always be attended by a bodyguard of lies.' How Bodyguard succeeded, how the Germans were false-footed everywhere in the summer of 1944 is now in all the histories. What is not in the books is a decrypt from Bletchley which in a few sentences illustrates, with an aesthetic perfection, how in this vital game of delusion Ultra enabled the deceivers, the Chiefs of Staff, all who were responsible for the critical launching of Overlord to share the enemy's thoughts and assess the effect of their delusive stratagems.

The signal is brief. Its Bletchley serial number is KV5689 and the decrypt was sent out from Station X at 9.31 in the evening of 29 May 1944. (D Day for Normandy was in the following week.) The original message was despatched on the 25th from von Rundstedt's headquarters. It is a report from the Commander-in-Chief West to OKW on fuel for the summer programme of defence-construction on the Western Wall, stating that the allocation from OKW was:

approximately 20% less than applied for on basis of summer programme. There would be sufficient for the concrete envisaged in the programme provided that it could be carried out without considerable disturbance

313

... C-in-C West therefore requests that as a precautionary measure a fuel reserve be made available for the construction ... recourse would only be had to this reserve if after the first ten days of June the situation can be reviewed as a whole.

What a wealth of irony in those few words! For there would certainly be a considerable disturbance, and after the first ten days of June the situation would certainly have to be reviewed as a whole. Yet here, even in a single complacent message, we can see how Ultra could bring reassurance to all the Allied deception agencies and battle-commanders whose nerves, so near to the launching of Neptune, were taut with anxiety lest the Germans, at this last minute, might have blown the invasion's cover. But no: the headquarters of the German High Command and the Commander-in-Chief in France are calmly discussing concrete and fuel and improvement of defences as though unconscious of time and danger. Bodyguard had achieved General Morgan's 'ultimate aim'.

There were two main elements within Bodyguard. Plan Zeppelin was the mission of 'A' Force: to pin down the large German forces in the Balkans, far from the critical beaches of Normandy. By the sustained threat of phantom British armies, the 9th and the 10th, which 'A' Force had imposed on the German mind as a reality ready to pounce from its assembly areas in the eastern Mediterranean, the enemy strength in Greece, Yugoslavia, the Dodecanese and Bulgaria was still some twenty-four divisions on D Day, 6 June 1944. Two dozen divisions diverted from the main front was a triumph: but the vital deception effort was naturally made along the great half-moon curving from the north of Norway round to the Cherbourg peninsula. The plan to contain the German forces in Scandinavia, Fortitude North, also involved selling the menace of a phantom army, this time the 4th, which was ostentatiously assembled in Scotland. Moreover, after a visit by Colonel Bevan to Moscow the Russians agreed to co-operate in mounting a fictitious Anglo-Russian threat. This was counter-productive: when the news came to Colonel Roenne, head of Foreign Armies West, he dismissed it as a plant on the grounds that the Russians would never want a British presence in Norway. But the news came too late and Fortitude North paid off, since no German divisions moved out of Scandinavia before D Day, and it was not until 16 June that Hitler ordered the 89th Infantry from Norway and the 363rd Infantry from Denmark – and then only to the Pas de Calais!

314

For here was the heart of the matter. On the Normandy front lay the German 7th Army. But the other half of Rommel's Army Group B, the 15th Army, was spread roughly between the Scheldt and the Seine with a strong concentration in the Pas de Calais. The problem, therefore, was to prevent its eighteen divisions – and particularly such dangerous units as 116 Panzer Division – from being used to reinforce in Normandy. The trick was to suggest that the Normandy landings were a feint and that the main assault, the *schwerpunkt*, would fall on the Pas de Calais. In this Fortitude South succeeded beyond expectation, for though Hitler himself had a last-minute intuition about Normandy his commanders in the west, von Rundstedt, Rommel, the 15th Army itself remained convinced before and for long after D Day that the key to Overlord was the Pas de Calais.

For the greatest orchestration of deception ever achieved in military history Fortitude South employed all the techniques polished and perfected over the years by LCS, B1A, 'Y' Service and other agencies both British and American. The central feature was another ghost. By carefully simulated wireless traffic, double agents' reports and the well-advertized presence in England of General Patton a solid conviction was built up in the German mind that a powerful force under Patton's command, First US Army Group or FUSAG, was to launch from south-east England an assault on the Pas de Calais. As a formation FUSAG was entirely imaginary – like its mission. And there was a double-take within the deception. A number of divisions in the notional FUSAG were real, but they were ear-marked for the battle in Normandy. Their identity, however, was supplied to the Germans as part of the FUSAG scenario and thus, when they came into action after D Day and were recognized by German intelligence, their visible presence on the 7th Army's front actually strengthened the credibility of the double agents who had first reported on them. (It was easy to sell the idea that these particular units had been shifted from FUSAG to Normandy because of the Allies' difficulties in breaking out of the beachhead).

FUSAG was thus a supreme application of what might be called the Magruder principle – the technique of telling the enemy what he already wants to believe. The German High Command, von Rundstedt, Rommel and even – until the last minute – Hitler readily accepted myth as reality. The battle is the pay-off: on D Day the

15th Army was still in the Pas de Calais – where it stayed. And why not? For in May 1944 the order of battle of the Allied forces waiting in Britain appeared in the German records as a vast array of eighty-five to ninety divisions plus seven airborne divisions, the true figures being thirty-five plus three airborne. And Patton was coming! Colonel Roenne of Foreign Armies West had indeed helped by multiplying the estimates he received before submitting them to OKW – perhaps, it is thought, because the plotters wished to preserve some 'safe' divisions intact in the 15th Army for use if the military coup succeeded. In any event, there on D Day was FUSAG, a credible ghost: and there, across the Straits of Dover, was a real but paralysed 15th Army.

The story of Bodyguard has taken a wide curve away from Ultra, yet even this summary account is essential to demonstrate that without Bletchley and all that Station X supplied D Day, the consummation of so long a prelude, might well have failed. No military student can assess with certainty the result if, during the early weakness of the Allied bridgehead in Normandy, the 15th Army had moved down from the north: still less the consequences if Rommel had shifted a significant number of divisions from the Pas de Calais into Normandy *before* D Day. But even an amateur at war games can perceive that in either event Eisenhower, Montgomery and Bradley would have faced an appalling and even a disastrous situation.

The historic fact is that without Ultra the weapons employed so successfully in Bodyguard could not have been forged and sharpened. In its deceitful armoury the double agents were of prime value. Colonel Bevan recognized this. On 25 October 1944, as the Allies advanced towards Germany, he wrote to the Director General Security Service: 'When the history of this war is written, I believe it will be found that the German High Command was, largely through the medium of B1A channels, induced to make faulty dispositions, in particular during the vital post-Overlord D Day period. The future can alone confirm or disprove this contention.'[12] Three subsequent decades, with their comprehensive revelations from the German records, have indeed confirmed Bevan's prophecy.

Though many other devices and agencies were employed in Bodyguard, the core of the deception consisted in convincing the Germans about FUSAG's existence through information passed by well-established double agents whom the enemy was known to trust. It was here that long-term preparation and practice paid off, for of the three chief agents employed Tate started to work in September 1940, Garbo in April 1942 and Brutus in October 1942. Without the Ultra intelligence derived from Bletchley's penetration of the Abwehr cipher it would have been impossible to build up the credibility of these men to a point where they commanded the absolute confidence of the Germans.

Indeed, the most elegant aspect of the FUSAG fiction was its durability. When D Day disembarked the Neptune divisions along the Normandy coast the Germans, and in particular the commander on the spot, Field Marshal Rommel, were led by the strength of their delusion into appreciating that this was merely a feint: the main assault was still to fall on the Pas de Calais. So absolute was the Germans' trust in the double agents who continued to feed them this misinformation that 'what is remarkable', Masterman noted, 'is that no single case was compromised by the grand deception for Overlord, but that, on the contrary, those agents who took a leading part in it were more highly regarded by the Germans after it than before.' And so the divisions of the 15th Army stayed out of the battle.

It might have been otherwise. On 8 June, D + 2, when Montgomery and Bradley were still struggling desperately to establish and expand their frail bridgeheads, Hitler yielded to Rommel's demand for reinforcements and ordered all available units from 15th Army to be put on the move. This threat provided the combination of Garbo and Ultra with its finest hour, for at seven minutes past midnight on the 9th a vast situation report was radioed by Garbo to his controller in Madrid, based, he declared, on careful consultation with his three best (but non-existent) sub-agents. Their joint view was that 'the present operation', ie Normandy, 'though a large-scale assault, is *diversionary in character.* ... The fact that the massive concentration of forces in east and south-east England remains inactive suggests that these forces are being held in reserve for other large-scale operations. The constant aerial bombardment which the sector of the Pas de Calais has been undergoing' (as it had: a calculated part of the deception scheme) 'and the disposition of the enemy forces would indicate *the imminence of an assault in this region.* ...'*

The details of the report's onward journey can now be traced in a

*Author's italics.

file of documents discovered by the Americans towards the end of the war, cached in a mountain cave in Thuringia. From Madrid it went to Berlin. By 10 pm on the 9th a summary had reached Hitler's command post at Berchtesgaden and von Rundstedt in France. The effect was instantaneous. Hitler cancelled his movement orders, and after a telephone call from General Keitel at Berchtesgaden von Rundstedt, at 0730 on the 10th, or D + 4, issued countermanding instructions. 'As a consequence of information which has just been received, C-in-C West has proclaimed a second degree alert for 15th Army in Belgium and northern France. The move of I SS Panzer Division will therefore be halted.' And not only I SS Panzer. 116 Panzer was actually directed from north-west of Paris towards the Somme, while 85 Infantry Division, already north of the Somme but about to move south, was told to stand fast. No wonder that Colonel Bevan, in that October letter to the Director General Security Service, placed particular emphasis on 'the vital post-Overlord D Day period'.

For though the precise way in which Garbo's misleading report had percolated to Hitler and his High Command was unknown at the time, its impact was immediately evident in Normandy and in London. In Normandy, for the obvious reason that the dreaded counter-attack by 15th Army on the vulnerable eastern flank of the Allied bridgehead never materialized. In London, because Ultra soon made plain the extent to which the Germans had swallowed Garbo's bait. Admiral Canaris no longer controlled the Abwehr. In February 1944 he had been defeated in his power-struggle with Himmler and the Abwehr had been assimilated within Amt Mil, the military intelligence division of Himmler's SS empire. So it was from the head of Amt Mil in Berlin that Bletchley deciphered a signal to the Madrid office stating that 'Himmler had expressed appreciation of the work carried out by the Garbo organization and that further efforts must be made to ascertain in good time the destination of the troops in the south-east of England.' It was from Berlin, too, that on 11 June another Ultra decrypt revealed continued appreciation: 'All the reports received in the last week from Arabel' (as the Germans called Garbo) 'have been confirmed without exception and are to be described as especially valuable.' Ultra, therefore, not only facilitated the Bodyguard deception plan. During 'the vital post-Overlord D Day period' it produced irrefutable evidence that the enemy was still deluded.

318

During the evening of 1 June, for example, Foreign Armies West signalled a long intelligence appreciation to Kesselring's headquarters in Italy. It was not decrypted and issued from Bletchley until the afternoon of the 11th, but its value as an index of German thinking was as plain then as it is now.

Paragraph One. Area of Great Britain. Identification of 7 Airborne Division (out of total eight) in southern England and transfer forward, reported by reliable source, of in addition 79 American Division from Yorkshire to S.E. England into area of 8 American Corps. An unquestionable *schwerpunkt* in that area. . . .

As has been seen, there were not eight airborne divisions in England, and in the south-east there was certainly neither a 7 Airborne Division or an 8 American Corps. Moreover, though the decrypt only came through on the 11th, it contained a useful indication that even by then the 15th Army's stagnation would continue. Referring to the 'dropping of uniformed officers who will be kept in hiding and direct activities', it commented: 'As enemy can hardly intend to keep Allied uniformed officers in hiding for long spell, *period from 12 June onwards must be considered the new danger period.*'*

To read, post-war, the teleprints and telephone logs recording this delusion is one thing: to be able, through Ultra, to assess it at the time was infinitely reassuring. And as the intercepts continued the picture, miraculously, remained the same. As late as the night of 22 June, for example, Bletchley sent out this decrypt.

Foreign Armies West. On 19th credible reports state 28 US Infantry Division moved back to Kent from Ipswich area. When in Ipswich division conducted landing exercise. A new US inf. division stated recently to have arrived Great Britain replaces 28th in Ipswich. This may be 8 US inf. div.

It is a kind of hallucination. No American division was ever in Ipswich: no American divisions were ever in Kent. And then, just twenty-four hours later, another Ultra disclosed a signal sent out earlier in the day from an obviously piqued 116th Panzer Division which showed that the lure of FUSAG was still seductive. The signal was presumably sent by the 'Flivo' or Air Liaison Office attached to the Division.

*Author's italics.

116 Panzer Div. on 23rd complained that it received last situation report on the 5th from Fliegerkorps 2. It requested information currently of air situation, intentions and recce results. *Division not engaged in the fighting.*[*]

That not only 116 Panzer but also the whole of the 15th Army was so neutralized, and that the decisive battle for Europe was fought not in the Pas de Calais but in the marshes of the Cotentin and the *bocage*, valleys and downlands of Normandy was a triumph which, in retrospect, seems scarcely possible without the aid of Ultra.

But Hitler, too, had his secret weapons. On 15 June 1944 the first flying bomb or V1 (*Vergeltungs* 1 or Retaliation 1) landed in London, the forerunner of 8617 launchings from which 2340 bombs reached the broad area of the London Civil Defence Region. On 8 September, the day that final victory over V1 was announced, the first of 500 V2 rockets arrived – all that were to drop in Greater London out of 1190 despatched. Neither bombardment seriously affected the landings in Normandy or the subsequent fighting. Nevertheless, before considering in the next chapter what actually happened in Overlord it is sensible to ask what might have happened, had the V1 and V2 'retaliation' been carried out earlier in a more effective and concentrated form – the real death-blow about which Hitler dreamed.

Germany fought on even though Bomber Command obliterated her centre of government in Berlin. The annihilation of London and an intensive rocket-bombing of British ports would not, presumably, have prevented the Anglo-American armies from ultimately landing in France. Yet a sustained and well-directed onslaught by the V-weapons must have had a grave effect, and could well have led to a postponement of D Day. The psychological and physical consequences of such an attack are difficult to assess. We can only speculate about how Churchill would have helped the country and Eisenhower his soldiers to overcome the trauma.

In the event, of course, the V-bombardment began later than the Germans intended. It was inaccurate, insufficient in volume to cause irrecoverable damage, and flawed by too many failures as the bombs and rockets aborted or strayed off course. Disaster was

[*]Author's italics.

averted: but only as a result of prolonged efforts by British scientific intelligence and intensive bombing of the launching sites in France. (These sorties, costly in crews and aircraft, also diverted the RAF and USAAF from their prime role of preparing for the invasion). The question is, how much did Ultra contribute to the anti-V effort which came to be summarized under the codename Crossbow?

R. V. Jones, who was continuously and indeed brilliantly immersed in the struggle of scientific intelligence, thought that in this case the contribution was less than that of other sources, and he is the most authoritative witness. A famous counter-measure was the great raid by Bomber Command on the V-weapon research and development station at Peenemünde on the Baltic. In his epilogue to *Most Secret War* Jones noted, 'At the end of every investigation I looked back to see how far we could have gone without Enigma. As the outstanding example, it was reassuring to find that we would very probably have raided Peenemünde without any help from Enigma.'[13] Hints and incidental pieces of information did, indeed, crop up in the Ultra signals, but the main reasons for discovering, and so preparing for what was afoot, were photo-reconnaissance and lynx-eyed interpretation of the results: superb collaboration by the Polish and French underground: the bombing of Germany, whose effect on industry and communications delayed manufacture and distribution of the weapons: the quality of the British scientific attack: and, not least, the internecine rivalries and inefficiencies within the relevant German agencies.

Nevertheless, in one particular instance Ultra was probably worth more than many of the heavy bomber squadrons blasting (and too often missing) the launching sites in the Pas de Calais. Jones saw an opening. The Abwehr spy-masters were telling their 'agents' in England to report both the time and the place of flying-bomb explosions in London. This was a crisis, for the double agents had a vital part to play in the continuing deception plan; if they reported falsely they might be unveiled. Yet it would have been foolish to let them send in accurate reports, as if they were Forward Observation Officers for this unique artillery. The profitable answer, Jones realized, was for them to report back the actual *point* of strike for bombs that had overshot London linked with the actual *time* of strike of bombs that had fallen short. The Germans, lacking the confirmation of photo-reconnaissance,[14] bought the idea and cut back the mean range of the flying-bombs, so that many more fell in the open southern suburbs and thousands of lives were saved – quite apart from the fact that governmental and military departments in the centre of London could continue to function normally.[15] Since, as has been seen, the viability of the double agents depended to a large degree on Bletchley's mastery of the Abwehr's signal-traffic, those who lived or worked in central London during the summer of 1944 owe a substantial debt to Ultra.

In any event, though the Channel was rough and the weather forecast uncertain, SHAEF's chief meteorologist Group Captain Stagg courageously backed a hunch and Eisenhower said 'Let's go'. All General Morgan's requirements had been fulfilled. The blow was to fall where the enemy least expected it, when he least expected it, and with a force altogether outside his calculations. But without the incessant decrypts from Bletchley neither B1A, nor LCS, nor the XX Committee nor the Middle East's 'A' Force could have cast their spells effectively. It was Ultra, above all, that enabled the deceivers to read the enemy's mind and twist it: to avert disaster from the Allies while arranging it for their opponents. By so doing they gave the British and American divisions on D Day the benefit which four centuries earlier Sir Francis Drake had considered paramount. 'The advantage of time and place in all martial actions', he said, 'is half a victory which being lost is irrecoverable.' What Hitler lost on 6 June, 1944, he was never to regain.

12 Finale and Curtains: from D Day to Victory

> 'The intelligence which has emanated from you before and during this campaign has been of priceless value to me. It has simplified my task as commander enormously. It has saved thousands of British and American lives and, in no small way, contributed to the speed with which the enemy was routed and eventually forced to surrender.'
>
> GENERAL DWIGHT D. EISENHOWER to Major-General Sir Stewart Menzies, July 1945, thanking him for Ultra and the achievement at Bletchley Park.

The greatest impediment for the Ultra organization on D Day was the invention of the telephone. As British and American airborne troops descended through the darkness on both flanks of the enemy front in Normandy and then, after the great armadas hove in sight, landing-craft and amphibious tanks worked their way shorewards, a mixture of paralysis and confusion seeped through all the German headquarters in the west. But the picture of their immediate reactions that has been built up since the war – the picture of an ant-heap slowly coming to life against a gradually identified aggressor – has been constructed essentially from telephone logs and teleprinter records.*

The land-lines were good, the exchanges were functioning, the situation was still static. And thus it was that the first puzzled communications passed between the command posts of von Rundstedt in Paris, Rommel's Army Group B at his château of La Roche Guyon on the Seine, Dollman's 7th Army HQ at Le Mans, Vice-Admiral Krancke at Naval Group West and General Hans von Salmuth at the 15th Army near Tourcoing. It was by telephone in the early hours of the 6th that Rommel's Chief of Staff, Speidel, informed his master that instead of celebrating his wife's birthday at his Bavarian home he must return to deal with an invasion. It was by telephone that Hitler received the news in his Berghof at

---

*Some of this reconstruction was soon possible. The telephone log-book for the headquarters of the 7th Army was captured at Falaise in August 1944, at the end of the Normandy battle.

Berchtesgaden – observing to Keitel 'It couldn't be better. As long as they were in England we couldn't get at them.' And it was by telephone next day that Rommel revealed the continuing mesmeric influence of FUSAG when he spoke to the Chief of Staff, General Jodl, at the Berghof and declared: 'My broad impression is that we must assume that the enemy is going to make an invasion elsewhere.' So it was not surprising that of the Ultra signals sent out from Bletchley on D Day – or at least of those in the only accessible file, DEFE3 in the Public Record Office, which contains the series of army/air decrypts issued from Hut 3 – the greater proportion comes from the Mediterranean rather than from the front in France.

Since these D Day signals were mainly brief and unco-ordinated reports from local commanders about events on their particular sector of the coast, with occasional general assessments from the more central headquarters, the news they brought to the Allies was not so much about what was happening, (for they were aware of this already), as of the late, patchy and imperfect picture the Germans were constructing. The signals were those of men caught in the confusion of surprise – from the intercepted report by Sea Defence Commandant Normandy at five minutes before midnight on the 5th, stating that 'some of the parachutists reported were straw dummies', to his remarkable signal later on D Day stating that there was 'no disembarkation yet on the east coast of the Cotentin': the American landings there on UTAH beach had started at 0630 in the morning and put over 23 000 men ashore in the course of the day. One useful piece of evidence from the early signals came from the various reports about the declining efficiency of German radar stations along the coast. Savage bombing and a barrage of jamming had this objective, and though the Official History says that 'it was too early to know how all these measures affected the enemy' the decrypt of a signal from the Sea Defence Commandant, made at 0221 on D Day and reporting 'no radio location in sea area to NE owing to failure of radar apparatus', must have brought reassurance. Such local blindness compounded the broad effect of the Bodyguard deception and the distraction of British airborne troops to the east and Americans descending from the western sky. At 1850 Bletchley issued the decrypt of a mid-afternoon signal from Naval Group West which revealed all. 'The proclamation by the Allied leaders and the disposition of Allied Forces point to further operations, *but no details available regarding their targets.'*

In many ways the most significant Ultra document issued by
Bletchley on D Day was not directly related to the landings. A long
signal from the Luftwaffe High Command, OKL, it stated bleakly
but firmly that owing to Allied air attacks on fuel installations and
the oil industry, and the paramount need to defend the heartland of
Germany itself, there was no prospect for weeks to come of any
increase in fuel stocks for commanders elsewhere. An immense
encouragement for Spaatz to know that the efforts of his Strategic
Air Command (so well serviced by Ultra) were neutralizing the
German war effort at this dramatic moment: an immense encouragement for Eisenhower, Montgomery and Bradley to know that
the panzer divisions opposing them could run dry and the weak
Luftwaffe become weaker still: and a terrible truth for von Rundstedt and Rommel at the close of Neptune's first twenty-four hours.
As at Alamein, so in Normandy fuel shortage would fatally restrict
the Germans' ability to manoeuvre both in the air and on the
ground.

Such Ultra intelligence could only be derived from radio-activity.
During the first day or two of the landings, therefore, Bletchley
could do little by way of tapping into the thoughts and over-hearing
the decisions of the German High Command and its generals in the
field. As the battle in the beachhead intensified, however, radio was
used more readily – often through *force majeure* – and a tide-race of
intercepts quickened into a flood. To anyone who, like the author,
served in the Normandy campaign and has subsequently studied it,
the volume and intimacy of the intelligence supplied by Ultra during those climacteric weeks is a revelation. How much more so must
it have been at the time for anxious commanders and their staffs!
For to read the signals is like sharing one of those experiments in
which, through a carefully placed sheet of glass, one is able to
observe in minute detail the behaviour-pattern of the ant-heap.

Pattern is the key word. Experienced intelligence officers, and
the generals they served, well knew that from time to time but
unpredictably Ultra would supply some dramatic piece of information about the enemy which would enable them to make decisive
moves on the battlefield, whether as a major stroke or in some
important local operation. But they also knew – as the senior intel-

*Author's italics.

ligence officers in Africa, Italy and Overlord have all confirmed to the author – that it was the remorseless *daily* flow of information from *all* sources that provided the continuous picture they needed of developments behind the enemy lines and inside the minds of the enemy commanders. They wanted, in fact, to watch patterns and trends. The Ultra signals relating to the Normandy campaign are rich in examples of such processes.

For Bletchley, as for Montgomery and Bradley, there was great significance in one pattern that emerged at an early stage and became progressively more vivid – the crumbling and degeneration of the German communication-system. The Allied air forces, the French resistance and, the fighting troops all played their part in sabotaging and severing the enemy's telephone-links and thus compelling him, willy-nilly, to use radio traffic whose transmitters could be located by direction-finding and whose messages could be intercepted and deciphered. Ultra decrypts revealed this deterioration. One, from D + 2, is characteristic. At 0851 next morning Bletchley reported that at 1345 on the 8th the Naval Communications Officer to Captain U-boats, West, had signalled: 'All lines to Berlin, Kiel, Wilhelmshaven, Paris, Brest, Aix, La Rochelle down as a result of enemy action. One teleprinter line to Paris limitedly effective.'

Communications by road and rail were simultaneously collapsing. Of course bomb-aimers' reports, air-photographs and reconnaissance established the scale of damage, but it was valuable to know how the Germans were reacting. On D + 1, Ultra disclosed that one thousand labourers had been urgently summoned from Luftwaffe construction sites for immediate repair of the railway stations Lyon-Guillotreu and Lyon-Venissieux: and the Luftwaffe in France, as will be seen, was in no condition on D + 1 to spare labourers. On the 8th, another Ultra revealed, the Highway Commission in France stated that all Seine crossings from Conflans to Rouen inclusive had been destroyed: 'In this sector traffic north and south was only possible through Paris.' The combined effect of the disintegration of all communications was perfectly demonstrated in a signal of the 11th, reporting on the painful movement of 2 Parachute Corps from Brittany towards the St Lo area. The signal ends: 'Delay owing to fuel. *Whereabouts of elements being brought up by rail (all tracked vehicles and one unspecified battalion) not known.'** But

*Author's italics.

the Germans were now in a world such that at midnight on the 8th a battalion of 2 SS Panzer Grenadier Division, inching its way from the south of France, discovered that its Colonel had vanished into thin air. 'At midday the Colonel's car was found parked in a village 40 miles back. There were no signs of sabotage or violence, not even a puncture. The village and the surrounding countryside were scoured in vain.' He had simply been pinched by the Resistance, who held up 2 SS Panzer for days.[1]

Nowhere was a pattern more evident than in the case of the drive by that old hand from Guadalcanal, General Collins, down the Cotentin peninsula towards Cherbourg from the beachheads established on D Day by the two American airborne divisions and the UTAH landings. The throat of the peninsula – and the telephone circuits – were soon in a stranglehold. Ultra reflected the increased radio-traffic. At first it was off target, with Admiral Atlantic Coast on the 10th appreciating 'hesitant and slow progress of Allied land operations in Cotentin and Seine Bay sector may indicate an intended second landing at another point'. FUSAG in action. But a cautionary (and surprisingly considerate) note is struck next day when Group West instructs the Admiral that all female staff of naval officers in Brittany are 'to be sent at once to appropriate offices in Germany'. By the 13th Ultra disclosed desperation, with the text of a signal sent by Group West at midday on the 12th to announce the policy which Hitler had imposed and Rommel perforce accepted. 'The fateful importance for Greater Germany of the battle for Cotentin requires each individual to fight to the last ... even fighting withdrawals are not to be countenanced.'

As Collins drove his three divisions northwards up the peninsula it was invaluable for him to know that German policy was to allow their indifferent troops on the Cotentin to be flushed out in the open rather than – as was militarily correct – to withdraw their whole force within the Cherbourg defences. And as the Americans encircled that formidable fortress it was no less important for Collins to be able to weigh the quality of its commander. This was General von Schlieben, who on 21 June rejected a demand for surrender although, it must be said, the 7th Army told him that six and a half American divisions were at his gates, an error of one hundred per cent. But this was bravado, as was swiftly revealed by two Ultra decrypts so instructive that they are worth quoting at length.

Early in the afternoon of the 22nd Bletchley issued two texts. The first was a signal from Hitler himself to von Schlieben, sent at six o'clock the previous evening and giving him full powers at Cherbourg.

I expect of you that you will conduct this action as Gneisenau once conducted the defence of Kolberg. As long as you still have ammunitions and rations, every enemy attack must be shattered by your inflexible will, the strength of your wisdom, your skill and the bravery of your troops. Even if the worst should happen, it is your duty still to defend the last pill-box and to leave the enemy not a harbour but a field of devastation. . . .

Epic words: but the less than heroic temper of their recipient came through in Ultra's decrypt of the miserable signal von Schlieben flashed to Rommel at eleven that night.

The troops of 709 Division who have taken part in the fighting are numerically and spiritually exhausted. Fortress garrison itself not fit to withstand a severe strain. Men are over age, untrained and pillbox-minded . . . leaderless groups of 77 and 243 divisions which have become separated from their formations are a handicap rather than a support . . . reinforcement regarded as absolutely necessary for a task which Hitler has declared to be decisive.

Never before in history, perhaps, has the pressure on a besieged commander from his head of state, and the commander's own despair, been so conclusively and so swiftly exposed to the besiegers as in these two Ultra documents. And so, when the end game was played on the 26th, von Schlieben was taken alive in his underground command post and a Psychological Warfare Unit effected the surrender of the virtually impregnable Arsenal. (In justice to von Schlieben it must be recorded that by stubborn but hopeless resistance he did indeed leave 'not a harbour but a field of devastation'. Waterfront installations were so destroyed and the waters themselves so infested that minesweepers, and divers specially trained over the mud-flats of the Thames, only opened the port to the first deep-draught ship on 16 July.)

It was this siege, incidentally, that produced the most amusing Ultra decrypt of the campaign – the text of a signal protesting that anti-tank bazookas had been dropped *again* on the Channel Islands. They were intended for and urgently needed at *Cherbourg*. Would the Luftwaffe commander take appropriate action? Dropped again! One hears the weary sigh of contempt with which the staff officer composed his signal: they can't even hit Cherbourg!

328

Yet the condition of the Luftwaffe was in truth irrecoverable. On D Day the whole 3rd Air Fleet in France, Luftflotte 3, had only 497 serviceable aircraft of which a mere 319 went into action. After four days 208 had been destroyed and 105 damaged. By the end of the first week, in spite of hectic reinforcements, there were still only about 1000 German aircraft of all types in the West. The full measure of the Luftwaffe's incapacity stands out in a single comparison: by 30 June, the day when the phase of the Neptune landings was reckoned to be complete and Germany became Overlord's realistic objective, the combined effort of the RAF and the USAAF had achieved 163 403 sorties in all operations while Luftflotte 3 managed no more than 13 829. A main reason, of course, was the decimation of the day-fighters over Germany by the USAAF and the shattering effect of the Combined Bomber Offensive on aircraft factories, ball-bearing plants and the sources of fuel.

But there was a more immediate reason. The original plan for the Luftwaffe in the event of an invasion was to rush westwards every available aircraft in Germany. But because of the imaginary threat of FUSAG to the Pas de Calais these were not released instantly: even by 10 June General Sperrle, commanding Luftflotte 3, had received no more than 300 extra fighters. Any hope of an initial superiority was lost and never recovered, for the airfields awaiting the newcomers were heavily bombed, impromptu landing grounds had to be organized, ground staff and technicians were delayed in their travel by train or road, and the signals network so essential for conducting air operations was disrupted. A Luftwaffe already weak and off balance was compelled, even more than was its habit, to employ radio and thus reveal its nakedness to a Bletchley already adept at reading its ciphers.

In consequence the Ultra decrypts for the Normandy campaign contain an astonishing profusion of intelligence about the condition and performance of the German air force. The regular strength returns reveal the growth or decrease in the readiness of individual units. Their locations are identifiable. The routine daily reports on operations carried out during the previous twenty-four hours were a useful check against actual experience, for they told the Allies what the Luftwaffe thought it had been doing as compared with what had happened: they told, too, of a pathetic inadequacy of endeavour, for to read them is to observe the Luftwaffe, once proudly all-powerful, now restricting itself mainly to reconnaissance flights, small-scale strikes, and the essential trivia of air warfare. Lack of fuel, lack of aircraft, lack of landing grounds form a continuing pattern of distress. Consider a single Ultra decrypt of 14 June describing the condition of the airfields at Epinay, Beauvais, Alençon, Argentan, Caen, Coulommiers, Rennes, Lorient – the outer perimeter, in fact, of the Normandy battlefield. The recurrent phrase is 'conditionally serviceable'. For some there is 'no night landing', or 'Serviceable by day. Great caution in landing'. Another field is 'closed for visiting aircraft owing to bomb craters'. Only two or three are said to be 'fully serviceable'. Yet Coulommiers was the Fighter Defence HQ and the base of a fighter division: Beauvais was the base of a Bomber Corps. Intelligence officers at RAF and USAAF headquarters were certainly able to monitor through a clear glass the bewildered activities of the Luftwaffe's ant-heap.

And there was other evidence, as important for the conflict on land as for the struggle in the air. By that illogicality which bedevilled the Germans' army commanders in all their theatres of war, Flak or anti-aircraft units were controlled by the Luftwaffe. Yet Flak included the most successful single weapon in Hitler's armoury, the dual-purpose 88 mm gun whose record against tanks is historic. In Normandy the chief formation was 3 Flak Corps – deployed almost entirely along the British front in anti-tank as well as anti-aircraft roles. It included, off and on, between 120 and 160 88 mm guns as well as many lighter weapons. As a Luftwaffe formation 3 Flak Corps used the Luftwaffe cipher, and since it was assiduous in registering by radio strength returns, unit locations, fuel and ammunition states and other domestic details, Bletchley was able to keep the Allied headquarters currently in the picture. If it was useful for the airmen to learn where the Flak guns were, it was even more important for Montgomery's armour.

To know the number and location of the 88s was of course profoundly important, even though the knowledge could not always be regular or precise. (In Montgomery's largest armoured attack, operation Goodwood, launched on 18 July to the east of Caen, the general area of the gun line was well identified by his intelligence, but this did not prevent eighty heavy anti-tank guns and 272 six-barrelled *nebelwerfer* mortars from halting three British tank divisions.) But other large benefits flowed from the communications-net of 3 Flak Corps. Because of its intimate association with the army it whispered the army's secrets.

Take the case of the ill-starred Panzer Group West which under the able General Geyr von Schweppenburg controlled the powerful 1st SS Panzer Corps and two infantry divisions. When this head-quarters advanced forward from Paris after the landings, fighter-bombers destroyed two thirds of its wireless gear. As it was coming into operation again a carefully directed bomb and rocket attack caught it, on the evening of the 10th, exposed among the orchards of its command post at Thury-Harcourt on the River Orne – whose beautiful château the author's guns were to help to pulverize a month later. By midday on the 12th the detailed results of this 'take out' were known from an Ultra decrypt – results about which the headquarters of 7th Army itself were not informed for many hours.

According to Flak Corps 3 at 21 hrs 10th all communications of Panzer Gruppe West out of action. Chief of Staff, 1A and 1C killed, GOC apparently slightly wounded. Chief of Staff of 7th Army who was there has entrusted 1 SS Panzer Corps with the former command tasks of Panzer Gruppe West.

It was certainly a relief for Montgomery to know not only that the nerve-centre of Rommel's toughest formation had been eliminated, but also that he had opposite him no longer the efficient Geyr but SS Gruppenführer Sepp Dietrich, the ex-butcher and 'old Nazi' at the head of 1 SS Corps, a man bound to Hitler by many years' service as his chauffeur and bodyguard, and a fighting animal rather than a commander at high level, whom von Rundstedt wrote off as 'decent but stupid'. And there were even more significant implications for Montgomery in these few lines from Ultra. They were vividly symbolized by Chester Wilmot in *The Struggle for Europe*.

Geyr's Chief of Staff and seventeen others were buried in one of the bomb craters over which the Germans were to raise a huge cross of polished oak, emblazoned with eagle and swastika – an appropriately impressive memorial, for this was the graveyard not only of these men but of Rommel's hopes for a major counter-attack before it was too late.

Two days later, moreover, Ultra brought news of the death of another first-rate general, the wooden-legged Eric Marcks, who in 1940 had drawn up the initial plan for the invasion of Russia. It was the 'Flivo' or Air Liaison Officer at his 84 Corps on the American front who reported at 12.30 on the 12th: 'GOC General of Artillery Marcks killed west of St Lo in fighter-bomber attack.' This signal

331

was deciphered and the decrypt sent out from Bletchley well before midnight.

Such swift intelligence was vital for the Allied staffs as they sought to build up the patterns of activity on the other side of the front line. But before the fighting spreads and intensifies, so that German army headquarters start to use their radios and thus supply Bletchley's cryptanalysts with abundant material, it is worth pausing to recall that even at this historic moment Normandy was only one of the sources for the signals which kept the men and women at Station X under a relentless pressure. June 7 or D + 1 is instructive.

For this day there is, of course, a variety of signals reporting the progress of the airborne landings, attempts to increase the Luftwaffe's effort, AA protection for the Seine crossings over which reinforcements must pass – and so on. But there is also Kesselring's summary of his intentions in Italy up to 8 June, and immensely detailed information about small ship movements around the northern Mediterranean. One signal warns that the German intercept service on the Russian front had been briefed on 5 June about the operations of the 15th US Army Air Force from its Italian bases, with specific detail about its different bomber groups. Another quotes an instruction from Army Group Ukraine that all German armoured transport will carry recognition marks on the side and rear, 'three 4-digit tactical numbers, height three nought cm., width 5 cm.' There is a report on sweeping gear by the Inspector of the Danube Minesweeping Service. Bletchley has become a universal provider.

But it was the land-battle in Normandy that mattered, and here, amid the many patterns that gradually emerged from Ultra and other intelligence, there was one above all that Montgomery watched consistently. After the early days, when it became clear that he was not going to take the city of Caen on the run, his undeviating purpose was to draw the main bulk of the German panzer divisions on to the British sector so that Bradley's army, once it had cleared the Cherbourg peninsula, could break out to the south and east and thus create the situation described in a famous wartime headline: 'Allies Push Bottles Up Germans'. Montgomery outside Caen, Grant outside Richmond: Sherman slicing through Georgia and Patton driving for Falaise. Every scrap of evidence about the panzers that came through on Ultra was therefore worth gold to Montgomery and his staff.

The movement of German divisions into the bridgehead was disclosed by Ultra slowly at first and then with gathering speed. On the afternoon of D + 2, for example, we have a signal of ZZZZ urgency: '17 SS Panzer Grenadier Division subordinated to 7th Army on 7th destination Villedieu.' What this meant was that at last Hitler had released 17 SS to Rommel from OKW reserve, and that it was now moving from its location south of the river Loire against the Americans in the Cotentin peninsula. At 0849 on the 11th Panzer Group West, restored from its traumatic experience, announces that it 'intends assuming command as soon as communications allow and asks to receive from von Rundstedt only "its general task" '. So von Schweppenburg is about to come into action again. At 0108 on the 12th comes an Ultra showing how interdivisional connections are beginning to emerge, in a signal issued at 1300 on the 11th which first gave the locations of 352 Division and continued:

Elements 3 Para Div engaged area T6065. Div to join up with right wing 352 Div both sides St Lo – Bayeux road as far west as possible. Operate in defence till complete fighting efficiency achieved. 17 SS PG Div assembly S and SW T4086. Mobile operations depending on situation.

Even more precise information about these divisional locations followed at 1419 and 1609. Here was Ultra reading with but a few hours' delay the small print of the Germans' plans.

June 13 is an admirable day for demonstrating Ultra's value as a mirror-image of the panzer situation. At 0547 a signal reports that during the previous afternoon 2 SS Panzer Division was on the march in the direction of Tours and expected at Poitiers the same day. (In distant Toulouse on D Day, the division was struggling northwards and still had not checked in by the 17th.) At 1425 Bletchley signalled a message from the Air Liaison Officer with 12 SS Panzer Division, engaged on the British sector. At nine o'clock the previous evening, it said, 12 SS Division's front line was running westward from Galmanche: then Panzer Lehr Division 'to bend in road T8870 ... then west ... communications with Panzer Division established'. Finally, at 2005, there came a plum: somewhat delayed, but still giving a complete breakdown of the SS Corps, opposite the British, and its links with the 84th Corps to the west whose task was containment of the Americans.

Information 11th following operationally subordinated to 1 SS Corps until further notice: Panzer Lehr, 12 SS Panzer, 21 Panzer and 716 Divisions, Werfer Brigade 7, Schnelle Brigade 30, Arko [artillery command] 474: dividing line between 1 SS Corps and 84 Corps Ht.361 Ht.194 Ht.142, E. edge Verney and Verney Wood, course of stream west of Bayeux, Port en Bessin: Hts. inclusive to 84 Corps, localities to 1 SS Corps.

Only a week after the landings, therefore, Montgomery was receiving full details of the command structure, and often precise and recent locations, in respect of every panzer division then in Normandy. And all commanders, staffs and military students are aware of the value of information about lines of junction between corps or divisions, since they notoriously offer to the attacker the point of greatest weakness in a defence line. Specific signals like these, moreover, were now being constantly reinforced and expanded by the routine full-scale returns about the units under his command in the west which von Rundstedt radioed to Germany. (See the Appendix for examples of the detailed information contained in such returns from von Rundstedt in France and Kesselring in Italy.) Bletchley was now deciphering these returns regularly.

Amid this stream, now in full flood, of massive German signals issuing in decrypt from Station X there were many shorter ones, sometimes of instant relevance. A perfect example of Ultra at work is supplied by one of these issued at 1533 on the 22nd. It was a report by the Abwehr officer at the 7th Army HQ on the 21st, that 'according captured documents in St Lo area American passwords and replies as follows: 20th to 22nd Chicken-Wire, 22nd to 25th Walking-Village, 25th to 26th Huddle-Time'. Within a relatively few hours the Americans in the St Lo sector knew that their passwords had been compromised and could change most of them forthwith.

Ultra in Normandy was thus proving to be an intelligence-system capable of providing information at every level on a scale ranging from the very small to the huge returns, often of five or six pages, that contained the unit strengths and locations of a corps, an army, and even the complete Germany military organization in the west. This was equally true of the Luftwaffe, whose signals about forthcoming attacks on Allied shipping or battle-zones were often deciphered in time for counter-action. How valuable, too, was the long signal from Fliegerkorps 9 (transmitted on the 21st but, as it had no great operational priority, not processed at Bletchley till the 23rd). This summarized the conclusions at a conference of senior Luftwaffe commanders on the 17th to review the air situation. For Air Marshal Coningham at the British 2nd Tactical Air Force or Major-General Quesada at 9th Tactical Air Command, as they gave close support respectively to the British and American sectors, it was instructive to know that already their opposite numbers, talking among themselves, believed that reinforcement pilots from Germany were useless: that the minimum for a safe strike into the bridgehead was 'a thrust by 12 to 15 fighters' – of which they had so few – and that anything less was dangerous: that under-trained pilots were jettisoning their bombs: that experienced flight leaders were lacking: and that aircraft should avoid ground held by their own troops as they were liable to be shot down!

Allied air superiority might well have become the supreme factor, for between 19 and 22 June the Normandy beaches were ravaged by the Great Channel Storm which, had it continued, might have produced the disaster Rommel failed to achieve. Even so, in those few tempestuous days the average daily landing of men fell from 15 774 British and 18 938 American to 3982 and 5865. The decline in the daily landing of stores and equipment was to less than a half for the British and to less than a quarter for the Americans, whose artificial harbours off the UTAH and OMAHA beaches had disintegrated. And this was the eve of the first major British offensive, EPSOM, which with two corps and 700 guns was intended to thrust fiercely inland beyond the crossings of the Odon and Orne rivers. The opening attack east of Caen was due on the 23rd: the main offensive, south west of the city, on the 25th.

Two Ultra signals now illustrate how Bletchley could bring the reassurance of precise information to battle-field commanders distracted by the elements as well as the enemy. (After the storm the British 2nd Army was already *three divisions* short on its planned build-up). At four minutes past midnight on the 23rd Ultra carried German situation reports, *in one case only seven and in the other only five hours old*, which showed the western boundary of the 21st Panzer Division and the eastern boundary of the 12th SS Panzer as following the railway running north from Caen: gave in point-to-point detail the boundaries between the 12th SS and the Panzer Lehr Division to the west: and set down, again with precision, the juncture points between the whole 1st SS Panzer Corps area and that of 47 Panzer Corps to the south east of St Lo. This was as good as having a spy in the enemy camp.

When the main attack began on the 25th it was obviously important for Montgomery to know the situation on his vulnerable left flank – that is to say, over on the east side of the River Orne as it ran northwards via Caen to the Channel. Here a new Corps headquarters, 86, had just moved in to control a fluid situation. At ten o'clock on the morning of Epsom, the 25th, Ultra showed 86 Corps taking shape, with a signal sent out only a few hours earlier. The 86th Corps, it said, had been put in command of General Reichert's 771 and General Distel's 346 Infantry Divisions (both previously under the 15th Army) while 16 Luftwaffe Field Division was on its way. The Corps area was defined as between the Seine and the Orne. The inter-divisional boundaries were spelled out in detail. Another unit, Battle Group Luck, was also posted to the Corps, and Bletchley added to the signal one of its characteristic informed comments. 'Rommel on 31st May requested that Major von Luck be entrusted with command of Panzer Grenadier Regiment 125 till health of Oberstleutnant Maempel restored: see KV 6343.' Meanwhile from far on the other flank, from the Sea Defence Commandant Brittany, there came on this same day an extensive and minutely particularized return of the large variety of guns, anti-tank guns, mortars, flame-throwers and ammunition under his authority. As he was unlikely to be replenished, certainly in his specialized equipment, such a stock-taking was of great interest to the American staffs looking ahead to the time of the break-out. (It was not, incidentally, the direction in which the Germans were looking. On the next day, 26 June, the Weekly Report from Rommel's Army Group B showed that Bodyguard and FUSAG were still at work. 'In England another 67 major formations are standing to, of which 57 at the very least can be employed for a large-scale operation.')

It was to achieve this break-out that the whole of the subsequent beachhead battle was directed. The British never relaxed their magnet-like attraction for the German armour. Patton, sustaining the FUSAG fiction, was held incognito for weeks in Normandy until the time was ripe for his 3rd Army to scythe into open country like Sherman from Atalanta. And it was to clear the breach for Patton that in Operation Cobra 1st US Army during the last week of July struck what Montgomery called 'the main blow of the Allied plan', the shattering offensive at St Lo which by tearing the German front apart caused a secret meeting at Hitler's headquarters about midnight on 31 July. Here withdrawal was seriously discussed, only to be dismissed, and the reliability of von Rundstedt's recent successor as Commander-in-Chief in the West, General von Kluge, was sceptically examined. Hitler threw out the fateful words 'I cannot leave the western campaign to Kluge'.

The words were doom-laden for the Germans because they contained the seeds of what historians must always consider as classic among Ultra's victories. To von Kluge their implications were immediately revealed. Two days later, at about one o'clock in the morning of 3 August, a signal arrived from Hitler indicating that the Führer was taking over the conduct of the battle. After instructing von Kluge to pull out the panzer divisions along the main perimeter of the beachhead, leaving its defence to the infantry, the message continued:

The armoured divisions which have up to now been employed on that front must be released and moved complete to the left wing. The enemy's armoured forces which have pressed forward to the east, south-east and south will be annihilated by an attack which these armoured formations – numbering at least four – will make, and contact will be restored with the west coast of the Cotentin at Avranches – or north of that – without regard to the enemy penetrations in Brittany.

When Ultra produced the text of this remarkable signal later in the day informed readers were at first incredulous. From the SHAEF headquarters at Portsmouth Eisenhower's deputy, Air Chief Marshal Sir Arthur Tedder, telephoned Group Captain Winterbotham in London to make certain that it was not a bluff. Winterbotham rang Hut 3 at Bletchley to confirm that the original German text was in Hitler's characteristic style.[2] But all was well. Kluge's troops, as its commandant knew, were being ordered to commit suicide. As Omar Bradley wrote of 'the Avranches offensive' in his memoirs, 'it was to cost the enemy an Army and gain us France'.

The Allied structure that Hitler intended to dismember had just taken a new shape. On 1 August, with the activation of the US 3rd Army (code-name LUCKY) Bradley became head of 12th Army Group (EAGLE), containing Hodges' 1st and Patton's 3rd Armies and equalled with Montgomery's 21st Army Group (LION), though Montgomery for the time being exercised overall control. By 6

August Bradley's generals had thrust no less than twelve divisions pell-mell through the twenty-mile gap at Avranches between the left flank of the German 7th Army and the sea. It was this picture, as presented on the maps at Hitler's headquarters, that stimulated his visionary order to von Kluge, for the Avranches gap looked like the narrow centre-piece of an hour-glass. Strike there, and all those American divisions in the south would be severed from their supplies.

For success the Führer's plan required three pre-conditions. Von Kluge must believe in it. He must be able to detach enough armour from the main front in Normandy to create an effective striking force. And he must achieve surprise. None of these necessities were attained, and the third of Kluge's failures was disastrous.

For the alert sounded by Ultra's decrypt of Hitler's initial instructions early on the 3rd was not followed by instant action. On the contrary, for three more days a series of angry communications passed between Hitler and the High Command on the one hand and Kluge on the other, reflecting the latter's doubts. His inability to assemble enough armour was now being increased by vigorous activity on the British front which pinned down the best divisions like 9th and 10th SS Panzer. But Hitler's will held, and the 'march to the sea' began just after midnight on the night of the 6th/7th August.

This prolonged dialogue between the Führer and his lack-lustre Commander-in-Chief had been steadily disclosed to the Allies by Ultra. Winterbotham has described Churchill's growing excitement and of how in London the Group Captain 'was awake at 5 am on August the seventh, waiting for the first news of the assault'.[3] But Ultra's real gift was to the commanders in the field, for it enabled them to design in comfortable time a death-trap for the enemy. In all the histories of the Normandy campaign, whether official or unofficial, the American victory in this battle appears as a fine example of improvisation, flexibility and courage. Courage was abundant, as ever, but it has not been realized previously how Ultra had given the Allies Sir Francis Drake's advantages of time and place: ample time to prepare exactly the right killing-ground. Instead of stunned opponents scurrying to the rear, the Germans found a cool, poised and fully briefed reception committee. The key American commanders were Bradley and Major-General Quesada, whose 9 Tactical Air Command with its Lightnings, Thunderbolts and Mustangs gave close support to 1st US Army. (Now under General Courtney H. Hodges, who had succeeded Bradley on 1 August, this army would take the direct shock of von Kluge's assault.) When discussing the value of Ultra during the Avranches battle General Quesada said to the author, in Washington in 1977, 'You know, Brad and I never used to talk together about our Ultra signals. We just took it for granted that each of us knew what was in them. But I can still see that moment when we stood with those signals in our hands, and grinned, and said "We've got them".'

In retrospect it all looks deceptively simple. Bradley held out an open sack and let the enemy march into it. During the early hours of 7 August von Kluge launched the assault that Hitler had ordered, but without conviction and almost in despair. His right-hand panzer division, 116, never even moved. 1 SS Panzer and 2 Panzer Divisions made a few miles, to be stopped in their tracks during the morning. A little further south 2 SS Panzer, advancing through persuasively light opposition (apart from a ferocious defence by 30 US Division) was drawn forward past Mortain on the opening road, as it seemed, to Avranches. By mid-day, however, the Americans on the ground had checked the German advance at every point. And then, suddenly, the mist and cloud that had prevented flying since dawn cleared away. In comfortably pre-arranged strikes the aircraft of Quesada's 9 TAC, working in concert with the British rocket-firing Typhoons, swarmed relentlessly over the unprotected panzer columns. The result was summarized in the Ultra decrypt of a report made that afternoon by the 7th Army. 'The actual attack has been at a standstill since 1300 hours, owing to the employment by the enemy of a great number of fighter-bombers and the absence of our own aircraft.' At 47 Panzer Corps 'the activity of the fighter-bombers is said to have been well-nigh unendurable'. 1 SS Panzer Division had had 'no previous experience of fighter-bomber attacks on this scale'. But there was a greater menace for the Germans. Working in complete and most praiseworthy confidence, Bradley remained undisturbed by the foray of four panzer divisions and continued, then and thereafter, to push his troops round and behind the enemy's southern front – particularly Patton's 3rd Army, which during the next week exploded like a bomb-burst in the rear of the German lines. The neck of the sack would soon be drawn tight.[4]

This Mortain/Avranches battle will long be studied as a technically perfect defensive operation – its course foreseen, the preparations sensible and sufficient, the shock of the enemy thrust swiftly absorbed, and the overall strategic plan continuing without interruption. But it must be studied as a prime example of the value to a commander of early and exact Ultra intelligence. Bradley and Montgomery were not flurried because they had been told in advance what was going to happen. Churchill in London, far from getting into a panic about an attack that, seen on the maps of his war room, might otherwise have seemed an appalling threat, actually looks forward to the event. And there is a deeper issue. Because of Montgomery's policy the German armour had so far operated consistently on the British front. By early August the Americans, for all their other fighting experience since D Day, had never known the power-drive of four panzer divisions advancing side by side. That they could handle the panzers was already clear: the main reason why the 116 Panzer Division never got going on the 7th was because it was exhausted by several days of engagement with the Americans. But it was an enormous bonus for Bradley and his tank commanders that through Ultra they could make their preliminary arrangements on the ground with such certainty, and tie into them with such devasting precision the strikes of Quesada's aircraft and the British Typhoons.

If Bradley's defeat of von Kluge's attempt to reach the sea was a model example of Ultra's power to guide a brilliant commander all the way to victory by supplying precise foreknowledge of his enemy's intentions, it was also the last of its kind in the European war. As the story of the advance to Berlin develops, it will be seen that conditions faded for so perfect a combination between intelligence and command decisions in respect of a single localized but decisive battle. And yet, oddly enough, by preventing von Kluge from cutting his 12th Army Group in half, and enabling his own drive into Brittany to continue, Bradley returned the compliment by giving Ultra itself a boost.

Angus M. Thuermer in the 1970s was a personal assistant to the Director of the CIA. In August/September 1944, however, he was a Naval Intelligence Officer attached to the staff of General Troy Middleton's 8th US Corps which was besieging the port of Brest. Overhead droned the usual Heinkel on a supply drop: but this time its package fell into the lines of 8 Corps. Weighted with Iron Crosses for the garrison of Brest (a common morale-builder: von

Schlieben at Cherbourg had scattered Iron Crosses like confetti) the parcel also contained the currrent Enigma-setting for a substantial period ahead: an obvious move, since like Cherbourg the beleagured Brest depended on radio. But thanks to Thuermer and sensible colleagues who appreciated their significance the papers were immediately rushed to Bletchley. As the German Army ciphers were always vexatious, this gift of the daily Enigma settings for the coming weeks was true treasure-trove.

But was Ultra's treasure now to be wasted? The question has a peculiar intensity as one considers the final days in Normandy – that confused and bloody period when the pincers of the Allied Armies (Montgomery from the north and Bradley from the south) seemed to be closing with decisive force on the retreating Germans. Since the cut-off was incomplete the 'battle of the Falaise gap', as it is called, has become one of the most controversial episodes of the campaign. At the time certain Allied Commanders, like Patton, misjudged the situation. In their post-war memoirs others, like Bradley, have put some of the facts in the wrong place. The picture is blurred and distorted. But at last it is possible to analyse what occured from a different viewpoint, by introducing a significant new factor in the shape of Ultra.

'August 15th', Hitler declared, 'was the worst day of my life.' It is a good cue, for on the 15th the situation of his armies in the west was irrecoverable. In Normandy a channel no more than fifteen miles wide remained for his 7th Army and the 5th Panzer Army to extricate themselves and make eastwards for the crossings of the Seine. On the northern side of the gap the Canadians, that evening, entered Falaise itself and to their left the Polish Armoured Division was pressing towards the road junction of Trun, a vital point of passage for the German retreat. On the southern side, Bradley's divisions were pushing against the mouth of the gap around Argentan while the bulk of Patton's Third Army was already sweeping through open country towards Chartres, Orleans and Paris. On that same day, moreover, the Anvil landings which the German High Command had anticipated were launched with one French and three American divisions along the Côte d'Azur. (Within three days Patch's 7th US Army had a bridgehead forty miles wide and twenty deep and would soon be driving northwards up the valley of the Rhône.)

But what caused Hitler the greatest anguish was the knowledge

341

that his suspect Commander-in-Chief in the west, von Kluge, was missing. Surely he was negotiating a surrender with the Allies. 'The measures taken by the Army Group', the Führer asserted, 'cannot be explained except in the light of this assumption.' The suspicion was false. On the 15th von Kluge was caught in an air attack while driving to the front from his headquarters at La Roche Guyon: his radio was destroyed, and for half the day he was out of touch. Montgomery, Eisenhower and their chief intelligence officers have confirmed that no approaches were made to them by von Kluge. Still, the 15th was a black day for Hitler. At the worst possible moment, when his western armies were in a crisis, he decided on a change of command. Early next morning a signal reached the hard-bitten Field Marshal Walter Model on the Russian front, ordering him to fly to France forthwith and take over the responsibilities of von Kluge who, though he had reported his survival, was not informed of the change.

The events that followed the worst day of Hitler's life were steadily illuminated by Ultra. To recreate for oneself the chaos in the German escape-pocket by reading the signals sent out from Bletchley is to see that whatever else Montgomery and Bradley may have lacked, it was not intelligence about the enemy. These messages confirm, in fact, that an explanation for the Allies' failure to cut off the Germans completely at Falaise must be sought elsewhere.

Throughout the 16th deciphered intercepts were eloquent. At 1105 the previous day's situation report from the 7th Army and a few minutes later, at 1114, news of the withdrawal of 10 SS Panzer Division at Brienze, opposite the 1st US Army. At 1305 another situation report from the 7th Army, with emphasis on the critical fuel shortage which recurs in the signals. At 1608 the location of 9 SS Panzer Division on the American front as at 1030 that morning. At 1618 an appreciation from 47 Panzer Corps to the west of Argentan: 'Owing to the bottleneck, losses of men, morale and material were uncommonly high. Supply difficulties increasing. Increasing tank losses owing to lack of fuel.' And then , at 1940, a report that General Bayerlein, the veteran of Russia and the Afrika Korps who now commanded the Panzer Lehr Division, was 'ill and at present at main dressing-station 277 Division'. Intermingled with these signals, moreover, was a succession of messages from the 19th Army in southern France disclosing the Germans' desperate reactions to the Anvil landings.

342

Before the end of the day the mood is even more disconsolate. A ZZZZZ message at 1042 reveals that 'a source with Eberbach' (commanding a panzer group west of Argentan) 'and Hauser' (commanding the 7th Army) 'confirms that total tank forces for aggressive action on a large scale which would turn the situation in the rear of the Army Group are no longer sufficient. Shortage in fuel supply contributing decisive factor. . . .' Another ZZZZZ at 2048 states that six hours earlier the Army Group had ordered 'that the armies withdraw in two or three nights beginning 16th/17th to the line of the Orne'. This meant that the whole of the German rear-guard was falling back into the Falaise pocket, and just after two o'clock next morning a signal from von Kluge demonstrated his despair. 'Situation at bottleneck still such that to certain degree orderly evacuation impossible. . . . Whole situation urgently demands evacuation west bulge without delay through the narrow channel still available. I request corresponding orders.'

It was not orders that von Kluge received, but a successor. By the 17th Model was in France. Kluge's position was now impossible. Aware of Hitler's rage over the failure of his Mortain offensive, and without hope now that the plot of July 20th (in which he was implicated) had failed, he set off for Berlin on 19th August and took cyanide on the way. But for the Allies Model's arrival presented a different proposition. During July, while commanding Army Group Centre, he had stopped the Russian drive for Warsaw and been christened by Hitler 'the saviour of the Eastern Front'. Until he too committed suicide, in April 1945 when the Allies surrounded the Ruhr, Model never brought less than ruthless energy and an admirable generalship to his command in the west. But his replacement of von Kluge was not overlooked by Bletchley, nor was its significance disregarded. At 1534 on the 18th Station X reported a signal from Army Group B during the evening of the 17th from 'the new Commander-in-Chief, Model, ordering conference of GOC or Chief of Staff of 7th Army and Panzer Group Eberbach'. The news was considered so important that, quite exceptionally, Hut 3 marked the message as 'personal for Airey, personal for Strong, personal for Williams, personal for Sibert': that is to say, it was being brought directly to the attention of the chief intelligence officers at the headquarters of Alexander in Italy and of Eisenhower, Montgomery and Bradley.

As usual, a selection of the Ultra signals despatched during the

343

Falaise battle cannot convey the full range of their evidence about what 47 Panzer Corps called 'the uncommonly high losses of men, morale and material', the repeated and anxious queries about the condition of ferries and bridges along the Seine, the paralysing lack of fuel: about everything implicit in the decrypt sent over by BP at midday on the 18th – 'C-in-C West to keep responsible departments of Reich Minister for Armaments and War Production in picture of military position and to give them a date by which destruction of armaments in the west must be completed.' It is abundantly clear, however, that neither Montgomery nor Bradley can have been in any doubt about the disintegration and desperation of their enemy. Why, then, did the pincers close too late at Falaise?

One answer lies in the word 'desperation'. No one who has not faced a German panzer army fighting for its life has the right to criticize these who have done so and apparently failed: at least, not without very careful consideration. Slim called the Japanese 'the most formidable fighting insects in the world': the Germans in Normandy, with their good tanks, their lethal 88 mm guns, their skilful techniques and high military qualities were even more formidable, particularly when struggling for survival. The Canadian and Polish divisions who should have smashed through the northern side of the escape corridor were gallant but inexperienced: neither they nor the Americans in the south had quite the cutting edge. Indeed, Bradley was prudent to refuse Patton's absurd telephone call after his troops were getting into Argentan: 'Let me go on to Falaise and we'll drive the British back into the sea for another Dunkirk.' Neither Patton nor his men had yet known what it was like to face expert divisions like those on their front, 116 Panzer or 2 SS Panzer for example, in a fight to the death. None showed greater ferocity than the Poles: but at this moment neither Polish self-sacrifice nor American self-confidence were sufficient.

A second answer lies somewhere within the fog of war. Ultra told Montgomery and Bradley the truth about what was happening between Falaise and Argentan, but they could neither be absolutely certain that their men could cut the corridor nor that the other German divisions which they knew to be outside the bag would not make their getaway eastwards. There were the Seine crossings to be secured. There was Paris. Only a small proportion of the superior Allied armies could in fact be brought to bear on the narrow fronts presented by the sides of the Falaise corridor, and in retrospect it seems not unreasonable to have used the spare British and American divisions to attain these other objectives. What is certainly clear is that the failure at Falaise – if it can be called a failure – was due to command decision and a simple inability, on the Allies' part, to destroy the German will to survive: it was not the result of an intelligence-failure. In any case, when Model's last rearguards crossed the Seine little more than a hundred of the panzers and assault-guns in Normandy had been rescued, while the campaign had cost the *Wehrmacht* about 250 000 casualties.

As the Allies broke into the Low Countries, and through eastern France towards the frontiers of Germany, the racing tanks and mobile columns created their own momentum. General Horrocks had no vital need of Ultra as his 30 Corps sped onward through Brussels to Antwerp, nor had Patton's 3rd Army as it rolled forward beyond Reims to Verdun. They cut through a soft resistance with the ease and speed of a cheese-wire. And then the unexpected happened. On the day after the fall of Paris, 26 August, the Intelligence Summary issued by Eisenhower's headquarters at SHAEF stated: 'Two and a half months of bitter fighting ... have brought the end of the war in Europe within sight, almost within reach.' Instead, by mid-September the German armies, far from scampering back to the homeland, established a more or less continuous defensive line still far to the west of the Reich's approaches – a thin line with some very strange constituents, 'stomach battalions' formed from those afflicted with ulcers, 'ear battalions' of the deaf, young recruits, aging men: but still a coherent line, particularly strong in areas like the Moselle front where American power-drives would be halted by German tenacity.

For Ultra, and for the future of the campaign, this remarkable recovery by an apparently shattered *Wehrmacht* had a profound significance. To begin with, as the Germans fell back eastwards towards their own country and stabilized a front against the Allies, their Army was able to use again – as it always preferred – a wide network of safe telephone and teleprinter links. The closer the front lay to Germany the less these were likely to be interrupted by saboteurs, as had happened so often in western France at the time of D Day. And there would not be flaws built into the system, as French technicians had contrived, for example, when laying the cables to German airfields in Normandy. Thus the Army's voice was less frequently heard on the air – and less radio, less Ultra. Of course the Navy's Enigma traffic in the Baltic and around Scandinavia still persisted,[5] and of course the Luftwaffe used the radio constantly. But for Ultra the law of diminishing returns took over in September 1944.

For the Allies a more immediate danger was the attack of excessive optimism which now infected all levels of command. Early in September, on the 5th, Eisenhower was saying that 'the defeat of the German armies is now complete' and his aide, Captain Harry Butcher, observed in his diary that Ike 'felt for some days it had been obvious that our military force could advance almost at will, subject only to supply'. In Washington and London the most senior intelligence staffs sang the same tune: at SHAEF, as has been seen, the mood was euphoric. On 6th September even the conventionally-minded Director of Military Operations at the War Office, Major-General Sir John Kennedy, made a note that 'if we go at the same pace as of late, we should be in Berlin by the 28th. . . .'[6] It was a sublime conception. But as Napoleon said to the Polish Ambassador after the retreat from Moscow in 1912, 'there is only one step from the sublime to the ridiculous'.

And by any objective standard the defeat which the Allies were about to suffer, (as they now sought to cross the Rhine and, by seizing the bridge at Arnhem, to burst into the north German plain), *was* ridiculous. By committing the other error against which Napoleon used to warn, and 'making a picture' of the enemy, they wasted the *crème de la crème* of their armies – the splendid young soldiers of 1 British and 82 and 101 US Airborne, the Poles, the Guards Armoured and 43 Wessex Divisions – in an operation where results were laughable in relation to the high hopes with which it was launched and the heavy cost involved.

One dominant theme runs through the planning of Operation Market Garden, the attempt to drive a narrow corridor from Belgium across a succession of rivers and link up with the British airborne troops dropped into Arnhem on the far side of the Lower Rhine. The theme is over-confidence. There exists in the Eisenhower Papers a manuscript note written by the General in 1966 which affirms, 'I not only approved Market Garden, I insisted on it.' Active in the highest command headquarters, this delusive influence also swayed the judgment of the airborne units. Since D Day they had been on the stand-by for no less than seventeen different operations, all of which had been cancelled. They were raring to go. At the head of the Allied Airborne Army which controlled the three divisions was General Brereton, USAAF, whose attitude was particularly urgent. When his British deputy, Major-General Browning, fell out with him on 4 September over the last of the aborted missions, Operation Linnet II, Brereton rejected Browning's complaint that the notice was too short by saying 'the disorganization of the enemy demands that chances be taken'. And during the briefing to his officers for Market Garden – at his headquarters near Ascot racecourse on 10 September – General Brereton announced that as time was short 'major decisions arrived at now must stand – and these have to be made immediately'.

Here are the elements – arrogance, impatience for action, and refusal to adjust a hastily frozen plan – that made Market Garden a disaster even before Sunday 17 September, when the British airborne division dropped beyond that 'bridge too far' at Arnhem, and the tanks of Horrocks's 30 Corps began their slow roll towards Holland as the US 82 and 101 Airborne floated out of the skies to clear their path. Many technical errors were committed before and after the 17th: ill-calculated tactical plans, inadequate wireless links, wide gaps in the air cover; errors now well-established. But no error was so grave as the failure to identify in advance the presence of a Panzer Corps in the area of Arnhem, for it was on this fact, beyond all that bad luck and bad judgement were to add, that the loss of the great bridge over the Rhine depended. This was a failure of intelligence, whose roots are to be found in the prevailing attitude of complacency. Nobody wanted to know.

In fact the armoured situation at Arnhem could scarcely have been worse. In April 2 SS Panzer Corps, containing 9 and 10 SS Panzer Divisions, had fought savage battles on the Russian front in General Model's Army Group North Ukraine. Transferred by Hitler to the west in mid-June, its menace in Normandy had always been exceptional. Now it was recuperating and re-equipping around Arnhem, and by a coincidental quirk of fate the Tafelberg Hotel at Oosterbeek – two and a half miles from Arnhem's centre – had actually been taken over on 15 September as the headquarters of the former commander of the Corps, General Model. Rommel's and von Kluge's successor at the head of Army Group B had planted himself unwittingly (for Model had no foreknowledge of Market Garden) at the heart of the area where two days later the

British paratroops would descend. Here, by pure coincidence, was the powerful combination of a commander and a corps who had learned it all together the hard way in the proving ground of Russia.

Since the Germans had a perfectly good telephone system from Holland to Berlin, and to Hitler and his High Command at the *Wolfschanze* or Wolf's Lair headquarters at Rastenburg in Prussia, it might seem unlikely that Ultra could offer much warning about this wasps' nest to the staffs most intimately concerned – to Montgomery's 21 Army Group, to the Allied Airborne Army, and to Eisenhower's supreme command post. Fortunately the decrypts sent out from Bletchley during the Market Garden period were made available in the Public Record Office early in 1978. In fact they contain a surprising amount of evidence which, had it been correctly interpreted by the intelligence staffs, might well have diminished their confidence.

For a start, the move of Model's headquarters to Oosterbeek was known through Ultra two full days before Market Garden was launched. At 0752 on the 15th Bletchley issued this message: 'New location Flivo Army Group B 07 hrs. 14th Oosterbeek 4 kilometres W. of Arnhem.' It seems extraordinary that this plain statement (derived, as so often, from the deciphered report of a Flivo or Air Liaison Officer) did not cause greater concern, for it not only revealed that Model's HQ was in the heart of the target area: it also disclosed that this critically important command post at Oosterbeek lay *between* the Arnhem bridge and the drop zones for the British airborne division. The puzzling fact that the signal was sent out from Bletchley with a low ZZ priority cannot, in itself, account for its failure to set alarm-bells ringing.

Moreover, there were strong indications from Ultra about German awareness of the likelihood of a thrust along what was to be Market Garden's centre-line. As early as the 13th a Bletchley decrypt referred to Army Group B's desire 'to establish whether Allies preparing formations for thrust to Aachen or against 1 Para Army for thrust to Arnhem'. Even more specifically, a signal sent out at 1612 on the 15th mentioned that German appreciations of Allied plans 'indicate probable intention is thrust mainly on Wilhelmina Canal on both sides Eindhoven into Arnhem'.

Of course we now know that this was not the final German appreciation – at least in the sense that when 1 Airborne arrived over Arnhem even Model himself was taken by surprise. But that is irrelevant: the Allied commanders did not know it *at the time*. Such signals, together with the Oosterbeek reference, ought surely to have induced a degree of anxiety. It is clear, too, as one examines the decrypts, that Ultra was producing a volume of information about the way that the German 15th Army in the north was extricating itself from the Antwerp region and filtering steadily eastwards towards what would be Market Garden's left flank. Taking the signals for this period as a whole, moreover, (and they cover the German front from Antwerp down to Aachen and the West Wall facing Bradley's advancing Americans) it must be said that while there are many references to shortages of fuel, ammunition and other supplies, and evidence of desperate efforts to reorganize a coherent defence, there is little to confirm that the Germans had lost the will to fight or to justify Montgomery's optimistic statements about the enemy streaming homewards in headlong disorder.

The contrast between the skilful assurance with which Ultra was applied to the battle in Normandy and the fumbling with its intelligence before Market Garden is striking. Over-confidence and a natural desire to 'finish the war before Christmas' were the evident cause. In March 1978 a conference on Market Garden assembled at the Royal United Services Institution in London a number of those who had a leading role in the operation – among them General Sir John Hackett, Major-General John Frost and Brigadier Charles Mackenzie of 1 Airborne Division: Major-General David Belchem, Montgomery's Chief Operations Officer: and Lieutenant-Colonel Antony Tasker, Chief Intelligence officer of the Allied Airborne Army. There was a consensus among the witnesses that euphoria had affected judgement. Not simply Ultra, but even the evidence from 'conventional' sources of intelligence had not been evaluated or even accepted with a proper alertness.

The most poignant instance is that of Major Brian Urquhart – who by chance had the same surname as the general commanding the division due to drop at Arnhem. An intelligence officer at 1 Airborne Corps, which under General Browning had executive command of the airborne part of Market Garden, Urquhart became deeply concerned as early as 12 September about the possible presence of armour at Arnhem. At first his concern was based on reports filtering through from the Dutch resistance about 'battered panzer divisions believed to be in Holland to refit'. But on the 15th five oblique-angle air photographs showed him indisputable evidence.

'There in the photos,' he said, 'I could clearly see tanks – if not on the very Arnhem landing and drop zones, then certainly close to them.' But when he took them to Browning he was brushed aside. He was held to be hysterical and shortly afterwards was ordered to take a rest and go on leave. 'Major decisions arrived at now,' General Brereton had said on the 10th, 'must stand.' This is an episode to compare with that of November 1941 when Rommel, obsessed with plans for his forthcoming attack on Tobruk, was shown photographs of the railway which the British were pushing westwards in prepartion for an offensive in which Rommel refused to believe. He hurled them furiously on the floor.

In the remoter stratosphere of Montgomery's 21 Army Group self-induced blindness also prevailed. In his memoirs Major-General Sir Kenneth Strong, Eisenhower's Chief Intelligence Officer, recalled that 'not long before the airborne drop on Arnhem, I told Bedell Smith that I had some doubts about its success as there was some evidence that elements of German armour, probably with new tanks, were within striking distance of Arnhem'.[7] Strong, a dour and deeply experienced Scot, who had been Eisenhower's adviser since Tunisia, could scarcely be dismissed as a youthful hysteric. So with 'Beetle' Smith, the Chief of Staff at SHAEF, he proceeded to Montgomery's headquarters in Brussels. But like the rejected Urquhart these two emissaries of the Supreme Commander found that their news was not even unwelcome: it was dismissed. The researches of General S. L. A. Marshall (Chief US Historian for the European Theater of Operations) confirm that Montgomery reacted with ridicule. 'I got nowhere,' Smith recalled. 'Montgomery simply waved my objections airily aside.' Bedell Smith saw Montgomery alone. This is what he put on record in 1945.[8] What could it matter, therefore, to minds closed like clams that on the 16th, the eve of Market Garden, SHAEF's Intelligence Summary at last declared that '9 SS Panzer Division, and presumably the 10th, has been reported withdrawing to the Arnhem area in Holland'?[9]

The Air Intelligence officer at Airborne Army was Wing Commander Asher Lee, a man highly skilled in making deductions from Ultra information, since from the days of the Battle of Britain he had worked in the Air Staff's section AI3b on constructing the Luftwaffe's order of battle: after 1945 Lee established himself by books and broadcasts as a widely recognized authority on the world's air forces. Since Airborne Army was not receiving Ultra material – at least in the volume to which Lee's previous work had accustomed him – he made it his business to rise very early in the mornings and brief himself at another source of Ultra to which he had the *entrée*. On one of these visits, so he told the author, he found evidence of armour at Arnhem so conclusive that he used every effort, without success, to bring its significance home to the authorities in England. Lee therefore made his way to Belgium and found that there, too, his warning voice fell on deaf ears.[10]

It would indeed have taken a very powerful pressure from Ultra to penetrate a wall cemented by confidence, complacency and an uncharacteristic refusal to weigh evidence. For the men on the staffs concerned were not fools: in the main they were astute and battle-hardened. In Normandy, and for some of them in North Africa and Italy, Ultra had descended daily like the Greek god Zeus dropping on his chosen Danaë in the guise of a shower of gold. Now that the shower was less copious, though still rewarding, were they thrown off balance? It is more likely – for the same, we shall find, was true at the time of the Ardennes battle – that the picture they had formed in September 1944 of a Germany tottering on the verge of defeat was so vivid and so universal that nothing could amend it.

One thing is certain. By noon on 17 September the first phase of the landings on Arnhem and its approaches had involved more planes than had ever been used in an airborne operation. There was a superbly confident comment by Captain Sweeny of 101 Airborne: 'It looked like we could get out on the wings and walk all the way to Holland.' Before dawn 1400 bombers had begun their softening-up. And then, throughout the morning, 2023 troop-carriers and glider-towing tugs protected by some 1500 fighters trundled towards the landing-zones. So vast an airlift, conducted mainly in broad daylight, was only feasible if command of the skies was absolute (16 977 sorties for all purposes were flown between 16 and 26 September by the RAF and the USAAF: the losses were only 261 aircraft and 658 crew, plus 152 Royal Army Service Corps supply-handlers). This is therefore an appropriate moment to ask what information Ultra was providing about the secret weapon with which Hitler was seriously hoping to erode, if not to abolish, the Allies' superiority over his enfeebled Luftwaffe: the Messerschmitt 262 jet-fighter, about which the German ace General Adolf Galland declared after a test-flight in 1943 that it flew 'as though an angel's

351

pushing'. 'It could', he reported, 'guarantee us an inimaginable lead over the enemy if he adheres to the piston engine.'[11]

In theory Hitler's hopes were justified. The Me 262 with its Jumo 004 engines was the first jet-propelled aircraft of any kind to go into battle. First flown on 18 July 1942, it made its first attack two years later – on an RAF Mosquito on 25 July 1944. Grave production difficulties had nevertheless not held it back as much as the problems of policy and output which were retarding its British equivalent, the Meteor. (Not until the New Year of 1945 would the Minister of Aircraft Production be able to give jets the highest priority.) It was thus of immense importance for the Allied air staffs to be able to monitor the expansion of the Luftwaffe's jet-fighter capability, for its potential threat to their swarms of day-bombers now streaming over Germany was incalculable. The exceptional speed of the jets, and their powerful armament, could prove a decisive counter to the miraculous Mustang and death to the fleets of Fortresses.

It was therefore fortunate that through Ultra, 'Y' Service and other intelligence sources the Allies were able to read the record of the German jets like an open book. The quality of their accumulating knowledge is demonstrated in one of those special appendices attached to the regular European Summaries issued (as described in Chapter Nine) by the German Military Reports Branch in Washington. The European Summary, it is worth recalling, was said by Brigadier General Carter Clarke in his post-war review to have been 'based on Ultra information, which formed about ninety per cent of the content'. The appendices were known as tabs, and the tab in question, headed 'Jet-Propelled Aircraft', was issued with a severely restricted circulation on 17 November 1944. (After it had been studied by the Commanding General Army Air Forces and the Chief of Air Staff Intelligence a 'sanitized' version was produced for the experimental centre working on jet aircraft at Wright Field: from this every Ultra-based item of information was scrupulously excluded.)[12]

The intelligence was encyclopaedic. First came the code-names of all jet-types in use or at an experimental stage. These were derived from a signal from Luftwaffe High Command of 27 October, which stated that 'for reasons of security' these 'secret designations' were to be used: *Silber* (silver) for the Me 262, *Zinn* (tin) for the jet-bomber Arado 234, *Blei* (lead) for the Me 163 fighter and *Kupfer* (copper) for the curious Dornier 335 with one engine in the nose and the other in the tail. The personnel and aircraft of the chief Me 262 fighter-bomber base, at Rheine in north-west Germany, are specified in exact detail. In this unit, 1 Gruppe of KG 51, crew strength was known to be thirteen on 13 October, rising to twenty-one 'operational' out of forty-eight on 31 October. The strength of this 'Ops Detachment', as it was called, (commanded by one Major Schenk) is shown in the daily returns listed between 13 October and 9 November to have risen, with fluctuations, from four jets serviceable out of eleven to twenty-four serviceable out of twenty-six. Maintenance problems and equipment failures are fully documented – a write-off when landing on 5 October with only one power unit, a crash from the rupture of a fuel induction pipe, a nose-wheel refusing to lower, and so on. This is only a sample of what was known about 1 Gruppe.

An outstanding fighter unit was Detachment Nowotny, based at Achmer and Hesepe to the north-west of Osnabrück. Nowotny was well known to the Allies as one of the highest-scoring pilots in the Luftwaffe – largely on the Russian front – whose 218th victory had earned him in October 1943 the 'Knight's Cross with Oak Leaves with Swords and Diamonds'. On 1 November a signal from Achmer revealed the unit's name and strength of twelve officers and 315 men. The Nowotny detachment and its base were still developing, as appeared from the proportion of unserviceable aircraft and a report on 31 October of elaborate works projects. On 2 November a signal went to the Air Officer for Bombers stating that the detachment intended to instal Robot 11 in its Me 262s – probably an automatic pilot known from reports on the Arado 234.

This aircraft, which could carry a one-ton bomb load, was also being used from September onwards for reconnaissance flights over England. It and the Me 262 were the only successful German jets, and 527 of them joined the Luftwaffe in 1944: a force worth investigating. As the tab to the European Summary shows, virtually everything was in fact known about the AR 234. The Allies' mastery of Japanese ciphers frequently made the signals from the Japanese embassy in Berlin a mine of information, and it was an extensive technical report on the Arado, transmitted by the Naval Attaché to Tokyo on 31 October, that provided a blueprint for the 234. Its dimensions, maximum speed at varying altitudes, reduction in speed by different bomb loads, rate of climb, ceiling, cruising range, landing speed, nature of automatic pilot, and descrip-

353

tions of the Luftwaffe units operating the machine are all there.

A similar detailed and explicit description of the Me 163 was also included in the tab. This was taken straight from a report radio-ed by the Naval Attaché in Berlin to Tokyo on 6 September. Of profound interest to Allied intelligence at the time, it had in fact less relevance to the air war than the data about the Me 262 and AR 234, since the 163 never matured into an effective fighting aircraft. But there was an intriguing tail-piece to the tab. On 11 and 12 October the Attaché had had a personal interview with a giant of the German aircraft industry, the great Professor Heinkel himself, who had held forth about the experimental Heinkel 'rocket plane'. This was being developed by the Hirth Company of Stuttgart whose 'new turbine factories are located, for the most part, in southern Germany and include a considerable number of underground installations'. In his full report to Tokyo on 19 October the Attaché stated that 'if everything progresses favourably, as many as 1000 of these aircraft should be produced by next spring'. They were not: but in any case British and American air intelligence officers were fully capable of evaluating such a claim in the light of their knowledge of Heinkel's prolonged, abysmal and disastrous failure to produce, in his He 177, a four-engined bomber that could actually perform.

In this mix of up-to-date and priceless intelligence about the most sophisticated advances in German air-technology we see the joint application, in a single field, of Allied mastery over the Luftwaffe and Japanese diplomatic ciphers – a mastery which resulted from what in 1944 seemed the far-distant conquest of Enigma by the Poles and British, and of the Japanese 'Purple' system by Colonel Friedman and his Washington cryptanalysts. Moreover, though this particular appendix to a European summary has been highlighted as an outstanding example of Ultra and associated signals-intelligence in action, it must not be supposed that it is a solitary case. From Justice Powell's witness, for example, we gauge the continuing value of Ultra for the Allied day-bombers as oil and aircraft production, road and rail communications, the manufacture of weapons and the ordinary business of daily life ground to a halt beneath those omnipotent wings. Early in December, indeed, SHAEF summed up its assessment of declining morale among German civilians by observing: 'As a nation they continue to struggle because there is no other option left to them, unless they desire death or a concentration camp.'

354

Yet exactly one month after the European Summary produced its appendix on jet aircraft, packed with information about Hitler's secret weapon, the Germans took the Allies by surprise in a great offensive. Between 16 December and the recovery of all lost ground by the end of January the Ardennes campaign cost the Americans 75 482 and the British 1408 in men killed and wounded. It was a major tragedy that before the Ardennes as before Arnhem Ultra was unable to produce those warning signals which, throughout the war, had so often averted disaster or pointed the way to victory. But the reason was basic, simple and indisputable. The Allies had been successfully deceived. The impartial historian is bound to recognize that if unstinted credit is to be given to the one side for the brilliance of Bodyguard, Fortitude, the double agents and all the other special means of deception, similar credit must be given to the Germans for the concealment of their forces and their intentions up to the last minute of 5.30 am on 16 December. As their tanks and infantry pressed forward through the mist, while shells and flying-bombs surged overhead, the old discipline and military skills of the *Wehrmacht* had achieved for two Panzer Armies, 5 and 6 SS, a surprise which can only be compared with Germany's great day of 21 March 1918. Like their catastrophic breakthrough on that day, 16 December 1944 was, of course, merely a well-staged prelude to imminent and absolute defeat. Nevertheless, the technical *bravura* must be saluted.

Hitler's child, the idea of a break-out through the Ardennes towards Antwerp (named *Wacht am Rhein* or 'Watch on the Rhine' to suggest that the armies assembled were meant to defend the river-region of Cologne against an Allied attack) was conceived in October and took shape with a formal directive issued on 10 November. Though von Rundstedt was the front man, as Commander-in-Chief West, all the meticulously detailed instructions came from Hitler and were stamped by his personal seal – the adjective 'unalterable'. The tightest security was imposed from the start, and only a handful of commanders and staff officers shared the secret. As all knew of Hitler's personal commitment, all had a special incentive to ensure what was in fact achieved – a total security blackout – for none had forgotten the slaughter of highly placed officers that had followed the failure of the 20 July plot. One mistake – and disgrace or the firing squad. Bodyguard was the product of men doing their duty in a free society, but the cover for

'Watch on the Rhine' was created by men who had also to watch for their lives. Fortunately for them it proved to be impenetrable.

The literature about the Ardennes offensive is enormous – histories, combat studies, autobiographies and biographies of the generals and their subordinates of several nations. But nothing has emerged to modify in any important way the verdict of the British Official History on the preliminaries of the battle: 'The well-kept secret of what had been going on behind the German scene was largely undiscovered or misunderstood by Allied Intelligence and so not anticipated by Allied commanders.' And few of the latter have sought to disguise their lapse. For how could they? Montgomery had asked to be allowed to go on leave for Christmas. On the day of the attack there was a conference in the SHAEF map room at Versailles, attended by Eisenhower, Tedder, Spaatz, Strong and others – to discuss the current shortgage of infantry reinforcements! Bradley, frankness itself, admits in *A Soldier's Story* that 'we were too much addicted to the anticipation of counter attack on the Roer to credit the enemy with more fanciful or ambitious intentions.' Even the mercurial 'Monk' Dickson, G2 or Chief Intelligence officer at Hodges' 1st US Army, whose alleged anticipations of what was to come have aroused much controversy, went off to Paris on leave on 15 December – scarcely the act of a man who knows that the army he serves is about to take the brunt of a Panzer assault.

The fact is that everyone was in the dark. A strict wireless blanket meant that there were no tell-tale intercepts for Ultra. As the Germans fell back on the Reich, intelligence from resistance movements or secret agents petered out. No German with knowledge of the offensive was allowed to fly west of the Rhine – in case of accidents. Troop movements were made by night. Bad weather brought down a shutter on the Allies' photo-reconnaissance. All of the best intelligence officers, Major-General Strong at SHAEF, Brigadier Williams at 21 Army Group and Dickson, too, felt in their bones that something was stirring, and retrospect has shown that there were in fact sufficient indicators available in the existing evidence for an offensive to be predicted. As Williams said to the author, 'we had it in the palms of our hands'. But such indicators only become meaningful to alert minds, and all headquarters were lulled into a comfortable sense of security by the feeling that even Hitler would not attempt an operation that looked like military suicide. The known presence of that solid conservative, von Rundstedt, seemed like a certain guarantee. The con was complete.

In scientific studies it is sometimes possible to weigh the effect of a particular factor or element by examining what happens in a given situation when it is absent. The Ardennes affair illustrates the value of Ultra to battle-commanders in precisely this negative way. If we take Normandy as an example, it was not just the exact forewarning about a coming attack that mattered – as in the case of von Kluge's drive on Avranches. Perhaps even more important, in terms of the conduct of the battle *from day to day*, was the manner in which Ultra could confirm, reinforce, qualify or expand the existing ideas of the staffs and their generals. But the practical value of intelligence depends on the attitude of mind of its recipients. In Normandy Montgomery and his team, committed to the broad concept of keeping the German armour concentrated on the British front, could read immediately the significance of those abundant signals that gave them the location, strength, equipment and leadership of the panzer divisions. It fitted into their mental picture. But this corroborative effect of Ultra was never more fatally absent than before the Ardennes offensive. Whether British or American, those officers who had to give critical advice or take critical decisions were looking at the wrong picture. They therefore failed to interpret correctly such evidence as was available to them from conventional sources, and there was no Ultra to shift their minds from a fixed position.

The lack of Ultra can be symbolized dramatically. Like the command headquarters in the field, Bletchley had come to feel that the war had entered its terminal phase and that the patient could not last much longer. The staff in the cryptanalytical and processing Huts had worked under relentless pressure both before and after D Day. As the autumn wore on, some were flagging from overwork, lack of leave, and concentrated effort. They were sustained by the general belief that victory was imminent. Ultra traffic on the German front had diminished to an encouraging degree. Suddenly and unexpectedly, in mid-December the Ardennes front was ablaze. There was more than one case of an individual collapsing at Station X from a simple inability to face 'going through it all again'. The point is that this natural reaction does not seem to have occurred until the attack began.

But though the Allies were in the dark about 'Watch on the Rhine' it is nevertheless just possible that, as in the case of Arnhem,

Ultra might have been able to open a chink of light. At Hodges' 1st US Army the Ultra Adviser was Adolph Rosengarten. It was his prudent habit to maintain close contact with Bill Williams at Montgomery's main 21 Army Group headquarters, and with Joe Ewart who handled intelligence at the Field Marshal's advanced HQ. After the tidal wave of the Ardennes offensive had recoiled Rosengarten, so he told the author, had a meeting with Colonel Ewart during which they reviewed all the information available before the battle began, to establish whether they had overlooked any major indicators. Not so: certainly nothing major from Ultra. Nevertheless they agreed that had their minds been tuned to the likelihood of an attack on the Ardennes front there was one small signal supplied by Ultra to which alert intelligence officers ought to have responded. It came, characteristically, from a Flivo or Air Liaison Officer attached to the main assault force, the 6th SS Panzer Army, the Army whose location and objective Allied officers had been seeking to identify since the autumn, knowing that it had been created to form a strong armoured reserve.

There was a revealing phrase in the Flivo's signal: it referred to something like 'the coming big operation'. (Presumably the strict wireless silence on the army nets did not apply to the Luftwaffe circuits which the Flivo would use, or perhaps it was a typical case of the Luftwaffe's lax security.) Since Allied thinking was directed southwards to the region of Cologne and the River Roer, a 'coming big operation' might naturally appear to be imminent in this area. But had their antennae, their sensors, their apprehensions been alive to the possibility of a Panzer thrust against the thin American line covering the Ardennes, what warning noises might such a signal have triggered off in the heads of perceptive men like Ewart* and Rosengarten! Look at a chess-board from one angle and the white squares attract the eye: seen from another view-point, black squares stand out. The Colonel and the Ultra Adviser – and everybody else – had concentrated on the wrong colour.

It has been estimated that the winter battle in the Ardennes and further south in Alsace cost the Allies between fifteen and twenty-five per cent of their weapons and supplies – guns, tanks, vehicles, fuel, shells – and about ten per cent of their effective manpower.

*By a wanton stroke of fortune, Colonel Ewart was killed in a car accident soon after the ceremony of the German surrender, which he had attended as a member of Montgomery's staff.

But such dramatic statistics are misleading. The losses were largely American: the resources and resilience of the United States were still incomparable. Within weeks of the conclusion of 'Watch on the Rhine' nine fresh American divisions were in Europe. Far more to the point was the fact that 'Hitler's last gamble' in the West had failed. His one powerful reserve formation had been shattered. Sepp Dietrich reckoned that the élite 6th SS Panzer Army had lost '37 000 men killed, wounded and frozen', as well as between 300 and 400 tanks. Along the whole western front German casualties were about 130 000 – 19 000 of them dead. And now Hitler, screaming 'I get an attack of the horrors whenever I hear that there must be a withdrawal somewhere or other', set about building a wall in the East as his frontiers crumbled: for on 12 January Stalin, in response to an urgent request from Churchill on the 6th, launched an offensive along the entire central front. On the 22nd Dietrich and his Panzer Army were on the move – to Hungary. In February 2000 tanks and assault guns were despatched from Germany to the Russian front, but only a hundred to the West.

In other words, from now on Eisenhower's armies would always be advancing and their opponents would either be on the defensive or in retreat. One of Ultra's most spectacular roles, the identification in advance of the enemy's plans for a major attack – as at Alam Halfa, or Medenine, or Mortain/Avranches – was now over, for there would be no more major attacks. Certainly there would be more hard fighting. During the month of February the successful battle of the Reichswald forest, Operation Veritable, cost the British and Canadians some 15 500 casualties as they forced their way to the banks of the Rhine in a close-quarter conflict reminiscent of the Wilderness campaign in the American Civil War. But this was essentially a slugging-match, a 'soldier's battle'. Ultra had ceased to be vital. And this remained true as the great sweeps into Germany began – the Ruhr surrounded, Hodges linking with the Russians at Torgau on the Elbe, Montgomery heading for Hamburg and Bremen, Patton hot-foot for Austria. In these irresistible manoeuvres the critical factors were now the preponderant strength of the Allies and the disintegration of the German Reich.

And just as well, for during the spring of 1945 Hut 6 at Bletchley faced a grave problem. Sir Stuart Milner-Barry and others have described to the author their concern when it was realized that an important modification had been introduced into the Enigma machine. This was a more sophisticated version of the *Umkehr-walze*, the 'return cyclinder' or reflector. After you pressed a letter on the keyboard of an Enigma, it will be recalled, an electrical impulse passed through the rotors or wheels and then, hitting the reflector, was returned by it through the rotors along a different path. The new version of the *Umkehrwalze*, by further complicating this process, meant that there would be a considerable delay, possibly amounting to months, before Bletchley revised its own technology, adapted the bombes, and acquired the facility to break signals enciphered by the latest machines. Two facts saved the situation. The first has been established: Ultra was now merely important, not vital. The second was the disintegration of Germany. The new machines could not be produced and distributed quickly enough – and the Germans made a simple and almost puerile mistake. A signal would be sent out from one station enciphered by the new machine, and then, if it had to be repeated to another station still using the older type of Enigma, it would be enciphered again on one of these unmodified machines before transmission. But this, of course, would be in a cipher that Bletchley had long been breaking, so all that Hut 6 required was an intercept of the repeated message, and the original text could usually be discovered. Presumably all signals were not repeated. In any case, though Bletchley, by these means, managed to keep abreast of the situation until Germany capitulated, it was a time of tension. For a team of professionals and perfectionists this was inevitable. Still, granted the terminal state of the war, the danger for the Allied cause was probably more imaginary than real.

During those last weeks, however, many seasoned soldiers were haunted by phantoms. 'Months before,' Omar Bradley recalled, 'G2 had tipped us off to a fantastic enemy plot for the withdrawal of troops into the Austrian Alps where weapons, stores, and even aircraft plants were reported cached for a last-ditch holdout. There the enemy would presumably attempt to keep alive the Nazi myth until the Allies grew tired of occupying the Reich – or until they fell out among themselves'.[13] This was the fairy-tale of the 'National Redoubt'. With the dogged honesty that characterizes his memoirs Bradley added, 'It grew into so exaggerated a scheme that I am astonished we could have believed it as innocently as we did.'

But the innocents did believe. At SHAEF their credulity was demonstrated by a large map, headed 'Unconfirmed Installations In

Reported Redoubt Area'.[14] This covered some 20 000 square miles, the Alpine meeting-point of southern Germany, northern Italy and western Austria, with Hitler's Berghof near Berchtesgaden in their midst. The qualifications in the map's title were hardly supported by the printed legend at the base of the map, for it displayed a whole range of symbols indicating food, ammunition and petrol dumps, headquarters and barracks, radio installations, factories, troop locations and a dump for chemical warfare. Such was the so-called 'National Redoubt' where the Führer's faithful, it was supposed, were to make a Wagnerian last stand: the SS, the 'werewolf' fanatics.

Dozens of intelligence reports sustained the myth, which particularly affected the Americans, from the War Department downwards. The British were cooler. As Alexander's armies drew close to the Alps from the south, they faced the disturbing prospect of having to fight their way into them – if the Redoubt existed. But though Alexander's Director of Intelligence, Major-General Airey, was supplied with the current rumours he has confirmed to the author that he never accepted them, on the grounds that the whole proposition made military nonsense. As it did: and as the Germans knew it did. The SS General Gottlob Berger, who was captured at Berchtesgaden on 7 May, and General of Mountain Troops George Ritter von Hengl, (who commanded in the Alpine area from April onwards, and was captured in the Austrian Tyrol on 6 May) were closely interrogated by the Americans. Their explicit and almost contemptuous denial that an *Alpenfestung* or Alpine fortress had existed or even been contemplated was confirmed by Allied troops when they over-ran the region. Every other post-war interrogation or captured document tells the same tale. The British Official History concludes its special appendix on the theme by observing that 'for Hitler the notion of a "redoubt" was no more than a momentary idea that passed through his mind, only to vanish again immediately afterwards'.[15]

On 11 March SHAEF intelligence had produced a fine imaginative essay. 'Theoretically ... within this fortress ... defended both by nature and the most efficient weapons yet invented, the powers that have hitherto guided Germany will survive to organize her resurrection.' But Hitler died in his Berlin bunker, and it was far away in Flensburg on the Danish border, at the headquarters of the newly appointed Reich president, Grand Admiral Karl Dönitz, that the glow-worm lights on the Enigma machines ceased to flicker and top-level radio signals, for the first time since 1939, were sent out in clear. The German armies in the north were surrendering to Montgomery, and three days later Eisenhower would make his historic report to the Combined Chiefs of Staff: 'The Mission of this Allied Force was fulfilled at 0241, local time, May 7th, 1945.' There was still Japan, and work to be done: but at Flensburg in Schleswig-Holstein Ultra was demobilized from the German war. The ceremonial farewell, however, was enacted in that land of myth and fantasy, the *Alpenfestung*, the 'National Redoubt': appropriately, by a man from Bletchley.

As Germany collapsed, many investigative teams raced into the Reich on urgent quests for the enemy's secrets – before they could be destroyed or acquired by the Russians. The American ALSOS group, for example, and its colleagues in British scientific intelligence successfully identified and commandeered the centres of German atomic research. By their swift capture of essential documents and the immediate removal to England of many leading physicists they made it possible for the Allies to establish – and establish with relief – the limited progress towards an atomic bomb that the Germans had achieved before they surrendered. Other papers, and other people, were stalked by special units whose mission was to discover the latest information about U-boat and aircraft development, or the effects of bombing, or stolen art treasures, or military archives. Most urgent of all was the search for concentration camps and Allied prisoners of war. The hunt was widespread, ranging from the Baltic to the Balkans, and the chase was naturally joined by officers from Bletchley Park. There was much to be discovered about German cipher techniques and technology, many questions to be asked, many documents to be rescued and explored.

From Hut 3 at Station X Oscar Oeser – then a Wing Commander in the RAF, and later a Professor of Psychology – pressed southwards to the mountain realm of the *Alpenfestung*.[16] A transmitter, he knew, was still operating in the Berchtesgaden area. He tracked it down, and without difficulty took over from the German staff a cipher van containing up-to-date Enigmas. These he handed over for safe keeping to puzzled troops of General Patch's 7th US Army which, on 4 May, had reached Salzburg, Berchtesgaden and the head of the Brenner Pass – linking up that same day with the 5th US Army from Italy. It was a time of great confusion, with some Ger-

mans happily surrendering, some stunned, some arrogant and belli-
cose. In the area were many chalets once used by Hitler's entourage, some wrecked by recent bombing, others set on fire by their SS
guardians. Oeser found Göring's: he found, too, a locked chapel
which, when the doors were forced, turned out to be crammed with
Luftwaffe records. There was a volume of topographical data about
the British coast, prepared for the 1940 invasion. For one beach the
illustration was a picture-postcard issued by a firm known to millions of British holiday-makers. It seemed incongruous, amid the
debris of a Reich that was to last a thousand years, to encounter by
chance the name of Raphael Tuck.

But Oeser also discovered a whole train ready for use as an operational headquarters – possibly the one used by Kesselring, to whom
Hitler had given command of all the forces in the South: or perhaps
the train which the Führer insisted on keeping near to the Berghof.
It stood in a little country railway station, abandoned. The lavishly
equipped compartment fitted out as a communications section contained several Enigmas and other cipher machines of the latest
design. Wing Commander Oeser ordered them to be lifted from the
carriage and laid out, in a row, on the deserted platform: silent,
beside the silent train. And with their silence, it might be said,
peace came to Ultra.

Notes

1. The Glow-lamp Machine (pp.25–50)

1. The idea of a glow-lamp machine using revolving wheels or rotors for encipherment had in fact been advertised as early as 1921 by an American in California called Edward H. Hebern. In his model, as in the Scherbius, the enciphered letters were displayed on an alphabetical panel illuminated from below. In the Hebern sales pamphlet in the author's possession he claims 'capacity without changing Code Wheels, approximately 40,303,146,321,064,147,046,400,000 Entirely Different Codes'. These lavish hopes were not fulfilled, although the US Navy purchased models from time to time. Some were actually in use until after Pearl Harbor, when two were captured by the Japanese. The Italians acquired an early version: the British inspected one. But Hebern never got off the ground, and Enigma's true line of development derives from Scherbius.
2. The relevant correspondence is in the National Archives, Washington.
3. For this paragraph see Ronald Clark, *The Man Who Broke Purple*, Chapter 6.
4. Professor I. J. Good, Lecture at the National Physical Laboratory on 'Early Work on Computers at Bletchley'.
5. Evans's report is in the National Archives, Washington.
6. Personal to author from Colonel Mayer.
7. *Ibid.*
8. Penelope Fitzgerald, *The Knox Brothers*, p. 230.

2. The British Breakthrough (pp.51–72)

1. Personal to author from Colonel Mayer.
2. All references to Welchman's part in this early period are based on the author's conversation and correspondence with him.
3. Ultra was essentially a word indicating highest-security classification. Though the main output of messages from Bletchley under this marking contained information from Enigma-enciphered signals, intelligence from the breaking of other ciphers and codes was also sent out under the same head. In an account of the classification of wartime documents at the Admiralty Captain Stephen Roskill has pointed out (*Churchill and the Admirals*, p. 290) that the endorsement Ultra on papers in the naval registry meant that their contents 'were derived from cryptographic intelligence *or other very secret sources*'. Nevertheless, since the publication of Winterbotham's *The Ultra Secret* Ultra has become the commonly accepted term to cover the procedures and events described in this book. There is no other word of equivalent precision.
4. Personal to author from MacFarlan.
5. Gort's changes of plan are well summarized in Brian Bond, *France and Belgium, 1939–1940*.
6. Personal to author from Winterbotham.

7. *Cadix* could transmit back to England any 'keys' or other relevant cipher-breaking information it could establish, but the traffic was one-way. For security, no information was sent back from England. (Source: Lieut-Col. Lisicki.)

3. A Plan Called Smith (pp. 73–110)

1. J. C. Masterman, *The Double-Cross System,* describes in detail the harvesting of the German agents.
2. Derek Wood and Derek Dempster, *The Narrow Margin.*
3. The appointment of R. V. Jones derived from three meetings of the Committee for the Scientific Survey of Air Defence in 1939 – on 9 February, 16 April and 17 May. With Tizard in the chair, this formidable group included distinguished scientists like Appleton, Blackett, A. V. Hill and Thomas Merton. Winterbotham, then a Squadron Leader, was in attendance to discuss 'scientific co-operation with the Intelligence Directorate'. Discussion revealed a weakness in liaison. At the third meeting the Director of Scientific Research, D. R. Pye, reported (Minute 390b) that 'approval had been obtained for the appointment of a Scientific Officer to his staff for liaison duties with the Intelligence Directorate, and that the appointment would be made as soon as a suitable man for the post could be found'. The man was R. V. Jones. He was initially attached to Winterbotham's section A.I.1(c), the Air Intelligence branch of the Secret Service, with which he moved to Bletchley at the outbreak of war. And here, through Winterbotham, he was introduced to Hut 3.
4. Ronald Clark, *Tizard.*
5. The MI 14 papers are in PRO file WO 199/911A.
6. Stephen Spender's poem beginning 'I think continually of those who were truly great' is in his *Poems,* 1933.
7. R. V. Jones, *Most Secret War.*
8. The Sealion memoranda are in the PRO file WO 199/911A. See also WO 166/3 'Original War Diary of GS1(x) GHQ Home Forces'.
9. Communicated to author by Sir John Martin.
10. For further details of the Air Staff and the Coventry raid, see the valuable article by N. E. Evans, 'Air Intelligence and the Coventry Raid', in the Journal of the Royal United Services Institute, September 1976.
11. Full text of Inglis report in PRO/AIR 40 2023.
12. Personal to author from Cavendish-Bentinck.
13. Ivan Maisky, *Memoirs of a Soviet Ambassador,* p. 149.

4. Station X (pp.111–37)

1. Letter to author from Shephard.
2. Milner-Barry's personal memoir is included in a symposium published, as a tribute to Alexander's achievement in chess, by the Oxford University Press: *The Best Games of C. H. O'D. Alexander,* ed. Harry Golombek and William Hartston, 1975.
3. Personal to author from Monroe. According to Good's Lecture, Wylie later transferred to 'the Newmanry' (see Chapter Four below).
4. Personal to author from Jean Alington (Mrs Roger Howard).
5. Personal to author from Telford Taylor.

6. Quoted in Arthur Marder, *From the Dreadnought to Scapa Flow*, Vol. III, p. 42.
7. Personal to author from Sir Edgar Williams. Among others who made formal visits were Field Marshal Alexander and the Chiefs of Staff.
8. The most detailed account of Colossus is the paper by Professor Randell (see bibliography). Good in his lecture said of Heath Robinson: 'Its vertical cross-section was about the size of a couple of doors. Its input was from two five-hole paper tapes which it read at 200 characters per second.... The tapes were driven by their sprocket-holes as well as by pulleys and analysis was carried out by photoelectric readers and electronic circuits.'

   About Colossus, Good observed: 'The Colossus had only one tape input because the function of the other input tape was incorporated in the internal electronics of the machine. One important advantage of this was that it avoided the need for a great deal of additional tape preparation. Another advantage of this was that the driving of the tape could be entirely by pulleys without the need to synchronize two tapes by any sprocket-hole driving. It read the tape at 5000 characters per second and, at least in Mark 2, the circuits were in quintu-plicate so that in a sense the reading speed was 25 000 bits per second.' Good also added that 'the Colossus produced quite a bit of heat and it was once proposed that the operators should be topless'.
9. For Cooper see Jones and Winterbotham.
10. This co-ordination described to author by Professor Vincent.

5. The Secret Limeys (pp.138–54)

1. Winterbotham.
2. Personal to author from Powell.
3. Personal to author from Poole, whose private papers and conversation provided many insights.
4. Reynolds to Winterbotham: letter in Winterbotham file.
5. Personal to author from Air Marshal Sir Edward Chilton.
6. Personal to author from Shearer.
7. Personal to author from Hamer.
8. See note 15, Chapter Nine, for relevant file.
9. Sir Leslie Rowan in *Action this Day: Working with Churchill*, Macmillan, 1968.
10. Crawshaw at Caserta: personal to author.
11. Personal to author from Robinson, who also went to the Yalta conference as the SLU officer. He could, however, recall no signals – 'perhaps two, but I thought they were for testing'. Ultra could not be risked in Russia.
12. SLU at Versailles: personal to author from Poole.
13. Quoted in Winterbotham. p. 173.

6. The Mediterranean Shores (pp.155–82)

1. Letter to author from Woodhouse.
2. Personal to author from Williams.
3. The best analysis of Freyberg's difficulties and mistakes is in I. McD. G. Stewart, *The Struggle for Crete*, Oxford University Press, 1966.
4. David Irving, *The Trail of the Fox*.
5. Shearer's mock-appreciation is in John Connell, *Wavell: Scholar and Soldier*.
6. Personal to author from MacFarlan.

7. Personal to author from Shearer.
8. *Ibid.*
9. David Hunt, *A Don at War.*
10. Shearer confirmed the details of this miscalculation to the author.
11. Personal to author from Powell.
12. For Fellers see Kahn, and also Irving.
13. Personal to author from Hood.
14. Personal to author from MacFarlan.
15. Hunt, *op. cit.*
16. Michael Carver, *El Alamein.*
17. Personal to author from Hood.

7. Mr Churchill's Secret Source (pp.183–94)

1. Source: private correspondence.
2. Personal to author from Jacob.
3. Martin Gilbert, *Winston S. Churchill*, vol. 5, *1922–1939.*
4. Letter to author from Sir Arthur Benson.
5. Personal to author from Sir Edgar Williams.

8. Ultramarine (pp.195–233)

1. Admiral of the Fleet the Viscount Cunningham of Hyndhope, *A Sailor's Odyssey*, p. 325 ff.
2. Sources: personal from Dr Giulio Divita, and transcripts of the court pleadings and judgements in the Lais hearings.
3. The relevant timings may be checked in Patrick Beesly, *Very Special Intelligence*, Chapter Five.
4. This account of the U 110 'pinch' is based on a long interview recorded in 1977, in which David Balme told his story to Peter Hennessy of *The Times.* Hennessy lent the tape to the author.
5. Until May 1941 the early naval decrypts are filed in PRO/DEFE3 under the Bletchley prefix ZTP. Thereafter the messages are serially numbered under the ZTPG prefix.
6. See Admiral Dönitz, *Memoirs*, and Cajus Bekker, *Hitler's Naval War.*
7. Personal to author from Marshal of the RAF Sir John Slessor, and see his introduction to Winterbotham, *The Ultra Secret.*
8. There was an agent, working at the entrance to Altenfjord, but he only transmitted reports at irregular intervals. Thus his silence at any particular time was not evidential.
9. See the valuable eye-witness account of the meeting at which Pound decided on the order to disperse, by a young RNVR officer of the keenest intelligence, Lieutenant Arthur Hutchinson. It is quoted as a note on p. 410 of Donald McLachlan, *Room 39.* 'My most vivid recollection is of a very tired-looking Dudley Pound sitting gazing in a mesmerized fashion at a small-scale chart of the Barents Sea area, calculating with a pair of dividers where the *Tirpitz* would be at that time.'
10. Jürgen Rohwer, *The Critical Convoy Battles of March 1943*, p. 242.

9. The American Involvement (pp.234–62)

1. For Friedman and Purple see David Kahn, *The Codebreakers*, and Ronald Clark, *The Man Who Broke Purple*.
2. Forrest C. Pogue, *George C. Marshall: Ordeal and Hope, 1939–1942*.
3. Kahn, *op. cit.*
4. William Stevenson, *A Man Called Intrepid*. Though carrying the apparent endorsement of a preface by 'Intrepid' (the code-name of Sir William Stephenson who is *not* to be confused with the author) this book's grasp of facts is wayward and uncertain. A less speculative account is in Montgomery Hyde, *The Quiet Canadian*.
5. Winterbotham, *The Ultra Secret*.
6. General Eaker discussed Ultra and the USAAF with the author in Washington in 1977.
7. The long delay in developing the Mustang and the opposition encountered are described in detail in Wesley F. Craven and James L. Cate, *The Army Air Forces in World War II, Vol. II*, University of Chicago Press, 1950.
8. Beesly, *Very Special Intelligence*.
9. Winterbotham.
10. This document, 'Synthesis of Experience in the use of Ultra intelligence by US Army Field Commands in the European Theatre of Operations', together with General Marshall's letter of instruction to General Eisenhower of 15 March 1944, are reproduced with certain excisions in a privately printed study by Ernest L. Bell, 'An Initial View of Ultra as an American Weapon'.
11. Personal to author from the Hon. Lewis Powell.
12. See note 10 above.
13. Churchill and Ultra security: personal to author from Winterbotham.
14. Sources for South-east Asia section: correspondence and conversation with the Hon. Inzer Wyatt; Benjamin King, personal to author; Winterbotham's visit to Wyatt is in *The Ultra Secret*, confirmed by Wyatt.
15. This report, 'Use of CX/MSS ULTRA by the United States War Department (1943–1945)' is also reprinted by Ernest L. Bell, *op.cit*, with excisions.

10. Alamein to the Alps (pp.263–91)

1. Personal to author from Powell.
2. Personal to author from Airey, Hunt and Williams.
3. David Dilkes, ed., *The Diaries of Sir Alexander Cadogan*.
4. Personal to author from Briggs.
5. Winterbotham, *The Ultra Secret*.
6. The tactical details, and the apartheid of Rommel and von Arnim, are well described in Martin Blumenson, *Kasserine Pass*.
7. Captain Harry C. Butcher's *Three Years with Eisenhower*, 1946, was an amended and abbreviated presentation of the personal diary which, on Eisenhower's orders, he kept from the time of his arrival in London in 1942 as Eisenhower's 'naval aide'. (Ike defined his actual function more realistically. 'Butcher's job is simple. It is to keep me from going crazy.') The original text of the diary, from which this quotation is taken, is in the Dwight D. Eisenhower Library, Abilene.
8. Sir David Hunt arrived in Tunisia at this time as a senior intelligence officer on Alexander's staff. He noted the contrast between the local intelligence from 'Y' Service and what he had been used to in the desert. Personal, Hunt to author.

9. Strong on spies: see *Men of Intelligence*, Chapter Six, 'Agents generally rank low in the hierarchy of useful sources.'
10. Personal to author from Allen.
11. Winterbotham.
12. At the last, there was anxious discussion about what would happen if the tide failed to sweep shorewards the canister containing 'Major Martin'. Churchill gave his verdict. 'You will have to get him back,' he said, 'and give him another swim.' Source: Colonel John Bevan to author.
13. Personal to author from Gavin.
14. Personal to author from Hackett.
15. Letter from Airey to author.
16. Sources for Caserta War Room: personal to author from Judy Hutchinson, Field Marshal Lord Harding, Lieut. General Sir Terence Airey.
17. Personal to author from Airey.
18. Nigel Nicolson, *Alex*. The book was published in 1973 and the interview with Clark was clearly recent.
19. The theory and technique of interdiction bombing had been worked out in North Africa and applied to the Italian communications system for the Sicily campaign by the distinguished zoologist Solly Zuckerman, who acted as scientific adviser to Eisenhower's deputy, Air Chief Marshal Sir Arthur Tedder. The techniques for taking out a railway system were continued during the Italian campaign. Before the great Diadem offensive in May 1944 20 000 tons of bombs were dropped to this end, ten railways were severed and substantial dislocation caused, but bad weather intervened and the Germans in fact were never defeated merely through shortage of supplies. The picture presented in Zuckerman, *From Apes to Warlords*, is naturally rosier. In his book, however, Lord Zuckermann is an explicit witness to the value of Ultra in planning such operations.
20. W. G. F. Jackson, *The Battle for Italy*, p. 228. This book and General Sir William Jackson's *The Battle for Rome* provided admirable accounts of Diadem and the Italian theatre.
21. Winterbotham.

11. Overture and Beginners (pp.292–322)

1. J. M. Stagg, *Forecast for Overlord*, Ian Allan, 1971.
2. Personal to author from Colonel T. Lisicki.
3. Personal to author from Golombek.
4. From a private file.
5. Winterbotham, *The Ultra Secret*.
6. The following passage on deception and double-agents is founded on discussions with Colonel Bevan, Colonel Robertson and the late Sir John Masterman, whose book *The Double-Cross System* is an essential point of reference.
7. Bruce Catton, *This Hallowed Ground*, Gollancz, 1957, p. 142.
8. Masterman, *op.cit.*, and Ewen Montagu, *Beyond Top Secret U*, Chapter Seventeen.
9. Professor Trevor-Roper's explanation to the author of the penetration of the Abwehr network clarified many points.
10. Beesly, *Very Special Intelligence*.
11. David Mure's *Practise to Deceive* is a light-hearted but instructive narrative of his experience in 'A' Force. In correspondence and conversation with the

author he amplified various points.
12. Quoted in Masterman, *op.cit.*
13. Jones was not denigrating Ultra, of which he was a leading beneficiary. His point was that, as a prudent scientist, he always allowed for the possibility that Ultra might be compromised and therefore, after each of his successful investigations, asked himself how far he could have got without Bletchley's aid.
14. There was no Luftwaffe photo-reconnaissance over London between January 1941 and September 1944.
15. The map charting the supposed fall of flying bombs on London was captured at the headquarters of Flak Regiment 155(W), which handled the operation. It is reproduced opposite p. 301 in Jones, *Most Secret War*. The centre of London is a mass of black dots – the false impacts reported by double agents.

12. Finale and Curtains (pp. 323–63)

1. Chester Wilmot, *The Struggle for Europe*, p. 305.
2. Winterbotham, *The Ultra Secret*.
3. *Ibid.*
4. From the Ultra signals in the PRO it is evident that Bletchley was providing Bradley with a prompt and continuous monitoring service which revealed the changing locations, frustrations and steady disintegration of von Kluge's divisions. In these signals the worried emphasis on the effects of attack from the air is impressive. It is considerably easier for a commander to keep cool, as Bradley certainly did, when he has so extensive a view of what is happening 'on the other side of the hill'.
5. Beesly, *Very Special Intelligence*, for details.
6. John Kennedy, *The Business of War*, p. 351.
7. Strong, *Intelligence at the Top*.
8. Quoted in Cornelius Ryan, *A Bridge Too Far*.
9. Ryan.
10. Asher Lee's experience, personal from Lee to author.
11. Quoted in David Irving, *The Rise and Fall of the Luftwaffe*.
12. The appendix on 'Jet-Propelled Aircraft' is reprinted in Ernest L. Bell, *An Initial View of Ultra as an American Weapon*.
13. Bradley, *A Soldier's Story*.
14. The map is reproduced in Cornelius Ryan, *The Last Battle*.
15. *Victory in the West*, vol. 2, Appendix X.
16. Oeser described his mission to the author. Subsequently he reverted to his profession and carried out in-depth psychological interrogations of some of the senior prisoners at Nuremberg.

Appendix

The signals that follow are intended to illustrate the variety and the operational value of the material deciphered at Bletchley and transmitted to appropriate headquarters in the field. Selected from a period of about four weeks in the summer of 1944, they represent a trivial percentage of the thousands and thousands of decrypts produced at Station X: but it may be helpful to the reader to see the form in which Ultra was actually circulated. The first signal is reproduced in the exact manner in which a message was sent out from Bletchley. From the rest all extraneous matter has been removed so that the contents of the message can be more easily grasped.

1

REF CX/MSS/T223/T54   KV 9177
                          ZZZ
KV 9177 £ 9177 SH58 £ 58 AG 87 £ 87 FU 44 £ 44 YK ZE EF 58 £ 58 TA 80 £ 80

INFORMATION ABWEHR OFFICER AOK £ AOK SEVEN ON TWENTYFIRST ACCORDING CAPTURED DOCUMENTS IN ST LO £ LO AREA AMERICAN PASSWORDS AND REPLIES AS FOLLOWS COLON TWENTIETH TO TWENTYSECOND CHICKEN - WIRE £ CHICKEN - WIRE, TWENTYSECOND TO TWENTYFIFTH WALKING – VILLAGE & WALKING – VILLAGE, TWENTYFIFTH TO TWENTYSIXTH HUDDLE – TIME £ HUDDLE – TIME.
PEP/AKW/KH   221533Z/6/44

Note

This is the normal layout for a signal issued from Bletchley. The CX/MSS number is the general reference number for Ultra material: KV 9177 is a specific reference number for Hut 3 where this decrypt was processed – for the Naval Section a typical reference would be ZTPG. The symbol £ is shorthand for 'repeat'. In the second line the figures SH58,AG87 etc are the signs for the particular headquarters to which this signal was transmitted. The time of origin from Bletchley, in the bottom righthand corner, (just after 3.30 on the afternoon of 22 June), shows that the knowledge of the American passwords acquired on the 21st by the Abwehr intelligence officer at the headquarters of the German 7th Army, (Oberkommando 7th Army or AOK 7), had been deciphered and the warning passed to Normandy in ample time for the American command to change most of its compromised passwords within twenty-four hours of the Germans' acquiring them. In the bottom lefthand corner are the initials of the individuals concerned with the issuing of this signal. The priority marking, ZZZ, indicated its urgency: priorities ranged from Z to ZZZZZ. The signal shows Ultra in action on an apparently small scale: but such swift intelligence, constantly flowing from Bletchley to the battle-fronts, saved many lives and prevented many mistakes. Certainly the Americans who might have been killed as a result of the enemy knowing their passwords for several days have cause to be grateful to Ultra.

2

ZZZ   KV 9241

ON TWENTYSECOND. 17 HRS. BOUNDARY 21 PANZER DIVISION – 12 SS PANZER DIVISION UNCHANGED ALONG RAILWAY FROM CAEN TO NORTH. BOUNDARY 12 SS PANZER DIV – PANZER LEHR DIV : WEST EDGE ST MARTIN T 8767 – EAST SLOPE HEIGHT 103 T 8570 – WEST EDGE DUCY T 8874. LEFT CORPS BOUNDARY WEST EDGE ANCTOVILLE CHURCH ST PAUL T7470. B). 19 HRS. (FAIR INDICATION 1 SS PANZER) CORPS EXPECTED ATTACK BETWEEN ORNE AND MUC. C). FROM DAY REPORT 14 HRS : NEW LEFT BOUNDARY 1 SS PANZER CORPS WITH 47 PANZER CORPS MAISONCELLES – PELVEY (TO 47 CORPS) – ST GERMAINS – GUESNON (TO 1 SS CORPS) – ST PAUL (TO 47 CORPS) – LE BAS (TO 1 SS CORPS) – NORON LA POTERIE (TO 47 CORPS). COMMENT : NEW 47 / 1 SS CORPS BOUNDARY GIVEN APPROXIMATELY IN KV 9200.

230417Z/6/44

Note

This deciphered signal, typical of so many issued from Bletchley during the Normandy campaign, illustrates the invaluable information supplied to Montgomery about the movement and location of the panzer divisions along his front. The last sentence, beginning Comment, is in the formula usually employed at Bletchley to indicate that what follows is not directly derived from a German text, but is elucidatory matter added to help the recipient either to understand the contents of a signal or to remember some relevant signal sent previously.

3

ZZZZ   KV 9202

WEATHER SURVEY 1230 HOURS TWENTYSECOND. GENERAL :
NO IMPORTANT CHANGE. COOL SEA AIR CONTINUING TO
FLOW IN FROM NORTH WILL EXTEND DURING NIGHT OVER
WHOLE REICH TERRITORY. OVER WHOLE REICH, MOSTLY
UNBROKEN SHALLOW LAYER OF CLOUD, BASE THREE
HUNDRED TO SIX HUNDRED METRES. NORTHERN FRINGE
OF MITTELGEBIRGE CLOUD BASE LOWER, IN PLACES DRIZ-
ZLE. VISIBILITY (EXCEPT DRIZZLE AREAS) FIVE
KILOMETRES ALL NIGHT. OPERATIONS BY TWIN/ENGINED
AIRCRAFT UNHAMPERED.

Note

Many thousands of meteorological reports were intercepted by the British
after transmission from weather-ships, aircraft on special weather-
observation flights, etc. U-boats, for example, would send in weather
reports as a matter of routine. This sample, sent out from Bletchley at 8.25
pm on the 22nd of June 1944 (or just eight hours after the German forecast
was transmitted) shows how valuable such up-to-date information about
weather conditions over Germany could be – in this case providing information about the condition of the German skies that night for any operations that Bomber Command might be undertaking. The signal has the
very high ZZZZ priority because obviously such information had to be got
to the Meteorological Office with the greatest urgency.

4

ZZZ   KV 5757

GERMAN ORDER OF BATTLE ACCORDING COMMANDER-IN-
CHIEF SOUTH WEST ON TWENTYSEVENTH. (A.) 14 ARMY.
COAST, RIGHT WING OF BRIDGEHEAD NOW ONLY GUARDED
BY 2/ 1060 OWING WITHDRAWAL ASSAULT REGIMENT.
1. I PARA CORPS (1) MAIN BODY 4 PARA DIVISION. (2). 65
INFANTRY DIVISION (LESS GROUP 145), ASSAULT GUN UNIT
AND ENGINEER BATTALION (LESS ONE COMPANY). (3) 3
PANZERGRENADIER DIVISION WITH INFANTRY LEHR
REGIMENT AND ONE FIELD ERSATZ BATTALION (LESS
GROUP ... MOTORISED... 8 AND RECONNAISSANCE UNIT
103). (4) 362 DIVISION: ELEMENTS GROUP 956 AND ELEMENTS
FUSILIER BATTALION 362, PANZER UNIT 508 (ONE COMPANY

374

HEAVY TANKS), ONE ASSAULT GUN UNIT 103, FUSILIER
BATTALION 65, ENGINEER BATTALION 65 LESS ONE COM-
PANY, PANZER RECONNAISSANCE UNIT 129, ELEMENTS
REGIMENT (STRONG INDICATIONS 1060), GROUP 145,3/8.
2. 76 CORPS. (1) GOERING DIVISION: PANZER REGIMENT I
WITH ONE BATTALION AND ELEMENTS TWO BATTALIONS,
PANZERGRENADIER REGIMENT 2 WITH TWO BATTALIONS.
ELEMENTS RECONNAISSANCE UNIT. IN COURSE OF BEING
BROUGHT UP 2/756, WERFER (heavy mortar) REGIMENT 56, HQ
WERFER BRIGADE 5, 1/15, 2/8, 1/29. (2) 29 PANZERGRENADIER
DIVISION: ELEMENTS GROUP 735, RECONNAISSANCE UNIT
103, GROUP 15 LESS ONE BATTALION............

Note

The above is less than half the signal; a routine report on the units under
his command sent to Berlin on 30 May 1944 by Field Marshal Kesselring,
supreme commander of the German armies in Italy. Such immensely
detailed returns were made habitually by German commanders in the
field, whether in Africa, Italy or Normandy. With great regularity they
were also deciphered at Bletchley, and the value of the information they
contained to Allied commanders and intelligence staffs is self-evident. It is
perhaps only by looking at an actual signal like this, and realising that it is
but one of very many, that it is possible to appreciate the full meaning of
Ultra. (Units like 2/1060, 3/8, 1/15 are presumably single battalions of
infantry regiments).

5

ZZ   KV 9597

AT (FAIR INDICATIONS VENICE) TWENTYFOURTH HOSPI-
TAL SHIP FREIBURG LEFT 20 HOURS FOR CESENATICO, AUX-
ILIARY SAILING VESSEL ENRICO ARRIVED 17 HOURS FROM
ANCONA. FREIBURG ARRIVED CESENATICO BY 0530 HOURS
TWENTYFIFTH. SECONDLY, LANDING CRAFT ML685 LEFT
PORTO GARIBALDI 13 HOURS TWENTYFOURTH FOR VENICE.
THIRDLY, RIMINI DEPARTS 18 HOURS TWENTYFOURTH:
AUXILIARY SAILING VESSELS SAN PIETRO FOR CATTOLICA,
MARIA PIA FOR RAVENNA. FOURTHLY, MOTOR COASTER
LIA LEFT CORSINI 17 HOURS TWENTYFOURTH FOR
ANCONA. LANDING CRAFT 813 RETURNED CORSINI BY 1845
HOURS TWENTYFOURTH, LIA 03 HOURS TWENTYFIFTH,
BOTH OWING WEATHER CONDITIONS. LANDING CRAFT 518

ARRIVED CORSINI 03 HOURS TWENTYFIFTH FROM VENICE.
FIFTHLY, REGIONAL COMMANDER ANCONA INTENDED
FORENOON TWENTYFOURTH TO TRANSFER TO MILANO
MARITTIMA NEAR CERVIA. SIXTHLY, FOUR HARBOUR
DEFENCE VESSELS ARRIVED ANCONA 0145 HOURS TWEN-
TYFIFTH HAVING CARRIED OUT SECOND PART OF OPERA-
TION.....

Note

.. And so this particular signal runs. Because of Allied dominance by sea
and by air German forces along the northern shores of the Mediterranean,
from southern France to the Dodecanese, relied to a very considerable
extent on coastal traffic – small ships sailing alone or in inconspicuous
convoys. From the autumn of 1943 onwards, with the start of the Italian
campaign, this traffic intensified. So did the immense flow of decrypts
produced in Bletchley which, as in this signal of 26 June 1944, recorded
the movements of Axis shipping with lethal precision. Besides registering
shipping movements, the decrypts also provided valuable intelligence
about the location of Axis minefields, the strength and location of German
gun-boats and other small warships, specific orders for air-cover by the
Luftwaffe and so on.

6

Z   KV 9179

INFORMATION TWENTYFIRST (A.) 3 PARACHUTE DIVISION
HAVING NO ARTILLERY REGIMENTAL STAFF ARTILLERY
STAFF ZBV 761 EMPLOYED FOR THIS TASK. 2 PARACHUTE
CORPS REQUESTED AOK SEVEN (Headquarters 7th Army) TO
BRING UP AN EFFECTIVE ARKO STAB (Artillery Command Staff)
TO WHICH BOTH ARTILLERY REGIMENTS TO BE SUBORDI-
NATED. (B.) PANZER LEHR DIVISION REQUESTED TRANSFER
OF HAUPTMANN PLUESKOW OR HAUPTMANN RAEMSCH
(BOTH SO FAR AT PANZER TROOPS SCHOOL BERGEN) OR
HAUPTMANN KOCHNIR (WITH MILITARY COMMANDER
PRAGUE) IN PLACE OF MAJOR MAROWSKY, COMMANDING
OFFICER 1 S PANZER LEHR REGIMENT 130. COMMENT: SUG-
GEST SUGAR MAY EQUAL SCHWER EQUALS HEAVY.

Note

From intelligence such as this (a decrypt of 22 June 1944) Bletchley was
able to build up an astonishing fund of knowledge about individual Ger-

man officers and their movements. Recorded in the Index, the details were available whenever the officer's name cropped up in later signals, and the background of exact knowledge about him could often give important significance to a signal that otherwise might have been obscure. This signal also, of course, shed light on the conditions of 3 Parachute Division in Normandy.

7

ZZ   KV 5825

REVIEW BY COMMANDER IN CHIEF SOUTH WEST ON TWEN-TYNINTH ON BATTLE EXPERIENCES IN PRESENT DEFEN-SIVE BATTLE. FIRSTLY, NOT ONLY FRENCH BUT ALSO BRIT-ISH AND AMERICANS HAD DEPARTED FROM THEIR METHOD OF CONDUCTING OPERATIONS. RECENTLY, ESPE-CIALLY WITH TANK FORMATIONS, THEY HAD IMMEDI-ATELY TAKEN FULL ADVANTAGE OF PENETRATIONS AND BREAKS THROUGH, AND ATTEMPTED TO EXPLOIT THEM TO MAKE A STRATEGIC BREAKTHROUGH. BY QUICKLY FOLLOWING UP WITH INFANTRY ON LIGHT TRUCKS BEHIND TANK FORMATIONS, AS THE RUSSIANS DO, TER-RAIN WON HAD BEEN VERY QUICKLY OCCUPIED IN SUCH STRENGTH THAT LATER COUNTER-ATTACKS BY LOCAL FORCES UNSUCCESSFUL. (COMMENT: INFORMATION HERE INCOMPLETE BUT INCLUDED REFERENCE TO OPERATIONS WITH UP TO FOUR HUNDRED TANKS IN FORMATION.) ESPECIALLY NOTEWORTHY WAS GREAT CROSS COUNTRY MOBILITY OF FRENCH (MOROCCAN) TROOPS, WHO QUICKLY OVERCAME EVEN TERRAIN WHICH HAD BEEN CLAIMED IMPASSABLE, TAKING ALONG THEIR HEAVY WEAPONS MAINLY LOADED ON PACK ANIMALS. THEY ALWAYS ATTEMPTED TO SURROUND GERMAN POSITIONS AND TO BREAK THEM UP FROM REAR. UNSPECIFIED FORCES CROSSED WITH AMPHIBIOUS VEHICLES (FLOATING LORRIES AND ACCORDING TO UNCONFIRMED REPORTS FLOATING TANKS). THEREFORE APPRECIATED THAT EVEN SECTORS OF SUCH COUNTRY MUST BE COVERED WITH AT LEAST WEAK FORCES. MINING OF REARWARD EDGES OF VARIOUS INUNDATED AREAS ETCETERA SEEMED EXPEDIENT...

Note

This first half of a report by Field Marshal Kesselring to Berlin conveys the reactions of himself and his staff to the way that Alexander's Allied

377

Armies had achieved the final breakthrough at Cassino. It went out from Bletchley just after midnight on 31 May 1944. Appreciations of this kind provided Allied commanders with an invaluable insight into the thinking of their opponents.

Bibliography

'As I conclude my work on this book (late in 1973),' wrote John Lukacs at the end of his encyclopaedic study *The Last European War,* 'I estimate that the number of printed items – that is, books and articles relating to its topic – approaches 60 000. . . . The usual practice of appending a large and seemingly scholarly bibliography at the end of a book such as this would be worse than hypocrisy since it would be devoid of practical usefulness.' In 1978, and in relation to a book spanning the whole war, these considerations apply with even greater force. I have not, therefore, attempted to illustrate my background of reading in relation to the general conduct of the war, but simply to mention sources which, in one way or another, relate directly to the story of Ultra. An essential frame of reference, of course, is provided by the series of British and American Official Histories. The Ultra signals in the Public Record Office at Kew are to be found in file DEF/E3. Otherwise, I have found the following relevant:

ALEXANDER, FIELD MARSHAL THE EARL, *The Alexander Memoirs*, Cassell, 1962

AMBROSE, STEPHEN E., *The Supreme Commander: The War Years of General Dwight D. Eisenhower*, Cassell, 1971

ASTLEY, JOAN BRIGHT, *The Inner Circle*, Hutchinson, 1971

BEESLY, PATRICK, *Very Special Intelligence*, Hamish Hamilton, 1977

BEKKER, CAJUS, *Hitler's Naval War*, MacDonald and Jane's, 1974

BELL, ERNEST L., *An Initial View of Ultra as an American Weapon*, TSU Press, Drawer F, Keene, New Hampshire,

BERTRAND, GUSTAVE, *Enigma*, Plon, 1973

BETHELL, NICHOLAS, *The War Hitler Won*, Allen Lane The Penguin Press, 1972

BIRKENHEAD, THE EARL OF, *The Prof in Two Worlds*, Collins,

BLUMENSON, MARTIN, *Kasserine Pass*, Houghton Mifflin, 1967

BÖHMLER, RUDOLF, *Monte Cassino*, Cassell, 1964

BOND, BRIAN, *France and Belgium 1939–1940*, Davis-Poynter, 1975

BRADLEY, OMAR N., *A Soldier's Story*, Eyre and Spottiswoode, 1951

BRIGGS, ASA, *The War of Words, The History of Broadcasting in the United Kingdom*, vol. 3, Oxford University Press, 1965

BRYANT, ARTHUR, *The Turn of the Tide*, Collins, 1957, *Triumph in the West*, Collins, 1959

BULLOCK, ALAN, *Hitler*, Odhams Press, 1952

CARVER, MICHAEL, *El Alamein*, Batsford, 1962
CAVE BROWN, ANTHONY, *Bodyguard of Lies*, W. H. Allen, 1976
CECIL, ROBERT, *Hitler's Decision to invade Russia, 1941*, Davis-Poynter, 1975
CHURCHILL, WINSTON, *The Second World War*, 6 vols., Cassell, 1948–54
CIANO, GALEAZZO, *The Ciano Diaries, 1939–1943*, William Heinemann, 1947
CLARK, RONALD, *The Man Who Broke Purple*, Weidenfeld and Nicolson, 1977
Tizard, Methuen, 1965
COLLIER, BASIL, *The Battle of the V-weapons, 1944–45*, Hodder and Stoughton, 1964
COLVILLE, JOHN, *Man of Valour: Field Marshal Lord Gort*, Collins, 1972
Footprints in Time, Collins, 1976
CONNELL, JOHN, *Auchinleck*, Cassell, 1959
Wavell: Scholar and Soldier, Collins, 1964
COSGRAVE, PATRICK, *Churchill at War: Alone, 1939–1940*, Collins, 1974
CRUICKSHANK, CHARLES, *The Fourth Arm: Psychological Warfare, 1938–45*, Davis-Poynter, 1977
CUNNINGHAM OF HYNDHOPE, THE VISCOUNT, *A Sailor's Odyssey*, Hutchinson, 1951

DAVIN, D. M., *Crete*. Official History of New Zealand in the Second World War, Oxford University Press, 1953
DEIGHTON, LEN, *Fighter: the True Story of the Battle of Britain*, Jonathan Cape, 1977
DEUTSCH, HAROLD C., 'The Historical Impact of Revealing the Ultra Secret', in *Parameters, Journal of the U.S. Army War College*, vol. 7, no. 3. *The Conspiracy against Hitler in the Twilight War*, Oxford University Press, 1968
DILKES, DAVID, (ED.), *The Diaries of Sir Alexander Cadogan*, Cassell, 1971
DIXON, NORMAN, *The Psychology of Military Incompetence*, Jonathan Cape, 1976
DÖNITZ, GRAND ADMIRAL KARL, *Memoirs*, Weidenfeld and Nicolson, 1958
DORNBERGER, WALTER, *V2*, Hurst and Blackett, 1954

EISENHOWER, DWIGHT D., *Crusade in Europe*, William Heinemann, 1949
EISENHOWER, JOHN S. D., *The Bitter Woods*, Putnam, 1969
EISENHOWER FOUNDATION, *D-Day: The Normandy Invasion in Retrospect*, The University Press of Kansas, 1971

ERICKSON, JOHN, *The Road to Stalingrad*, Weidenfeld and Nicolson, 1975

FARAGO, LADISLAS, *The Broken Seal*, Arthur Barker, 1967

FEIS, HERBERT, *Churchill, Roosevelt, Stalin*, Oxford University Press, 1957

FITZGERALD, PENELOPE, *The Knox Brothers*, Macmillan, 1977

FLEMING, PETER, *Invasion, 1940*, Hart-Davis, 1974

FOOT, M. R. D., *S.O.E. in France*, H. M. Stationery Office, 1976

FRIENDLY, ALFRED, 'Confessions of a Code Breaker', in *The Washington Post*, 27 Oct. 1974

GILBERT, MARTIN, *Winston S. Churchill*, Vol. V, 1922–1939, William Heinemann, 1976

GREENFIELD, KENT ROBERTS, *American Strategy in World War II*, Johns Hopkins Press, 1970
Command Decisions, (Ed.), Methuen, 1960

GRETTON, PETER, *Convoy Escort Commander*, 1964
Former Naval Person: Winston Churchill and the Royal Navy, Cassell, 1968

HARRIMAN, W. AVERELL, *Special Envoy to Churchill and Stalin*, Hutchinson, 1976

HIBBERT, CHRISTOPHER, *The Battle of Arnhem*, Batsford, 1975

HINSLEY, F. H., *Hitler's Strategy*, Cambridge University Press, 1951

HOFFMANN, PETER, *The History of the German Resistance 1933–1945*, Macdonald and Jane's, 1977

HOWARD, MICHAEL, *The Mediterranean Strategy in the Second World War*, Weidenfeld and Nicolson, 1968

HUNT, DAVID, *A Don at War*, William Kimber, 1966

HYDE, H. MONTGOMERY, *The Quiet Canadian*, Hamish Hamilton, 1962

IRVING, DAVID, *Breach of Security: The German Secret Intelligence File on events leading to the Second World War*, William Kimber
The Mare's Nest, William Kimber, 1964
The Destruction of Convoy P.Q.17, Cassell, 1968
Hitler's War, Hodder and Stoughton, 1977
The Rise and Fall of the Luftwaffe, Weidenfeld and Nicolson, 1974
The Trail of the Fox, Weidenfeld and Nicolson, 1977

JACKSON, W. G. F., *Alexander of Tunis*, 1971
The Battle for Rome, 1969
The Battle for Italy, Batsford, 1967

JAMES, D. CLAYTON, *The Years of MacArthur*, 2 vols., Leo Cooper, 1970

JONES, R. V., *Most Secret War*, Hamish Hamilton, 1978

KAHN, DAVID, *The Codebreakers*, Weidenfeld and Nicolson, 1974
KENNEDY, JOHN, *The Business of War*, Hutchinson, 1957
KENNEDY, LUDOVIC, *Pursuit: the sinking of the Bismarck*, Collins, 1974
KESSELRING, FIELD MARSHAL, *Memoirs*, William Kimber, 1974

LASH, JOSEPH P, *Roosevelt and Churchill, 1939–1941*, André Deutsch, 1977
LEE, RAYMOND E., *The London Observer: The Journal of General Raymond E. Lee, 1940–1941*, Hutchinson, 1972
LOEWENHEIM, FRANCIS L. (ED.) with HAROLD D. LANGLEY and MANFRED JONAS, *Roosevelt and Churchill: their secret wartime correspondence*, Barrie and Jenkins,

MCLACHLAN, DONALD, *Room 39: Naval Intelligence in Action, 1939–1945*, Weidenfeld and Nicolson, 1968
MAISKY, IVAN, *Memoirs of a Soviet Ambassador: the War, 1939–1945*, Hutchinson, 1967
MARDER, ARTHUR, *Winston is back: Churchill at the Admiralty*, Longmans, 1972
MASTERMAN, J. C., *On the Chariot Wheel*, Oxford University Press, 1975
The Double-Cross System, Yale University Press, 1972
MONTAGU, EWEN, *Beyond Top Secret U*, Peter Davies, 1977
The Man Who Never Was, Evans, 1966
MONTGOMERY, FIELD MARSHAL THE VISCOUNT, *Memoirs*, Collins, 1958
MORGAN, FREDERICK, *Overture to Overlord*, Hodder and Stoughton, 1950
MURE, DAVID, *Practise to Deceive*, William Kimber, 1977

NICOLSON, NIGEL, *Alex*, Weidenfeld and Nicolson, 1973

PAGE, BRUCE with DAVID LEITCH and PHILLIP KNIGHTLEY, *Philby*, André Deutsch, 1968
PATTON, GEORGE S, *War as I saw it*, W. H. Allen, 1950
POGUE, FORREST C., *George C. Marshall*, 3 vols., Viking, 1963
POPOV, DUSKO, *Spy/Counterspy*, Weidenfeld and Nicolson, 1974
POWNALL, SIR HENRY, *Chief of Staff: the Diaries of Lieut-General Sir Henry Pownall*, 2 vols. (Ed. Brian Bond), Leo Cooper, 1973
PRICE, ALFRED, *Instruments of Darkness*, William Kimber, 1967

RANDELL, B., *Report on Colossus*, Statistical Dept., Newcastle University
ROHWER, JÜRGEN, *The Critical Convoy Battles of March 1943*

Chronology of the War at Sea, 2 vols., Ian Allen, 1972, 1974

ROMMEL, ERWIN, *The Rommel Papers*, (Ed. B. H. Liddell Hart), Collins, 1953

ROSKILL, STEPHEN, *Churchill and the Admirals*, Collins, 1977

RYAN, CORNELIUS, *A Bridge Too Far*, Hamish Hamilton, 1974
The Last Battle, Collins, 1973

SEATON, ALBERT, *The Russo-German War, 1941–1945*, Arthur Barker, 1971

SHIRER, WILLIAM, *The Rise and Fall of the Third Reich*, Secker and Warburg, 1960

SLESSOR, SIR JOHN, *The Central Blue*, Cassell, 1956

SPEER, ALBERT, *Inside the Third Reich*, Weidenfeld and Nicolson, 1970
Spandau: the Secret Diaries, Collins, 1976

STEVENSON, WILLIAM, *A Man Called Intrepid*, Macmillan, 1976

STRAWSON, JOHN, *Hitler as Military Commander*, Batsford, 1971
The Battle for the Ardennes, Batsford, 1972

STRONG, SIR KENNETH, *Intelligence at the Top*, Cassell, 1968
Men of Intelligence, Cassell/Giniger, 1970

TEDDER, SIR ARTHUR, *With Prejudice*, Cassell, 1966

THOMPSON, R. W., *Churchill and Morton*, Hodder and Stoughton, 1976

TREVOR-ROPER, HUGH, *The Philby Affair*, William Kimber, 1968

WHEELER-BENNETT, SIR JOHN (ED.), *Action this day: Working with Churchill*, Macmillan, 1968

WILMOT, CHESTER, *The Struggle for Europe*, Collins, 1965

WINTERBOTHAM, F. W., *The Ultra Secret*, Weidenfeld and Nicolson, 1974

WINGATE, SIR RONALD, *Lord Ismay*, Hutchinson, 1970

WOHLSTETTER, ROBERTA, *Pearl Harbor: Warning and Decision*, Stanford University Press, 1962

WOOD, DEREK and DEMPSTER, DEREK, *The Narrow Margin: the Battle of Britain and the Rise of Air Power, 1930–1940*, Hutchinson, 1969

WRIGHT, ROBERT, *Dowding and the Battle of Britain*, Macdonald, 1969

ZUCKERMAN, SOLLY, *From Apes to Warlords*, Hamish Hamilton, 1978

Index

385

PENGUIN ONLINE

READ MORE IN PENGUIN

In every corner of the world, on every subject under the sun, Penguin represents quality and variety – the very best in publishing today.

For complete information about books available from Penguin – including Puffins, Penguin Classics and Arkana – and how to order them, write to us at the appropriate address below. Please note that for copyright reasons the selection of books varies from country to country.

In the United Kingdom: Please write to *Dept. EP, Penguin Books Ltd, Bath Road, Harmondsworth, West Drayton, Middlesex UB7 ODA*

In the United States: Please write to *Consumer Sales, Penguin Putnam Inc., P.O. Box 12289 Dept. B, Newark, New Jersey 07101-5289*. VISA and MasterCard holders call 1-800-788-6262 to order Penguin titles

In Canada: Please write to *Penguin Books Canada Ltd, 10 Alcorn Avenue, Suite 300, Toronto, Ontario M4V 3B2*

In Australia: Please write to *Penguin Books Australia Ltd, P.O. Box 257, Ringwood, Victoria 3134*

In New Zealand: Please write to *Penguin Books (NZ) Ltd, Private Bag 102902, North Shore Mail Centre, Auckland 10*

In India: Please write to *Penguin Books India Pvt Ltd, 11 Community Centre, Panchsheel Park, New Delhi 110017*

In the Netherlands: Please write to *Penguin Books Netherlands bv, Postbus 3507, NL-1001 AH Amsterdam*

In Germany: Please write to *Penguin Books Deutschland GmbH, Metzlerstrasse 26, 60594 Frankfurt am Main*

In Spain: Please write to *Penguin Books S. A., Bravo Murillo 19, 1° B, 28015 Madrid*

In Italy: Please write to *Penguin Italia s.r.l., Via Benedetto Croce 2, 20094 Corsico, Milano*

In France: Please write to *Penguin France, Le Carré Wilson, 62 rue Benjamin Baillaud, 31500 Toulouse*

In Japan: Please write to *Penguin Books Japan Ltd, Kaneko Building, 2-3-25 Koraku, Bunkyo-Ku, Tokyo 112*

In South Africa: Please write to *Penguin Books South Africa (Pty) Ltd, Private Bag X14, Parkview, 2122 Johannesburg*

READ MORE IN PENGUIN

PENGUIN CLASSIC MILITARY HISTORY

This series acknowledges the profound and enduring interest in military history, and the causes and consequences of human conflict. Penguin Classic Military History covers warfare from the earliest times to the age of electronics and encompasses subjects as diverse as classic examples of grand strategy and the precision tactics of Britain's crack SAS Regiment. The series will be enjoyed and valued by students of military history and all who hope to learn from the often disturbing lessons of the past.

Published or forthcoming:

Corelli Barnett	**Engage the Enemy More Closely**
	The Great War
David G. Chandler	**The Art of Warfare on Land**
William Craig	**Enemy at the Gates**
Heinz Guderian	**Panzer Leader**
Heinz Höhne	**The Order of the Death's Head**
Anthony Kemp	**The SAS at War**
Martin Middlebrook	**The Kaiser's Battle**
Philip Warner	**Sieges of the Middle Ages**
Cecil Woodham-Smith	**The Reason Why**